GONE TO THE COUNTRY

MUSIC IN AMERICAN LIFE

A list of books in the series appears at the end of this book.

GONE TO THE COUNTRY

THE NEW LOST CITY RAMBLERS AND THE FOLK MUSIC REVIVAL

RAY ALLEN

UNIVERSITY OF ILLINOIS PRESS

Urbana, Chicago, and Springfield

FRONTISPIECE

Tom Paley (banjo), Mike Seeger (fiddle), John Cohen (guitar).
Photograph by Robert Frank, New York City, 1960.
© Robert Frank.

Publication of this book was supported by a grant from the
L. J. and Mary C. Skaggs Folklore Fund.

1 2 3 4 5 C P 5 4 3 2 1

∞ This book is printed on acid-free paper.

Library of Congress Cataloging-in-Publication Data
Allen, Ray.
Gone to the country : the New Lost City Ramblers
and the folk music revival / Ray Allen.
p.   cm. — (Music in American life)
Includes bibliographical references and index.
ISBN 978-0-252-03560-9 (cloth : alk. paper)
ISBN 978-0-252-07747-0 (pbk. : alk. paper)
1. New Lost City Ramblers.
2. Folk musicians—United States.
I. Title.
ML421.N515A75   2010
781.62'1300922—dc22 [B]   2010015369

To

LAURIE, RUBY, AND ROSE,

and in memory of

MIKE SEEGER (1933–2009),

the best friend old-time music ever had

THE
NEW LOST CITY RAMBLERS
JOHN COHEN, MIKE SEEGER, TRACY SCHWARZ

Folkways

Gone To The Country

PHOTO: LAURENCE SIEG

CONTENTS

ACKNOWLEDGMENTS

Gone to the Country was made possible by the efforts of many. First and foremost, my gratitude to the four Ramblers: Mike Seeger, John Cohen, Tom Paley, and Tracy Schwarz. Without their patient cooperation during hours of interviews and informal conversations this book could not have been written. My greatest disappointment is that Mike Seeger did not live to see the completion of this work. My deepest condolences to the entire Seeger family, and special thanks to Mike's wife, Alexia Smith, for helping me sort through and copy portions of his personal archive.

Thanks to the Ethyle R. Wolfe Institute for the Humanities and the Office of the Provost at Brooklyn College, CUNY, for their generosity in providing me with the released time from teaching that made this project possible. I am grateful to Judith Tick and Ellie Hisama for introducing me to Ruth Crawford Seeger's work during a conference we coordinated honoring the centennial of her birth in 2001. That event, where I first met Mike Seeger, became the impetus for this project. Thanks also to my colleagues in the Hitchcock Institute for Studies in American Music at Brooklyn College—Jeff Taylor, Stephanie Jensen-Moulton, Salim Washington, and David Grubbs—for constantly challenging me to think about American music in innovative new ways and to ponder where folk music fits into the larger puzzle.

Steve Weiss and his staff at the Southern Folklife Collection at the Wilson Library, University of North Carolina, Chapel Hill, and Dan Sheehy, Mary Monseur, Jeff Place, and Stephanie Smith of Smithsonian Folkways gave graciously of their time to help me secure many of the recordings, photographs, and written sources that are the foundation of this book. Thanks to Bill Ferris and Marcie Cohen Ferris at the University of North Carolina for their encouragement and for putting me in touch with their research assistant, Aaron Smithers. Elijah Wald generously shared recordings of early Ramblers concerts from his personal collection. Laurie Matheson and her staff at the University of Illinois Press skillfully guided the manuscript through the entire publication process. Thanks also to Angela Gibson and to Mary Hill for their superb copyediting work on the initial drafts of the manuscript and to John Cohen and Suzy Thompson for their assistance in locating photographs.

I am deeply indebted to Ronald Cohen for his unflagging support over the past five years. *Gone to the Country* is a far better book thanks to the volumes of material and the insightful criticism he shared with me throughout the writing process. My appreciation to Judith McCulloh for her initial encouragement and her astute suggestions on the final manuscript and to Kip Lornell, Michael Scully, Burt Feintuch, Alan Jabbour, Bill Malone, and George Cunningham for their helpful comments on early portions of the work.

My deepest gratitude goes to my family. My daughters, Ruby and Rose, grew up with this book and were subjected to more old-time music than most teenagers in Brooklyn could tolerate. And finally to Laurie Russell, who kept me going over the course of the project. Without her love, good cheer, and editorial prowess *Gone to the Country* would never have happened.

GONE TO THE COUNTRY

INTRODUCTION
REVIVING TRADITION IN MODERN AMERICA

Readers familiar with American folk music have probably heard the story of Bob Dylan's controversial appearance at the 1965 Newport Folk Festival. When Dylan came onstage, sporting a leather jacket and backed by members of Paul Butterfield's electric blues band, Pete Seeger flew into a rage. Appalled by the band's high volume and Dylan's distorted vocals, he allegedly threatened to chop the electric cables with an ax (a rumor he later denied). Seeger, the reigning godfather of the folk music revival, viewed Dylan's brash display as an invasion by the rock barbarians, who personified the ills of commercial music that he and the old-guard devotees of folk song detested. Dylan's betrayal, Seeger's wrath, and the death of folk music have become urban folk legend.

Dylan's presence so overshadowed the 1965 Newport Folk Festival that few people remember the other artists who appeared that year, many of whom had little or no connection with commercial folk music. All but forgotten is the serenade from the old-time Texas fiddler Eck Robertson that greeted festival participants as they filed into the opening Thursday evening concert. Robertson, unknown at the time to most city folk musicians, was legendary among old-time music buffs as the first hillbilly artist to make a commercial recording—his 1922 Victor rendition of "Sallie Gooden" remains a classic.

Robertson performed later in the program backed by the New Lost City Ramblers, a trio of New York–born musicians consisting of Pete's half-brother Mike Seeger, John Cohen, and Tracy Schwarz. Robertson landed in Newport after John and Tracy "rediscovered" him in his piano shop in Amarillo, Texas, in 1963. Mike returned to Amarillo later that summer to record

Robertson and to convince him to come out of hiatus to play for college and festival audiences "up north."

Eck Robertson was not the only traditional musician to appear at Newport in 1965 at the behest of the Ramblers. Roscoe Holcomb, whose modal banjo tunes and archaic vocal style offered a window into nineteenth-century Appalachia, had been located by John on a trip to eastern Kentucky in 1959. Cousin Emmy, another Kentucky banjoist and songster, ran into the Ramblers in California in 1961. Mother Maybelle Carter, the mellifluous voice of the original Carter family of Virginia, had connected with audiences at folk festivals and coffeehouses at the prompting of Mike and John. And the old-time string band of Sam and Kirk McGee with Fiddlin' Arthur Smith, a favorite of Nashville's Grand Ole Opry, had been brought to the attention of northern folk enthusiasts by Mike, who recorded them in 1956. In addition to these artists the festival's daytime workshops and evening concerts featured southern bluesmen Mississippi John Hurt and Son House, West Texas songster Mance Lipscomb, a Texas work gang, bluegrass legend Bill Monroe, and Appalachian balladeer Horton Barker. The workshop schedule read like a survey course in southern roots music, with offerings ranging from Appalachian ballad singing and string-band music to blues guitar and bluegrass banjo styles to Negro spiritual singing, blues origins, and psalmody.

Robertson and the cadre of traditional artists who shared the stage with Dylan found themselves in Newport that summer thanks to the efforts of the Ramblers and the Newport Folk Festival board, which included Alan Lomax, Ralph Rinzler, and Pete and Toshi Seeger. The festival board had encouraged the Ramblers and others to locate, document, and invite traditional artists to Newport, a venue that many used as a springboard to the urban audiences who fueled the 1960s folk music revival. Though Dylan's performance did signal a shift in popular tastes toward electric folk rock and away from acoustic folk music, by 1965 the Ramblers and their like-minded cohorts at Newport could take solace in the enthusiastic reception that traditional artists like Robertson received. The fate of commercial folk music was of little concern to them, for their mission to promote traditional southern music and musicians appeared to be coming to fruition.

Gone to the Country chronicles the life and music of the New Lost City Ramblers, pioneers in the resurgence of southern mountain and bluegrass music during the postwar folk music revival. The original trio was formed in 1958 by Mike Seeger, John Cohen, and Tom Paley, with Tracy Schwarz replacing Paley in 1962. Though city born and suburban bred, the Ramblers immersed themselves in the sounds of traditional southern mountain music, initially through scratchy old records and Library of Congress field recordings and later through visits south to meet, record, and commune with rural artists.

FIGURE 1. John Cohen (banjo) and Eck Robertson (fiddle) at Newport Folk Festival, 1965. Photograph by Diana Davies. Image courtesy of the Ralph Rinzler Folklife Archives and Collections, Smithsonian Institution.

The Ramblers' early recordings on Folkways Records and live appearances at coffeehouses, folk festivals, and college campuses propelled the trio's rise to prominence as the preeminent northern interpreters of old-time string-band and early bluegrass music. Their attempts to faithfully replicate southern folk styles and to champion a group of rural artists who they believed embodied a genuine folk sensibility opened up critical debates over the nature of authentic folk expression. *Gone to the Country* examines those debates in the context of the search for an idealized folk sound and cultural experience that neither the commercial revival nor the popular media could deliver.

The self-conscious revival of traditional music among urban Americans that peaked in the postwar years has, until recently, received surprisingly little scholarly attention. During the decades following the great folk music boom of the early 1960s folklorists and cultural historians remained relatively silent on the subject. Some questioned the legitimacy of the revival, while others feared their own personal brushes with the movement might preclude objective study. For folklorists the dam finally broke in 1993 with the publication of *Transforming Tradition: Folk Music Revivals Examined*, edited by folk music scholar and bluegrass musician Neil Rosenberg. Like most of the folklorists and ethnomusicologists who contributed to his volume, Rosenberg had come to the formal study of folk music by way of the revival. He and his cadre of aging revivalists turned scholars penned deeply self-reflective essays that probed their motivations for playing folk music and the multiple meanings transformed traditions held for them and their contemporaries. Works that followed, particularly Robert Cantwell's personal and provocative *When We Were Good: The Folk Revival* and Ronald Cohen's meticulously sourced *Rainbow Quest: The Folk Music Revival and American Society, 1940–1970*, provide long-overdue road maps for historicizing the peak years of the postwar revival. More recently, Benjamin Filene's *Romancing the Folk: Public Memory and American Roots Music*, Michael Scully's *The Never-Ending Revival: Rounder Records and the Folk Alliance*, and Thomas Grunning's *Millennium Folk* have laid to rest the spurious myth that folk music died following the demise of the 1960s commercial boom. They argue convincingly that diverse forms of American roots music remain a vibrant part of our modern landscape. These volumes, along with the plethora of fresh memoirs by key figures Bob Dylan, Dave Van Ronk, George Wein, Dick Weissman, Bess Lomax Hawes, and Hazel Dickens, have further enriched our understanding of the postwar revival and its place in twentieth-century American life.[1]

Emerging from these studies is a picture of a tremendously complex social phenomenon not easily reducible to a single category of music, a particular political ideology, a common set of values, or even a shared cultural perspective. The postwar folk music revival was at once a commercial boom, a protest song movement, a rebellion by disillusioned college students, a search for cultural roots, a do-it-yourself approach to homemade music, and more. Throughout the 1950s and 1960s millions of Americans swooned to (and purchased) the sounds of sweet-crooning commercial folk groups like the Weavers, the Kingston Trio, and Peter, Paul and Mary. Drawn to music they perceived to be more genuinely humane than the pop culture pap of the late 1950s, thousands of college students across the country picked up guitars and banjos to sing and socialize with kindred spirits. A small but vocal contingency embraced the legacy of the old singing Left, writing their own songs of significance as the turmoil of the civil rights movement and the Vietnam War engulfed the country. As the idealism of the 1960s turned into the malaise of the 1970s, the idea of homegrown music became increasingly appealing to those seeking lifestyles on the edges of conventional society.

The folk revival spawned endless debates over exactly what constituted folk music, who should play it, and how it should be played. It was this last question that became a central concern for those musicians who would come to be known as the "purist," "traditional," or "neo-ethnic" camp of the movement. These were the city players who were simply mesmerized by the sounds of traditional music and the exotic cultures and bygone eras those sounds evoked. City musicians like the Ramblers felt transformed when they first heard the shuffle of an old-timey fiddle, the brush and pluck of a frailing banjo, the rolling arpeggios of a bluesy, fingerpicked guitar, the reckless abandonment of a mountain string-band breakdown, and the high lonesome wail of a backwoods balladeer or a bluegrass vocal duet. Southern ballads, blues, string-band music, and bluegrass were the first regional styles to grab the attention of urban traditionalists and to ignite among some an insatiable desire to emulate those sounds.

Gone to the Country focuses attention on this vital wing of the revival, which to date has been marginalized from the standard historical narratives. The struggles and achievements of the traditionalists can only be understood from a broad cultural perspective that recognizes the interconnectedness of the seemingly disparate strands of the revival. While the Ramblers sought to position themselves in opposition to commercial folk music, they were financially dependent on Folkways Records and the national network of clubs and festivals that allowed them to survive as a touring band for over a decade. They denied their songs and tunes had overt political overtones, yet in the act of performing the music of downtrodden Appalachian mountaineers they implicitly offered a critique of modern urban and suburban society. The Ramblers and like-minded traditionalists were loath to portray themselves as cultural crusaders, but they did see themselves as part of a broad social movement that folklorist and traditional fiddler Alan Jabbour likened to "a quest for cultural roots" that reflected "our admiration of democratic ideals and values, our solidarity with the culturally neglected, and our compulsion to forge our own culture for ourselves."[2]

My investigation of the Ramblers is further guided by recent folklore and cultural studies scholarship focusing on contemporary Americans' search for authentic experience and our penchant for the self-conscious display of folk traditions through festivals, exhibitions, and staged performances. Works with such provocative titles as The Invention of Tradition, Transforming Tradition, Staging Tradition, Romancing the Folk, In Search of Authenticity, Folk Nation: Folklore in the Creation of American Tradition, and Folklife and the Representation of Culture suggest a growing consensus that the terms authenticity and tradition are slippery constructs that serve a variety of social and cultural agendas.[3] My aim, then, is not to render absolute judgments about the authenticity of the Ramblers' music or the traditional artists they championed but rather to examine how they ascribed notions of cultural and artistic authenticity to certain musical styles, repertoires, and performers and how they presented their perceptions of what constituted genuine folk culture to urban audiences who initially had little knowledge of southern mountain music.

Romancing the Folk, Filene's insightful study of the cultural mediators Alan and John Lomax, Willie Dixon, Charles Seeger, Benjamin Botkin, Pete Seeger, and Bob Dylan, is particularly useful in understanding this process. "Eager to promote the authenticity of the performers they worked with," Filene writes, these influential figures positioned themselves as "cultural funnels channeling the musicians' raw, elemental power to popular audiences."[4] Strictly adhering to regional performance styles when presenting carefully selected southern songs and tunes to northern folk enthusiasts, the Ramblers served as just such a cultural funnel, connecting middle-class Americans with the practitioners of rural roots music. Unfolding against the backdrop of the southern civil rights, anti–Vietnam War, and utopian back-to-the-land movements, their music and cultural advocacy offer fresh insights into the role that tradition played in the social upheaval of midcentury America.

Gone to the Country draws on a variety of primary sources, first and foremost the personal recollections of the four Ramblers. Over the past seven years, Mike, John, Tom, and Tracy have offered themselves up for countless hours of interviews, informal conversations, and e-mail exchanges. In turn, I have sought to leave ample room for their voices to be heard throughout my narrative. When their accounts of certain past events do not agree, I have done my best to present their divergent recollections without rendering judgments or playing favorites. That said, I beg their forgiveness for those instances where my interpretations of their experiences and their music do not coincide with their own.

Fortunately, Mike, John, and Tracy kept thorough financial records. Their ledgers provided a baseline chronology of their sojourns across the country, and occasionally the globe, from the late 1950s through the early 1970s. These records, along with royalty statements for Folkways Records, allowed me to probe the financial realities of the most successful old-time string band of the period; indeed, they were the only touring string band of the period, for reasons that will soon become clear. Their personal collections of posters, flyers, reviews, photographs, and correspondence, ferreted out from the rafters of attics and barns, proved invaluable in fleshing out the details of their story.

The Ramblers left behind a rich trove of musical recordings, releasing twenty LPs and EPs on Folkways Records between 1958 and 1975. I occasionally digress from the main narrative to examine these recordings in detail. My purpose in doing so is twofold: to chart the Ramblers' musical development and to assess their efforts to emulate traditional styles and establish a canon of southern songs and tunes. I encourage readers to listen along to the songs and tunes, which are all available on the Smithsonian Folkways Web site. I have also dug deeply into the copious liner notes that accompany each Rambler Folkways album. These writings provide contemporaneous commentary on the group's artistic and cultural goals as well as valuable source material for their tunes and songs.

The compilation *The New Lost City Ramblers: 40 Years of Concert Recordings* (Rounder Records CD 0481, 2001) introduced listeners to the rollicking world of live performances, stretching from the group's first 1958 radio broadcast through shows taped in the early 1970s. An even more detailed picture of the trio's performance practices emerges from the study of several dozen unedited concert tapes from Mike's collection currently archived in the Southern Folklife Collection (SFC) of the University of North Carolina at Chapel Hill. These concert tapes reveal not only the musical skills of the individual Ramblers but also the wit and wisdom they collectively employed from the stage in their struggle to educate and inspire their listeners.

Gone to the Country is organized chronologically, with the first two chapters focusing on the early lives and musical experiences of the three original Ramblers, Mike Seeger, John Cohen, and Tom Paley. Chapters 3 and 4 recount the formation of the trio in 1958 and their attempt to carve out a niche for themselves as the late 1950s folk revival evolved into a full-blown commercial boom in the early 1960s. Chapter 5 turns to Tom's stormy departure and his replacement by Tracy Schwarz in 1962, while chapter 6 chronicles the "new" New Lost City Ramblers' busy touring schedule and their work with traditional southern artists. Chapter 7, "Gone to the Country," follows the Ramblers' mid-1960s efforts to relocate themselves, both geographically and spiritually, in rural environs more congruent with their music.

The gradual decline of the Ramblers from the late 1960s through the mid-1970s is the subject of chapter 8. The collapse of the commercial folk boom, coupled with changing personal interests and internal personality clashes, led the band to cut back significantly on its touring and recording activities after 1969. Chapter 9 turns to the Ramblers' legacy as the perceived progenitors of the old-time music revival and assesses their ongoing individual efforts to perform, promote, and document traditional American folk music. Finally, chapter 10 reexamines the term *folk revival*, reflecting on the challenges it posed for the Ramblers as well as academics and cultural preservationists.

The Ramblers' story is best told through the interweaving of biography, history, and music criticism. *Gone to the Country* thus unfolds as a narrative, with interpretations emerging from the deep contextualization of the specific historical texts and musical practices encountered along the way. With this perspective I seek to provoke fresh thinking about the role that so-called traditional folk music has played in modern American life. More specifically, I want to understand how and why so many young people became infatuated with music they perceived to be old and antiquated during the 1960s, the twentieth century's most turbulent decade of social change. Unpacking this history will, I hope, shed light on why traditional folk music in general and old-time music in particular have continued to resonate with Americans more than fifty years after the Ramblers first appeared.

THE SEEGER FAMILY DISCOVERS THE FOLK

When Mike Seeger, John Cohen, and Tom Paley stepped into the broadcast booth of Washington, DC's WASH-FM radio station on the Sunday evening of May 25, 1958, they had only played together for about half an hour. One of the numbers the nameless trio performed that night was a mountain dance tune called "Colored Aristocracy." Mike, who led the piece on fiddle, explained this was an old tune "from way back in the hills of West Virginia" that was recorded at the Arthurdale Folk Festival by an obscure fiddle band known as the Rich Family. Time did not permit him to recount how his father, Charles Seeger, had made the recording for the Library of Congress (LOC) in 1936 while working for the federal Resettlement Administration. "Colored Aristocracy" was one of the many field recordings made by Mike's father and the Lomaxes that turned up in the Seeger family home during his childhood. As an eight-year-old, Mike had been mesmerized by the swinging fiddles of Sanford and Elmer Rich that jumped off the scratchy aluminum disk recording. Years later he dubbed the Rich Family disk onto quarter-inch tape, learned the main fiddle line, and hastily rearranged the tune with John and Tom before going on the air that evening.

The Seeger-Cohen-Paley trio that broadcast on WASH-FM was something of an anomaly for the urban folk music scene in 1958. By that time the revival had splintered among old-guard proponents of topical songs, younger singer-songwriters, ballad singers often trained in classical technique, small ensembles performing popular arrangements of folk material, and a fledgling contingent of bluegrass enthusiasts. A raucous fiddle, banjo, and guitar trio that played and sang in a rough style reminiscent of southern mountain string bands was indeed a rarity in city circles. John and Tom had come to the music primarily through the reissue of commercial hillbilly and blues records and LOC field recordings that had become available to the public in the early postwar years. Mike, on the other hand, had grown up with field recordings like "Colored Aristocracy" in his home. He and his sisters, Peggy, Penny, and Barbara, were quite possibly the only children in urban America who were literally reared on folk music field recordings during the 1930s and 1940s. What other youngsters gathered together regularly with family and friends to sing traditional American folk songs from books their parents had helped compile? Charles Seeger and Ruth Crawford Seeger's intense involvement with American folk music during the first twenty years of Mike's life shaped not only his own musical sensibilities but those of the nascent folk revival that would eventually make possible the emergence of a group like the New Lost City Ramblers.

Michael Seeger was born in New York City on August 15, 1933. His parents were both musicians, although at the time of his birth neither had shown much inclination for folk music. His father, Charles Seeger, was born in 1886 into a monied New England family that traced its lineage back to the *Mayflower*. Charles, against his father's wishes, insisted on studying music when he enrolled in Harvard in 1904. After graduation he completed three years of postgraduate work in Germany and then returned to the States, where in 1911 he was hired by the University of California at Berkeley. There he taught music theory and composition, conducted orchestras and accompanied singers, and struggled to incorporate the revolutionary ideas of early-twentieth-century moderns like Claude Debussy, Arnold Schoenberg, and Igor Stravinsky into his own compositions. One of his students, the sixteen-year-old piano prodigy Henry Cowell, would become a leader of the American ultramodernist movement that Charles and Ruth would eventually be associated with.[1]

Following his dismissal from Berkeley in 1918 over his outspoken opposition to World War I, Charles and his first wife, the classically trained violinist Constance Edson Seeger, relocated to New York. In 1919, shortly after their move east, Constance gave birth to their third son, Peter, who would grow up to be the leading figure of the postwar folk music revival. Meanwhile, Charles immersed himself in New York's music scene, teaching at the Institute of Musical Art (later Juilliard) and the New School. Growing increasingly discontented with conventional classical music, he was drawn into New York's modernist movement and labored to refine his own compositional theories based on dissonant counterpoint. In 1929, two years after his divorce from Constance, he agreed to take on a promising composition student, twenty-nine-year-old Ruth Crawford.

Student and teacher became husband and wife in 1932, at the height of Ruth's own compositional career.

Dismayed by the atrocities of the Depression, Charles and Ruth gravitated toward socialist politics. Charles helped organize the Composer's Collective in 1932, a leftist organization dedicated to composing "people's music" that would foster progressive social change. He composed a number of political songs and wrote criticism for the communist *Daily Worker* under the pseudonym Carl Sands. Despite his interest in music that supposedly reflected the ethos of the common man, he remained skeptical of the value of folk music as a foundation for revolutionary art, noting in 1934 that many folk tunes were "complacent, melancholy, defeatist."[2]

Charles's attitude toward folk music would soon be radically transformed. In late 1935 he and Ruth, along with their two-year-old son, Mike, and their infant daughter, Peggy, relocated to Washington, where Charles took a position with the New Deal's Resettlement Administration. Charged with finding ways of bringing music to Depression-ravaged rural communities, he quickly realized that, contrary to the views held by many of his academic colleagues and modernist associates, American folk music was neither dead nor limited to the archaic survivals of Elizabethan ballads or African work songs. As he visited small communities throughout the American South he discovered that folk music and dance were quite alive and well, woven deeply into the social fabric of contemporary rural society.[3] He soon joined progressive New Deal colleagues Alan Lomax and Benjamin Botkin as an outspoken advocate for the collection of rural folk music and its dissemination to a broad American public. Charles, Ruth, Lomax, and Botkin began to develop what historian Jerrold Hirsch identified as a "cultural strategy" aimed at using folklore toward the "promotion of a new and more expansive vision of American nationality that would be inclusive and democratic rather than elusive and coercive."[4]

Charles served as deputy director of the federal Music Project of the Works Progress Administration from 1938 through 1941 and as chief of the music division of the Pan American Union from 1941 through 1953 before returning to academia with a position at the Institute of Ethnomusicology at the University of California at Los Angeles. His contributions to the fields of musicology and ethnomusicology were vast, and his prolific writing on American folk music helped reshape the way scholars approached the subject.[5] He was one of the first established figures in musicology to recognize the intrinsic aesthetic value of folk music itself instead of viewing it simply as inspirational grist for the composer's mill. But even more importantly he became an early and persuasive voice for shifting the focus of folk music scholarship away from the structural and literary analysis of antiquated texts and toward the study of folk music style as practiced by tradition bearers whose performances had been captured on tape. He was also one of the first to stress the dynamic and processual nature of folk music, arguing that in twentieth-century America oral traditions did not exist in isolation from written and mediated expressions. In the modern world musical idioms were interconnected, and he envisioned a highwaylike continuum along which so-called folk, popular, and fine art expressions traveled. The midcentury folk music revival, which he famously characterized as "an American shotgun wedding of oral (folk) and written (fine and popular art) idioms," was an ideal arena in which the three forms met and mingled. While rural folk migrants were adopting city ways, urban folksingers were discovering rural traditions.[6] Charles urged city people, including his own family, to listen to "the voices of authentic folk singers" on record, to sing folk songs to their children, and to participate in making folk music themselves. Yet he maintained a somewhat ambivalent stance toward the postwar revival itself. Charles chastised rural singers who modified their singing and instrumental styles solely to please urban audiences and disparaged urban singers who affected nasal twangs while questioning their ability to completely embrace rural music styles, quipping, "Inheritance always shows."[7]

Mike's mother, Ruth Crawford, followed a similar trajectory in her journey from high art to folk music. The daughter of a Methodist minister, she was born in East Liverpool, Ohio, in 1901. Following the family's move to Jacksonville, Florida, she began piano lessons and demonstrated such promise that she accepted a job offer at a local music school on graduation from high school. Two years later, after earning a reputation as a brilliant performer, she moved to Chicago to attend the American Conservatory of Music, where she studied piano and composition.[8]

In Chicago Ruth's talents blossomed, and by 1924 she was teaching piano and harmony at the conservatory. Although her musical training was centered on Western classical and romantic traditions, she came in contact with individuals who opened her up to the possibilities of alternative ways of viewing the world and composing music. Her piano instructor and mentor, Dejane Herz, introduced her to the mystical aesthetic philosophy of Theosophy, which championed the intuitive, spiritual nature of existence. The works of radical composers Henry Cowell and Dane Rudhyar challenged her to rethink the tonal, harmonic, and structural conventions of Western classical music and introduced her to new ideas about dissonance and experimental forms.[9]

While in Chicago Ruth was befriended by the great American poet Carl Sandburg, who welcomed her into his family as an "informal unadopted daughter" after she began giving piano lessons to his own daughters.[10] She became an admirer of Sandburg's populist vision of art and culture and contributed piano arrangements for four folk songs to his classic 1927 collection, *The American Song-*

bag. Ruth's work with Sandburg marked her initial efforts to notate folk music, an activity that would consume her latter years.

In the fall of 1929, following a summer at the MacDowell Colony, Ruth relocated to New York, where she joined a growing movement of ultramodernist composers that included Aaron Copland, Henry Cowell, Carl Ruggles, and Marc Blitzstein. After a year of study with her future husband, Charles Seeger, she was granted, at the urging of Cowell, a Guggenheim Fellowship in composition to study in Berlin, the first to be awarded to a woman. Her compositions of this period exemplified the ultramodernist impulse to replace conventional harmonic consonance, diatonic tonality, and sonata-form structures with dissonant counterpoint, radically independent polyphonic textures, and irregular rhythmic patterns. Her Piano Study in Mixed Accents (1930), Diaphonic Suites nos. 1–4 (1930), and the much celebrated String Quartet 1931 have been hailed as influential works that "anticipated and enabled the achievements of subsequent generations of American Composers."[11] Her Three Songs to Poems by Carl Sandburg (1930–32) and her 1932 music settings of H. T. Tsiang's radical texts "Sacco, Vanzetti" and "Chinaman, Laundryman" united her interest in leftist politics with her modernist inclinations.[12]

After moving to Washington and giving birth to her second and third daughters, Barbara (1937) and Penny (1943), the pressures of raising a family and supplementing Charles's income through teaching piano forced Ruth to curtail her composing. But Charles's work through the Resettlement Administration programs opened up a new musical world for her, ushering in a phase of her life devoted to studying, transcribing, publishing, and teaching folk music. In 1937 she compiled Twenty-two American Folk Tunes, a collection of piano arrangements of southern ballads, play-party tunes, and African American songs that she hoped would "acquaint the piano student with at least a small part of the traditional (i.e., 'folk') music of his own country."[13] That same year she would begin work as the transcriber of John and Alan Lomax's field recordings, a project that eventually resulted in the 1941 publication of the Lomax folk song collection *Our Singing Country*.[14] The proposed preface to the Lomax volume, published in 2001 as *"The Music of American Folk Song" and Selected Other Writings on American Folk Music*, revealed Crawford's struggles to squeeze the sounds of performance-centered folk music into the language of Western music notation as well as her keen observations regarding folk song structure and performance style.[15] An unexpected by-product of the Lomax transcribing project were the hundreds of LOC field recordings that made their way into the Seeger home, where they delighted the ears of Mike and his sisters.

Ruth built on the success of the Lomax project, going on to compile her own collections of children's folk material in *American Folk Songs for Children* (1948), Animal *Folk Songs for Children* (1950), and *American Folk Songs for Christmas* (1953), each including song arrangements for voice and piano accompaniment. The volumes played an immense role in introducing youngsters of the postwar generation to a breadth of American folk songs, leading cultural historian Robert Cantwell to characterize them as "master texts of the expanding folk revival."[16]

Toward the end of her life Ruth sought to unite her interests in folk music with her earlier passion for modernist composition. Tragically, she only produced one complete piece, her 1952 Suite for Wind Quartet, before succumbing to cancer in 1953. Although her dream of merging modern and traditional idioms in composition eluded her, she is remembered as a leading composer of ultramodern music and a pioneering scholar, innovative teacher, and successful popularizer of American folk music.

The Seeger home in Silver Spring, Maryland, where the family moved in 1938, was by all accounts overflowing with music.[17] Mike recollected that Ruth and Charles refused to allow a radio in the house because they believed "you should make your own music."[18] His parents "played 'Get Along Home Cindy' on the piano to get us to go to bed at night. They played European piano music and southern folk songs for us as we danced a circle around the couch and family desk in the middle of our huge living room. Singing was always around the house, and by the time I was five or so I knew all the words to 'Barbara Allen.'"[19]

Learning ballads was apparently great fun for five-year-old Mike, but two years later he discovered the unusual sound recordings that his parents were beginning to collect:

> When I was around seven, I was given the great honor of being allowed
> to use the variable-speed record player that my mother used for folk song
> transcription. . . . I couldn't use it on her desk, so I sat on the floor with it. I
> sharpened the cactus needle we used to play the two hundred or so alu-
> minum field recordings that made up the largest part of our family record
> collection and listened to Jimmie Strothers, Leadbelly, and the Ward Family
> of Galax, Virginia. I also listened to our very few commercial recordings,
> which included Dock Boggs's "Pretty Polly," Gid Tanner's "Fiddler's Con-
> vention in Georgia" (I almost wore it out), and artists such as Sonny Boy
> Williamson, Fats Waller, Norman Phelps and the Virginia Rounders, Billie
> Holiday ("Strange Fruit"), Meade Lux Lewis, Sidney Bechet, Josh White, and
> Winifred Christie playing Bach's Toccata and Fugue in D Minor.[20]

By the time the Seeger family moved to Kirk Street in Chevy Chase, Maryland, in 1944, eleven-year-old Mike was steeped in a variety of musical traditions, ranging from his mother's classical European piano repertoire to the jazz and folk music he listened to on disc. But Mike's enthusiasm for music was not matched by any interest in formal musical instruction. At the age of six, when his mother attempted to sit him down at the piano, he rebelled: "I couldn't stand the idea of practicing and wouldn't do it. Perhaps I was already absorbing my parents' new devotion to traditional music and the informal ways one can pick it up."[21] Mike did learn to strum the autoharp to accompany songs during the family song sessions, but he had no other lessons during his elementary and junior high days in Silver Spring and Chevy Chase or at the Woodstock Country School in Vermont, where he was sent for high school. His one musical experience at Woodstock was winning a talent contest his senior year singing a folk song, probably "Goodnight Irene," to the accompaniment of autoharp.

Although he shirked formal lessons and refused to learn to read music, as a child Mike absorbed fundamental ideas that would shape his attitudes toward music for the rest of his life. Through family singing sessions and listening to recordings he became familiar with a wide range of southern folk music, from ballads and blues to spirituals and dance music. He would return to these songs throughout his career as a soloist and with the Ramblers. But equally important, the field recordings and early hillbilly discs exposed him to a variety of southern regional folk music styles that had not been rearranged and tidied up for distribution to urban audiences. As he "wore out" Gid Tanner's fiddle records and the Rich Family's "Colored Aristocracy" he soaked up the subtle nuances of vocal inflections, melodic variations, and rhythmic irregularities that characterized much southern mountain music. The family singing sessions demonstrated that folk songs were not merely words and notes on paper but rather living expressions that could be performed and reinterpreted by even those with little direct contact with rural southern culture. For Mike and his sisters, singing a ballad or dancing around the couch to a fiddle tune seemed as natural as hearing a church choir or attending a recital. Finally, he began to embrace Ruth and Charles's belief that American folk music was aesthetically and culturally as valuable as Western art music and that efforts must be taken to ensure that this music did not disappear as the result of the homogenizing effects of an ever-expanding commercial media that was coming to dominate postwar American life.

The Korean War was in full swing in the spring of 1951 when Mike graduated from the Woodstock Country School in Vermont and prepared to enter the University of Maryland. But as the fall term was about to begin he was shocked to learn of the university's ROTC requirement. Perhaps having inherited Charles's pacifist sentiments, Mike refused to enroll and a week later was admitted to George Washington University, a private school with no military obligation. The summer of his high school graduation, at his mother's urging, Mike agreed to try guitar lessons. His first instructor, the soon-to-be-renowned jazz guitarist Charlie Byrd, taught him rudimentary chords and allowed him a great deal of freedom to interpret individual pieces. But after Byrd left to pursue his career as a performer, the music school's other guitar teacher, Sophocles Pappas, took over Mike's instruction. Pappas insisted Mike adhere to strict classical technique and written notation, and when he suggested a bland arrangement of "I Gave My Love a Cherry" for nylon-string banjo, Mike terminated the lessons. Although Pappas dampened Mike's interest in further music instruction, he did sell him his first banjo, an SS Stewart 5-string.[22]

Mike showed little interest in academic studies, and to his parents' dismay he dropped out of GWU in early 1952. What followed was a pivotal time in Mike's life; in the midst of applying for conscientious objector status and of dealing with the onset of his mother's cancer, his interests in traditional music resurfaced: "My mother was very upset that I didn't go to college, but what I was doing in a way was going to my own version of college." He began to teach himself the banjo, listening to his parents' records and LOC recordings and watching Mike Vidor, Peggy's boyfriend, who played in a traditional frailing style. Peggy also encouraged him to work with their half brother Pete's manual, How to Play the 5-String Banjo, but Mike recalled having little success with it.[23] By that time Pete Seeger had emerged as a leading force in the New York City folk revival. He had apprenticed himself to Woody Guthrie and Lead Belly in the late 1930s, worked to meld folk song and progressive politics through his activities with the Almanac Singers and People's Songs in the 1940s, and helped usher in the first wave of popular folk song through the commercial success of the Weavers in the early 1950s. While the half brothers would maintain a friendship throughout their lives, Pete and Mike traveled different roads in their approaches to folk music—Pete the "popularizer" and Mike the "preservationist," as Pete's biographer, David Dunaway, would later put it.[24] But in the summer of 1952, while visiting Beacon, New York, where Pete was finishing his log house overlooking the Hudson, Mike did pick up some basic fingerpicking techniques watching Pete play the banjo.

Mike continued to live at home, taking a part-time job as an office boy at the Brookings Institution and painting houses. Sometime in late 1952 he heard about a weekly square dance on a local country music radio show hosted by Curley Smith. He found his way to a public school gymnasium on Eleventh Street and Pennsylvania Avenue in downtown Washington, DC, where a small band fronted by Virginia fiddler Blackie Morgan was playing for a group of southern-migrant dancers. Mike began hanging around the dances and eventually joined the group playing banjo, just "sitting in the background playing chords, trying to get rhythm and learn to play with a group." He bought a cheap mandolin soon after meeting

Morgan and then glued together an old fiddle a friend had found in the garbage. He practiced at home, banned to his third-floor room by his sisters, trying to play like Morgan by fitting dance tunes into a simple shuffle rhythmic patter (de, de-de; de, de-de; etc.).

Although the Seeger family did not have a record player and Mike rarely bought records at that time, he was impressed upon first hearing the *Anthology of American Folk Music*, compiled by filmmaker Harry Smith for Moe Asch's Folkways Records and released in 1952. The compilation of eighty-four hillbilly string band, ballad, blues, and spiritual numbers, culled from Smith's prodigious collection of 78 rpm records first released in the 1920s and 1930s, was hailed by critics as introducing genuine southern folk music to the burgeoning folk revival. As Cantwell put it: "The Folkways Anthology was a kind of curriculum in mystical ethnography, converting a commercial music fashioned in the twenties out of various cultural emplacements and historical displacements into the 'folk' music of the revival." Armed with the *Anthology*, "revival musicians [like Mike and the New Lost City Ramblers], in turn, became themselves living anthologies, purveyors not only of a repertory of songs, but of instrumental and vocal styles."[25] John Cohen, Mike's future collaborator, would later recall that the *Anthology* "gave us contact with musicians and cultures we wouldn't have known existed," hillbilly and blues performers who would become "like mystical Gods to us."[26] At the time neither Mike nor John could have guessed that in just over a decade they would locate *Anthology* artists Dock Boggs, Eck Robertson, and Maybelle Carter and eventually introduce them to new urban audiences.

In 1956, having worn out the *Anthology*, Mike and a young Swarthmore student named Ralph Rinzler volunteered to catalog Smith's collection of thousands of old 78 blues and hillbilly records that he had donated to the New York Public Library. While Rinzler cataloged, Mike began dubbing choice tracks onto his quarter-inch reel-to-reel recording machine, which he had brought into the library, but he was ordered to stop by the head librarian, William Miller. Undaunted, Mike and Rinzler decided to smuggle out a batch of 78 records the next night:

Ralph hatched the idea that I'd bring a suitcase in and fill it up with boxes full of the Columbia and RCA Victor 78 discs that we were forbidden from copying. That evening we went out with my tape recorder and the box [of records]. So the guard at the door said, "Oh, I want to look at the box." So Ralph went into kind of like a frenzied dance, looking for a card or something to show him. So he got the guard, who was this sixty-year-old, like a cop doing his retirement, so flustered and confused, and I just walked out with the box. So we took these absolutely fantastic discs out, spent the night at Ralph's in Passaic, New Jersey, dubbing them all. And I brought my suitcase with the records back in the next morning.[27]

By transferring old records onto tape and making his own recordings of traditional players, Mike gradually compiled a substantial library of traditional material for listening and learning.

Rinzler, who had studied classical music as a youth, proved to have a keen ear for traditional music. By the mid-1950s he had become one of the organizers of the Swarthmore Folk Festival and would go on to play mandolin with one of the first urban bluegrass bands, the Greenbriar Boys. Rinzler remembered meeting Mike and Peggy at one of the Swarthmore festivals, probably in 1954.[28] He stayed in contact with Peggy, who sent him a mimeographed copy of Pete's original banjo manual and invited him to come to Beacon to visit Pete and Mike in June 1954. Rinzler became one of the legions of folk enthusiasts who helped with the building of Pete's log home and who picked and sang with his fellow workers. In early 1955 Mike sent Rinzler a postcard suggesting he bring the Stanley Brothers to the next Swarthmore festival. Later that spring he visited New River Ranch country music park with Mike to hear the Stanleys, Bill Monroe, Grandpa Jones, and the McGee Brothers.[29] Within a few years the two would become close collaborators on various music projects, including Mike's *American Banjo* album and Mike and Peggy's initial 1957 recording for Folkways. Rinzler later recalled Mike's intense commitment to traditional music:

> Mike [back] then had a vision of forwarding old-time music. He had a missionary sense of, "Look, if you are going to do things for the Swarthmore Folk Festival, deal with people who are still playing the music." Then he took me a year or two later to hear the Stoneman Family, and then he took me to record this Washington fiddler. I looked at how Mike had a van and a tape recorder, a whole studio, everything organized. Mike had a sense in his own mind of progressing in his own way. He already played mandolin, fiddle, banjo, guitar, and mouth harp. He seemed to me like a whole catalog of experience, information, and collected archival recordings and a whole world of information about these things. Mike was clearly a guided missile, and I got very much a sense of missionary zeal from him.[30]

By 1953 Mike's skills on the banjo and guitar had advanced to the point that he would play in public with his younger sister Peggy, who was by then proficient on piano, banjo, and guitar. In June 1953 they performed at a talent show for Peggy's high school graduation. On November 18 of that year, the day their mother succumbed to cancer, the siblings sang at a Washington book fair to promote their mother's newly published volume, *American Folk Songs for Christmas*. The *Washington Post*, in an announcement of the upcoming book fair, reported that Mike felt a "special thrill" to be performing songs from his mother's new book.[31]

In the spring of 1954 Mike left the Seeger home in Chevy Chase, moving to Pikesville, Maryland, where he began his conscientious objector alternative service, working in the kitchen of Mount Wilson State Hospital. He was not allowed to play music in his hospital living quarters, so after he finished his shift he would take his Chevrolet Carryall (a trucklike station wagon) out to a nearby Tasty Freeze parking lot, where he would practice the banjo, mandolin, and fiddle. At Mount Wilson he met a group of working-class Appalachian migrants who played old-time and bluegrass music. One patient, a singer and guitarist named Robert Dickens, invited Mike home to meet his family. Transplanted from the hills of West Virginia to a tenement building in downtown Baltimore, the Dickens family played traditional styles that Mike associated with the field recordings he had grown up with. He quickly befriended Robert's sister, Hazel, who sang in a searing Appalachian voice and was just starting to write her own songs. Mike recalls supplying all the instruments—guitars, banjos, mandolins, and fiddles— for evening music sessions with the Dickens family. Hazel and Robert's parents, Hillary and Sara, and their two brothers, Arnold and Guy, often joined in. The music was a bit rough but gave Mike a firsthand introduction to early bluegrass and the transitional country music of the 1940s, whose roots were firmly anchored in older mountain singing and instrumental styles. Making informal music with mountain people was a transformative experience for Mike, who found the Dickenses' warm hospitality "like family" at a time when his own family was splintering apart in the aftermath of his mother's death.[32]

Through the Dickens family Mike discovered what he commonly referred to as Baltimore's "underground country scene." At local music parties and square dances that resembled those he had experienced in Washington, DC, he encountered migrants from rural areas of Maryland, Virginia, and West Virginia. He was introduced to Bob Baker, a singer and guitarist whose family was originally from eastern Kentucky. Mike played banjo, mandolin, and occasionally fiddle with Baker for several years in what he described as an informal bluegrass band that performed at "some of the worst downtown dives" and music parties in and around Baltimore. Mike, sometimes accompanied by Baker or members of the Dickens family, also showed up at more folk-oriented sing-alongs and hoots. There they enjoyed "breaking up the party," often to the consternation of ballad singers, with their raucous bluegrass and old-time dance music. Sometime in 1957, while attending a hoot hosted by Myron Edelman in a fancy carriage house in downtown Baltimore, Mike was introduced to Tom Paley. Mike was familiar with the recording of old-time southern songs that Tom had made several years earlier for Elektra Records and was impressed by his flashy guitar and banjo picking. The two jammed informally at Edelman's hoot more than a year before they would play together on John Dildine's radio show.

Sometime in the early fall of 1954 or the late spring of 1955 Mike made his first visit to the country music parks to the north of Washington. Sunset Park, located near Oxford in southern Chester County, Pennsylvania, was an eight-acre spread built by Roy Waltman on his family farm in 1940. In the postwar years the park became a mecca for country and bluegrass musicians. Bill Monroe, Flatt and Scruggs, the Stanley Brothers, and the Stoneman Family were among the stellar bluegrass bands that played the open-air stage.[33] A second, more rustic park was New River Ranch, located just south of Sunset Park on Highway 1 near Rising Sun, Maryland. Run by Ola Belle Reed and Alec Campbell, the park was a mixing ground for country people as well as urban and suburban fans who were discovering country and bluegrass music by the 1950s.[34] Richard Spottswood, then a young bluegrass buff and nascent record collector from Silver Spring, traveled regularly to New River Ranch with Mike, Hazel Dickens, Gerry Foster, Alice Gerrard, and Lamar Grier. On one memorable day they were awed to hear the Monroe Brothers and Grandpa Jones with Sam and Kirk McGee on one show. The unpretentious country sounds and the rural ambience were striking to suburbanites like Mike and Spottswood, the latter recalling "the thrill of sitting on splintery boards resting on upturned cinder blocks, to then see the Amish buggies coming in and out and these people in these ancient-looking, wonderful costumes who would then just move off by themselves in a part of the audience and enjoy the Martin guitars, the Gibson banjos, and the high lonesome sound along with the rest of us. The music was wonderful because it was very un–class conscious."[35]

Mike and his friends soaked up the sights and sounds of country and blue-grass music at Sunset Park and New River Ranch. By 1955 he was hauling along a forty-pound Magnecord tape recorder that he had bought with a royalty check from his mother's songbooks. He recorded hundreds of hours of music, rang-ing from performances by obscure honky-tonk and bluegrass singers to such legends as Bill Monroe, Flatt and Scruggs, the McGee Brothers, and Grandpa Jones. As he became more confident as a musician he would occasionally sit in, playing string bass, guitar, or mandolin, with lesser-known groups who were short a player. At the time Mike had no plans to use the material he recorded; he simply wanted to document the bluegrass music that he viewed as an "emerg-ing country music" based on the older forms of string-band music and ballad singing he had heard as a child.[36]

In the fall of 1956, when Mike completed two years' service at Mount Wilson, he moved into a small apartment over an automotive garage in downtown Baltimore. Soon after he enrolled in the Commercial Radio Institute, a trade school, hoping to obtain a first-class radio/telephone license and eventually find work as a radio announcer. Despite help from his father with tuition, money was tight, and in early 1957 he took a day job working as a clerk for the Social Security Administration in Washington. He left after three months but returned again in early 1958. But during this second stint he was put through a complete FBI screening, probably because of his Seeger name. Halfway through the investigation he quit in frustration and went on unemployment.

Just before enrolling in the Commercial Radio Institute Mike received an offer that would mark the beginning of his career as a serious documenter of traditional music. In the summer of 1956, probably at the prompting of his half brother Pete, Moe Asch of Folkways Records wrote Mike about recording and producing an album of southern banjo styles. The idea, Mike later reflected, was to document the evolution of the driving, arpeggiated three-finger picking style popularized by Earl Scruggs among bluegrass banjo players in the late 1940s. Accepting Ash's invitation and one-hundred-dollar production fee, Mike traveled to the South Carolina home of Snuffy Jenkins, whose early recordings of three-finger picking undoubtedly influenced Scruggs. After five days of recording in the South, Mike returned to the Baltimore–Washington, DC, area to document several of the local banjo players he had played with. The album, released by Folkways in early 1957 under the title *American Banjo: Tunes and Songs in Scruggs Style* (FA 2314), included ten pieces by Jenkins as well as performances by J. C. Sutphin (a southwestern Virginia native), Junie Scruggs (Earl's older brother and a North Carolina native), and twelve others. The *American Banjo* LP was quite successful by Folkways standards. Writing for *Bluegrass Unlimited* in 1985, Spottswood called the record "a landmark LP. . . . one of the first 33⅓ discs devoted to bluegrass," and noted that Folkways' distribution to city specialty shops made it "a significant influence in spreading the bluegrass sound to an emerging generation of young city pickers."[37] The companion booklet, clearly aimed at urban consumers, included an informative introductory essay on the three-finger banjo style by Rinzler and notes on the artists and tunes by Mike.[38]

The *American Banjo* LP provides an initial glimpse at Mike's skills as a documenter and performer of traditional music. A snappy rendition of the dance tune "Cindy," played in a loose bluegrass style by the Baltimore-based Baker band, featured Baker on guitar and vocal, Mike and Dick Rittler on banjos, Hazel Dickens on string bass and chorus, and Bob Shanklin on mandolin. Both Rittler's and Mike's banjo breaks stuck close to the basic melody of the old dance tune, with

Rittler up-picking in Scruggs style and Mike using the older frailing drop-thumb technique. Mike also picked Scruggs-style banjo while Baker sang and played guitar on "Ground Hog." Mike's finger work was concise but not overly imaginative, alternating the basic melody line between low and high registers off the banjo. In a nod to the New York scene the two final cuts featured the fancy banjo picking of Eric Weissberg, accompanied by Mike on mandolin and Rinzler on guitar. Mike's mandolin break on "Hard Ain't It Hard" demonstrated his ability to embellish the melody with simple but tasteful ornamentations.

In early 1957 Rinzler arranged for Mike and Peggy to make a recording at the Swarthmore radio studio. The results of that session are heard on the 1957 Folkways release, *American Folk Songs Sung by the Seegers* (FA 2005). In the accompanying liner notes Charles Seeger commented on the interplay of survival and revival among country singers embracing city ways and city singers adopting country styles, emphasizing the crucial role of mass media in the complex process. He noted that his own children, who appear on the album, were "representatives of a second generation in the Anglo-American revival-survival complex." Although they were of "strictly urban, unhybridized musical ancestry," they were exposed to a broad swath of traditional material at a very young age, thanks to his and Ruth's obsession with southern folk music recordings. The implication, although never stated outright, was that his children's unique background allowed them to avoid the tendency of many city singers to consciously adopt concretized styles of folksinging or to affect poor imitations of "nasal twang or dialect pronunciation of rural singers."[39]

Mike appeared with Peggy and Rinzler on five selections, with the rest of the album filled out with songs by Peggy and her younger sisters, Penny and Barbara. Mike's first recorded fiddling was heard on the Scots-Irish dance tune "Old Molly Hare." The playing was straightforward and a bit scratchy, evoking the spirit of an undistinguished square-dance fiddler. The simple, unornamented melody was bowed in short, choppy strokes accompanied by Peggy's lively frailing banjo and Rinzler's steady guitar. Mike sang in a clear tenor, pinching his vowels in a slightly self-conscious manner that might have elicited a wince from his father. Mike played a bluegrass arrangement of "My Home's Across the Smokey Mountains" with solid Scruggs-style banjo; following Rinzler's mandolin break, Mike dropped the picks and frailed the melody. Mike's singing on the verses was tentative and occasionally slipped off pitch, while the trio chorus with Peggy and Ralph was solid but lacked the tension associated with traditional mountain singing. Mike and Peggy presented the Child ballad "Lord Thomas and Fair Eleanor" in tight but unpretentious harmony. Interspersed among the verses chronicling the tragic love affair were instrumental breaks featuring Peggy thumbpicking the melody on the bass strings of the guitar and Mike answering in the higher register of the mandolin. Mike seemed most at ease singing "Kicking Mule," a hoedown tune learned from the LOC recording by the King Family of California. His mandolin break was clean and energetic; following Peggy's banjo break, he returned with the fiddle, squeezing the uncomplicated melody into a shuffle-style rhythmic pattern. The final selection on the album was the sentimental country song "Goodbye, Little Bonnie." As with the previous song, Mike's mandolin playing was solid and his vocal chorus with Peggy tight. But he seemed uncertain on the lead verse lines, especially when the melody jumped to the higher register.

Mike's performances on the *American Banjo* and *American Folk Songs* albums reveal that the twenty-four-year-old had a strong feel for bluegrass-style mandolin as well as Scruggs-style and drop-thumb frailing banjo. His fiddling was adequate but lacked the melodic ornamentation and rhythmic complexity of the more experienced old-time and bluegrass fiddlers he emulated. His vocals were uneven, at times demonstrating a genuine feel for traditional phrasing and timbre and at others failing to hit and sustain the tense, high-range notes characteristic of bluegrass and mountain singing. In sum, his singing and playing on these early recordings were adequate but unremarkable—Mike was still in the early stages of mastering southern folk style and finding his own voice.

Encouraged by the success of *American Banjo*, Mike stepped up his recording and production activities. In early 1957 he made a series of recordings of North Carolina guitarist Elizabeth Cotten, who had worked as a domestic in the Seeger family's Chevy Chase home. The result was *Negro Folk Songs and Tunes* (FG 3526, 1958), a collection of Cotten's guitar instrumentals and songs issued by Folkways. Later that year and again in the summer of 1958 Mike returned south to record more bluegrass and traditional players, assembling materials that would eventually be released on Folkways as *The Stoneman Family: Old Time Tunes of the South* (FA 2315, 1957), *Mountain Music Bluegrass Style* (FA 2318, 1959), and *Look! Who's Here: Old Timers of the Grand Old Opry—The McGee Brothers and Arthur Smith* (FA 2379, 1964).

In the spring of 1958 the future was anything but certain for Mike; he had dropped out of the radio school, quit his second shift at the Social Security Administration, and gone on unemployment. His hopes of becoming a radio announcer were not materializing, nor did he have any other immediate job prospects. He continued to devote his energies to his Folkways documentation projects and playing music, but neither brought him ample income or offered opportunity for steady employment. Then, in May of that year, while playing at a music party at Myron Edelman's house in Baltimore, he had a conversation with a young banjo player and radio engineer that would prove to be pivotal to his musical career. John Dildine, impressed that a city-bred player like Mike demonstrated such knowledge of bluegrass and old-time music, asked him if he would like to perform live on his WASH-FM Sunday evening folk music show. Mike jumped at the chance, and two weeks later he found himself cramped in a small DC studio with two other city pickers he hardly knew, John Cohen and Tom Paley.

2
YALE HOOTS AND WASHINGTON SQUARE JAMS

When seventeen-year-old John Cohen took his seat at Town Hall for the Lead Belly memorial concert, he witnessed a historic gathering. It was January 1950, and New York City's folk music community was in the throes of transition. Lead Belly's death, Woody Guthrie's declining health, Alan Lomax's imminent departure for England, and Pete Seeger's involvement with the pop-oriented Weavers all contributed to the growing tension between the movement's leftist Depression era roots and its more recent commercial aspirations. Six months later, the Weavers' arrangement of Lead Belly's "Good Night Irene" would top the pop charts, demonstrating folk music's commercial viability, which would resurface in the late 1950s as a full-blown national fad.

But schisms in the folk revival were not on John's mind; in fact, he recalled that night as "a seminal moment" in his life when he witnessed a parade of folk legends who had come to define the New York scene. In addition to the people's songs of Guthrie and Seeger, he savored the down-home blues of Sonny Terry and Brownie McGhee, the plaintive balladry of Kentucky-born Jean Ritchie, the bouncy calypso tunes of Lord Invader, and the hard-edged gospel blues of Reverend Gary Davis. A relative newcomer to folk music, John was mesmerized by the gathering of folk luminaries to honor Lead Belly, the first southern folksinger to establish himself in New York.

John had no way of predicting that January evening that many of the performers onstage would play important roles in his future career as performer, documentarian, and folk music activist. Three years later he would visit and record Reverend Gary Davis in the Bronx, thus beginning his lifelong commitment to documenting traditional music. A decade later he would enlist Jean Ritchie to help organize New York City's Friends of Old-Time Music, a loosely knit organization that hosted concerts of southern folk music in Greenwich Village. Pete Seeger was destined to become John's brother-in-law following his marriage to Pete's half sister Penny in 1964. Pete's half brother, Mike, would soon become his longtime partner in playing and promoting old-time mountain music. But the most immediate presence that evening was Tom Paley, a twenty-two-year-old guitarist from the Bronx who was accompanying Woody Guthrie. Two years later John and Tom would connect at Yale University hoots and begin a decade-long musical collaboration that culminated with the formation of the New Lost City Ramblers.

John Harris Cohen was born in Sunnyside, Queens, on August 2, 1932. Sunnyside, a haven for political progressives, was a consumer cooperative and one of the first planned developments with communally owned land. His father, Israel E. Cohen, was the son of Russian Jewish immigrants. After graduating from City College, Israel worked as a surveyor and eventually owned and ran a shoe store in downtown Brooklyn. John's mother, Sonya Shack, was born in Russia and brought to New York at the age of three. She and Israel had met while square dancing in the Lower East Side at Madison Settlement House, where, like many eastern European immigrants, they were introduced to American cultural activities such as square dancing and folksinging as part of a self-conscious nod toward acculturation. Later they organized square dancing in Sunnyside with the help of Margot Mayo, the founder of the American Square Dance Association who would occasionally drop in to lead dances. Though neither of his parents had formal music training, both liked to sing around the house, occasionally to the accompaniment of Israel's rough, stride-style piano. John heard Russian folk songs, Yiddish show tunes, Gilbert and Sullivan light opera ditties, and even spirituals gleaned from a copy of James Weldon Johnson's Book of Negro Spirituals. Unlike the Seegers, the Cohens did listen to the radio, where John was first introduced to the voices of Burl Ives, John Jacob Niles, Josef Marais and Miranda, and Paul Robeson.[1]

John's mother eventually attempted to develop a more formal singing voice that consciously employed the classical techniques of vibrato and coloratura. "It made me uneasy to hear it," John later recalled. "There was something there that smothered her joy. She sang European folk songs in her natural voice, with an open pleasure that I connected with the beauty of nature." This was probably John's first inkling of folk song style, as he recognized the aesthetic merit of rendering a traditional song in what sounded to him like a natural, untrained voice.[2]

In 1941 the Cohen family moved to the suburban town of Great Neck, nestled on Long Island's north shore, just over the Queens line in Nassau County. Shortly after the move John recalled that his older brother, Mike, started taking accordion lessons and then began teaching himself guitar. While he enjoyed listening to folk music on the radio, John showed no interest in actually playing an instrument at the time. In 1945 the family began spending summers at Camp Turkey Point near Kingston, New York, where his mother taught folk dancing and his father worked in the camp office. It was there in the summer of 1948, at age sixteen, that John had the first of several transformative musical experiences. A group of progressive young people associated with the Henry Wallace presidential campaign were counselors that year. One was Woody Wachtell, a New Yorker who had learned to build and play five-string banjos following a trip to eastern Kentucky with Margot Mayo, who was visiting her uncle Rufus Crisp. John, who had recently taken up the guitar under the informal tutelage of his brother, was fascinated by the drop-thumb, frailing banjo style that Wachtell had learned from Crisp. Later that summer he was inspired by another urban banjo picker, Pete Seeger, whom he heard for the first time at a gathering sponsored by the Progressive Party in nearby Woodstock.

Another Turkey Point counselor, Helen Silber (the sister of long-time *Sing Out!* editor Irwin Silber), had brought to the camp that summer a batch of 78 LPs that she had borrowed from the WNYC radio station. For the first time John heard the gritty voice of Woody Guthrie on a volume called *Dust Bowl Ballads*.[3] Equally influential were two album sets of reissued 78s of hillbilly recordings compiled by Alan Lomax for Brunswick Records in 1947, *Mountain Frolic* and *Listen to Our Story*.[4] These collections were John's introduction to southern mountain music played by traditional performers who happened to be recorded by commercial record companies in the 1920s and 1930s. Lomax's Brunswick collections included lively fiddle-guitar-banjo breakdowns by Uncle Dave Macon and his Fruit Jar Drinkers, the Crockett Family, the Tennessee Ramblers, and Al Hopkins and his Buckle Busters. Also featured were bluesman Furry Lewis, spiritual singer Reverend Edward Clayburn, and banjo-accompanied solo singers Buell Kazee and Dock Boggs. John was bowled over by what he heard on those scratchy records: "The stuff would just burn into me! It was such a vivid thing!"[5]

That fall his Great Neck High School art teacher heard John talking about his hillbilly record discovery and gave him an even older collection that John Lomax had compiled for Victor Records in 1941. *Smoky Mountain Ballads* included reissues of the driving fiddle-banjo-guitar trio led by Wade Mainer, the tight duet singing of the Monroe Brothers, the plaintive harmonies of the Carter Family, a banjo stomp by Uncle Dave Macon, the rollicking double fiddles of Gid Tanner and the Skillet Lickers, and the comical vocalizing of the Dixon Brothers.[6] As a soloist and later with the Ramblers, John would return to many of the hillbilly artists featured on the three Lomax collections for source material. The string bands provided John with a new model for folk music grounded in a fiddle-driven ensemble, a striking alternative to the guitar- and banjo-accompanied songs he had heard on the radio and around the campfires.

While Harry Smith's 1952 six-record Folkways release, *The Anthology of American Folk Music*, is widely credited for providing the folk revival with southern source material, the Lomax collections made hillbilly and blues artists available to city listeners like John years earlier. The packaging of the recordings, especially the two Brunswick sets, was unquestionably aimed at city listeners. The accompanying booklets are festooned with caricatures of a straw-hatted hillbilly guitarist, a bearded fiddler perched on a keg of whiskey, and a high-stepping square dance caller clutching his bottle while shouting his calls to a throng of frolicking hillbilly dancers. *Listen to Our Story*, subtitled *A Panorama of American Ballads*, included printed material assuring listeners that, while commercial singers had "replaced these awkward country folk in the catalogues of big companies," these recordings had captured "the timeless breed of the folk artist."[7] Lomax described *Mountain Frolic* as "an album of reels, sinful ditties, square dance pieces, hoedowns and devilish banjo tunes from the Southern mountains." The accompanying booklet included his highly romanticized fictional account of "the tale of a rip-roaring square dance that took place on Sugar Hill in Tennessee about 1840 or thereabouts." The purpose of the volumes, noted Lomax, was to "give you authentic folk songs performed by genuine folk singers." Each of the booklets accompanying the recordings was identified as a "Sing-Along Book" and contained simple melodies, guitar chords, and words to the songs. Lomax invited readers to use the notated musical examples "to study and learn to perform these songs for your own pleasure." But he warned, "Only the skeleton of the melody is given. Try it out on your guitar or piano and then sing along with the performers on the recordings. Only in this way will you capture the true style and real flavor of American Folk Music."[8] John and the Ramblers would take Lomax's suggestion to heart by focusing on "true style" instead of printed notes and words.

John was so excited by the Lomax reissues that he began to look for more old recordings. In a small record shop in Manhattan he came across a Disc Records release of Hobart Smith and Tex Gladden called *Blue Ridge Ballads*. At Macy's he found *Kentucky Mountain Ballads Sung by Cousin Emmy*, recordings made by a Kentucky banjoist whom the Ramblers would later promote. On a family vacation to San Francisco he discovered a store that sold old 78s for five cents apiece and recalls buying recordings made by Charlie Poole and Fiddlin' Arthur Smith. On another family excursion, this time to Washington, DC, he purchased several LOC field recordings that had been issued on 78 rpm record sets. By the time he had completed high school John described himself as "hungry" for old string-band and blues recordings.[9]

Following his graduation from Great Neck High School in 1950, John began attending Williams College in North Adams, Massachusetts. The school, which he recalled was dominated by fraternities, was not a good social fit. He did, however, run across an ample collection of LOC field recordings at the Williams Library and was inspired to finally buy a five-string banjo at a local junk shop. Having already acquired an eight-dollar Stella guitar, he set about trying to reproduce the sounds he heard on the old 78 discs and the LOC field recordings as well as the frailing banjo style Wachtell had introduced him to at Camp Turkey Point.

Disillusioned with the scene at Williams, in the spring of 1951 John applied to and was accepted at Yale University, where he planned to study art. That summer he and his cousin Peter Herman set out to hitchhike to Florida to visit relatives. On the way they stopped in Washington to listen to more LOC recordings and were advised to visit singer and folk festival producer Bascom Lamar Lunsford in Asheville, North Carolina. They hitched down the Blue Ridge Parkway, spent the night in a ditch in Danville, Virginia (a town they had heard sung about in ballads), and finally reached Asheville, where they hoped to fulfill their hobo fantasy of sleeping in a jail. John and his cousin were turned away from the jail but were finally able to reach Lunsford on the phone. After John explained that his name was Cohen, he was from New York, and he knew Pete Seeger and Alan Lomax, Lunsford brushed him off. John's initial attempt to hear southern mountain music firsthand ended in disappointment.

John found the social atmosphere at Yale more to his liking and completed a successful freshman year. In the summer of 1952 he took a job as a counselor at Camp Woodland in the Catskills, an experience that further broadened his musical horizons. Growing out of a New Deal program and founded by Norman Studer in the late 1930s, Woodland stressed progressive politics and a strong interest in regional cultural and folklore.[10] Storytellers, craftspeople, and musicians visited the camp regularly. John vividly recalls weekly square dances featuring local callers and bands of fiddlers and accordion players. The Jamaican folklorist and writer Louise Bennett-Coverley introduced him and fellow campers to West Indian folksinging during a residency. Woodland provided John with firsthand contact with rural tradition bearers, and the experience left a lasting impression of how city people could appreciate and participate in rural folk culture.

John's discovery of old recordings and frailing banjo at Turkey Point, along with his experiences with local singers and square dance musicians at Woodland, combined to shape a more expansive view of folk music than that held by most city listeners. Just as Mike was learning through his contact with the Dickens Family, John was coming to the realization that folk music was far more than a set of antiquated words and musical notation from a songbook. Instead, it was a dynamic, living expression that had been and was still being practiced by individuals with strong ties to regional traditions. Moreover, he had absorbed the essential sounds of southern folk styles from the Lomax reissues of mountain string-band music, ballads, and blues. These southern musicians sounded nothing like the popular folk music of Burl Ives, Oscar Brand, or the Weavers; they sang and played with an emotional immediacy that moved John like no other music.

Toward the end of the summer of 1952 John took a job as a waiter for a week at a resort in the Catskills. There he ran into two other waiters from the city who shared his passion for folk music: Izzy Young, whose Greenwich Village Folklore Center would become a focal point of the New York City revival, and Tom Paley, the young guitarist whom John had heard two years prior at the Lead Belly memorial concert. On learning that they were both living in New Haven, John and Tom agreed to get together and play some music.

Allan Thomas Paley was born in New York City on March 19, 1928. His father, David Paley, was a Jewish immigrant from Belarus. The elder Paley first found work as a clerk for Standard Oil and eventually pursued a successful career as a copy editor for the New York Herald Tribune. Although Tom's father did not play an instrument, there was plenty of music in the Paley family. Tom's paternal grandfather, Phipha Palaeus, played piano, accordion, and mandolin back in Europe, and his American-born uncle, Martin Paley, was an accomplished double-bass player who performed in orchestras and jazz bands. His mother, Sylvia Rosamund Leichtling, was a classically trained piano teacher. The Paley family lived at several different Bronx addresses, and, following his parents' separation, Tom spent two years in California with his mother. He returned to New York City in 1944, enrolled in the Bronx High School of Science and Math, and graduated in the spring of 1945.[11]

Tom resisted the formal lessons on piano and violin offered by his mother and Aunt Birdie. He was far more interested in picking out tunes on the harmonica and listening to the political folk songs he occasionally heard in the upstate Long Pond community where his parents summered. Tom's family was politically left of center and encouraged him to participate in Folksay, a branch of the American Youth for Democracy, the youth group of the American Community Party. For Tom, Folksay's greatest draw was its bimonthly square dances, where he first witnessed live folk dancing to piano, guitar, and banjo accompaniment. Unlike many teenagers of his generation, Tom developed an aversion to pop singers who he felt privileged star persona over artistic integrity. The folksingers he would soon come to admire—Woody Guthrie, Cisco Houston, Pete Seeger, and Lead Belly—were those who put the songs first.

In January 1945 sixteen-year-old Tom purchased a seven-dollar guitar from a fellow high school acquaintance and began to teach himself to play. He consulted a booklet called *The Five Minute Guitar Course*, which included diagrams of fingering for basic chords and a series of familiar songs with chord changes. In the summer of that year he acquired a five-string banjo and, again with the help of a manual, learned the rudiments of Pete Seeger's up-pick and strum style to accompany simple songs. Around that time Tom began attending informal hoots, often referred to as wingdings in the Greenwich Village scene, and playing at the Sunday afternoon jam sessions in Washington Square Park. He also played several times on a folk music show hosted by Oscar Brand on the public radio station WNYC.

In the fall of 1945 Tom matriculated at City College, where he majored in math. His interest in folk music continued to expand as he listened to David Miller's *Home Town Frolic* show on a New Jersey–based radio station. Miller occasionally played old hillbilly recordings by the Carter Family, Wade Mainer, Uncle Dave Macon, and the Skillet Lickers in addition to Woody Guthrie and Pete Seeger. Tom soon discovered that these recordings were available on the aforementioned Lomax reissues and on a series of field recordings issued by the LOC that he located in the City College library. Like John and Mike, he was deeply moved by the raucous sounds of the southern string bands that employed fiddles and banjos as well as guitars, and he collected additional hillbilly 78s he found in midtown used record shops. He began to draw distinctions in his own mind between the styles of Guthrie, Lead Belly, and the rural fiddlers and banjo players he heard on the reissue recordings and those of the city players, who tended to soften the rough edges of the music in order to make their songs more palatable to their audiences.

Tom's chance to meet Guthrie personally came about in the summer of 1949, when his friend guitarist Victor Traibush invited him along on a trip out to Brooklyn to visit the Oklahoma legend. Tom returned on several occasions to play with Guthrie at his home on Mermaid Avenue on Coney Island and accompanied him at the Lead Belly memorial concert in early 1950. That spring he and Guthrie performed a few more dates at union halls, where Tom played second guitar, banjo, or mandolin and occasionally sang harmony. He was impressed with Guthrie's unpretentious voice and his voluminous repertoire but soon grew frustrated with his mentor's failure to appear at prearranged engagements. With Tom's imminent departure for graduate school, their brief musical collaboration came to an unceremonious end.

By the time Tom relocated to New Haven in the fall of 1950 to begin graduate studies in mathematics at Yale, his passion for traditional southern mountain music was firmly established. Following their brief meeting at a summer resort in the Catskills, he and John connected in New Haven in the fall of 1952. Aware that Swarthmore, Cornell, Oberlin, and other colleges were forming folk song groups and holding informal gatherings called hoots, they decided to find a space for student folk enthusiasts to meet. After a successful party at an architect student's cramped apartment where a dozen guitars showed up, John was able to acquire a room in the Yale art school for what would become a regular Friday-night hoot. The gatherings were informal and at times chaotic, but according to John everyone was encouraged to participate:

> The early hoots were held in the architecture department and in the art school, where 200–300 people would come around and sing with us on Friday nights. All kinds of folk music were represented: calypso, blues, union songs, hobo songs, hymns, parodies, dirty limericks, an occasional Dixieland band, a Russian chorus, group precipitation numbers, real and fake flamenco, old-type Elizabethan ballads, old-time string band and country music. The idea was seldom for everybody to sing along—more it was to encourage each person to be able to sing and play for himself and not to be afraid to perform for everybody else.[12]

John and Tom would often sit together, trading off on guitar and banjo and leading songs they had learned from old hillbilly recordings. Tom's fancy picking and frailing added a vital instrumental component to the otherwise song-dominated hoots.

Peggy Seeger occasionally came down from Radcliffe, and Tom recalled that she once brought her brother, Mike, along. Woody Wachtel, John's former banjo-playing counselor from Turkey Point, and other aspiring folksingers John knew from camp and New York showed up among the throngs of students. Given the tensions of the McCarthy era, the early hoots were viewed with skepticism by the Yale administration and some students. John claimed he heard that students were warned against attending the hoots for fear of tarnishing their future reputations through association with leftist folk-singing organizations. But attitudes gradually changed as the Friday-night hoots became popular spots for Yale students looking for a cheap date. The hoots would continue after John and Tom departed from Yale in the mid-1950s, and a second folk organization formed the Indian Neck Folk Festival, which sponsored concerts by Pete Seeger and other well-known folk artists. The success of the early Yale hoots demonstrated the tremendous enthusiasm that folk music could evoke among college students, an audience that would become loyal supporters of John, Tom, and the Ramblers.

While studying at Yale and teaching at Connecticut College, Tom continued to visit New York on weekends and during summers, where he became a regular fixture in the Sunday Washington Square Park sessions. Dating back to the mid-1940s, when George Margolin began leading sing-along sessions, the Sunday afternoon gatherings at the park became a focal point of the Village folk scene. As the crowds grew, so did tensions with the police. Eventually, a permit allowing only singing accompanied by stringed instruments between 2:00 and 6:00 P.M. was negotiated with the New York Parks Service. Sunday afternoons offered fledgling folksingers an opportunity to swap songs and tunes and to hone their playing skills in front of an informal audience.[13]

Folk singer Dave Van Ronk, who arrived on the scene in the mid-1950s, called the Sunday Washington Square gatherings "a great catalyst for my whole generation." He recalls that between the arches and fountain various groups of musicians would gather, including singing and dancing Zionists, People's Songs devotees, bluegrass and country musicians, and soloists playing topical songs, blues, and ballads.[14] One Sunday afternoon when he wandered into the park he "noticed this guy playing an old New York Martin, a very small, very sweet guitar, and he was doing something that sounded an awful lot like 'Stakolee.' It immediately grabbed my attention, because he was doing the whole thing by himself: his thumb was picking out the bass notes, while he was playing the melody with his fingers. I'd never seen anything like that."[15]

The player turned out to be Tom Paley. He dazzled Van Ronk and other parkgoers with his intricate fingerpicking and was often heard playing with Roger Sprung, Eric Weissberg, and Harry West. Sprung, a native New Yorker, was one of the first to study Scruggs-style banjo and bring it to Washington Square. In 1957 he formed a folk and bluegrass trio called the Shanty Boys with Lionel Kilberg, a park regular, and John's older brother Mike Cohen. Sprung's lively renditions of the North Carolina ballad "Tom Dooley" and the minstrel-derived tune "Raise a Ruckus Tonight," recorded with Bob Cary and Eric Darling for Stinson's *Folksay II* volume, demonstrated his mastery of Scruggs-style picking.[16] Weissberg, a classically trained musician turned bluegrass maven, went on to play with two other park regulars, banjoist Bob Yellin and singer-guitarist John Herald, as a member of the bluegrass-oriented Greenbriar Boys.[17] Weissberg's banjo work on "Jesse James/Hard Ain't It Hard," recorded for Mike Seeger's 1957 *American Banjo* LP, was an early indication of his creative approach to three-finger Scruggs-style picking, which would eventually make him one of the instrument's finest practitioners. West, a native of Virginia, moved to New York in the early 1950s and began selling records and instruments from his upper Manhattan apartment. He and his wife, Jeanie, made a series of recordings for Stinson Records that introduced many city folks to frailing-style banjo and tense mountain harmonizing.[18] John attended wingdings at the Wests' apartment and recalled hearing one of the first old-time string bands in New York, composed of West on mandolin and guitar, Tom on banjo and guitar, and Artie Rose on mandolin, guitar, and Dobro.[19] Such ensembles, where musicians played mountain dance and bluegrass tunes instead of simply accompanying folksinging, had become an integral part of the Washington Square scene by the mid-1950s.

By the fall of 1956, when he moved to College Park to take a teaching position at the University of Maryland, Tom had become legendary for his guitar and banjo picking. Barry Kornfeld, penning his reflections for *Caravan* in 1959, described Tom's arrival as something "akin to the appearance of the Messiah."[20] But Tom's influence was equally felt through a recording of old-time country songs and tunes he made for Elektra Records in 1953.

Tom was invited to accompany banjoist Roger Sprung at an audition for Elektra, but producer Jac Holzman decided to make the recording with just Tom after he heard him play a few pieces. The ten-inch LP, titled *Folk Songs from the Southern Appalachians*, featured eleven songs and tunes sung by Tom with guitar and banjo accompaniment. It marked the first recording of old-time southern music by a native New Yorker.[21] But Tom's face was nowhere to be seen on the recording. Instead, the jacket and the accompanying song-lyric booklet present a cartoonish image of a barefoot, overall-clad hillbilly with a guitar strung across his back, peering plaintively toward a cluster of roughly hewn cabins and barns nestled at the foot of a mountain. In the liner notes Tom explained that southern Appalachian folk songs were primarily of British extraction and that at least half of the eleven pieces were variations of British ballads. Tom also noted a rich body of native American folk songs and made a pitch for the "borderland music" that fell between the "pedigreed [British] traditional ballads" associated with "pure folk songs" and the "enormous mass of modern commercial hillbilly and cowboy music." Although he did not identify any of the music as borderland, it is clear that the courting song "Shady Grove," the troubled tale of "Little Maggie," and the hot guitar arrangements of "Buck Dancer's Choice" and "Wildwood Flower" fell into this category. While stressing the traditional nature of the material, Tom admitted originally hearing three of the pieces from city singers John Cohen, Harry West, and Rod Moffett. The complicated threads tying city musicians to country sources were revealed in his explanation of "Shady Grove," a banjo tune Tom learned from John Cohen, who learned it at camp from Woody Wachtell, who learned it on his visit with eastern Kentucky banjoist Rufus Crisp.

In the album notes Tom introduced himself as a folksinger who "accent[s] my instrumentals." This was astute self-criticism. While he sang in a clear tenor, his vocal delivery was marked by little phrase variation and at times became a bit monotonous. This understated approach seemed conscious and in keeping with his philosophy of putting the song, not the singer, out front, but the results were not always satisfying. His slightly nasal vowel enunciations on songs like "Deep Water" and "The Girl on the Greenbrier Shore" sounded affected, suggesting he was trying too hard to sound like a southern hillbilly or perhaps like Woody Guthrie. His voice was more relaxed and natural feeling on "The Miller's Song" and "Jackaro," where little twang is heard. Tom's instrumental work, on the other hand, set high standards for city players at the time. His banjo style was unique, drawing on Pete Seeger's pick-and-strum style, traditional frailing, and Scruggs-influenced three-finger picking. His banjo accompaniments for "Shady Grove" and "Old Grey Goose" alternated between fingerpicked rolling arpeggios and brushing clawhammer; "Coal Creek March," "Old Joe Clark," and "Flop Eared Mule" were rendered with rapid-fire, tight precision. His intricate guitar fingerpicking on "Buck Dancer's Choice" was flawlessly executed, while his arrangement of "Wildwood Flower" demonstrated his mastery of Maybelle Carter's style of picking the melody on the low strings while strumming chords in the higher register. Although the guitar playing sounds a bit stiff and the banjo a tad mechanical by today's standards, they were marked by such technical virtuosity that it is no wonder his playing elicited high accolades from the Washington Square crowd. Released in 1953, Tom's Elektra recording, combined with his regular appearances in the park, pushed the New York revival deeper into southern mountain music several years before the appearance of the Ramblers and the Greenbriar Boys.

While Tom was settling into his teaching duties in College Park, John spent the fall of 1956 in the Peruvian highlands, documenting Quechua weavings and culture for a project that would become his MA thesis in photography. In early 1957 he returned to New York and was greeted by a letter from his draft board. On advice from friends who had successfully evaded the draft, he showed up at his induction in lower Manhattan carrying a battery of cameras to "document" the process. His load of cameras and trembling hands landed him in a session with a psychologist who deemed him unfit to serve, and he left the induction center with a 4F deferment.

That summer John rented a loft on Third Avenue and 9th Street in Manhattan, where his neighbors included abstract expressionist painter Willem de Kooning and photographer Robert Frank. He plunged himself into a Greenwich Village scene filled with avant-garde artists, Beat poets, and jazz musicians.[22] Following a successful one-man exhibition of his Peruvian photographs at the Limelight Gallery in November 1957, he tried to eke out a living as a photojournalist, selling his work to *Life* and *Esquire*. He relished photographing the Beat poetry and abstract art scenes in and around his neighborhood but grew increasingly disconsolate with the mentality of the commercial publishing business and the banal assignments he was offered by magazine editors.

In addition to living in the center of the downtown art world, John found himself at the hub of the burgeoning Greenwich Village folk music scene. By 1957 the Sunday jams at Washington Square had grown into huge gatherings, and coffeehouses were springing up that welcomed folksingers, who would pass the basket. The old-guard socialist and union songs were on the wane, but interest was growing in contemporary topical songs and all sorts of traditional music, from string band and bluegrass to ballads and blues. A steady stream of releases from Folkways, Elektra, Stinson, and Riverside records featured a broad array of folk styles. Inspired by Smith's *Anthology of American Folk Music*, a small but devoted group of players had gravitated toward rural blues and hillbilly music.

In February 1957 Izzy Young opened the Folklore Center on MacDougal Street, a store that sold folk music records, books, and magazines. Located a few blocks from John's loft, the Folklore Center quickly became a popular hangout for Village folk musicians.[23] Young soon moved into the promotion business, beginning with a Peggy Seeger concert at the Actors' Playhouse in Sheridan Square. He would go on to produce a number of small concerts, often in his store, including some of the first formal performances by Tom and John. That same year Dave Van Ronk and Roy Berkeley organized the Folksingers Guild, a loose-knit group that sponsored concerts at the Young People's Socialist League's Hall in the Village. In early 1958 Art D'Lugoff opened his now legendary Village Gate, a large cabaret that featured folk and jazz acts.[24]

New York City, the initial epicenter of the postwar revival, was hardly alone in terms of urban folk music activity. Folk music historian Ronald Cohen describes a "national folk music infrastructure" congealing by late 1957 and early 1958.[25] Folk music clubs and festivals at Yale, Swarthmore, Oberlin, the University of Wisconsin, the University of Chicago, UCLA, Berkeley, and other college campuses were attracting growing numbers of students. Clubs and coffeehouses, including the Gate of Horn in Chicago, the hungry i in San Francisco, the Second Fret in Philadelphia, the Ash Grove in Hollywood, and Club 47 in Cambridge, had begun featuring folk music on a regular basis. Folk acts like the Weavers, the Tarriers, Burl Ives, Josh White, and Harry Belafonte had gained national exposure, foreshadowing the chart-busting success of the Kingston Trio and the commercial boom that would shortly erupt. Radio programs devoted to folk music, following the pioneering efforts of Alan Lomax and Oscar Brand, were cropping up in Washington, Chicago, and San Francisco. The fan magazines *Sing Out!* (1950) and *Caravan* (1957) chronicled the proliferation of folk music activities across the country, reviewed recent recordings, and provided a forum for debates over the role of the urban folksinger and the growing commercialization of folk music.

Roger Lass caught the prevailing mood in a provocative piece on urban folk-singers penned for *Caravan* in the spring of 1958. Sketching a brief history of the urban revival, he pondered the conundrum of urban folksingers, who were generally removed from indigenous folk culture, and their involvement in the pursuit of various social, political, and cultural agendas. Surveying the scene in the late 1950s, he identified four separate, though not totally exclusive, categories of urban folk musicians: arty adaptations of folk music shaped by classical music sensibilities, as personified by Richard Dyer-Bennet; the legions of middle-ground devotees of Pete Seeger who sang a wide range of American folk material with relatively simple and non-region-specific banjo and guitar accompaniment; the ethnic professionals like Jean Ritchie, Woody Guthrie, and Lead Belly who hailed from a particular cultural or regional folk group and who had found their way to urban venues where they specialized in their native folk style; and the self-consciously ethnic artists, who, though presumably not originally members of a particularly ethnic or regional folk group, "devote themselves, in their own playing, to the imitation of existing ethnic styles. Their aim is idiomatic faithful-ness." Lass heralded Tom Paley and Roger Sprung as representing this final group. Such self-conscious ethnic singers, located in northern cities, would need to play a vital role if regional folk styles were to be preserved. Lass pointed to southern mountain music as a case in point, claiming that local styles were dying out in their home communities.[26] In a follow-up *Caravan* article Lass argued further that urban folksingers must pay close attention to instrumental and vocal styles of the culture whose material they are interpreting, for popular arrangements of folk songs "are incongruities. They are the sort of thing that would produce laughter, revulsion, or utter puzzlement in a member of the folk from which the song came."[27] Lass's challenge, written precisely at the time of the formation of the Ramblers, in retrospect reads like an early mission statement for the group.

After leaving New Haven, Tom maintained his friendship with John and contin-ued to visit New York on weekends to play in Washington Square and occasionally to perform at concerts. Lee Shaw heard the two play for a Folksingers Guild con-cert in early June 1958 and reported to *Caravan* readers that "Paley and Cohen are a fine team, both as musicians and as end men," a reference to their "entertaining patter."[28] They also performed in small concerts organized by Young's Folklore Center and Mike Cohen through the American Youth Hostel and informally at Washington Square. In such appearances they sang many of the songs from the Yale hoots, accompanying themselves on two guitars or rotating between guitar and banjo.

One of Young's earliest concerts took place in November 1957 at the Carnegie Chapter Hall. John Cohen, Jeanie and Harry West, and Gina Glaser were featured. Young was pleased with the show and the following spring wrote a tribute to John in *Caravan*. He intuitively understood John's contributions to the revival, foreshadowing his work with the Ramblers: "[With John] I also know I will get a sense of tradition, a feeling of continuation and permanence I rarely get in concerts. It is as if the Folk Music recordings of the Library of Congress were restored to their importance, if only for a night; as if picking 500 notes a minute isn't the only way to play a banjo; as if Alan Lomax's collections 'Listen To Our Story' and 'Mountain Frolic' were translated into present day life without self-consciousness."[29]

Meanwhile, Tom was finding plenty of folk music activity around Baltimore and Washington. He began attending weekend music parties held in the home of Myron Edelman, a guitarist who owned a carriage house in downtown Baltimore. The scene was a mix of balladeers, topical song singers, and string-band instrumentalists. It was at an Edelman party, sometime in 1957, that Tom first met and jammed with Mike Seeger, who he recalled at the time was a superb bluegrass banjo and mandolin player. Mike, who was familiar with Tom's 1953 Elektra record of old-time southern music, was likewise impressed with his guitar and banjo playing, describing Tom as a "legend among city players."[30]

Occasionally, Tom would venture into Washington and its suburbs to attend hoots organized by John Dildine, a young banjo player and radio engineer who hosted a Sunday evening music show on the DC radio station WASH-FM. Once a month Dildine rented a space from the Maryland Parks and Planning Commission in the small town of Cabin John. According to Dildine, as many as sixty people would sit in a large circle, with various individuals or small groups taking turns leading songs. There were tensions between the "greensleevers," who sang ballads and topical songs, and the "bluegrassers," who played mostly instrumental bluegrass and old-time tunes. But Tom, who could fingerpick guitar and sing or play along with the string-band folks on guitar or banjo, was quite comfortable with both groups.[31]

In mid-May 1958 Dildine ran into Mike at one of Edelman's music parties and broached the subject of Mike's coming on his folk music show the following Sunday evening. Mike had heard that John would be visiting Tom that weekend to dub records and to attend Foshag's Fertility Rites, a weekend-long folk music gathering near Hagerstown, Maryland. Suspecting John and Tom might enjoy playing with a fiddler, Mike suggested to Dildine that the three of them perform together. Dildine, who had been impressed by Tom's playing at the Baltimore and Washington hoots, quickly agreed. Following several phone calls, arrangements were made for Mike, Tom, and John to appear on WASH-FM on Sunday evening, May 25.[32]

The trio rehearsed briefly for the first time in a small space adjacent to the station's broadcast booth. Tom and John already had a repertoire of shared songs from their Yale hoots, Washington Square jams, and Village concerts. Mike and Tom had played informally at Edelman's place and other music parties around Baltimore. In a short time they figured out who would play which instrument on what tune. They stepped into the small broadcast booth with Dildine and huddled around a single microphone.

Fortunately, the full radio program was recorded.[33] Dildine opened his program by introducing his guests as a trio of wandering folksingers with no name (Mike later refers to them as the "Song Swipers"). John identified the first piece as a "military number," and the group launched into the fiddle tune "Soldier's Joy," with Mike on fiddle, Tom on guitar, and John on mandolin. The unusual configuration was one of the few times that John played mandolin with the group instead of guitar or banjo. Next John and Tom played twin guitars on "Weave Room Blues." Learned from a Dixon Brothers hillbilly recording, the piece featured tight-harmony singing and yodeling. Dildine commented that he associated yodeling with commercial recordings, prompting Mike to explain that country yodeling was made popular in the 1920s by the Alabama singer Jimmie Rodgers. Dildine pressed the point, inquiring if the song stems "from the people" or from some record company trying to reap a profit. John responded unequivocally that the former was the case, noting that the lyrics contained so many esoteric terms about weaving-industry techniques that the song would have had little popular appeal.[34]

As Mike picked up his banjo and finger picks, Dildine reflected on the greensleevers/bluegrassers dichotomy and asked for an explanation of bluegrass. Mike clarified that bluegrass comes out of the old-time fiddle and banjo music of the southern mountains, as opposed to the electric guitars and Tin Pan Alley sounds of Nashville that had been "corrupting the Grand Ole Opry" of late. He identified the next tune, "Molly and Tenbrooks," as an "old-time bluegrass number" by Bill Monroe, the originator of the tradition. About halfway through the piece Mike shed the finger picks and switched to an older-style frailing strum. At Dildine's prompting, Mike demonstrated the difference between the two styles of banjo picking and reminded his host that this was an old song that had been given a new melody and arrangement by Monroe and his band.

Following John's solo rendition of the hillbilly hobo song "Make Me a Pallet on Your Floor," Mike and Tom joined him to perform "Colored Aristocracy." The lively dance tune featured the trio in what would become one of its standard configurations—Mike on fiddle, John on five-string banjo, and Tom on guitar. Mike and John traded banter and speculated on the brand of Tom's strings while he tuned his guitar and finally commenced with "The Boll Weevil." The final number featured Mike and Tom playing autoharp and guitar to accompany the ballad "Little Moses." Dildine thanked the three singers and reminded listeners that Tom would be appearing on a concert at Pierce Hall with Paul Clayton later in June. Tom played "Railroad Bill" as an outgoing theme, accompanied by John vocalizing scratchy-old-record sounds.

Mike, John, and Tom's initial 1958 radio broadcast foreshadowed performance practices and attitudes that would become hallmarks of the Ramblers for years to come. While the Ramblers were technically a trio, they envisioned themselves from the beginning as three individual artists who could perform as soloists or join together in different configurations. Only two of the eight pieces on the broadcast, the instrumentals "Soldier's Joy" and "Colored Aristocracy," were played by the trio; three other pieces were duets, and three were solo performances. Each individual musician demonstrated mastery of southern folk styles on multiple instruments—Mike on the fiddle, five-string banjo, and autoharp; John on the guitar, banjo, and mandolin; and Tom on guitar (his fancy banjo picking would be heard later). The singing was a bit rough, but it attempted to stay true to southern sources and contained none of the artsy or pop sweetening associated with commercial folksingers. The repertoire was drawn from various sources, including old hillbilly and not-so-old bluegrass records, LOC recordings, and songs in currency around the New York and DC folk scenes. While characterizing their music as generally old-timey, they did not hesitate to dip into hillbilly and bluegrass recordings, sources their host Dildine intimated were perhaps not pure folk music "from the people." Mike and John vehemently defended commercial hillbilly and bluegrass songs, noting that the roots of those genres were in traditional mountain music. They would have to continue to deflect such criticism stemming from folk purists who remained skeptical of any material drawn from commercial recordings. And finally, the group's humorous patter, often covering Tom's bouts of tuning anxiety, was heard for the first time.

3

THE RAMBLERS TAKE THE STAGE, 1958-1959

Mike, John, and Tom had no plans to form a band when they left the broadcasting booth of radio station WASH-FM in late May 1958. Not that they were displeased with their performance that night—John and Tom were thrilled to play with a fiddler and experience the full sound of an old-time string band, a rarity in New York's folk music scene at that time. A year later Mike would write wryly that the program "went off at least with spontaneity" and that before they went their separate ways that night they "concluded that maybe [they] ought to do this more often, maybe sometime even for money."[1] Money was certainly a concern for Mike, who, currently unemployed, returned to Baltimore to continue his search for a radio engineer position. John headed back to Greenwich Village to work on his photography, and Tom went to College Park and the University of Maryland.

John took the initiative to bring the trio together sooner rather than later. Earlier in 1958 he had provided a second guitar accompaniment for Guy Carawan on his first Folkways recording. While picking up his copy of the record, John ran into Folkways' owner and director, Moe Asch. The two men ended up having lunch together, and in a moment of critical reflection John admitted that the Carawan release lacked the spontaneity and energy of the earlier Folkways recordings he greatly admired, particularly the Woody Guthrie, Cisco Houston, and Sonny Terry sessions. Asch agreed, explaining that Guthrie and Houston had been out playing for Eighth Avenue bar crowds just before their recording session, which probably accounted for their exuberant moods.

After performing on Dildine's radio show, John visited Asch again to report how this new trio seemed to capture the earthy feel of those earlier Folkways recordings. Asch inquired who the other two musicians were. When John answered that they were Mike Seeger and Tom Paley, Asch immediately agreed to record the group.[2]

John then dropped by Izzy Young's Folklore Center. Young, a strong proponent of traditional, noncommercial folk music, was intrigued by John's account of the Washington radio broadcast and grew increasingly interested on learning of Asch's commitment to record the group. Swayed by John's enthusiasm, he agreed to organize a concert for the trio later that summer. Young quickly realized that neither his store nor the small Village theaters he normally used for folk music concerts would suffice for this show, so he booked the Carnegie Chapter Hall, a venue where he had successfully presented John with Harry and Jeanie West the previous year. Young had good reason to suspect that the Seeger-Cohen-Paley trio was worth moving uptown. John and Tom were well known around Washington Square Park and Village hoots, and their previous concerts, produced by Young and the Folksingers Guild, had been well attended. Mike's *Seeger Family* and *American Banjo* albums, both released on Folkways in 1957, had gained him a small following among New York's bluegrass and old-time string-band aficionados. In addition, Pete's fame with the Weavers and more recently as a soloist had put the Seeger name on the map. Young's instincts were right—ticket demand for the concert was so high that at the last minute he switched the show from the intimate Chapter Hall to the four-hundred-seat Carnegie Recital Hall, which came close to selling out.

In late June Mike wrote John in New York, thanking him for making the recording and concert arrangements and expressing his hope to visit during July "to work out a dozen or two numbers with you and Tom." He also invited John to the Fourth of July banjo contest at Sunset Park and to consider accompanying him on "a swing through the mountains during the first two weeks of August with tape machine and banjo."[3] John came down and photographed the Sunset Park concert but could not join Mike on the southern sojourn because he had been invited to be an artist in residence at the Yale Norfolk Summer Art School. In a second letter dated August 19 Mike wrote to confirm that he would arrive in New York on September 7 or 8 so the trio would "have time to practice together and polish a little." He added, "I've begun working on my solos so they won't require much time there. I'll bring tapes and recorder and song sheets." Mike also reported that he had won the banjo contest at the Galax Old-Time Fiddlers Convention and that he was off to Nashville to finish his McGee Brothers recording project.[4]

FIGURE 2. Roger Sprung (banjo), Mike Seeger (mandolin), and John Cohen (guitar) in Washington Square, 1958. Photograph by Aaron M. Rennert of Photo-Sound Associates.

Mike did visit New York several times that summer and accompanied John to Washington Square Park, where the two men jammed with Roger Sprung (figure 2). John recalled the sheer exuberance of playing clawhammer banjo with a live fiddler. With Mike fiddling and Tom plunking out bass runs on guitar, the trio for the first time could approximate the sounds of the old string bands they had heard on field recordings and hillbilly records. Mike's recollections of the group's initial rehearsal in John's Third Avenue loft that summer captured the epiphany of that moment: "The excitement of playing this type of music, old-time music, with a group was indescribable. I'd played bluegrass before in a band. But to try and get certain instrumental sounds and feelings that we were trying to get, especially on the Charlie Poole stuff [with fiddle, banjo, and guitar]—that's what we really worked on, getting that close-knit feeling."[5] The week before the concert the three gathered for more serious rehearsal, aiming to come up with enough material for the program and the Folkways recording session scheduled for the following day. They worked on repertoire and began thinking about how to transform their informal playing into a more serious and organized stage show.

Writing for the folk fan magazine *Gardyloo* the following year, Mike reflected on preparing for the Carnegie concert:

> We attempted to practice the music and learn to play together, then the words, and then how to get the instruments ready for the next song. Obviously, with the variety of types of songs that we play, we have [our] hands full just keeping our instruments tuned (@!?*), remembering who does what song on what instrument, and in what key and when. And we forgot that we would be watched between songs. We could have cut down on variety as do many bluegrass bands down here in order to speed up the show, or we could have accented talk and song background as do so many city-folk. We're working towards a balance we hope, since both are desirable.[6]

Young's flyer for the September 13 concert was Spartan, announcing simply "An Evening of Old Time Songs, Ballads, and Breakdowns" with Mike Seeger, Tom Paley, and John Cohen. Tickets were $1.65, and the show was scheduled to begin at 8:40 P.M. No recording or full review of what unfolded that evening exists. A brief note in *Caravan* reported that the recent Paley, Cohen, and Seeger concert "jammed Carnegie Recital Hall to the rafters with an eager audience."[7]

Whatever planning the trio did in terms of stage production was clearly not enough. "I remember the terrible feeling of utter chaos on the stage—we had never done that before, never figured out how to choreograph anything. It was like the floor of my loft—everywhere you stepped there was another instrument," John recalled. Mike added, "It was almost like a jam session. I don't think we had any idea of how to program." The problem was, John explained, "on every song we'd switch instruments. That was the disaster, but funny. The floor was littered with instruments, and after every song we'd switch and have to tune again."[8] *Gardyloo* editor Lee Shaw confirmed these recollections in a review of a later Ramblers concert in which she remarked that the trio's debut Carnegie Recital Hall show was "severely criticized for the disorganized quality of their performance—the wandering, onstage switching of instruments, tuning up, etc."[9] But John would later defend the group's informal stage presence: "And maybe that was all wrong but it set a certain tone, saying it was more important to present things as they are supposed to be presented rather than saying, 'Here's a slick group that puts them together in one sound.'"[10]

Mike introduced the songs and served as the group's primary spokesperson, while Tom interspersed humorous quips over periods of extended tuning. John remembered the concert ending with enthusiastic applause, but, rather than performing an encore, the trio invited the audience up on stage to look at the instruments and even jam, a practice that was common at Young's informal concerts at the Folklore Center. "Instead of saying, 'We'll do another one, we're the stars,' we said, 'This is your music, come on up and either play by yourself or play with us.' It was an interesting idea for the audience."[11] The Carnegie Hall concert marked the Ramblers' initial effort to present informal music in a formal stage setting while underscoring their struggle to educate as well as entertain.

The following day Moe Asch took Mike, John, and Tom into the Cue Records studio, located in the WEVD building in midtown Manhattan. Asch served as recording engineer, a role he would not repeat on future Ramblers albums. By all accounts the session proceeded smoothly, although several songs required multiple takes.[12] As recording engineer and producer, Asch adopted a laissez-faire attitude, basically giving the group full rein over choosing and arranging material. The only criticism would come from Mike, whose own experience as a recording engineer led him to object to what he perceived to be Asch's excessive use of echo and high-fidelity filters.[13]

As the group prepared to record the final number, "Crossed Old Jordan Stream," John, perhaps embarrassed at their choice of a religious number, explained somewhat sheepishly to Asch that this was a gospel hymn. Asch, who was familiar with the Fisk Jubilee Singers, answered back that he knew about "that Jubilee stuff." John misheard, thinking Asch had said "Jew-billy stuff" instead of "Jubilee stuff," and broke into hysterical laughter. Historian Peter Goldberg interpreted the incident as a "mischievous encapsulation of the incongruity of Asch and Cohen toiling together over the music of poor white Appalachians."[14] But perhaps the exchange revealed not a cultural incongruity but rather a level of comfort that an acculturated immigrant Jew like Asch and a second-generation immigrant Jew like Cohen (and presumably Paley) had with American folk music, including a Christian folk spiritual.

During the lunch break Asch suggested that the trio consider coming up with a name for itself to facilitate marketing the album. This precipitated a lengthy discussion that would not be resolved until several months later, when John was ready to lay out the type for the album design. Although no one can recall with certainty, the name New Lost City Ramblers was apparently a combination of terms drawn from various sources: "New Lost" from the Mainer's Mountaineers song "New Lost Train Blues"; "City" as a nod to the group's urban origins; and "Ramblers" from a favorite group, the North Carolina Ramblers.[15] Mike and John liked the overall flow of the sounds, while Tom was amused at the semantic ambiguity inherent in the name: "Were we the *New* Lost City Ramblers, as if there had been a group called the Lost City Ramblers before us? Or were we the *New Lost City* Ramblers, that is, the Ramblers from New Lost City?"[16]

Mike and Tom returned home after the concert and recording session. Tom

FIGURE 3. Mike Seeger (autoharp) and John Cohen (banjo) at their
September 1958 recording session. Photograph by Tom Paley.

resumed teaching, and Mike finally landed a job with a Baltimore radio station
as a transmitter technician. The three got together once in Baltimore to rerecord
several songs that were not to their liking and to talk about sequencing and the
liner notes. On one trip John visited the LOC to look through the Farm Security
Administration collection of Depression era photographs, which he envisioned
as a visual complement to the group's music.

Folkways had no art department, so John took on the job of jacket designer, a
role he would continue throughout his career with the Ramblers. For the album
cover he chose an FSA image by photographer Russell Lee of a young man and
woman, presumably about to enjoy a country picnic (figure 4). The man sits in the
sunshine on a blanket, holding a Gibson guitar, while the woman peers out at him
with apparent indifference from the passenger side of an old Model T car nestled
in the shade of a tree. The photograph depicts a country scene that is bucolic but
unsettling given the unresolved mystery of the woman, who appears reluctant
to leave the dark confines of the car and move into the sunshine to join the man
with his guitar. The names Mike Seeger, Tom Paley, and John Cohen appear under
the title *The New Lost City Ramblers*, all in white letters across a red horizontal strip

FIGURE 4. Cover of *The New Lost City Ramblers* Folkways LP (1958).
Farm Security Administration photograph by Russell Lee. Image courtesy of the
Ralph Rinzler Folklife Archives and Collections, Smithsonian Institution.

that sits above the photograph. The decision to use the Lee photograph instead
of images of the actual band members on the album cover revealed much about
the sensibility the Ramblers brought to their record project. "It was about the
music, not us!" John explained. "It was about the ambience from which this music
came. It was the Depression; it was virile, country. What it was trying to make a
case for is the look of things: the way we dressed, the typeface, the images, the
photographs."[17] Evoking an atmosphere of a bygone era, when hard times and
uncertain love might be soothed with the balm of music, was more important
to the Ramblers than foregrounding themselves as featured artists. The choice
of the Lee image acknowledged the power and mystery that rural Depression
era music held for the group and demonstrated John's sophisticated eye, which
recognized the photograph's aesthetic merits.

Pictures of the actual Ramblers shot at the September Carnegie Recital Hall concert appear in the eight-page booklet that accompanied the album. Mike wore a plaid shirt with a snap-on western tie (an artifact of his bluegrass performing); John, a shirt and conventional tie; and Tom, a shirt open at the collar. The mismatching outfits were in keeping with the three personal statements found in the booklet, a pattern that would be repeated in all future Ramblers liner notes. Each Rambler viewed himself as an individual with his own distinct perspective on the music and the group's mission; thus, no communally authored statement appeared on any of their early albums. Mike later quipped, "The reason that all three of us write notes separately to accompany our discs is that we don't agree what and why we are and especially what to write for notes."[18]

The album booklet opened with Mike's brief historical sketch of southern old-time music, titled "About the Music and Its Times." He began with a concise description of the music: "The songs on this album were recorded by commercial companies and the Library of Congress between 1925 and 1935, and show the first attempts of the hill musicians to 'make a hit' with old traditional songs that had been in the mountains since pioneer days."[19] Listeners, particularly those purists who might be dismissive of commercial country music, were reminded that the roots of hillbilly recordings were in the music played at "small dances, around home, and contests held by local groups." Before the earliest hillbilly musicians were recorded or heard on radio broadcasts, "their fame was limited to the immediate area in which they lived and worked, where people could see and hear them at local parties and corn-shuckings." Mike never used the word "folk" to describe the music, nor did he view the musical practices of rural people as static or antiquated, noting, "This was a period of great experimentation, when country people were learning new instrumental and vocal techniques, affected sometimes by urban or Negro music." Though often pigeonholed as antiquarians, Mike and the Ramblers understood from the beginning that innovation, experimentation, and mass media all played a crucial role in the traditional country music they had come to admire.

John's statement, titled "About Us," began on a more philosophical note:

There is a side of us all which goes about trying to make the world over in our image.

There is another side—where one searches to encounter his own image in the world. In this process one examines all kinds of elements which come in his path.

John clearly chose to pursue the latter side, and his encounter with traditional music would become his personal path to understanding the wonders of the wider world. Despite his love for things old-timey, he maintained a modernist sensibility that stressed the sanctity of the individual. He identified the individual Ramblers as "coming from different backgrounds and know[ing] many separate worlds." He described himself as a photographer, painter, and global traveler; Tom as a scholar and teacher of mathematics; and Mike as a civil servant, radio technician, and part-time bluegrass musician. (Mike would later add that his own pedigree included growing up in a family of classically trained musicians.) But through old-time music "we have found a place where we can bring together our separate experiences in picking and singing," even though "many of our individual styles" were "arrived at independently." Individualism and independence would turn out to be both assets and liabilities for the Ramblers as they carved out a unique niche in the folk music revival and struggled to keep their strong personal tastes and egos in check in order to function as a group.

The second half of John's statement cut to the heart of the Ramblers' mission. John chastised city folksingers who tried to make folk tunes "more musical with the addition of complicated chord transitions. This intrusion of Art (capital A) is done with the intent of making the music more palatable, so that the folk songs can fit in with the décor of the living room or what have you. But this becomes the death of the songs and returns us to a point which we were trying to avoid in the first place." The Ramblers were not about "watering down and smoothing off" or adding excessive "emotional messages" to the music; rather, they sought to "present" rather than to "interpret."

Tom's statement, titled "About Our Singing Style," picked up on John's line of thought, noting that unlike the "slick, modernized, carefully arranged approaches of the Weavers and the Tarriers," the Ramblers "avoid the most commercial aspects and try to stay fairly close to genuine 'folk' material." While recognizing that the music on this recording reflects "the broad front along which folk music was coming into contact with commercial performances and mass media," he differentiated the Ramblers from their hillbilly sources. "We are performing what we like best," he declared, "rather than tailoring the music to the available market, while many of the earlier performers adapted the music to the expected tastes of their audiences; and, as the audiences were enlarged through radio and recordings, they became even more commercial." This paradox of trying to make a living playing traditional music without compromising style and succumbing to the pressures of the commercial market would haunt the Ramblers, and particularly Tom, in the ensuing years.

Tom reflected on his attraction to the sound of the old-timey string bands, whose multiple melodic instrumental and vocal lines are intertwined to produce a "contrapuntal feeling" instead of to emphasize showy solos. Unlike much urban folksinging, where instruments are subservient to the singer, the Ramblers chose to make their instruments and voices equal partners in the overall texture of the piece. These older approaches to folk music, he feared, "have just about disappeared from the current folk music scene." But he maintained a degree of optimism, surmising that with the sudden resurgence of interest in folk music, older sounds and styles might become recognized as "deserving of resurrection."

Although each Rambler attempted to explain the group and its music from a slightly different perspective, their three statements reveal a shared sensibility. They were united in their love for the sound of southern old-time music, which they perceived to be endangered from an onslaught of commercial folk and country music. As a result, they shared an unwavering commitment to perform such music in the style in which it was originally sung and played. So important were their musical sources that the album booklet included, in addition to the words for each song, annotations and discographic citations to lead listeners back to the original commercial hillbilly and LOC field recordings. Ironically, their own meticulous annotations were clearly borrowed from the conventions of the stuffy folk song collectors they were fond of poking fun at.

The statements accompanying their initial album also made it clear who the Ramblers were not. They were adamant in differentiating themselves from the artsy and popular urban folk artists who in the late 1950s were coming to dominate the commercial revival. They objected to the self-conscious reinterpretation of folk material that stressed the pure tonalities and complex harmonies of the Western art tradition or overblown attempts to smooth out the rough edges of the original folk songs to create popular, Tin Pan Alley–sounding arrangements. Yet they were neither purist greensleevers nor antiquated Luddites. They recognized the dynamic nature of southern mountain music and the role that mass media had in both preserving and accelerating the evolution of that music.

A close listen to the eighteen pieces that comprise *The New Lost City Ramblers* reveals how these aesthetic and cultural commitments shaped the group's choice and arrangement of material. Five commercial records and a 1939 LOC field recording of Virginia fiddler H. L. Maxey were listed as sources for the album's opening dance piece, "Forked Deer." Mike played fiddle, John banjo, and Tom guitar on what would become one of the Ramblers' standard configurations. Mike's fiddling had progressed significantly since his initial 1957 Folkways recordings with his sisters. His squeaks and slurs added subtle variations to the melodic line, while his choppy, slightly syncopated bowing propelled the piece forward with a strong rhythmic drive. John's nimble three-finger banjo picking outlined the chord changes and provided a skeletal version of the melody, and Tom's counterpart guitar bass lines occasionally mirrored the fiddle's main melody. There were no flashy solos but rather a rich polyphonic mix of interlocking sounds. The same fiddle-banjo-guitar configuration was heard again on the popular hillbilly song "Don't Let Your Deal Go Down," on which John sang lead and Tom provided a tenor harmony on the chorus. The accompanying commentary about "the influence of jazz and sophisticated 'popular' songs, particularly in its chord progression," was undoubtedly a reference to the use of VI and II chords, commonly found in ragtime and Tin Pan Alley songs but generally absent from older mountain songs and dance tunes, which revolved around variations of simple I–IV–V chord progressions. The lilting guitar, banjo, and fiddle accompaniment, along with John's understated and slightly pinched lead vocal, closely followed the original 1925 recording by Charlie Poole and the North Carolina Ramblers (the first of five commercial recordings listed as sources).

The mournful love song "I Truly Understand You Love Another Man" featured Tom accompanying himself on frailing banjo and backed by a three-part vocal chorus. Tom's lead tenor was full and rich, but the chorus sounded forced and uneven. "The Dallas Rag," a bouncy ragtime instrumental taken from a Columbia recording of the Dallas String Band, had Mike and Tom trading the melody on mandolin and banjo, respectively, while John provided chordal accompaniment on the guitar. Mike's syncopated melodic lines and improvisations on the stop-time sections gave the piece a particularly jazzy feel. "Tom Cat Blues" introduced a new configuration, with Tom on Hawaiian slide guitar and John on guitar. The humorous piece, filled with sexual innuendos about a stud cat named Tom, was delivered with a laid-back voice interspersed with tasteful blues licks on the Hawaiian guitar. Described in the notes as a "white folk blues" learned from Bob Clifford, the piece's melodic line emphasizes blues tonality, but the lyrics are cast in an eight-bar verse rather than the more familiar twelve-bar blues structure.

The first solo on the album was John's version of Uncle Dave Macon's "Railroading and Gambling." The frailing banjo is crisp and lively, but, perhaps because the song was pitched low, the vocal falters slightly in the lower register and lacks the energy of the Uncle Dave original. The fiddle-banjo-guitar ensemble returned, this time with Tom on banjo and John on guitar, to play "Colored Aristocracy," the aforementioned West Virginia fiddle tune that was recorded by Charles Seeger for the LOC in 1936. Played at a medium tempo, the piece had a slight ragtime flavor, given the use of the flatted seventh VI chord (E) and the II chord (A) in the progression. The clash of the G-natural of the fiddle line and the G-sharp of the accompanying E7 guitar chord provided a surprising moment of dissonance. "Sailor on the Deep Blue Sea," learned from the Carter Family and a Lomax LOC recording by Kentucky ballad singer Lilian Napier, was accompanied by autoharp and banjo played by Mike and John, respectively. The ballad was sung in Carter-style two-part harmony, with Mike leading and John bassing. The interplay of autoharp and banjo created a light, shimmering texture that served as a pleasant counterpoint to the coarse voices and made the occasional harmony slips less annoying.

"East Virginia," the album's only multitracked piece, showcased Mike on guitar, mandolin, and multiple vocal parts. The high, tight, two-part harmony was evocative of the Stanley Brothers, while the bass-lead picked guitar was borrowed from the Carter Family arrangement. The song was unquestionably the most bluegrass-sounding piece on the album. Tom sang "Battleship Maine," a satirical ditty narrated by a soldier in the Spanish American War who, when confronted with the enemy, "dropped my gun and run" because "I cannot fly." Following an uncertain start, the song settles into a bouncy lilt that again suggested the influence of Charlie Poole and the North Carolina Ramblers.

"Davy" was a rollicking breakdown displaying the tight interlock of Mike's fiddle and Tom's fingerpicking banjo. Though starting on a sour note and failing to keep a steady tempo throughout, the piece had the ragged-but-right feel of an informal square-dance number. Mike sang the ballad "Roving Gambler" to the unusual accompaniment of a banjo picked in a rolling, three-fingered style and a harmonica (played on a rack) doubling the banjo's melody between sung verses. The jagged melody came across in a relaxed, natural voice.

The fiddle-banjo-guitar trio returned for another Charlie Poole number, "Take a Drink on Me." The piece chugged along, driven by Mike's shuffling fiddle and punctuated by John's plucky banjo and Tom's assertive bass runs on the guitar. In keeping with the spirit of the subject matter, John's lead baritone and the vocal chorus were rough but compelling. In response to the boisterous drinking song came the lamenting "Likes Licker Better than Me," the sad tale of a girl whose beau prefers whiskey to her charms. Mike, accompanying himself on autoharp, crooned the verses, while John and Tom joined in on the three-part-harmony chorus, which stayed on pitch but failed to achieve a smooth vocal blend.

The fiddle-banjo-guitar configuration was again used for the Fiddlin' John Carson ditty "It's a Shame to Whip Your Wife on Sunday." Sung with another loose three-part vocal chorus, the piece equates wife beating with card playing and drinking and satirically denounces all three—a reminder that the late 1950s were much closer to the 1930s than the 1960s in terms of attitudes toward women. Tom and John played twin guitars on another blues-tinged number, "Brown's Ferry Blues," learned from recordings by the McGee Brothers and the Delmore Brothers. The guitars, one played in standard position, the second capoed up, interlocked with great precision, and the vocal harmony was among the tightest on the recording.

Mike was heard on an unusual arrangement of an Old Testament ballad about Jonah and the whale. Titled "The Old Fish Song," the piece was learned from a Lomax LOC recording of Blind James Howard of Harlan, Kentucky. The haunting modal tune was delivered in a spare voice and accompanied by droning fiddle. The final number, the gospel tune "Crossed Old Jordan's Stream," was taken from a recording by Bird's Kentucky Corn Crackers. The slightest hint of sarcasm was perceptible in John's voice as he lamented the good old neighbor, mother, and Christian who have "crossed old Jordan's stream." The three-part vocal chorus evoked the spirit of untutored country church singing, while the guitar, mandolin, and Hawaiian slide guitar provided a lilting accompaniment with a slightly bluesy feel.

The music on *The New Lost City Ramblers* set in place the tropes of repertoire and style that the trio would closely adhere to in subsequent recordings. The choice of songs and tunes was broad, ranging from string-band breakdowns and rags to ballads, love songs, songs of drinking and gambling, blues, and gospel numbers. Elements of prebluegrass were heard in the Carter Family and Stanley Brothers songs, although no full-blown bluegrass arrangements appear. The focus was almost exclusively on southern Anglo-American rural material as captured on commercial and field recordings from the 1920s and 1930s.[20] Although blues- and ragtime-influenced pieces were included, the sources for the material were consistently white, not black, southerners, the former having absorbed the influences of African American blues, jazz, and ragtime into their music.

The discographic sources included in the album booklet suggested that the Ramblers had little in common with the typical urban folksingers of the time who learned their material from songbooks or at informal song swaps. Twelve of the eighteen selections sourced commercial hillbilly recordings; four more sourced hillbilly and LOC field recordings; the remaining two, "Colored Aristocracy" and "Old Fish Song," came solely from LOC field recordings. The degree to which the Ramblers' arrangements replicated their original sources varied. They were reasonably successful at duplicating the fiddle-banjo-guitar sound of the early Charlie Poole recordings on "Don't Let Your Deal Go Down" and the twin guitar and duo harmonies of the Delmore Brothers on "Brown's Ferry Blues." But many arrangements, such as the trio's version of "Forked Deer" and "Battleship Maine" as well as Mike's rendition of "East Virginia Blues" and "Roving Gambler," were clearly composites drawn from multiple sources. They could not replicate the exact sounds of four- and five-piece string bands like Dykes Magic City Serenades and the Dallas String Band, nor could they reproduce the precise harmonies of groups like the Carter Family, which featured female voices. Apparently, their aim was to capture the spirit and energy of the original recordings, not to render arrangements note for note. As journalist and longtime admirer Jon Pankake would put it years later: "Far from imitating, they [the early Ramblers] managed the feat of learning the musical syntax of old time song—the instrumental attacks and licks, the vocal shadings, the interplay of ensemble lead and support—and then used their mastery of this syntax to recreate in their own voices new performances which boasted all the spirit and sweetness and bite the old masters such as Sara Carter and Charlie Poole bequeathed to history in their recordings."[21]

The Ramblers' arrangement of "Colored Aristocracy" provides a useful example of creative re-creation without rigid imitation. The original source, a Rich Family LOC recording, featured an ensemble of two lead fiddles backed by guitar and strumming mandolin, whereas the Ramblers used fiddle, banjo, and guitar. The fiddles carried the melodic line throughout the Rich Family original, but Mike (fiddle) and Tom (banjo) rotated the lead melody. The guitar and mandolin on the Rich Family original played a simple I–VI–I–V (G–E–G–D) chord progression, while Tom (banjo) and John (guitar) added a IV (C) and a II (A) chord to the mix. The resulting Ramblers arrangement was unquestionably derived from the Rich original but had its own unique, slightly more modern feel.[22]

Musically, the three Ramblers demonstrated great competence on a variety of instruments, including guitar, Hawaiian slide guitar, banjo, fiddle, mandolin, autoharp, and mouth harp. Given their adherence to the loose polyphonic texture that characterized much old-time and prebluegrass music, their arrangements rarely featured solos. Indeed, at this stage of their careers none of the three could be described as a true virtuoso on the instrument(s) he played. As impressive as Mike's fiddling and mandolin work were, neither could approach the technical or creative level of the likes of Arthur Smith or Bill Monroe. Tom was highly proficient on the guitar but hardly equal to the extraordinary ability of the soon-to-be-discovered Doc Watson. Nor could Tom's or John's banjo playing match the sound of Earl Scruggs or, for that matter, Eric Weissberg. But technical virtuosity was secondary to the group's primary goal of re-creating traditional ways of playing the instruments. The subtle bowing patterns of the fiddle, the intricacies of two- and three-finger banjo picking and frailing, the complex three-finger and flat picking guitar techniques, and the alternative banjo and fiddle tunings employed by traditional musicians demanded close study and practice. In addition to their mastery of traditional playing techniques, the Ramblers achieved a variety of textures and sonorities through varied and at times unusual combinations of instruments. This set them apart from other folk ensembles and would become a hallmark of the Ramblers' sound. Where else in the early revival could one hear banjo paired with autoharp or mouth harp or a ballad accompanied by a drowning fiddle?

These early recordings revealed that the Ramblers were initially more accomplished players than they were vocalists. All three were adequate singers, with Tom possessing the richest voice and widest range. But none had a particularly distinguished voice by urban folk or country music standards. Their vocal harmonies were consistently on pitch, but the trio singing lacked the clarity of vocal blend that Tom and John approached on "Brown's Ferry Blues" and that Mike achieved on his overdubbed singing in "East Virginia." Occasionally, the singing sounded affected, as if they were trying too hard to replicate the tense, vibratoless, slightly nasal vocal timbre typical of southern mountain singers. The question of just how much of a southern accent they, as nonsoutherners, should adopt in their singing would nag them throughout their careers. They certainly sang in more natural voices than did the classical-influenced folksingers or the pop-oriented folk ensembles of the period. At best, their early vocal arrangements had a loose, spontaneous feel that would prove better suited for live performance than the unforgiving environment of the recording studio.

Arguably, *The New Lost City Ramblers* was the first recording by a city-bred revival group to pay serious attention to southern regional performance practices. Thus, the album's significance went beyond the Ramblers' skilled rendering of the material. Equally important was their presentation of what they perceived to be authentic southern mountain repertoire and styles—that is, a way of selecting and playing a body of tunes and songs that could, with practice, be replicated by urban folk musicians like themselves. Moreover, the careful choice and sequencing of material emphasized the breadth of southern mountain music and provided a satisfying listening experience for those who did not play or sing but simply enjoyed the sound of rural folk music.

Despite or perhaps because of its pioneering focus on regional folk style, *The New Lost City Ramblers* album initially received little attention outside of the small circle of old-time music aficionados who were willing to pay the $5.95 price for the Folkways LP at a time when most popular albums were selling for around $2.95. Fewer than 350 copies of the record were sold in 1959, the first full year of its availability.[23] The album received no full reviews in the folk music magazines or the popular press. The recording did, however, garner favorable mention in the scholarly *Journal of American Folklore*, where record-review editor D. K. Wilgus characterized the work as a "stylistic re-creation" with "able performances from the hillbilly period."[24] A second scholarly journal, *Western Folklore*, also mentioned the recording. Record-review editor Ed Cray seemed perplexed about how to categorize a group of "citybillies" who played "primarily hill-billy" songs whose origins are "clearly folk." But he praised the Ramblers for "master[ing] the playing styles of the Nashville recording industry, ca. 1925–1935" and concluded, "If they are not authentic hill-billies, whatever that may be, they remain a good copy of a vigorous tradition."[25] Cray's commentary went straight to the thorny issues of cultural and stylistic authenticity that would plague the Ramblers' efforts to forge alliances with professional folklorists. With a few exceptions (most notably, Wilgus, who would eventually support the Ramblers' work), folklore scholars were at best skeptical and at worst dismissive of folk revival musicians.

It is not coincidental that the Ramblers' self-conscious attempts to re-create southern folk styles came on the heels of efforts by folklorists Alan Lomax, Charles Seeger, and Ruth Crawford Seeger to redefine the idea of folk authenticity in terms of performance style. The criteria for judging the authenticity of folk songs employed by early folk song scholars and collectors like Francis Child and Cecil Sharp were based purely on issues of age, supposed anonymity, and certain textual features, including rhyme, meter, theme, and so forth. Critical printed collections of American folk songs by John and Alan Lomax, Vance Randolph, Malcolm Laws, and Tristram Coffin, as well as the classic compendiums by Sharp and Child, followed this textual model. But as Neil Rosenberg has persuasively argued, notions of what constitutes authentic folk music would change with the advent of recording technology capable of capturing the full range of aural performance style, which annotation by pen and paper could not hope to rival.[26]

Writing in 1940, only seven years after he and his father had embarked on a trip across the rural South to collect folk music with a three-hundred-pound "portable" tape recorder in tow, Alan Lomax noted how recordings could reveal "a complete authenticity of performance" that included, in addition to elements of melody and text, "rural singing and playing styles" that dated back at least fifty years before the recordings.[27] Lomax's early infatuation with style led him to develop critical models for comparing and analyzing the world's folk music in articles written for the *Journal of the International Folk Music Council* (1956) and *American Anthropologist* (1959) and eventually in a provocative monograph, *Folk Song Style and Culture* (1968). His 1959 article compared the stylistic characteristics of African American and Anglo-American folksinging. "Southern Negro Folk" tend to sing with a relaxed, resonant voice that employs multiple timbre variations (from grunts and groans to falsetto swoops). They favor strong rhythms and improvised, fragmented text and most often sing in groups, where the music functions to coordinate work, dance, or worship activities. "Southern White Folk," in contrast, tend to sing solo, with a rigidly pitched, harsh, hard, nasal timbre, while employing simple rhythms and structured texts with minimal variation.[28] It was this latter singing style that the Ramblers would most closely attempt to emulate.

Charles Seeger, who was a friend and collaborator with Lomax during his Resettlement Administration days in Washington, similarly emphasized performance style in scrutinizing folk authenticity and strongly advocated the use of recording technology to determine the parameters of style. Writing for the *Journal of the International Folk Music Council* in 1953, he took folklorists and city revivalists to task for "stressing written tradition almost to the exclusion of oral tradition," warning that overemphasis on written sources might sound the death knell to the oral-transmission process. He concluded: "The disc and tape, for example, at last puts in the hands of folklorists and revivalists alike, a means of bypassing the bottleneck of the notation of folk song. Millions are now learning to sing from hearing the voices of authentic singers."[29] In a 1958 article for the journal *Western Folklore*, appropriately entitled "Singing Style," he argued for more precise analysis of structural concepts of pitch, loudness, timbre, tempo, proportion (division of sung syllables), and accentuation and suggested the use of electronic devices for the comparative graphing of sound performances.[30]

Similar discussions over the limitations of written sources and the import of recorded material in denoting folk music style and authenticity were also cropping up in popular folk song collections and magazines. Ruth Crawford Seeger, who meticulously transcribed the Lomaxes' field recordings for the popular 1941 folk song collection *Our Singing Country* and later published three widely distributed collections of children's folk songs, realized the shortcomings of printed notation in capturing the intricacies of folk song style. Her original 1941 introduction to the Lomax collection encouraged readers to sing in a "natural" as opposed to a "trained, bel canto" voice and to accompany the songs whenever possible on traditional instruments such as the guitar, banjo, fiddle, or dulcimer as well as to avoid obtrusive piano.[31] In her introduction to the 1950 *Animal Folk Songs for Children* volume she claimed that after years of listening to recordings "I have come to feel that the way folk singers sing and play their music is almost as important as the music itself." She readily admitted that "listening of this sort can yield an enjoyment and understanding which reading of notes or words cannot give."[32]

Crawford Seeger's folk song collections were used primarily by teachers and parents of young children, but Lomax pointed his provocative pen directly at the urban folksingers who were fueling the late 1950s revival. Writing for *Sing Out!* in 1959, he admonished city "folkniks" for their overdependence on written collections and their ignorance of traditional style: "The American city folk singer, because he got his songs from books or from other city singers, has generally not been aware of the singing style or the emotional content of these folk songs, as they exist in tradition. . . . When songs are ripped out of their stylistic contexts and sung 'well,' they are, at best changed. It would be an extreme form of cultural snobbery to assert, as some people do, that they have been 'improved.' In my view they have lost something, and that something is important." Lomax went on to explain to his *Sing Out!* readers that singing style cannot be written down in conventional musical notation "but can be heard and felt in a recorded or live performance." He encouraged city singers to "experience the feelings that lie behind it, and learn to express them as the folk singers do." He warned that such an undertaking is time-consuming but ultimately worthwhile, for serious folk musicians who pay attention to style could become vital links between rural and urban audiences.[33] John wrote a response in the same *Sing Out!* issue, reminding Lomax that there were city musicians like himself who were undertaking fieldwork and listening closely to recordings of regional folk music.[34] Although John did not admit it, Lomax's piece articulated a strategy that the Ramblers wholeheartedly embraced and were just starting to put into action.

In redefining folk authenticity with aural stylistic criteria that could be captured through recordings, Lomax, Charles Seeger, and Ruth Crawford Seeger presented the possibility that urban musicians might—and in Lomax's mind should—aim to re-create rural vocal and instrumental folk styles as accurately as possible. Their position called into question the validity of popular folksingers who gleaned material from written collections and performed in styles shaped by conservatory training or Tin Pan Alley experience with no connection to the original source of the music. The Ramblers, in turn, would move this new theory of folk authenticity beyond the pages of scholarly and popular literature, taking the folk style paradigm directly to lay urban audiences through their stage performances and Folkways recordings. They aimed to answer Lomax's challenge by demonstrating that city folk musicians could, through careful study of aural sources, emulate rural styles with a high degree of accuracy.

In January 1959, concurrent with the release of *The New Lost City Ramblers*, John Dildine helped Mike land a job at a private Washington recording studio, Capitol Transcriptions. Mike moved back to DC and began what would turn into a year-and-a-half-long stint recording commercials and news stories for the Westinghouse Broadcasting Network. With Tom preoccupied with his teaching duties at the University of Maryland, the responsibility of setting up another engagement again fell to John. His brother, Mike Cohen, had recently taken a job with the American Youth Hostel and was in charge of the organization's cultural activities, which included the production of small folk music concerts. At John's prompting, Mike was able to arrange a program with the Ramblers and the Virginia ballad singer Andrew Rowan Summers for February 28 at elementary school PS 41 in Greenwich Village.

Folklorist Lee Haring reviewed the AYH concert for the folk magazine *Caravan*. He was thoroughly impressed by Summers, who sang Child ballads to the accompaniment of dulcimer, interspersing the songs with historical commentary.

Summers was a favorite of the ballad-singing crowd, but neither his singing nor his dulcimer playing were grounded in regional style. Haring's review of the Ramblers was more tepid: "After the expectations raised by their superb Folkways record, the group proved to be a bit disappointing in performance." While admitting that the trio had achieved "great accuracy and the authentic sound of the records on which they model themselves," he lamented, "One could only have wished for more enthusiasm or vitality in the concerted numbers." He did go on to praise Mike's complex Travis-style guitar picking, concluding that "both parts of the program were thoroughly enjoyable."[35]

A second, more sympathetic review of the AYH program was written by Lee Shaw for Gardyloo, a spin-off of Caravan that would become something of a fanzine for the Ramblers. Shaw peppered her review with laudatory adjectives such as "excellent," "superb," and "humorous," but she criticized their stage presence. Unlike their first September concert, which she characterized as chaotic, this show suffered from "their over awareness of staging," resulting in the group seeming "a little tense, uncertain of themselves and the audience's reaction to them." Their banter between songs seemed "apologetic" to Shaw, who preferred a less formal staging where the group would feel "freer to make the performer-audience contact that is so vital to a concert of this kind."[36]

Parts of the AYH show were recorded, providing the first sound of a live Ramblers concert and reinforcing Haring's and Shaw's observations. Musically, the AYH performance was not as tight as the Folkways recording. The starts and endings were sloppy, the vocal parts were not always well blended, and Mike's fiddling was tentative, particularly on the slower songs. Yet the program conveyed a feeling of informal spontaneity, and one can feel the audience enthusiasm for faster songs like "Don't Let Your Deal Go Down," "Battleship Maine," and "Leaving Home" (a variant of the familiar "Frankie and Johnny"). Tom emerged as the strongest singer in the group, although he was best as a song leader and tended to oversing on the background-harmony parts. Songs were prefaced by brief introductions and interspersed with nervous banter and excessive tuning. At one point Tom told a joke about renaming the group "The Weevil Brothers: Bill, Bowl, and Bull, or better known as see no, hear no, and speak no weevil." The pun fell flat when Tom and John tried to tell the punch line in unison. A sense of uncertainty surrounded their stage presentation as the trio searched for a formula to balance music, humor, and informative talk.[37]

The Ramblers' first Folkways album caused enough buzz that the group immediately began work on a second recording, this one focusing on children's folk songs and tunes. Then in March Mike received an invitation from Alan Lomax to appear at Folksong '59, an ambitious musical extravaganza he was organizing at Carnegie Hall for early April. In addition to Mike, the program featured an eclectic mix of performers, including Pete Seeger, bluesmen Muddy Waters and Memphis Slim, the Selah Jubilee Singers, the Virginia bluegrass ensemble the Stony Mountain Boys, and others. This was Mike's first high profile appearance as a solo performer, a practice he would continue throughout his years with the Ramblers. John was irked that Lomax had chosen only Mike instead of the whole band to perform at Folksong '59; the event foreshadowed a tension that would fester between them regarding Mike's commitment to the Ramblers as a full-time enterprise. Mike's mention in the *New York Times* concert review and the Carnegie Hall program booklet, which listed him as "the leader of the New Lost City Ramblers," only exacerbated John's apprehensions.[38]

Meanwhile, Mike set up a concert for the Ramblers in Washington's Pierce Hall, a small venue attached to All Souls Unitarian Church, located on Fifteenth and Harvard streets. He issued a brief press statement describing the April 17 show as a presentation of "old ballads, blues, fiddle breakdowns, rags, and children's songs." The statement went on to explain that the group played "folk music as it was being done in the 20's and 30's" and that "most of their material is traditional, but they give more importance to their instruments than the older, 'purer' traditional singers did." The latter reference was undoubtedly a reminder that this would not be a concert of ballad singing, which was popular among the DC folk crowd that attended Dildine's hoots. The press release also announced the appearance of Elizabeth Cotten, "best known for her ragtime style of left-handed guitar picking and for her composition 'Freight Train.'"[39] Cotten, an elderly African American woman originally from North Carolina, had worked as a domestic for the Seeger family for several years before Mike and his sister Peggy discovered she was an expert two-finger guitar picker with a broad repertoire of traditional folk songs. An album of Cotten's superb guitar and banjo playing, produced by Mike, had been issued on Folkways the previous year, and her lilting fingerpicking arrangement of "Freight Train" was rapidly becoming a standard among urban guitar players.[40]

Shaw was again in attendance and wrote about the concert in the second edition of *Gardyloo*. She noted that the Ramblers' first two numbers "didn't quite get off the ground," and it was not until their third piece, a rag (probably "Dallas Rag"), that things picked up and "carried on with the usual New Lost vim, vigor, and enthusiasm," adding, "They swung." The Ramblers' presentation included a skit about the New Lost City Lease Breakers, a humorous account of the group being thrown out of various city apartments for making too much noise during rehearsal. The skit apparently "petered out," and Mike and John confirm that such musical minidramas were generally failures.

Shaw was quite taken with Cotten's guitar playing and understated singing. In language that today might sound slightly patronizing she extolled the virtues of Cotten's "simplicity and sincerity," which lay at the heart of her genuine folk performance, untainted by "acquired craft" and "professionalism." The Ramblers played a second set, and the program ended with Cotten returning to the stage to join them on "The Wreck of the Old 97." Lack of time evidently "prevented the encore that the audience roared for."[41] Mike recalls that the program only drew around fifty people, and the experience discouraged him from organizing further concerts in Washington. But the show was significant, marking the first time that the Ramblers would share the stage with a traditional performer who, unlike themselves, actually grew up and learned his or her music in a southern community. Over the next two decades Cotten would perform on a number of occasions with the Ramblers at concerts, clubs, and festivals.

The spring of 1959 continued to be a busy time for the Ramblers. The recording for the *Old Timey Songs for Children* LP was completed in New York just prior to the Pierce Hall concert. In a letter to John, Mike recounted completing the notes for the children's album, continuing to work on the notes for his second Folkways bluegrass compilation, and beginning work on the notes for the Ramblers' next recording, which would focus on songs from the Depression. He also reported getting together with Tom every week to select songs for the Depression project and closed by offering John several contacts for traditional singers whom he might visit on his upcoming trip to Kentucky.[42]

In late May and June 1959 John spent five weeks in eastern Kentucky near the small town of Hazard. There he recorded and photographed traditional musicians Roscoe Holcomb, Bill and JC Cornett, the Granville Brothers, and others for what would eventually become the Folkways LP *Mountain Music of Kentucky* (Folkways FA 2317, 1960). This was the first of many journeys John would make to rural Appalachia, and it marked his initial search "to encounter his own image in the world." Writing years later, John recalled a transformative moment when he first heard Holcomb sing and play:

> On the day I exhausted the list of names, I decided to drive down the first dirt road which led off the hardtop and into the hills. In this random way I met Roscoe Holcomb. The dirt road led over a small bridge, then crossed the railroad tracks of the L&N leading into a row of wooden houses. I asked a kid standing there, "Are there any banjo players here?" He pointed to the second house in the far row, and from the distance I could hear a banjo. I visited there with Odabe Holcomb and his aunt Mary Jane, who both played some tunes. At some point they said, "Oh, there; Rossie [Roscoe]. He

plays." They called him in and he sang. The first impact of his sound was puzzling and very moving, for it was as if I'd felt this music already even though I had never heard it before.[43]

The emotional immediacy and sublime intensity of Holcomb's singing stunned John: "I know this was what I had been searching for—something that went right to my inner being, speaking directly to me. It bridged any cultural difference between us."[44] This sort of deeply personal, "lightning-strike reaction" to the initial sounds of unfamiliar but appealing folk styles has been reported by other city musicians who, like John and the Ramblers, had consciously embraced traditions outside of their own cultural spheres.[45]

Two years later John would bring Holcomb to perform at the University of Chicago Folk Festival and to New York City's Friends of Old-Time Music, establishing him as a favorite among urban aficionados of mountain banjo. Holcomb was destined to become an iconic figure for the traditional wing of the revival, and John's depiction of the Kentucky songster in his later films and audio-documentary projects would eventually come under close scrutiny. Appalachian culture historian Scott Matthews suggested that John's documentary work "strived to produce a humane picture of Appalachia, but it also created a new romantic mythology." According to Matthews, John presented Roscoe Holcomb as both "a signifier of pure, powerful folk expression, of authenticity" and as an eccentric, "visionary folk musician" who remained on the periphery of his local community. John and Little Sandy Review editors Jon Pankake and Paul Nelson, argued Matthews, romanticized Holcomb "for his seeming imperviousness to popular culture and his resemblance, in his lonely quest to maintain a meaningful life in a meaningless society, to the existential hero of literature."[46] This complex interweaving of folk romanticism and existential angst shaped John's view of southern mountain music and society as well as his efforts to serve as a cultural liaison between traditional performers and urban audiences.

Shortly after John's return from Kentucky, the Ramblers played a June 13 program at Mills College Theater in Greenwich Village. A promotional flyer promised an evening of "Ballads! Blues! Breakdowns! Sacred Songs! Ditties! Old-Timey String Band Music!" as well as "an outstanding display of fast and fancy picking on: guitar, banjo, fiddle, autoharp, twelve-string guitar, and mandolin" for $1.65. Winnie Winston reviewed the Mills College Theater concert favorably for Gardyloo, carefully chronicling both sets, which were drawn from the Ramblers' first Folkways album and from their forthcoming albums of children's and Depression era songs. Next he recounted a hilarious scene. During one of Tom's extended tuning bouts, Mike and John pulled out a second guitar from backstage and began "turning pegs on the second guitar, madly." Finally "John seems completely frustrated. Violently, he raises his guitar and smashes it down on the stage, splinters flying. Then he jumps on it." Tom, refusing to be pulled into the ruse, clearly aimed at his tuning neurosis, eyed the broken guitar and wryly commented, to the audience's delight, "John, that's flat!" "Now yours," shouted John, staring at Tom's guitar. Without skipping a beat Tom launched into the next song, "The Girl I Left Behind Me." Winston concluded that the concert was "the greatest thing I have ever attended."[47]

Harriet Goodwin also reviewed the Mills College concert for *Caravan*. She praised the Ramblers' trio work and then commented: "With equal versatility all three perform solos and take the lead voice with laconic countrified grace. Their honest exuberance and appealing, direct stage manner might well give other groups pause. Without any vestiges of either amateurism or disturbing slickness they filled the tuning interludes of their fast-paced programs with relaxed tom-foolery and anecdotal patter that was both informative and amusing." Goodwin's only criticism was that some of their singing "suffers from weak or uneven projection" and that "the instrumental work is often more exciting."[48]

An unedited recording of the Mills College concert reveals that the Ramblers were beginning to work out a simple model for structuring their stage presentations.[49] Their first set opened with a foot-stomping fiddle-banjo-guitar breakdown, "Up Jumped the Devil," followed by several trio vocal numbers and a series of individual and duet pieces. The trio returned for several more numbers, ending the set with the rollicking song "I'm Going Home." The second set began with an up-tempo bluegrass instrumental, "Holston Valley Breakdown," and repeated the pattern of several vocal-trio numbers followed by solos and duets. The show ended with the bouncy trio number "Don't Let Your Deal Go Down" and the comical kazoo-driven "Too Tight Rag."

Although an inordinate amount of time was devoted to tuning, the Ramblers seemed much more at ease than in their previous concert, filling the space between songs with humorous quips and anecdotes, which were warmly received by the audience. They also engaged in informative talk about themselves and their music. Following the opening breakdown, Mike stepped up and introduced the group:

> Thank you very much. That [breakdown] is a good definition of what the New Lost Ramblers are—we were lost most of the way through it [audience laughter]. This is the New Lost City Ramblers, Mike Seeger, Tom Paley tuning on my right [audience laughter], and John Cohen. Last night we played for an enthusiastic audience at the New Lost Century Auditorium in

Philadelphia [audience laughter]. Seriously, it was the Century auditorium. And we decided we should make some sort of statement about what kind of music we play while we're up here making fools of ourselves—city boys playing old country music. Simply, for no reason at all, we just heard some old records from back in the twenties and thirties of this old country music they used to play back in the hills. This was from the time when they were beginning to learn to play the guitar and mandolin; it had been mostly banjo and fiddle music up to that time. And they had begun getting a little up-tempo a little bit, like the first piece we played for you, "Up Jumped the Devil." So there's not much more that I can say about that. We're playing country music the way it sounded twenty or thirty years ago. And later we'll play it more the way it sounds today, bluegrass style.

Mike's statement about the group's urban origins, coupled with his brief history lesson on old-time music, reflected a conscious effort to identify, up front, the Ramblers' mission and music. On the one hand, by declaring the group's willingness to draw material from old commercial hillbilly records, Mike reminded his audience that the Ramblers did not embrace a purist philosophy. On the other hand, by noting that the roots of those hillbilly records "are back in the hills," he underscored the Ramblers' commitment to styles and repertoire anchored in regionally based traditions. Specific song and tune sources were painstakingly noted. Of the twenty-six pieces performed that evening, seventeen were introduced as being learned from particular commercial hillbilly or field recordings. An image of mountain culture that is both humorous and exotic was conveyed by the names of groups such as Gid Tanner and his Skillet Lickers, Earl Johnson and the Dixie Clodhoppers, the Dixie Crackers, and Fisher Hendley and his Aristocratic Pigs.

John introduced "Shady Grove" with a narration about his recent trip to Kentucky, which was followed by a demonstration of banjo tunings and fingerpicking techniques, creating a moment of informal instruction:

I wanted to tell you a little bit about what I've been doing in the last few weeks. I've been down in Kentucky recording music and taking photographs. Mostly in Jean Ritchie territory. She was looking for old ballads and I was looking for banjo pickers and coal miners and that. It's pretty rich country for this kind of music. And I was very interested in seeing how these people approached the music, and how they felt about it, and how they used it, and what it meant to them. And they just sat around the house and played a lot of the time, nothing too professional, not too many concerts. I guess the really good banjo players, the ones who get flashy or the ones who do bluegrass, they move out of the mountains and come to the city and make their money. But there are a lot of old men around there, and old ladies too, who know how to pick the banjo and do some very wonderful things on it. And I got a great kick out of how they approached it. And they used a great many different tunings and very interesting styles with their fingers. . . . Here's one I heard in this tuning I heard an old fellow play. [Tunes high string.] That's "Shady Grove" tuning, but he played it in the key of F instead. [Plays three-finger banjo picking tune.] I thought it was a wild tune. I told him I was interested in old songs. And he said here's a really old song. So he sang in this little voice, "Charlie's neat and Charlie's sweet, and Charlie he's a dandy." [Sings song and plays on banjo.]

John's interlude was musically and culturally instructive for audience members, who were reminded that he had actually been south and communed with the "old men" and "old ladies" who sing and play genuine "old songs." These field sojourns to the southern sources of the music would play an increasingly significant role in the Ramblers' future.

Musically, the Mills College concert was tighter than the earlier AYH show. Mike's Scruggs-style banjo picking on "Holston Valley Breakdown" was superb, as was his haunting solo voice-fiddle arrangement of "The Old Fish Song." John displayed his best three-finger banjo picking to date during the "Shady Grove" demonstration and on the tune "Rabbit Chase." Tom's guitar and banjo picking were strong throughout, and the trio swung hard on the instrumental piece "Dallas Rag." The harmony singing was occasionally sloppy, partly due to the "weak or uneven projection" previously identified by Goodwin, but throughout the program there was a sense of spontaneity and audience enthusiasm missing from the earlier shows. The Ramblers were developing a concert persona that one observer would later describe as "a curious mixture of stage show, illustrated lecture, academic and creative folklore, corny country jokes, and complicated patter improvised on the spot. . . . It was an odd combination of seriousness, antiquity, intensity, and hilarity."[50]

In the summer of 1959 the Ramblers' second album, *Old Timey Songs for Children*, was released on Folkways (FC 7064). Despite the title, explained Tom in the liner notes, "the songs on this record are not just children's songs, but they are songs that children will enjoy." He suggested that adults will like the songs too, as long as they "haven't become so pseudo-sophisticated that they can't enjoy things which are simple and direct anymore," an ironic dig at intellectuals from a college instructor. Tom concluded by ramping up his earlier critique of commercial folk music, remonstrating, "You will not find slick commercial arrangements on this record—you can hear that kind of pap on the juke box and the pot-luck juke box called radio any day—we prefer to leave the songs with their original vigor and feeling." Mike used the notes to recount his own childhood experiences listening to LOC field and hillbilly recordings, but, surprisingly, he does not mention his mother's three volumes of children's songs. Only one selection on the album, "Old Bell Cow," appeared in one of her songbooks. John refrained from discussing the music and simply contributed a poem that began, "This record has some of the songs and sounds that would be fine to grow up with."

Roger Abrahams's short but superlative review of *Old Timey Songs for Children* in *Caravan* confirmed that "the level of performance is up to their other record and is in no way geared down to children's level."[51] With the exception of the animal ditty "Old Bell Cow," the lullaby "Eyes Are Blue," and the nonsense song "Jennie Jenkins," the selections fell squarely into the ballad, breakdown, spiritual, and love-song categories heard on their first recording. Although blues and ragtime material were noticeably absent, perhaps deemed inappropriate for children, "Beware, Oh Take Care" dealt with drinking and card playing, and "Soldier, Soldier Will You Marry Me?" flirted with the theme of infidelity.

While the positive reviews of their Mills College concert and second Folkways release brought local attention to the Ramblers, another event that took place that summer would earn them national visibility and propel them toward a commitment to full-time performance. On June 11, 1959, Mike received a letter from Albert Grossman asking the Ramblers to participate at the first Newport Folk Festival to be held on July 11 and 12.[52] The band would play two sets on Sunday afternoon and evening for the sum of $150. The invitation came unsolicited and was something of a surprise—Mike assumed that favorable responses to their first record and perhaps a good word from brother Pete had led to the offer. Newport was known for its prestigious jazz festivals dating back to 1954, but neither the Ramblers nor anyone else could have predicted the immense national attention that the first Newport Folk Festival would bring to folk music. The idea of sharing the stage with commercial stars like the Kingston Trio and the Clancy Brothers undoubtedly gave them pause, but the chance to play on the same bill as bluegrass legends Earl Scruggs and the Stanley Brothers was too much to pass up, and the Ramblers eagerly accepted Grossman's invitation.

4

SEEGER, COHEN, AND PALEY PERFORM THE FOLK, 1959-1961

When the Ramblers arrived at Newport, Rhode Island, in July 1959, they found themselves in the middle of what *New York Times* critic Robert Shelton called "perhaps the most ambitious attempt ever made at delineating a cross-section of the nation's folk music."[1] Festival producers George Wein and Albert Grossman envisioned a midsummer outdoor gathering that would bring together members of New York's and Boston's grassroots folk music scenes as well as fans of southern blues, gospel, ballad singing, and bluegrass. The headliner was the Kingston Trio, whose 1958 recording of the North Carolina murder ballad "Tom Dooley" topped the pop charts and helped ignite the current folk music boom. Professional urban singers the Clancy Brothers, Odetta, and Pete Seeger were joined by an array of lesser-known city acts as well as Kentucky balladeer Jean Ritchie, bluegrass stars Earl Scruggs and the Stanley Brothers, bluesmen Memphis Slim and Sonny Terry and Brownie McGhee, and gospel singers Alex Bradford and Reverend Gary Davis. A young, unknown singer named Joan Baez would stun the audience with a performance that propelled her to national prominence. The festival featured three stage concerts as well as a workshop on traditional instrumental styles and a seminar with Willis James, Alan Lomax, and Moe Asch titled "What Is American Folk Music?" Attendance estimates varied between twelve and fourteen thousand for the weekend of events, making Newport the largest gathering of folk music enthusiasts to date.[2]

Where the Ramblers fit into this potpourri was a conundrum. They did not identify with the showy arrangements of the Kingston Trio and the Clancy Brothers or the concert singing of Martha Schlamme and John Jacob Niles. Even Pete Seeger, since his Weaver days, showed little regard for traditional instrumental or singing styles. On the other hand, the Ramblers could not claim the authentic roots of Davis, Memphis Slim, Ritchie, Terry and McGee, the Stanley Brothers, or Scruggs. City-bred practitioners of southern mountain music, they were an anomaly.

Despite their apprehensions, Mike recalled "a great deal of excitement there; people were really interested in our music; it was fast and furious and full of energy." Playing for a concert audience of approximately four thousand fans was certainly a new experience for the Ramblers, who saw themselves as virtual unknowns in a sea of established folk figures. John recalled being literally "in a state of shock" when they came off the stage. Mike remembered, "I think we were a little sloppy and we played too fast—I know I was nervous."[3] But loose and lively rather than sloppy was the feeling conveyed on the three selections drawn from the Ramblers' 1959 Newport sets that were released on a 1961 Folkways compilation. "Up Jumped the Devil," "Hop High Ladies," and "Take a Drink on Me" were high spirited, with the latter featuring John's energetic vocal and a well-blended chorus.[4] Likewise, the band's renditions of "Beware, Oh Take Care," "When First into This Country I Came," and "Hopalong Peter," appearing on a Vanguard recording of the festival, suggested Newport fans were treated to strong performances. In the liner notes to the Vanguard LP Studs Terkel recognized the Ramblers' contributions as artists, researchers, and advocates, predicting that their efforts to revive old-time music would bear fruit:

> The New Lost City Ramblers have set themselves a double task as sprightly performers and as devoted young scholars. Tom Paley, John Cohen and Mike Seeger (youngest of the Seegers, that fantastically talented family) are uncanny in their re-creation of the mountain music, so popular in the Twenties and Thirties. Obviously dedicated, these three urban-conditioned musicians have caught the flavor and the fire of another era. Of even happier note is their building of a new audience for this style that is far from dead.[5]

The Sunday-night concert ended in an incident that revealed a deep cleavage between the "city-bred folksingers" and the "authentic singers" that Billy Faier identified in his festival-program essay.[6] When members of the Kingston Trio finished their set, a group of overly enthusiastic fans would not let them off the stage to make room for the final bluegrass act led by Earl Scruggs. The host, Oscar Brand, had to spend fifteen minutes restoring order, and only after he promised to bring the Kingstons back for a finale would the crowd quiet down so Scruggs could finally play. The occasion disgusted Izzy Young, who told *Caravan* readers,

"Only one person was heard booing (this writer) when the Kingston Trio returned to another great ovation." Mark Morris, writing for *Gardyloo*, hailed the Sunday-night concert but was dismissive of the Kingston Trio's performance, sniping, "What connection these frenetic tinselly showmen have with a folk festival eludes me."[7] While not mentioning the Kingston-Scruggs collision directly, Robert Shelton commented on the larger problem of how to "transplant the 'root' singers and put them on side by side with the large-voiced, polished and earnest professionals who are not indigenous folk singers but who have been drawn to the music." He lamented that solo ballad singer Jean Ritchie and spiritual songster Reverend Gary Davis "were unable to perform as effectively" on the large Newport stage.[8] Shelton's concerns were taken seriously by the festival organizers, who would, in the future, feature more intimate workshops where soloists and less-polished performers could share their music.

The first Newport Folk Festival received wide media coverage and brought a glimmer of national attention to the Ramblers. Shelton reviewed the festival for the *Nation*, mentioning the Ramblers alongside Scruggs and the Stanley Brothers as "the representatives of Bluegrass country music."[9] Shelton also described the Ramblers as "three city performers [who] captured a moment in time twenty-five years ago with verisimilitude" in his *New York Times* review.[10] Critic Frederic Ramsey, Jr., devoted two paragraphs of his Newport commentary in the *Saturday Review* to the Ramblers, offering brief biographies of the three men and noting that they "perform in sprightly, lively dance tempi." Commenting on the sources of their repertoire, he observed, "They have learned a lot of their music from recordings, and refer to records of the Twenties and Thirties, in explaining sources of certain selections."[11]

"I think when it dawned on me that we'd done something important was when I saw reviews in the *Nation* and the *Saturday Review* that we were there. That's when I woke up a little bit and got some perspective," reflected John.[12] The experience of Newport and the press that followed brought him to the realization that there might be a larger audience for the sort of traditional music the Ramblers were promoting and perhaps a niche for them in the burgeoning folk music boom. But it would be nearly two years before all three Ramblers would make a firm commitment to full-time music making.

The following month the group received more accolades in the *New York Times*, again from Shelton. In an August 30 piece he introduced his readers to bluegrass music by reviewing a number of recent albums, including Mike's second bluegrass Folkways LP, *Mountain Music Bluegrass Style* (FA 2318). He called the collection "a fine introduction to this heady music" and lauded the work as "well recorded and exhaustively annotated by Mike Seeger." In commenting on bluegrass's early roots,

Shelton praised the first New Lost City Ramblers LP, characterizing it as "a finely wrought bit of musical archeology and reconstruction. The trio have recaptured the past of the old-time string bands with considerable flavor and wit."[13]

Shelton's comments were a mixed blessing to the Ramblers. They certainly welcomed the high visibility that the *New York Times* publicity brought and the recognition of their mission to champion the much-neglected southern string-band tradition. But they took umbrage at the label "musical archeology and re-construction" with its implications that they simply imitated, note for note, the music on old records. Such characterizations, they complained, downplayed their creative abilities to select and rearrange traditional material. The press's tendency to emphasize the sources of their material while ignoring their musicianship surfaced again in a review of their performance on a September 19 Carnegie Hall show. John Wilson of the *New York Times* commented on the Ramblers' "spirited renditions of country tunes, which were originally recorded by Southern hill people in the Twenties and Thirties."[14]

The Ramblers played three more concerts in the fall of 1959, all within a day's drive of home, allowing Mike and Tom to continue their jobs. On December 19 Izzy Young produced his second Ramblers concert in New York City at Carl Fischer Hall on West 57th Street. Young was confident that the group would draw a crowd and scheduled two separate performances at 8:30 P.M. and 11:30 P.M., each with an admission of $2.00 (up from $1.65 in 1958). The flyer featured a graphic of an old-time mustachioed street worker brush pasting a large photograph of the Ramblers on a city wall (figure 5). Such iconography suggests a synergy between nostalgia and contemporary urban culture, the latter represented by the image of the youthful and slightly offbeat Ramblers.

During the fall of 1959 the Ramblers began work on their next album, *Songs from the Depression* (Folkways FH 5264), which was released in early 1960.[15] At first glance an album of Depression era folk songs might suggest a nod to the singing unions, Woody Guthrie and the Almanac Singers, People's Songs, and other elements of the progressive, old-guard wing of the folk music revival. This so-called singing Left had roots in Depression and World War II era ideology that championed the music of the "common man" and attempted to use folksing-ing as a means of organizing a leftist political movement for social change.[16] Though beaten back by anti-Communist McCarthyism throughout the 1950s, the singing Left still looked to Pete Seeger and *Sing Out!* editor Irwin Silber as torchbearers for politically relevant topical songs. But Mike and John made it clear that neither they nor the mountain musicians who originally recorded the songs were interested in political organizing or overt protest that might lead to social upheaval. "It was just a topic," recalled John, who was adamant that the

FOLKLORE CENTER PRESENTS

ONLY NEW YORK CONCERT THIS SEASON

SAT., DEC. 19 1959

2 PERFORMANCES ⁚ 8:30 & 11:30 P.M.

at Carl Fischer Hall—165 West 57th Street, N.Y.

★ OLD TIME
  FOLK SONGS

★ BALLADS

★ BREAKDOWNS

★ FAST & FANCY

Picking on:

Guitar

Banjo

Fiddle

Auto Harp

Mandolin

Exclusive on
Folkways Records

JULES HALFANT

THE NEW LOST CITY RAMBLERS

MIKE SEEGER ★ TOM PALEY ★ JOHN COHEN

TICKETS $2.00 • ON SALE AT FOLKLORE CENTER • 110 MACDOUGAL ST. • GR 7-5987

FIGURE 5. Flyer for December 19, 1959, concert at Carl Fischer Hall, New York City. Photograph by Robert Frank. Flyer courtesy of John Cohen.

songs were simply records of how poor, disenfranchised mountain people dealt with the adversities of the Depression. "The evidence was there in the records, the commercial records and the LOC recordings. It wasn't coming from our desire to bring about social change."[17]

In the accompanying booklet to Songs from the Depression John argued that these were not "songs with conscious messages, composed with a calculated awareness, from sophisticated industrial and urban sources," and he dismissed such efforts as "often sound[ing] self-conscious and sometimes un-musical."[18] He also pointed out that the selections on the album differed in intention from the popular Tin Pan Alley songs of the 1930s, which to his mind were inherently "escapist in nature." He envisioned the songs as accounts of hard times that "didn't offer pretty dreams to take the mind away from the problems of reality, but neither do they attempt to offer much of a solution to the problem. Rather they offer a way of living through and dealing with the actuality of the times." Mike concurred, noting that with the exception of Aunt Molly Jackson's 1937 "Join the C.I.O." "these songs were not anything but protest or comments about hard times, and they did not often propose a solution, especially the organization of a trade union, since they were musicians, not organizers." Given the conservative nature of the recording industry, Mike admitted being "amazed that so many of these songs were actually recorded and released by the commercial companies during the Depression."

John further distanced himself and the Ramblers from any overt political agenda, warning that contemporary listeners who embraced "fashionably romantic notions attached to the thirties, with overtones of action and reform" and who are "looking for such a bandwagon to jump onto" would be disappointed. The material on the record "won't provide any marching songs for the arguments of social reform or provide anyone with a cause to pursue." Such musings on folk song and politics were probably not well received in some quarters of the folk music world, especially following the resurgence of political folk songs in the early 1960s as the civil rights and antiwar movements expanded their reach.

There was certainly nothing overly romantic about the stark, social-realist imagery that John chose for the album's cover and booklet. Yet the shadowy Depression era figures conveyed a sense of gritty authenticity that apparently appealed to an expanding number of young listeners who were growing uneasy with the banality of middle-class life. A striking Ben Shahn photograph of three young Okie-looking men, sitting curbside in front of what appears to be an old Model T Ford, adorns the LP cover (figure 6). Two are hunched over their guitars, strumming G chords and harmonizing, while a third looks on intently. The angle of their bodies projects a sense of motion, as if these three young men, perhaps historical surrogates for the Ramblers, are about to hit the road in search of better lives. The accompanying booklet is illustrated with photographs taken by Walker Evans and Dorothea Lange from the Farm Security Administration collections that reveal the deprivation of rural life in the 1930s: a haggard-looking southern family singing in front of their cabin and a disheveled Oklahoma child desperately clutching a cotton sack. The plight of the oppressed is clear in the reproduction of a lithograph by social-realist artist Harry Gottlieb that depicts a group of poor men hunkering over a campfire while factory chimneys belch out foul black smoke. Iconography of the famous National Recovery Administration Blue Eagle and "We Do Our Part" logo, along with a photograph of Franklin Delano Roosevelt sitting with a hillbilly string band in Georgia below headlines announcing his repeal of Prohibition ("Roosevelt Insists on Immediate Beer"), add to the mystique of the period and suggest that efforts for social action and reform were afoot. But even if the album's city listeners were not interested in the political struggles of the 1930s, they could not help being transported to a faraway place and time by images of these poor rural "folk" who were clearly the source of the music heard on the album. The NRA Blue Eagle logo would later turn up on a Ramblers publicity card, with the defiant bird clutching a guitar and banjo in its sharp talons. The back of the card read: "I am lost. Please return me to 1932."

Whatever the Ramblers thought regarding the social message of the songs, the first two selections on the album did raise the specter of escapism. "No Depression in Heaven," from the Carter Family, predicted that the pains of the Depression would only be eased in the next life:

> I'm going where there's no depression,
> To the lovely land that's free from care.
> I'll leave this world of toil and trouble,
> My home's in Heaven, I'm going there.

The next song, "There'll Be No Distinction There," written by Blind Alfred Reed, reflected a similar message of delayed gratification in heaven:

> There'll be no sorrow on that heavenly shore,
> There'll be no woes at the cabin door.
> We'll all be wealthy and the poor will all be there,
> We'll be rich and happy in that land bright and fair.
> There'll be no distinction there.

Such glorification of heaven at the expense of social action here on earth played into the classic Marxist critique of religion as the opiate of the masses, an attitude that was certainly prevalent among many progressives in the 1950s and 1960s.

FOLKWAYS RECORD FH 5264

THE NEW LOST CITY RAMBLERS: MIKE SEEGER, JOHN COHEN, TOM PALEY

SONGS FROM THE DEPRESSION

PHOTOGRAPH: BEN SHAHN, FSA   DESIGN: SHELDON BRODY

FIGURE 6. Cover of *Songs from the Depression* Folkways LP (1959).
Photograph by Ben Shahn. Image courtesy of the Ralph Rinzler Folklife
Archives and Collections, Smithsonian Institution.

John recalled that the ire of an old friend was directed at him when he sang one
of the songs at a folk festival:

> Sometime in the early 1960s we did the Berkeley festival and they had a topi-
> cal song workshop, so I thought I'd do a song from our Depression album,
> "There'll Be No Distinction There." So the words went: "We'll all be white
> in that Heavenly Light / The white folks and the Gentiles, the colored and
> the Jews / Praise the Lord together and there will be no drinking booze /
> There'll be no distinction there." Joan Baez sang next, and she said, "Now
> I'd like to sing a song for the colored people." I'll never forgive her for that.
> She totally missed the point about good intentions, and our awareness of
> the South and religion—it wasn't supposed to be a solution.[19]

Not all the songs on the album were escapist or apolitical. Bob Baker's "White House Blues" did not hesitate to skewer President Hoover, who "let the country go to ruin," while Uncle Dave Macon's "Wreck of the Tennessee Gravy Train" wagged a finger at corrupt bankers and government officials who misplaced five million dollars in state funds. Hoover's successor fared better in "Franklin D. Roosevelt's Back Again," which commended FDR for his concern for working people and his repeal of Prohibition ("Since Roosevelt's been elected moonshine liquor's been corrected / We've got legal wine, whiskey, beer, and gin"). "NRA Blues" and "Old Age Pension Check" sang the praises of two popular New Deal programs, and "Taxes on the Farmer Feeds Us All" and "How Can a Poor Man Stand Such Times and Live?" chronicled the woes of working people at the hands of predatory lawyers, merchants, and preachers. "Serves Them Fine" and "All I Got's Gone" poked fun at country people who leave their mountain homes for the lure of mill work and others who overextend their credit to buy automobiles, tailor-made suits, and satin dresses. The narrator of "Breadline Blues" implored "us good old folks" to vote, for "we've got to do something or we're all going to croak," and Aunt Molly Jackson's "Join the CIO" was one of the few examples of a southern union song.

Songs from the Depression presented a politically mixed bag. John and Mike were certainly correct in asserting that those searching for a call to arms for social change would be disappointed in the material on the album. But even the most radical proponents of the singing Left could not deny that the songs had an intrinsic value as historical snapshots of working people grasping for ways of dealing with the miseries of unemployment, poverty, and class exploitation. Writing for the Journal of American Folklore a decade later, Jens Lund and Serge Denisoff suggested that, by identifying with the Depression, the Ramblers "attempted to satisfy the folk revival's social consciousness." Songs from the Depression, they contend, successfully "provided a common ground on which the 'ethnic' and 'protest' folkniks could meet."[20]

The Ramblers demonstrated a genuine sense of musical comfort with the Depression material. Their vocalizing was more relaxed and natural than in past recordings, and with few exceptions they did not oversing or seem to try too hard to sound southern. The instrumental work, although relegated to more of a supportive role than in the previous two albums, was consistently well executed and never overwhelmed the vocalists. The slithery steel guitar on "Breadline Blues" and "Old Age Pension Check" and the plucky-textured mandolin-banjo-guitar configuration on "Serves Them Fine" and "NRA Blues" presented intriguing new instrumental sonorities.

Songs from the Depression received several favorable mentions. Writing for Caravan, Roger Abrahams confirmed that "the instrumental and vocal performances on this disc are up to the usual high standards of this outstanding group." Jazz and folk music critic Nat Hentoff commented on the album's eclectic assortment of historical samplings and paid a high compliment by identifying the Ramblers as "the most intriguing of the city-billy revivalists in the current folksong renaissance."[21]

The most quirky review of *Songs from the Depression* came from Jon Pankake, writing in the first issue of the fanzine *Little Sandy Review*. Pankake gushed over the Ramblers, who "need only to put bow to fiddle and finger to string to put on the greatest group show in the folk field." Lauding the album as "superb," he noted that the Ramblers "make the time [the Depression] sound like a lot of fun in that the hard-luck humor of the country man is emphasized rather than the grimmer aspects of the era." He blithely observed that "the message that the Ramblers project is that to those in touch with the humor and crazy unpredictability of American life, the Depression is not a catastrophe; but rather a passing phase inflicted upon America by the uppity city Dude, who, despite his illogical ways, cannot prevent the wacky life of the Folk from marching on, triumphant and singing." It is difficult to judge how seriously to take Pankake's comments. In hindsight he described the *Little Sandy Review* as more fiction than journalism, a publication meant to "portray the absurdities of the folk music revival," including the incongruity that "city people drenched in popular culture—movies, pop music—would embrace rural and oral tradition." But it is hard to imagine the Ramblers agreeing with his assessment of the Depression as a passing phase through which the "wacky" American folk happily marched with a smile and a song. Pankake's observations, couched in his own ironic view of American culture, reveal the inherent difficulties the Ramblers faced in presenting accurate representations of southern mountain culture to city dwellers whose romantic preconceptions of "the folk" did not always coincide with reality.[22]

By the time *Songs from the Depression* was released in early 1960, the Ramblers faced an uncertain future. Proliferating networks of commercial clubs, coffeehouses, and college folk music societies presented opportunities for the best musicians and those who could hustle to eke out a living. The temptation for Mike, Tom, and John to pursue music full time was further fueled by discontent with their current jobs. Tom, who had the longest record of steady employment, had left the University of Maryland to take a position as a lecturer at Skidmore College the previous fall, but with an incomplete dissertation his academic future was far from secure. Mike trudged along, working as a recording engineer at Capitol Transcriptions, but the company was not financially sound, and by June he had been let go. On top of this both Tom and Mike had recently married and now faced new family responsibilities. Tom married Claudia Lane Lingafelt, an

English major and writer originally from Hyattsville, Maryland. In December of that year Mike married Marge Ostrow, a graduate of Antioch College whose own interest in country music had led her to Sunset Park, where she had met Mike the previous year. John, who remained single, had made enough money selling photographs to *Life* and *Esquire* to finance his recording trip to Kentucky that spring. But he had little enthusiasm in pursuing a career in photojournalism, a profession he feared would force him to compromise his artistic vision for the demands of the commercial publishing world.

Despite their passion for music and their misgivings about conventional work, none of the Ramblers could feel sanguine about the prospects of making a living playing old-time music, given their 1959 earnings. John's financial records from the period were sobering. Although the group's relationship with Folkways allowed them tremendous creative freedom in the way they recorded and produced their music, remuneration was minimal. John had spent countless hours in the fall editing and assembling the music and visuals for *Mountain Music of Kentucky*, for which Asch paid him nothing (he would eventually receive minimal royalties of ten cents per record). Over the course of the year he received $85 in session fees for recording the *Children* and *Depression* albums and $33 and $5, respectively, in royalty payments for record sales of the two albums. In addition, he made approximately $500 for the twelve engagements the Ramblers played that year. Even for John's bohemian lifestyle, an annual income of slightly over $600 was hardly enough to live on in 1959.

In the early spring of 1960 the Ramblers took a handful of jobs, tapping their personal networks of traditional music supporters to arrange programs at Columbia University and the Indian Neck Folk Festival at Yale. A review in the *Yale Daily News* commented on the unique role the Ramblers played in the increasingly commercial folk revival: "If Saturday's concert is any indication, a sizeable audience exists for this [early hillbilly] music. This is to be applauded as the New Lost City Ramblers serve a very valuable function in bringing old traditions onto the modern folk-music stage. Moreover, they combine their unique musical talents with an informality of approach which is sorely missed in this era of cute, contrived witticisms."[23]

In late March the Ramblers appeared at Manny Greenhill's Ballad Room in Boston for a night and then moved over to the Golden Vanity in Kenmore Square for a full week. The Vanity was one of the original Cambridge coffeehouses and a hangout for Joan Baez when she was a student at Boston University. Critic Robert Gustafson reviewed a show for the *Christian Science Monitor*, praising the Ramblers as "highly skilled on a variety of instruments" and noting that they sang "in the high, nasal tone of mountain singers." He then offered an astute observation: "The New Lost City Ramblers are doing more than simply presenting a program of entertaining music. They are recreating the era of the 1920s when bluegrass had its flowering. They are once again playing and singing the music of the mountaineer who farmed, or perhaps worked in a coal mine, perhaps in Harlan County, KY."[24] Why a sophisticated, coffeehouse audience in Cambridge, Massachusetts, would want to be transported back in time to a far-off mountain land of subsistence farmers and poor miners was a vital question that cut to the heart of the Ramblers' appeal to their city listeners. Gustafson did not venture an answer but made it clear that in addition to the songs and tunes themselves such extramusical associations were crucial to the allure of old-time music outside the rural South.

A live recording of two of the Ramblers' sets at the Golden Vanity reveals the Ramblers were still struggling to work out a smooth show. The group was introduced by an emcee, who read a portion of Gustafson's review from the previous day's *Monitor*. In a quick moment of self-deprecating wit Mike dismissed the reporter's comments as overly complimentary, chortling, "Those guys [the Ramblers] sound so good, I don't know if I want to pick with them or not. Sounds like they're out of our class." The band launched into a lively rendition of the fiddle tune "Colored Aristocracy," which Mike, perhaps self-conscious about the racial overtones of the title, identified simply as "Aristocracy." He then introduced himself as the fiddle player by default, John as a photographer and artist from New York, and Tom as a mathematician and photographer. The first set moved along at a fairly good clip, although often nearly a minute or more ticks by between each song as instruments are switched and tuned. Song introductions were kept to a minimum, but the second set bogged down with wasted tuning time. One highlight was a song-skit introduced as "The New Lost City Ramblers Visit Arkansas," with John (playing banjo) as the traveling city slicker who runs across Mike (playing fiddle), the local Ozark mountaineer who sits on his porch dispensing witty retorts to the traveler's foolish queries. The words to the three-and-a-half-minute skit were taken primarily from the Tennessee Ramblers' version of the story, which was reissued on Alan Lomax's 1948 *Mountain Frolic* recording. Other memorable moments were Mike's fancy picking on the bluegrass instrumental "Hard to Love" and his bluesy three-finger rendition of Elizabeth Cotten's "Going Down the Road." On these numbers Mike demonstrated tremendous technical competency on the banjo and guitar, respectively. But he had yet to achieve such command on the fiddle, the instrument he had to play, in his own words, by "default."[25]

The Ramblers' fourth album, titled simply *The New Lost City Ramblers Volume II* (FA 2397), was released in the late spring of 1960. For the first time the Ramblers

THE NEW LOST CITY RAMBLERS
MIKE SEEGER ★ JOHN COHEN ★ TOM PALEY   VOL. II

DESIGN: JOHN COHEN   PHOTO: ROBERT FRANK

FIGURE 7. Cover of *The New Lost City Ramblers Volume II* Folkways LP (1960).
Photograph by Robert Frank. Image courtesy of the Ralph Rinzler Folklife
Archives and Collections, Smithsonian Institution.

themselves appeared on one of their album covers thanks to a dramatic portrait
taken by the well-known photographer and John's neighbor Robert Frank. The
group was posed in the courtyard of John's Third Avenue loft in front of a moldy
brick wall. With fiddle, banjo, and guitar in hands, the three were dressed in
plain jackets and ties (figure 7). The idea, John explained, was to emulate old
photographs of country musicians who dressed up to go to town.[26] Whatever the
Ramblers' intent, for the citybillies who would buy the record the photograph
sent an unambiguous message that country music was indeed flourishing in the
city and that the Ramblers were hip enough to have drawn the interest of one of
New York's most noted contemporary photographers.

In the notes to *Volume II* Mike paid homage to the record collectors who helped put the Ramblers in touch with countless old hillbilly records. These slightly eccentric characters "obtained these rare discs in the long neglected field of southern American folk-music at considerable personal cost, time, and expense. Their sources were old stock at retail stores, auctions, other collectors, and Salvation army and other goods stores, or through canvass of neighborhoods likely to have this type of record." They were, Mike noted, "no less important than the collectors of the Library of Congress Archives of the 1930s. . . . Certainly this music would go unheard if it were not for them."[27] Richard Spottswood, Pete Kuykendall, Harry Smith, Joe Buzzard, and Gene Earle were given special thanks for providing the Ramblers with source material. John recalled that Earle's New Jersey home "was stacked wall-to-wall with old hillbilly 78s. . . . On many occasions I would strap a tape recorder to the back of my Vespa motor scooter and drive across the George Washington Bridge for an evening of listening to and taping old records." One of John's "astounding discoveries" was the 1922 recording of "Sallie Gooden" by Eck Robertson, the traditional fiddler the Ramblers would later locate and coax out of retirement.[28] Although John and Tom had small collections of 78 recordings, the Ramblers were heavily dependent on a handful of collectors for their material. Copies of quarter-inch tapes filled with songs and tunes culled from these collections, rather than the actual records themselves, were the medium of choice for the three musicians.

John used his notes to *Volume II* to offer a short retrospective on the past two years of the Ramblers' activities, noting a small network of old-time music devotees emerging across the country: "We have been singing in concerts and at colleges and clubs all over, and seem to be finding friends where we never know we had them. In many colleges small country string bands have been springing up and have taken a real place in the general field of folk music."[29] In a lengthy letter he penned to *Mademoiselle* reporter Susan Montgomery that August, John remarked that in the Ramblers' wake old-time string bands were now active at Harvard ("three at last count"), Yale, Amherst, Dartmouth, Oberlin, Antioch, the University of California, and the University of Michigan.[30] In his mind the seeds the Ramblers had planted were starting to sprout.

In his notes to *Volume II* John also commented on the Ramblers' increased immersion in the traditional styles of singing and playing and the group's attempts to be creative within those confines: "We have encountered certain clear-cut almost rigid styles of sliding notes singing, picking banjo, pushing guitar runs, squalling fiddles. We have found that once having recognized these traditions, one can make many variations upon them. Having recognized the symmetry of the music, and the regularity of its phrasing, there comes an excitement of finding never-ending possibilities of asymmetrical and irregular structures—but only in relation to the tradition."

This struggle to generate new variations of southern mountain music without violating the stylistic parameters of the tradition was an ongoing challenge for John and the Ramblers, who saw themselves as creative artists, not simply imitators of old records. His remarks may have been aimed at the previously mentioned newcomers to the music scene in hopes of encouraging college and city players to become deeply conversant with traditional styles and structures—what he identifies as the "symmetry" of the music—before progressing on to the creation of new variants.

While the music was generally strong, much of the singing on *Volume II* did not live up to the expectations raised in John's discussion of style. There were bright instrumental moments, including Tom's vigorous mandolin playing on "Hawkins Rag," Mike's intricate guitar picking on "Everyday Night," the tasteful steel guitar and mandolin fills on "Louisville Burglar," and the fiddle-banjo-guitar frenzy "Up Jumped the Devil." But the solo singing was consistently unsatisfactory, with Tom and John occasionally oversinging and affecting hillbilly accents. John was too exuberant in his desire to sound like Uncle Dave Macon on "Whoop 'Em Up Cindy," and his lead vocals on "Didn't He Ramble" and "Tom Dooley" were self-consciously dry. Tom was convincing when he sang in a relaxed voice that advantaged his rich tenor, but on songs like "Late Last Night," "Leaving Home," and "Raging Sea" his efforts to pinch his intonation in the style of a mountain singer fell flat. Most of the choruses were well executed, with the exception of Mike's shrill falsetto part on the "Raging Sea"—obviously an attempt to duplicate the high female harmonies of the Carter Family. The result was one of the trio's most forgettable vocal performances.

These vocal deficiencies seemed to escape the ears of contemporaneous critics, or perhaps they simply chose to ignore them. D. K. Wilgus, writing for the *Journal of American Folklore*, declared that the album "re-presents in superb fashion rural Southern music, taken primarily from the 1940s," and noted that "their presentations are not always exact imitations." In his typically rambling style Jon Pankake declared the album "fantastic" and mused about the group's ability to capture the vanishing American attributes of "optimism, painful honesty, joy, and humor that come with self-knowledge, toughness, innocence, strong affirmation, pragmatism, simplicity and love of life that are inherent in our folk music." Such reviews emphasizing sources and mission over artistry reflect the investment a small group of folk music scholars and enthusiasts had in promoting hillbilly and old-time music.[31] It was a viewpoint the Ramblers themselves, at least in their rhetoric, tended to share.

In May 1960, when Tom's semester at Skidmore had ended, the Ramblers set out on a brief swing through the Midwest. John recalled that Pete Seeger's manager, Harold Leventhal, advised them not to undertake such a long trip for a few engagements with no guaranteed pay arrangements. In what would turn out to be a wise decision, the Ramblers ignored Leventhal's advice. Progressive colleges, many with folk music clubs and festivals, had provided important venues for folksingers like Pete Seeger throughout the 1950s. The Ramblers, with their emphasis on historicizing American folk music by blending art and education, found receptive audiences at colleges where interest in folk music was escalating in the early 1960s. John recalled: "Traveling as three men in a Volkswagen beetle with suitcases and seven instruments (two guitars, two banjos, fiddle, mandolin, and autoharp), we played at Oberlin College, in Ann Arbor, and at the University of Chicago."[32] A review in the *Michigan Daily* called the Ann Arbor concert "one of the liveliest musical evenings the cultural Mecca of the Midwest has seen in years—probably since the 1930s," alluding to the period from which the Ramblers drew their material. The author assured readers that in dress, demeanor, and music the Ramblers would not be confused with another more popular folk act, "for even in their wildest moments, the Kingston Trio could not hope to match the musical frenzy produced by fiddle, mandolin, and banjo working on 'The Man Who Wrote Home Sweet Home Never Was a Married Man.'"[33]

On May 21 the Ramblers were greeted by an enthusiastic group of students who were members of the University of Chicago's Folklore Society. The organization's leader, Mike Fleischer, organized the Ramblers' Saturday evening concert with only three days' notice. For student folk music enthusiasts like Fleischer the Ramblers were a godsend. Here were three educated, articulate, middle-class young men from New York who appeared to have mastered the art of southern mountain music. Moreover, they could play and present the material in a way that inspired and invited young college students like Fleischer and his cohorts to take up the music themselves. Despite the short lead time and lack of publicity, the concert was a huge success. An overflowing crowd of students piled into the three-hundred-seat auditorium for two shows. Following the concert, Fleischer and the Ramblers began to discuss the possibility of a larger event that would take place later that winter, the first University of Chicago Folk Festival.[34]

The next day college students packed the Gate of Horn, where the Ramblers had been invited to audition. The Horn had served as the center of the Chicago folk music scene since Albert Grossman and Les Brown opened the club in 1956 and helped launch the careers of several important folk stars, including Odetta.[35] The audition was a success, and the trio was booked for an extended three-week engagement in early June, their longest to date.

When Mike returned to DC in late May 1960, he parted ways with Capitol Transcriptions for good, receiving a portable tape recorder as severance pay. A week later he and Marge, who was four months pregnant, packed up their belongings from their Georgetown apartment and headed west to Chicago, where they crowded into a small, shabby apartment with John, Tom, and Claudia. "And we just played show after show, between nine in the evening and four in the morning," recalled Mike. "And that's when we really got broken into showbiz."[36]

Concerns over the Ramblers' appearance by the Horn's proprietors became the genesis of what would become the band's trademark vest uniforms. "We realized we couldn't keep coming on looking like schlumps, and we had to have something that looked presentable," recalled John, "and that's where we cooked up the idea of vests and ties, based on an old photograph that Eck Dunford had taken of the Stoneman Family, the one that ended up on the cover of the *New Lost City Ramblers' Songbook*. And we studied old photographs and also old catalogs of what Gid Tanner and those guys looked like in their suits and vests and ties. Up till then the image of old southern singers was guys in blue jeans, hillbillies with long beards, and straw hats and barefoot."[37] As a result, the trio embraced "the attitude of old-time farmers who might have gone to town to perform a show and decided to dress in our best, rather than in blue jeans or work clothes. . . . We came up with white shirts, ties, and differing vests as our garb."[38] A writer for the *Montreal Star* would later comment: "Put them all together, solemn-faced, black vests separated from unpressed pants by a frill of rumpled shirt, and you have a period print: a trio of country music men just arrived from the pea-pickers' festival in a battered Model T."[39]

Reviewers from the mainstream press took notice of the Ramblers' engagement at the Gate of Horn, with the *Chicago Tribune* proclaiming, "They sing none of the old warhorses, they affect none of the standard garb, and their impact is fresh and strong."[40] The *Chicago Sun-Times* declared that the Ramblers "have been responsible for bringing the music out of the mountains" to college students and observed that their music presented an alternative to the "tired popular music of the day." The piece reflected further on the larger question of the music's appeal to young city people: "There is also more than a suggestion of a search for roots in the turning away from synthetic music. It's also interesting that most of the people who dig folk styles are city-born and bred. Perhaps they see honesty and a purity in these styles that becomes more and more elusive in a society that condones payola at many levels."[41] This search for roots, honesty, and purity in musical expression was becoming central to the romantically tinged discourse that positioned the Ramblers as purveyors of genuine, as opposed to commercial, folk music.

Three weeks later Mike, John, and Tom flew back to New York and on to Newport while Marge and Claudia drove west to California, where Charles Seeger had taken a position at UCLA. The second annual Newport Folk Festival placed increased emphasis on commercially proven groups such as the Weavers, the Brothers Four, the Tarriers, the Clancy Brothers, and the Gateway Singers along with rising stars Joan Baez and Odetta. More traditional performers included gospel stars Clara Ward and Alex Bradford; bluesman John Lee Hooker; Earl Scruggs, this time with Lester Flatt and the Foggy Mountain Boys; and the Ducorans African Trio from Nigeria. The Seeger clan was represented by Pete, Peggy (with her husband and British singer-songwriter Ewan MacColl), and Mike and the Ramblers. A Sunday afternoon hootenanny and a panel discussion debated what Robert Shelton described as "the thorny questions of authenticity versus ersatz folk music."[42] The evening concerts and daytime workshops attracted a total crowd of more than ten thousand fans, and the event was recorded by Vanguard, Elektra, and Folkways records.

Stacey Williams—a pen name for Robert Shelton—commented in the liner notes to the live Vanguard LP that the Ramblers' second appearance at Newport was well received: "Of the host of faces and performing styles, none were more distinctive than that irrepressible trio, the New Lost City Ramblers, Mike Seeger, Tom Paley and John Cohen, with their mountain songlore and their droll wit. Here are some of the great 'old timey' string band numbers culled from recordings by the great performers from the mountains in the 1920s and '30s. Hear Mike Seeger's hard-cider voice on 'Man of Constant Sorrow' and hear the whole aggregation singing and playing with the strength of thirty on 'Foggy Mountain Top.'"[43]

While Izzy Young and others fretted over the increasingly commercial nature of Newport (the triumph of "ersatz" over "authentic" folk music, to use Shelton's language), the Ramblers flew directly to California to take part in another folk festival that purported to offer a different approach.[44] From his earliest days as a folk music host on radio KPFA and a concert presenter at the University of California at Berkeley, Barry Olivier gravitated toward noncommercial folk music. "With popularizers all about—the Kingston Trio and its school—we had almost a religious fervor about laying out what we considered to be real folk music, so it would be fully appreciated and so that people wouldn't waste time and energy with the watered-down, 'impure' stuff," he would later reflect.[45] Stressing the historical and educational value of folk music, Olivier convinced the University of California to stage a four-day folk festival in late June 1958 that combined concerts and educational workshops. The second annual Berkeley Folk Festival, held over five days in June 1959, brought in Alan Lomax, Pete Seeger, Jimmy Driftwood, and for the first time an African American blues singer,

Georgia native and Oakland resident Jesse Fuller. Among the workshops were "The Negro's Influence in American Folklore," led by Alan Lomax, and "The Commercialization of Folk Songs," moderated by Jimmy Driftwood. The latter theme hit a nerve with *San Francisco Chronicle* critic Alfred Frankenstein, who asked, if the university-based folk festival was so "deeply concerned with questions of authenticity and esthetic significance," then why was Jesse Fuller "the only genuine folk musician" on the program?[46]

Into this milieu came the Ramblers on June 30, 1960. In keeping with the spirit of the festival, the program booklet touted the trio as proponents of "a type of folk music that has all but disappeared from the American folk music scene . . . the old string bands prevalent in the rural areas of our country in the early part of this century." The Ramblers shared the stage with British songsters Ewan MacColl and Peggy Seeger, city singers Sandy Paton and John Lomax, Jr., cowboy singer Slim Critchlow, and bluesman Lightning Hopkins. The Ramblers performed two evening concerts and participated in two festival workshops, "Folk Song Accompaniment—Types and Taste" and "Hill-Billy Music and Its Place in Folk Music." In the latter they attempted to demonstrate the connections between traditional folk music and the material recorded by commercial hillbilly players in an effort to convince ballad-oriented folk enthusiasts that early country music recordings had aesthetic as well as cultural integrity.[47] The Ramblers were paid $750 for their two days of participation.

Frankenstein was more complimentary of Olivier's efforts in his *Chronicle* review of the 1960 festival but grumbled that the event "still brings far too few folk artists and draws a bit too heavily on that intermediary borderland where the Seegers take mainly from the Lomaxes and the Lomaxes mainly from God." He praised the Ramblers as skilled musicians who "play and sing in the fashion of hillbilly string bands of the Twenties, with great precision and a very high polish of virtuosity." Then, in a moment of sublime insight into the Ramblers' quirky mix of pedagogy and ironic humor, Frankenstein noted, "If they really were a hillbilly string band, they would be intolerable for more than a few minutes at a time, but because they are actually eggheads exercising a genius for mimicry, their performance takes on about 87 different nuances of satire all at once and rises to monumental stature in the process."[48]

A July 11 story in *Time*, "Folk Frenzy," announced that the five-day Berkeley festival had attracted twelve hundred "ardent fans" each day. Surveying the national scene, the article singled out the Ramblers as one of seven "currently popular or promising" folk music acts; the six others were Odetta, Theodore Bikel, Pete Seeger, the Brothers Four, the Weavers, and Joan Baez.[49] Meanwhile, the Ramblers had headed south for a concert with Peggy and Ewan MacColl at the Santa Monica Civic Center on July 8 and settled in to spend the remainder of the summer in southern California. In late July they spent a week in residence at the Idyllwild Arts Foundation School of Music and the Arts summer camp near Palm Springs, teaching group lessons for traditional banjo, guitar, and singing styles. The music camp, where Bess Lomax Hawes and Sam Hinton had taught, was becoming a summer center for folk music. But the most important hub for folk music activity in Los Angeles was Ed Pearl's Ash Grove, where the Ramblers opened up a four-week stretch in early August.

Ed Pearl began playing the guitar as a student at UCLA in the mid-1950s. Eventually, he joined the UCLA Folksong Society, where he led the effort to bring Pete Seeger to the college during the blacklist period, when many institutions refused to hire him. He taught guitar and coordinated folksinging sessions at the college, and after producing a successful concert of flamenco music he raised money to convert an old furniture factory on Melrose Avenue in Hollywood into a folk music club. In July 1958 he opened the Ash Grove with a series of concerts featuring his guitar teachers Bess Lomax Hawes and Geronimo Villarino, bluesman Brownie McGhee, and topical folksinger Guy Carawan. The 250-seat club quickly became a popular spot for folk music as well as jazz, poetry, and dance and doubled as a music school where country and blues guitar and folk banjo classes were taught during the day. Pearl made contact with Midwest and East Coast folk music promoters Albert Grossman, Manny Greenhill, Harold Leventhal, and Alan Lomax and began serving as a West Coast booking agent for touring acts.[50]

Early on, professional folk music acts like the Limeliters, the Tarriers, Odetta, and Bud and Travis were big draws that kept the club going. But Pearl quickly realized that his real love was the traditional country and blues music that he had first heard on Smith's *Anthology of American Folk Music*. In 1959, while attending the Newport festival, he was amazed to hear a city-bred group actually replicating the mountain styles he had heard on the *Anthology*. He immediately invited the Ramblers to perform at the Ash Grove. Unfortunately, Mike and John had prior commitments, so only Tom traveled west and spent August performing and teaching guitar for Pearl.

When the Ramblers opened at the Ash Grove in August 1960, Pearl quickly realized that they could connect with students and young city kids in a way that the commercial folk acts could not: "The Ramblers actually knew about the music, its history, its nuances. And they could play and sing, and make it enjoyable and intelligible to sophisticated city kids who could then pass it on to others. . . . They became wonderful in Johnny Appleseeding old-time country music." Based on the strength of the Ramblers' first stint at the Ash Grove along with successful presentations of traditional blues singers Sonny Terry and Brownie

McGhee and Lightning Hopkins, Pearl began to shift his emphasis toward traditional music. Then one night Mike and Pearl ventured to Burbank and made a monumental discovery:

> In 1960 or maybe 1961 Mike had heard about this group of kids, and he and I went out to this hillbilly bar in Burbank. At that time it was strictly cow country. And we saw Clarence and Roland White playing, who became the Kentucky Colonels. So we brought them to the Ash Grove, and they jolted the country music movement here in Los Angeles. Clarence was the best guitarist that anyone had ever heard, and they were the same age as the kids that Clarence began teaching. And suddenly they found a community. And that helped me put my stake in traditional music of all kinds and to discard my early stars like Bud and Travis, and the Limeliters, and folks like that.[51]

In the early 1960s the Ash Grove was the only venue in Los Angeles featuring traditional folk music, as Pearl introduced audiences to such luminaries as Bill Monroe, Flatt and Scruggs, the Stanley Brothers, Doc Watson, Maybelle Carter, Roscoe Holcomb, Eck Robertson, Skip James, Mississippi John Hurt, Reverend Gary Davis, Junior Wells, Arthur Crudup, Bessie Jones and the Georgia Sea Island Singers, and the Chambers Brothers.

During their initial engagement at the Ash Grove the Ramblers found themselves sharing the program with professional singers Bud and Travis. This experience was crucial, according to John, in shaping what they did and did not want to do onstage:

> We came in to the Ash Grove following the Limeliters, and that was kind of interesting, because they were very popular and we didn't like that kind of thing. And we were booked with Bud and Travis, these two local boys who were very smooth, and funny as can be. They had the most incredible patter. Except we noticed that every night it was exactly the same, and we didn't want to do that. But since we had to follow this real smooth act, we'd come out and have to work out something for ourselves. That's when our stage act was being worked out. We already had personalities from these concerts, but to do it in a forty-five-minute set was amazing! But playing behind them was important in honing our own stage style and deliberately not repeating ourselves.[52]

The Ramblers' mix of traditional music, informative patter, and sardonic humor was appreciated by a reviewer for the local *Canyon Crier*, who exclaimed: "These three young men look like chemistry, or math, or sociology professors (as indeed I am told they are) but approach their music with a fervor that is far from academic. They must have combed every swing-floor dance hall in Kentucky, every shack in the Allegheny Mountains, and a goodly portion of the farm hoedowns in Iowa to glean their current repertoire. They impart a side meat and pot likker quality to their music which is knee-slappin' authentic . . . but they perform with the wry smile of the college town suburbanite."[53]

By the end of the summer of 1960 the Ramblers had taken pause to contemplate their future. *Time* had named them one of the country's seven most promising folk acts, they had been well received at the Newport and Berkeley festivals, and their summer income, including their extended gigs at the Gate of Horn and the Ash Grove, had netted them nearly $2,000 each. Despite strong reviews, sales of their initial four albums remained spotty. A June 30 statement from Folkways shows that just over 500 copies of their four albums had sold during the first six months of 1960, and by year's end the figure would climb to only 1,090 copies.[54] At the Folkways' royalty rate of thirty cents per copy their total annual income for record sales just topped $100 per person. There were other practical concerns, not the least of which was that the group had no manager and no prospects for steady work in the fall. On a more philosophical note, they were having a hard time squaring their passion for down-home music and the rural mountain culture that spawned it with the demands of the commercial show-business world. The idea of even having a manager or a booking agent at that time, recalled Mike, "drew more heat than light."[55] Tom, who remained the most skeptical about playing folk music for a living, had taken yet another teaching position for the 1960–61 academic year, this time at Rutgers University in New Jersey. Shortly after the Ramblers' final night at the Ash Grove he and Claudia returned east for the beginning of the fall semester. John departed for New York and his Third Avenue loft, where he continued work on various music and photography projects.

Marge gave birth to Kim Seeger in Los Angeles on September 6, 1960. The couple and their newborn son moved into an inexpensive apartment for a month while Mike performed a few solo engagements that Pearl arranged for him. With no job in DC to return to, Mike began to pursue his solo career more aggressively, and on the way back to the East Coast he played at Ann Arbor and Chicago. Mike and his family remained homeless for the next six months, staying with Pete and his wife, Toshi, in Beacon and with Bill Clifton and Jeremy and Alice Gerrad in Virginia. Finally, in early 1961 they settled in the small New Jersey town of Roosevelt.

The fall of 1960 was a relatively quiet time for the Ramblers. In late October they played Harvard and Yale, and in November they performed at the Ethical Society and at Sheraton in the Square in New York City. In December 1960 *Mademoiselle* ran an impressive spread by Susan Montgomery on the growing popularity of folk music among young college students, quoting heavily from a three-thousand-word letter John had sent her filled with his observations on college hoots, folksinging societies, and festivals. A dramatic David Gahr photo of the Ramblers appeared on the opening page, with a caption identifying the group as "folk music's crusaders. Their cause: Bluegrass and country music (favorites now with students)." Montgomery's thoughtful piece probed student motivations for embracing the folk music that expressed "the ideas and emotions of the downtrodden and the heartbroken, of garage mechanics and millworkers, and miners and backwoods farmers." Likening the "communal euphoria" of group folksinging to a revival meeting, she concluded that young people's need to set themselves apart from the debilitating effects of mass culture accounted for much of the music's appeal. Her observations clarified why college campuses, where social discontent was just beginning to percolate in the early 1960s, were becoming fertile ground for the Ramblers and their advocacy for "downhome" country music.[56]

On Friday, December 23, Izzy Young sponsored his third Ramblers concert in New York, this time at the Union Hall at 13 Astor Place. The decision to have Elizabeth Cotten make her New York City debut on the program turned out to be more significant than the Ramblers or Young might have predicted. The concert was well attended by an audience that included Ralph Rinzler, who had helped Mike with several of his earlier bluegrass LP projects and was currently playing with the New York City–based bluegrass band the Greenbriar Boys. A week later John and Rinzler were marveling over the enthusiastic crowd response to Cotten. Out of that conversation was born the idea for the Friends of Old Time Music (FOTM), a loosely knit organization that would eventually sponsor more than a dozen concerts of traditional country, blues, and spiritual singers in New York. The purpose of the organization, as John, Rinzler, and Young told readers of Sing Out!, was to pay tribute to the rural musicians who were the "original source" on which the folk revival was built. Urban audiences who had heard only recordings and city interpretations of traditional music were ready, they believed, to experience "the real thing" in person. Taking a shot at the Kingston Trio and the Newport Folk Festival, they groused, "So much is being made from folk music while almost nothing is being put back into it. There have been millions for exploitation and profit and scarcely a penny for tribute."[57] The FOTM group incorporated under the legal name The Society for Traditional Music, and with an advisory committee that included square dance instructor Margot Mayo and balladeer Jean Ritchie in addition to Rinzler, Young, and John, plans were put in motion for the first concert to be held in February 1961.

But just prior to the FOTM debut concert the Ramblers would participate in a college festival destined to become the country's most prominent venue for traditional folk music. Inspired by his previous summer's discussions with the

Ramblers, Mike Fleischer organized the first midwinter University of Chicago Folk Festival (UCFF) on February 3–5, 1961. "The key words were tap-roots, tradition, authenticity, and non-commercial," Shelton reported in the *New York Times*.[58] John brought the Kentucky banjoist and singer Roscoe Holcomb, and Mike invited Elizabeth Cotten, fresh from her Greenwich Village success with the Ramblers. Horton Barker, a seventy-one-year-old blind ballad singer from Chilihowie, Virginia, who had recorded for the LOC in the 1930s, came with storyteller Richard Chase. Folk song collector Frank Warner brought the traditional North Carolina banjoist Frank Proffitt, whose recording of the ballad "Tom Dula" was believed to be one of the sources for the 1958 Kingston Trio commercial hit. Street singer Blind Arvella Grey, Quebec fiddler and clogger Jean Carignan, bluesmen Memphis Slim and Willie Dixon, and the bluegrass luminaries the Stanley Brothers were also featured, along with a handful of city singers, including Sandy Paton and of course the Ramblers.

In addition to the evening concerts, the festival included a series of daytime workshops on traditional banjo and guitar styles led by Mike and John. Lectures included "The Value of Tradition in Folk Music," "The Growth and Development of Bluegrass," and "Field Collecting in Folk Music." The bluegrass presentation, led by Mike, evolved into an informal music session, as Jon Pankake and Paul Nelson described in the *Little Sandy Review*: "After the lecture, Mike hung around answering questions and autographing banjos. Some youngsters talked him into singing a few numbers for them; and Mike amiably complied, doing a beautiful 'Butcher's Boy' on the banjo. When we left, he was still sitting in a stream of sunlight, singing and playing for his rapt audience in the large, empty room." Tom participated in another unscheduled session with his guitar after hearing a discussion that a group of students were having about guitar technique: "Tom hurried off to fetch his beat-up Martin, and was soon picking and singing and slapping in his galoshes up and down to keep time. He sang us a nicely flavored 'Jackero,' and then played 'Buck Dancer's Choice' and went through some of Sam McGee's old routines. When the talk got around to guitar picking heard on old country 78's, Tom began playing samples of everything from McGee to Gary Davis." Mike and Tom were held in high esteem by the students who attended the festival, and their willingness to engage in both formal workshops and impromptu sessions underscored the Ramblers' commitment to passing the music on to fledgling city players.[59]

As they planned their folk festivals and FOTM concerts, Fleischer, Rinzler, and the Ramblers wondered if city audiences would respond to the raw, unprocessed sound of rural performers who might not be accustomed to playing in formal stage situations. After viewing the UCFF Shelton answered unequivocally yes:

"It is possible to produce an artistically and commercially successful event rely-
ing mainly on unknown, unheralded genuine folk singers. The translation of
authentic music for city audiences is no longer necessary, the weekend demonstrated. A preface and an occasional subtitle helped, but the folk can speak and
sing eloquently for themselves."[60] Sandy Paton, one of the few city singers on the
UCFF stage, reiterated Shelton's argument that traditional performers and urban
fans could connect, even in a formal concert setting:

> The audience was alternately enchanted and electrified by each of these
> great artists. The producers of the festival must have known moments of
> trepidation prior to the first program, for people who were active in the
> field had long assumed that, in order to get urban audiences to listen to
> folk music, one had to "interpret" them—that is to say, translate them into
> a more familiar vocal style, namely that of "art" or "pop" music. That first
> evening in Chicago proved, without a doubt, that this was no longer true, if,
> indeed, it had ever been true at all. Urban audiences not only could but most
> certainly *would* appreciate the opportunity to hear genuine folk artists in live
> performances.[61]

Studs Terkel, who emceed the Friday- and Saturday-night concerts, recalled: "The
audience, consisting primarily of college students, acclaimed the Appalachian
men over the slick pros. It was not out of sentiment; rather, it erupted from the
excitement of a rare experience: seeing and hearing men reveal themselves."[62]

While the Ramblers were certainly heartened by the students' enthusiastic
response to traditional ballad, blues, and bluegrass musicians, Shelton's and
Paton's comments undoubtedly gave the three men pause. If indeed city singers
were no longer necessary to translate and interpret traditional music for city audiences, then what, exactly, was the role of the Ramblers in this new folk music
milieu? Were they destined for demotion to "consultants, advisers, workshop
organizers, and panel discussers," as John described their role in the festival two
years later for *Sing Out!* readers?[63]

The Ramblers would serve as both performers and interpreters the following
week when they returned to New York with Holcomb for the first FOTM concert.
Concerns that Holcomb was an unknown entity to New York audiences prompted
the FOTM organizers to include the well-established Ramblers along with the
Greenbriar Boys and Jean Ritchie in order to attract a respectable crowd. The
strategy worked, with nearly four hundred folk music fans crowed into PS 41 on
February 11. Following a brief set by the Ramblers, John introduced the audience
to Holcomb: "Well, thank you very much. And now, it's my great privilege—and
I guess all our great privilege—to meet Roscoe Holcomb who . . . He's a con-

struction worker, he lives down in Kentucky near Hazard, in a little town called Daisy. I met him several years ago when I was down there collecting songs and trying to find out what the music was about, see where it came from. And now I guess we're giving you and ourselves a chance to hear what it really sounds like. So here's my friend, Roscoe Holcomb."[64]

John established Holcomb as bona-fide folk from small-town Kentucky—a purveyor of genuine folk music, "what it really sounds like," directly from the source, "where it came from." He also reminded the audience of his own credentials as an adventurer who journeyed to the hill country of Kentucky in order to "collect songs and to find out what the music was about" and finally to befriend a backwoods musician and bring him out of the mountains to the city for their appreciation.

Holcomb, clearly nervous, addressed his audience apologetically: "Well, I've been on the road now about two weeks, and I'm little hoarse tonight and I don't know what kind of sound I'll make, but I'm gonna try." He quickly launched into a driving rendition of "East Virginia Blues" with a banjo accompaniment that blended three-finger up-picking with brush stroke, an esoteric sound that clearly predated the popular Scruggs bluegrass style. The audience reacted with fervent applause, an unambiguous affirmation that they wanted what Holcomb had to offer. John, who remained sitting at Holcomb's side onstage, introduced the next song: "So we'll do another song that you might know, but not this way, it's called, 'Old Smokey.'" Holcomb chimed in, "This is one of those old-time tunes, that's played way back" while retuning his banjo. As he moaned the tale of losing his own true love "for courting too slow" there was no mistaking his version of the ballad for the Weavers' slick arrangement, which reached the pop charts for twenty-three weeks in 1951. Jean Ritchie joined Holcomb to sing what she described as an old, regular Baptist hymn, and the duo lined out "Amazing Grace" in the traditional church style. Holcomb moved through his set of ballads, mountain blues, and dance pieces, with John occasionally joining him on guitar and interjecting bits of information about the songs and banjo tunings. "What we were doing was a public interview—not just to extract information but to convey to people who were sitting there how to approach these instruments—trying to give things they could use," John later recalled. "That was an essential thing that the Ramblers and the FOTM were doing: how to tune the banjo, how to play different picking styles and techniques so people could get at the music. That was the assumption. Sometimes [in between sets] members of the audience would go into the hallway and start picking their banjos."[65]

Holcomb's angular, modal vocal lines evoked a sense of ancient mystery, especially when sounded against his droning, repetitive banjo riffs, which rarely

FIGURE 8. Friends of Old Time Music flyer with Roscoe Holcomb (1961). Photograph and flyer design by John Cohen.

moved off the tonic chord. His tensely pinched voice was dangerously close to cracking when he soared into the high register with a shrill, vibratoless timbre that violated all Western conventions of tonal beauty. While the aficionados of mountain music saw Holcomb's style as personifying the high, lonesome sound, some in the audience apparently found his singing too raw for their tastes. Rinzler recalled: "I remember some people who came thought Roscoe was a mistake, that he was too harsh and shrill, at least the middle-class people who were our kin. My cousin Richard's parents came, and they didn't understand why Roscoe was there. Everyone else was nice to listen to, they said, but Roscoe was very harsh, and they couldn't deal with that."[66]

It is doubtful that Holcomb, as a soloist inexperienced in stage performance, could have sustained an entire evening in front of a city audience. But presenting him in the informal "public interview" format somewhat akin to a workshop, having John serve as presenter, and wrapping his presentation around performances by popular city bands like the Ramblers and the Greenbriar Boys resulted in a highly successful program. Planning for further FOTM concerts began immediately.

The Ramblers continued to work the college circuit in March, playing the University of Illinois, Washington University, the University of Virginia, and the Rhode Island School of Design. They were not in town on March 25 for the second FOTM concert, which featured a string band led by Clarence "Tom" Ashley that included a then-unknown blind guitarist named Arthel "Doc" Watson. Ashley was known among folk music aficionados for his haunting 1929 recording of the "The Coo Coo Bird," which appeared on Smith's *Anthology of American Folk Music*. In the spring of 1960 Rinzler, while playing at the Union Grove Old-Time Fiddlers Convention in North Carolina with his Greenbriar Boys, had been shocked to find Ashley alive and still performing.[67] Rinzler arranged for Ashley and his band to come to New York and served as the presenter for the concert. Shelton, who had missed the first FOTM program, gave the Ashley show a rave review in the *New York Times*, describing the group as purveyors of "real folk music, without any personal or commercial axes to grind." They were utterly "down-to-earth" performers whose music had "the well-worn quality of fine antiques, a rut and a scratch here and there only heightening the character of a family heirloom."[68] Over the next four years the FOTM would sponsor more than a dozen concerts of traditional musicians, including Doc Watson, Maybelle Carter, Dock Boggs, Bill Monroe, the Stanley Brothers, Mississippi John Hurt, Fred McDowell, and Bessie Jones, many of whom would move on to successful second careers performing on the burgeoning folk music circuit. The efforts of John, Mike, and Rinzler to stage traditional musicians for urban audiences at the FOTM and the UCFF would be further refined at the reconstituted Newport Folk Festival, where Mike and Rinzler served as advisors and field workers between 1963 and 1967. The FOTM concerts and early 1960s folk festivals were the models Rinzler would draw on when he became director of the first Smithsonian Festival of American Folklife in 1967.[69]

On March 17 the Ramblers played at the University of Virginia in Charlottesville. It was a significant occasion because it was the first time that the group had performed below the Mason-Dixon Line (with the exception of Washington, DC), close to the source of their music. Among the receptive audience was Professor Arthur Kyle Davis, Jr., the author of several collections of Virginia ballads and a venerable collector of folk songs during the 1930s. The presence and approval of a man John identified as "an old southern folklorist and Child ballad scholar" was gratifying to the Ramblers.[70] In a review he wrote for the *Charlottesville Daily Progress* Davis described the Ramblers as "spirited, musically competent, and entertaining" but inexplicably concluded that the group "would invite comparison with the Kingston Trio"![71]

While traveling between Washington and Charlottesville on old Route 29, a troubling incident occurred when they pulled into a restaurant in Warrington, Virginia. According to Tom,

> We were driving back home, and not too far from DC we wanted to make a stop to get something to eat. But I saw a sign at the place we stopped at—I said, "Look, it says 'No Blacks.'" It was a segregated place, and I said, "I'm not going in there." I said, "We can wait until we get back to Washington, it won't take that long." But Mike and John wanted to go, so they went in and I sat in the car. . . . Of course it wasn't because they wanted to support segregation. Now Mike, even though his parents were Left, he was pretty much apolitical—he never talked about politics, spoke about politics. John I was a little bit more surprised at.[72]

John, who recalled that the incident took place on the way down to Charlottesville, offered a different perspective:

> I'll never forget that first trip south in 1961. We pulled out of Washington, DC, in Mike's van. And there was this diner we wanted to go in, and Tom suddenly found himself incapable of getting out of the van and eating in a place that might support segregation. I was very amazed and puzzled and struck by the position that he took. Because it suddenly told me about the conflicting things within our own message. Which was yes, we like southern music, we like country people, we like country songs, we're going to play that way, and that's what we're doing. But then when confronted with the actual society, he [Tom] had some blockade on that. And for me it was an adventure to step over that line. Finally I was stepping into this area that I'd been appreciating and looking at but had never really dealt with, and now we were going to deal with it.[73]

Mike apparently did maintain an apolitical view of the situation; even years later he recollected: "It was the restaurant where you could eat between Charlottesville and Washington. It did have a sign on the door that said 'Due to lack of facilities, we can only serve whites' or something like that. A friend of mine wrote in: 'Due to lack of "mental" facilities!'" Mike claimed that by working at Mount Wilson Hospital with an integrated staff and hanging around rural folks at the country music parks and at Baltimore bluegrass sessions, he had a more realistic perception of racial problems in the south than Tom did.[74] John agreed: "I think it was the difference between perception and experience. We were all aware of this social inequity and this horrible situation of inequity between the North and the South. And Tom had remained in the North and hadn't had the experience of dealing personally with it. Mike had dealt with it through music and work at the hospital, and I think I jumped into it in my east Kentucky collecting trip in 1959. I certainly got a big dose of dealing and of having a very interesting time with country people."[75]

While admitting that they had encountered "all sorts of seemingly racist remarks" and "old southern stereotypes" in the music, John concluded: "But still the spirit, and the virtues of the music overrode that. Tom hadn't had that personal experience. He'd never put himself on the line. And it wasn't just Tom; it was a whole bunch of city people."[76] Mike and John felt strongly that their firsthand experience with southerners, black and white, had given them a deeper understanding of racial dynamics that Tom and other northern liberals could not fully comprehend. At the time neither saw any inconsistency in recognizing the "horrible situation of inequity" that existed in the South and eating at a whites-only restaurant.

Given his concerns about segregated eating establishments, it should come as no surprise that Tom was adamantly opposed to any playing before segregated southern audiences. Although the Ramblers performed only three times in the South during the early 1960s with Tom (at the relatively liberal urban campuses of the Universities of Virginia, North Carolina, and Texas), Tom would later charge that his strong feelings about segregation deterred the group from taking additional southern dates. This, he concluded, was one of the main reasons that Mike and John would force him out of the group.[77] But there is little evidence for his claims, and the Ramblers rarely played below the Mason-Dixon Line even after Tracy Schwarz replaced Tom the following year. As it turned out, very few southerners at the time were interested in a trio of city-bred Yankees playing what they perceived to be antiquated hillbilly music.

The incident underscored issues of race that would increasingly challenge the Ramblers. As the nation plunged into the heat of the civil rights movement, the Ramblers continued to champion the music of southern whites, considered by much of the Ramblers' progressive northern audience as the villainous per-petuators of racial injustice. John recalled an uncomfortable moment at Izzy Young's Folklore Center when a group of students wondered out loud whether an upcoming Stanley Brothers FOTM concert would showcase "those south-ern guys in white sheets." Another time he was confronted by a radio host who claimed Dave Van Ronk had criticized old-time music as "lynching music." John dismissed such attitudes as naive, claiming that the Ramblers, in their role as cultural liaisons, hoped to "find linkages between people who would otherwise be opposed to one another. . . . We were putting our stamp of approval on these white guys who, until that time, had been stereotyped as racists, lynchers, and all those nightmarish things about the South. We were trying to turn Ashley and Watson and the Stanleys into real people, and I thought this was a good thing—acknowledging those people and their culture was political. . . . We were looking for deeply human, positive connections rather than confrontations."[78]

John's search for "deeply human" linkages between southern whites and northern progressives was well intentioned, but making this point to audiences who would soon be singing the civil rights anthems by Pete Seeger, Bob Dylan, and Tom Paxton was not always an easy sell. The aforementioned dismissal of John's "There'll Be No Distinctions There" by Joan Baez, who commented, "Now I'd like to sing a song for the colored people," was a case in point.

The night after the Charlottesville performance the Ramblers played at the Washington Theater Club and were recorded by John Dildine. After greeting the audience Mike noted: "No, we're going to do a little bit of very informal kind of playing here, nothing high pressure like the University of Virginia last night, where we had folklorists watching us, and we had to impress with our acumen or some-thing like that [laughs]." After playing "The Battleship Maine" Mike remarked:

Not all the folk music we do is that high pressure; it's not all commercial hits. You can tell we're commercial, right from the beginning. . . . There are lots of ballads and blues and all kinds of indefinable songs that we do. Most of the songs that we play were learned off of old commercial record-ings, believe it or not. The commercial recording companies recorded a lot of old-time folk music in the early days of recording, back in 1925 through the 1940s. They did this without knowing this or realizing it, that they were documenting the time. And I'm sure they wouldn't have done it if they had known about it. They were just trying to make a dishonest dollar, and I'm sure they did. They copyrighted the songs in their own name, something like that. We didn't mean to get bitter. I'm just making up a little folklore here.

Following "Willow Garden," Mike delivered a rambling commentary:

> Thank you, that was "Down in the Willow Garden." In the early days of
> what we call country music it used to be called hillbilly music sometimes.
> But folklorists have been learning more about this [hillbilly music] lately.
> Actually, their old definition of folk music used to be something that is
> dead. But they've been redefining it lately, realizing that there is really
> folklore around and a continuing folk. What I'm trying to say is that in the
> earlier days of folk music in the country they played a lot of banjo and fiddle
> duets. That was a lot of the type of dance music they had around, and a lot
> of the ballads were accompanied by banjo or a fiddle. Here's just a dance
> tune that's on our latest record, "Fly Around My Blue-Eyed Miss," that's
> on our latest record. I'd like to also put in a little commercial, saying we're
> as commercial as the Kingston Trio, we'd like to sell a million records too.
> And some of ours will be on sale outside in the lobby at vast discount prices.
> We recommend our latest record; it's much easier to take than the other
> four, especially if you have four dollars [audience laughter].[79]

Mike's remarks revealed that the Ramblers straddled a fine line between
entertainment and education. They felt obligated to let their audiences know
something about their music and its sources, but they did not want explanations
to turn into boring lectures or show-and-tell sessions. Thus, Mike's commentary was always delivered in a deadpan, slightly sarcastic tone, often including a
self-conscious apology about "making up folklore" to cover for Tom's extended
tuning sessions.

The Ramblers certainly did not want to be viewed as stuffy academic folklorists who viewed folk songs to be "something that is dead." John elaborated on
this point in the notes to The New Lost Ramblers Volume 3 (Folkways Records FA
2398, 1961), where he stated: "Coming from the scholars and academicians, the
terms 'folk music and traditional' have also meant a death certificate—as if such
titles were guarantee that the music was finished and belonged only to history."[80]
Despite this criticism, the Ramblers approached their discographies with the
same sort of meticulous care that folk music scholars used in annotating their
"dead" ballad collections, and they did not hesitate to share that information
with their audiences during live performances. Moreover, Mike acknowledged
that some folklorists were broadening their perspectives and now viewed hillbilly
music as a type of modern folklore. In their following release, The New Lost City
Ramblers Volume 4 (Folkways Records FA 2399, 1962), Mike would acknowledge
the efforts of Charles Seeger, Alan Lomax, and D. K. Wilgus in articulating the
parameters of instrumental and vocal performance styles that were central to

the Ramblers' approach to folk music as well as their support for the study of commercial hillbilly recordings.[81]

Mike's comments to the Washington Theater Club audience also underscored the deep distrust the Ramblers had for the recording industry. Even the early record companies, who inadvertently documented the hillbilly music that would become the primary source of much of the Ramblers' material, were criticized for "trying to make a dishonest dollar" and engaging in the disreputable practice of copyrighting traditional folk songs in their own name. Mike next took a dig at the Ramblers' favorite villains of the contemporary commercial scene, the Kingston Trio. He sarcastically quipped that the Ramblers wished they too could sell millions of records like the Kingstons and later criticized the popular trio for trying to copyright a version of the traditional tune "Leaving Home" (a variant on "Frankie and Johnny"), which they learned from the Ramblers' Volume II. After positioning the virtuous Ramblers in opposition to the exploitive Kingstons, Mike felt free to engage in his own "commercial" and hawk Ramblers' Folkways recordings, which they now sold at their concerts. The group faced the paradox of trying to "make it" playing esoteric traditional music on the fringes of an entertainment business that increasingly demanded smooth arrangements to maximize profits from record and ticket sales. The Ramblers did not hesitate to comment on their dilemma of trying to make it playing traditional music, albeit couched in a self-deprecating humor that was appreciated by their small but sympathetic audiences.

Volume 3 returned to the tradition of an FAS photograph on the cover, this time a shot of an unidentified fiddle-banjo-guitar country string band joined by a cellist in a jacket and tie who looked as though he had just arrived from Carnegie Hall (figure 9). The title, The New Lost City Ramblers Volume 3, and the names Mike Seeger, John Cohen, and Tom Paley appeared above the picture, creating a sense of ambiguity. Did the album feature the three hillbilly performers in the picture? Or would Mike, John, and Tom be performing the music of this unknown trio? Or, for the uninitiated, were the three hillbilly musicians actually Mike, John, and Tom? Perhaps the urban trio was impersonating, or wished to be, the trio in the picture? The matter is resolved in part by the accompanying booklet, which featured a dramatic David Gahr photo of the real Mike, John, and Tom in their now familiar vests and white shirts.

In separate statements John and Tom continued the conversation about the Ramblers' commitment to replicating an "authentic quality" in the band's arrangements of hillbilly music that did not sacrifice individual creativity. On the one hand, the purist ballad collectors needed to be reminded that the Ramblers' hillbilly sources were anchored in traditional vocal and instrumental styles, but styles that were constantly evolving. On the other hand, urban audiences steeped

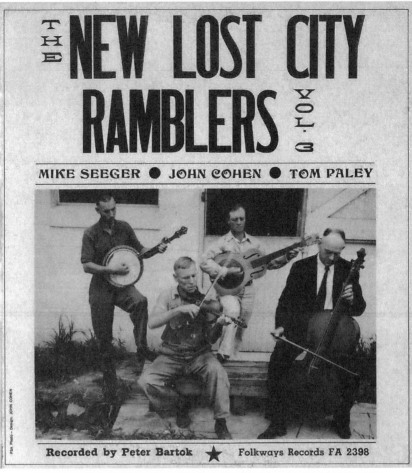

FIGURE 9. Cover of *New Lost City Ramblers Volume 3* Folkways LP (1961).
Farm Security Administration photograph. Image courtesy of the Ralph Rinzler
Folklife Archives and Collections, Smithsonian Institution.

in modernist sensibilities needed to understand that the Ramblers were artists
who did not simply imitate or replicate the sounds of old recordings or, as Shelton and Wilgus had suggested, practice a rigid sort of "musical archeology and
reconstruction" or "stylistic re-creation."

Trying to link past and present practices, John observed that "the commercial
singers of thirty years ago are considered 'traditional' today." He asserted that
many of the musicians the Ramblers most admired, including Charlie Poole,
Bill Monroe, Earl Scruggs, and the Stanley Brothers, "were not reactionary in
their desire to preserve the old way, rather, they were some of the most artisti-

cally progressive innovators" of their time. "None of them ever presented their music as 'folk' music. To them it was, and is, alive." Like Scruggs, John argued, Mike took a traditional banjo tune and added his own licks to it or combined several versions of the tune in order to "bring his own ideas to the music, which makes it directed and meaningful to the present as well." Finally, he addressed his urban listeners directly: "In the city, we seem to be missing the possibility of understanding newness and creativity within traditional terms."

Tom tackled the imitation question head-on: "There is always the temptation to learn everything note for note and inflection for inflection from old recordings, but this leads down a completely blind alley from any artistic standpoint." However, a city player "cannot expect to achieve an authentic quality unless he is steeped in the sound he wishes to reproduce. We have tried to get around this problem by listening to enormous amounts of old-timey music in order to be able to sound authentic without note for note copying." Regarding regional accents, Tom admitted that he "always feels a little phony when I try and put on a very obvious accent. Actually, a little bit of southern accent has rubbed off on us, and I believe that now, without sounding contrived our accents are not glaringly out of place."

Volume 3 conveyed a warmer sound than the earlier albums, perhaps due to the new recording environment, the Pequot Library Auditorium in Connecticut, and a new recording and mixing engineer, Peter Bartok (previous albums were recorded by Moe Asch at the Cue studios in New York City). For the first time a number of the pieces were mixed in stereo, with significant vocal and instrumental separation resulting in a fuller sound. Musically, Volume 3 featured some of the Ramblers' most innovative and well-rendered material. Mike played the fiddle with more assurance, drive, and precision than on previous recordings. "Black Mountain Rag," "Fly Around My Pretty Little Miss," and "Hog Eye" stood out as superb breakdowns featuring choppy, syncopated bowing patterns that broke the standard shuffle beat and varied phrasing on the tastefully ornamented melodic lines. In the middle of "Black Mountain Rag" he set down his bow and picked the A and B sections of the tune with a delicate pizzicato technique. "Hog Eye" proved to be one of the group's more unusual tunes, with an atypical harmonic progression that opens in the key of A with the tonic (A) chord alternating with the VII (G) chord and then suddenly modulates to the key of D for the second strain. The bluegrass numbers "Rolling in My Sweet Baby's Arms" and "Long Journey Home" galloped along as Mike's lead and Tom's tenor harmony blended with an edgy tension. John's rendition of "Talking Hard Luck" captured the feel of a laid-back Guthrie talking blues, delivered with just the right mix of humor and cynicism without overstating the case. The harmony singing on the comical "Three Men Went a-Hunting," the easy swinging "Hot Corn, Cold Corn," and the suggestive "Sal's Got a Meatskin" was well pitched and tightly blended. Mike and Tom's fiddle-banjo duet, "Fly Around My Pretty Little Miss," conveyed the exuberant energy of an informal square-dance performance without sounding too slick, while their voices were just tense enough to emulate mountain singing without sounding contrived. The Ramblers seemed completely at ease with their material, suggesting that their efforts to immerse themselves in the sounds of mountain music were paying off. D. K. Wilgus, who reviewed *Volume 3* for the *Journal of American Folklore*, was impressed. He praised the collection for its "superlative performances of material seldom familiar to the purchasers of 'folk' recordings" and complimented the Ramblers for "absorb[ing] the tradition amazingly well" and for "stimulating study as well as performance."[82]

Toward the end of the Ramblers' Washington Theater Club performance Mike thanked the audience for coming and apologized for the small turnout, noting: "As many folk music groups, we have a problem of managership. Our manager, or one of our managers, we have about twenty—anybody who gives us a job, we'll take it—he only informed us about ten days before our concert that somehow he couldn't find us a place to give us a concert here in DC." Mike's joke belied a serious problem for the Ramblers, whose network of contacts at times must have felt like twenty managers. On a publicity flyer that John put together with the help of Folkways Records he listed himself as the main contact for "concert arrangements" and Manny Greenhill for concerts in the New England area. Harold Leventhal occasionally booked their engagements in and around New York, while Ed Pearl was their most important West Coast contact. Their growing networks of friends in folk song clubs and coffeehouses, often associated with colleges, provided them with most of their work. But setting up a profitable tour to the Midwest or West Coast took time, and most of the work fell to John.

This would change in the spring of 1961, when John ran into Jim Richmond, the proprietor of the Record Hunter shop in Greenwich Village. Richmond introduced him to Charlie Porterfield, who managed a handful of folk acts, and Herb Jacoby, who owned the swank Blue Angel club on East 55th Street. Together, Richmond, Porterfield, and Jacoby offered to take over management of the Ramblers and to hook them up with International Talent Associates (ITA), an agency that booked commercial acts like the Kingston Trio and the Limeliters. "They were promising us the world, and we signed up," recalled John. "So the first job they got us was at Jacoby's Blue Angel."[83]

The Ramblers opened a week's stay at the Blue Angel on Saturday night, June 17, 1961. Mike recalled that the Blue Angel "was a very slick, chichi place—it was very sophisticated, not our class at all."[84] John remembered "this very sophisticated, or posh, or bored, or stupid audience, whatever you wanted to call them—that high-priced, uptown audience—listening to us guys. It was a little strange." The Ramblers' show was not fast paced and predictable enough for Jacoby. Following a squabble that ended in Tom walking out of a sound check, the trio agreed among themselves to work out a more structured stage presentation. They would start each set with a fast breakdown followed by a brief greeting from Mike. Next would come several vocal trio numbers and then a series of solos and duets. The entire group would next return for more trio vocals and instrumentals. The set would end with an up-tempo number. With this template they could substitute a variety of songs while keeping the Blue Angel staff satisfied.

No less a distinguished publication than the *New Yorker* took note of the Ramblers' residency at the Blue Angel, identifying them as "real rings-on-their-fingers-and-bells-on-their-toes hillbilly singers."[85] A more serious review came several days earlier from Shelton. His four-hundred-word piece for the *New York Times* and its accompanying Robert Frank photo-portrait of the trio (see the frontispiece) were hard for browsers of the Arts section to miss. Shelton immediately noted the incongruity of the Ramblers playing an Upper East Side club: "The sophisticated confines of the Blue Angel were invaded last weekend by one of the least sophisticated forms of entertainment, old-time country music." The audience, he bemused, "was part quizzical and part enchanted. 'It's not the sort of thing I ordinarily expect to hear at the Blue Angel,' one slightly mystified habitué remarked." After offering a short biography of the group, Shelton commented that their music "has the archaic, quaint but durable quality of an antique. . . . They sing in tawny, nasal upper-register voices that evocatively re-create a far-off time and place." He later noted: "The rough-hewn quality of the Ramblers' playing and singing is purposeful, for the trio is ardent about authenticity." Shelton concluded on an optimistic note: "There have been so many ways of changing and sweetening the recipe for serving folk music to night-club patrons that the Ramblers' undiluted blend is as acerbic as hard cider. But watching members of the audience at the Blue Angel start to tap feet and swizzelsticks as they got into the rural swing of things, it appears that the Ramblers hopefully will broaden the beachhead they've established."[86]

Just how far the group could broaden that beachhead remained to be seen, but the Ramblers certainly had reason to be optimistic by the summer of 1961. Shelton's glowing review in the *New York Times*, a full-month run booked at the Ash Grove for August, and the promise of more lucrative work through ITA were enough to finally convince Tom to take a year's leave of absence from his teaching duties at Rutgers. The Ramblers would finally have a go at playing music full-time.

PALEY
DEPARTS AND
SCHWARZ ARRIVES,
1961–1962

On August 3, 1961, *Variety* informed its readers that Ash Grove
"folksong buffs should find unusual pleasure in a solid bill link-
ing the New Lost City Ramblers with Salli Terri and nicely supple-
mented by Frank Hamilton." The review went on to describe the
Ramblers as "enthusiastic and dedicated, delivering a selection
of authentic traditional southern mountain music. Students of
folklore, they have taped most of the material in its locale before
adding to their repertoire and, perhaps more honestly than any
other group in the field today recreate with faithful flavor. Expert
instrumentalists as well as singers, the trio uses violin, guitar,
banjo and autoharp to advantage. Country style stuff features
yodeling and a running mixture of homespun comedy patter
add to their appeal."[1]

The Ramblers surely appreciated the popular press recognizing the "authenticity" of their repertoire and the "honesty"
of their arrangements. But, more important, such accolades
from the leading commercial entertainment publication in the
country, coming on the heels of Robert Shelton's superlative
feature in the *New York Times*, must have been reassuring as the
Ramblers looked to the future. Their month-long engagement
at the Ash Grove was met with enthusiasm by growing throngs
of young students and citybillies who recognized the Ramblers
as the premiere urban gurus of old-time mountain music. The
trio received rave reviews at the Berkeley Folk Festival that September. Previews of the Berkeley engagement echoed their recent
Variety review, suggesting two images of the group that appealed
to college students. First was the Ramblers as purveyors of au-

thentic down-home mountain traditions: "Ever have a yen to sit in the twilight of a southern mountain country evening on an old wooden porch and listen to music handed down through generations, played by local inhabitants on home-made string instruments?" asked the *Daily Californian* of Berkeley. The Ramblers presented a "reasonable facsimile" of such music and would, the editors assured their readers, deliver "a concert of the music of your dreams." A second vision from the *Berkeley Daily Gazette* cast the Ramblers as educators who "bring with them an impressive scholarship; there is nothing dry or acrid in their treatment of the material. . . . They are known for being entertaining as well as informative—and thoroughly professional."[2]

All the positive press attention did not, unfortunately, immediately translate into more lucrative engagements. Even more disturbing was the realization that International Talent Associates (ITA) was not delivering on its promises of steady work. The Ramblers remained in California throughout September and October, playing in addition to the Berkeley Folk Festival five club and college gigs arranged by Ed Pearl. In November they had a one-night concert in Ann Arbor and a week at the Gate of Horn in Chicago. But with no further bookings from ITA, John recalls that things had become "desperate," for "here was this situation with a contract that had us tied up and no work. It was almost the end of the Ramblers."[3]

Ironically, a note on the Ramblers' November 18 concert that appeared in the University of Michigan Folklore Society's *Folkways* magazine characterized them as "a part-time group and as such, folk music is a wonderful hobby rather than a desperate business. They feel that while they have no objection to making money, this allows them to be more honest in their music." The commentary concluded that hearing the Ramblers was "not only an enjoyment but an education. You cannot help but learn something from them, not only of the music, but of the people and the emotion behind it. And this is the trademark of the truly great folk musicians."[4] The *Folkways* magazine piece unknowingly exposed a painful dilemma for the Ramblers. They certainly were not willing to compromise the "honesty" of their music by sweetening their sound or broadening their repertoire to include more popular material. And they detested the "desperate business" of commercial entertainment while maintaining an unwavering commitment to not just entertain but educate. But pursuing these noble goals on a "part-time" basis as a "wonderful hobby" that somehow placed them above the fray of com-mercial corruption was simply not practical. Mike's second son, Christopher, had arrived in September. Tom, who from the beginning had voiced his skepticism about playing folk music for a living, was becoming increasingly concerned about financial matters. According to John, Tom was now making noises about leaving if the fiscal situation did not improve.[5]

In addition to financial concerns, personality issues and subtle disagreements over musical tastes had become sources of ongoing friction within the group. All three Ramblers possessed strong dispositions, which often precluded easy compromise. John's enthusiasm and energy were essential to the group's chemistry, but he could be domineering and vindictive if he didn't get his way. Tom could be charming and humorous but also obsessive and uncompromising when it came to politics, tuning, choice of repertoire, and the distribution of solos in a program. Mike tended to be stubborn, intense, and deeply set in his ways regarding anything to do with playing and recording music; he could quickly turn temperamental in tense social situations.

Mike's love of and Tom's general ambivalence toward bluegrass proved divisive. Tom found Scruggs-style banjo too "flashy" for his tastes, and he was put off by the competitive, showy nature of bluegrass players.[6] As a result, the Ramblers' bluegrass repertoire was limited to vocal duets from the Monroe and Stanley Brothers as well as Carter Family tunes generally perceived to be predecessors of bluegrass. Rarely did Mike get a chance to exercise his superb banjo skills on a full-blown bluegrass number. Mike, while admiring the technical precision and rhythmic drive that Tom brought to his playing, found his idiosyncratic banjo style too "stiff," sometimes "square," and often lacking in "a country feel." Nor could he abide the old English ballads and folk songs that Tom occasionally tried to introduce to the group.[7]

On the practical side, John was the Rambler who showed the most inclination toward management. His insatiable curiosity and proclivity to take on too many projects at once, however, could result in an atmosphere of disorder that wore on Tom and Mike. Indeed, it was John who seemed the most committed to the Ramblers as a full-time project. Mike continued to augment his income with solo appearances and his Folkways documentation projects, while Tom, now without his teaching salary, grew more and more uneasy.

In late November and early December 1961 Pete Seeger organized four high-profile Seeger Family Reunion concerts in Madison, Chicago, Boston, and New York. "That saved us!" recollected John. "Pete being very generous split the income—each person got the same amount. That kept us from going under."[8] Robert Gustafson, who reviewed the Boston concert, praised the Ramblers for their "prowess in instrumental music. Mike's fiddling and Mr. Paley's banjo playing were particularly noteworthy. A high point of this section, however, was Mr. Cohen's singing of 'The Cuckoo is a Pretty Bird.'" Gustafson approved of Pete's interjection of politics by singing "We Shall Overcome" and was moved by the show's finale, "with the audience joining all the performers in the stirring 'Mary Don't You Weep.'"[9] Shelton, who reviewed the December 23 Carnegie

Hall program for the *New York Times*, noted that the actual Seeger family—Pete, Mike, Peggy, and Penny—were at their best as soloists rather than as a family performing unit, describing the latter as "a bit raggedy." He was more generous with Mike and the Ramblers: "The trio had a group spirit and cohesiveness that gave the concert several needed lifts. The Ramblers' 'Foggy Mountain Top,' 'Bill Morgan and his Gal,' 'Coo-Coo Bird,' and 'Crow Black Chicken' proved them to be a harmonious musical family, even though unrelated."[10] The four-city Seeger Family tour netted each Rambler nearly $3,000, keeping them afloat while John was able to get an old Yale friend, entertainment lawyer Russell Karp, to help extricate them from their disastrous ITA contract.

Amidst these tensions came a brief moment of levity when the Ramblers made their first (and only) X-rated recording, *Earth Is Earth*. Eventually issued as a 7 inch EP (Folkways Records FF 869, 1963), the record featured four bawdy old-timey songs: "Bang Bang Lula," a tribute to an infamous prostitute; "My Sweet Farm Girl," the tale of a young farm boy who loved to plow fields and sow seeds; "Then It Won't Hurt," the story of a licentious country dentist; and "Women Wear No Clothes," a call for universal nudity. In keeping with the tradition of hillbilly bands changing their names when recording prurient material, the musicians are identified as Wilbur Seeger, McKinley Cohen, and Delmore Paley, collectively known as the New Lost City Bang Boys. Delmore (Tom) described the group as "three young men who were born and raised in and around New Lost City, which is famous for earth and old-time songs." Folkways issued another EP that year simply titled *The New Lost City Ramblers* (Folkways Records EPC 602, 1961). The EP included four of the trio's best recordings of the period: a highly charged bluegrass arrangement of "Foggy Mountain Top," a bouncy rendition of Charlie Poole's "Milwaukee Blues," the humorously understated "Talkin' Hard Luck," and the spirited Carter Family ballad "Waves on the Sea." Neither recording sold well, and the two EPs were later repackaged as a compilation under the *Earth Is Earth* title.[11]

Sometime in late 1961 or early 1962 another incident occurred that further stirred the pot and, according to Tom, raised an issue that eventually led to his leaving the Ramblers. On the strength of their recent publicity the Ramblers had been invited to make a second appearance on the nationally broadcast NBC television program *The Jack Paar Show*. Just before they were to go on, Tom was suddenly confronted with two documents, one of which he would have to sign before the group could perform. Tom recalled:

> This was because there was a guy named Harvey Matusow, who worked as a volunteer at People's Songs, and then suddenly became a great American hero, revealing these dangerous communists. I didn't know for sure he had

given my name, but considering other things he said, I wasn't surprised when later I found out. . . . So they asked me to sign one of these papers. One said that what Matusow said about me is a lie—he said that Tom Paley is a member of the Communist Party and as such is a member of the Soviet espionage apparatus in America. In the first place, I never was a member of the Communist Party because of the dogma of the guy who once tried to recruit me. So I could have honestly signed the one that said what Matusow said was a lie, but not honorably, because I felt it was none of their fucking business what my politics were. The other choice wouldn't have been honest—what Matusow said was true, but in those days I was young and innocent and misled by bad companions, and then I would have had to have given names and dates of these companions. But that wouldn't have been true. So I refused to sign either one, and we got booted off the program.[12]

Neither Mike nor John was served loyalty papers, and both recalled supporting Tom's decision not to sign and not to perform on the show. Tom, however, claimed his refusal to sign had long-term repercussions: "Later on it was one of the reasons they [Mike and John] wanted to get rid of me, because it was my fault we had been blacklisted from TV shows."[13] In retrospect the accuracy of his claim is questionable, since the Ramblers only appeared on one national television broadcast show, ABC's *Hootenanny*, in the years after Tom left the group. Despite Pete Seeger's years of blacklisting and his pending jailing for contempt of Congress in his earlier appearance before the House Un-American Activities Committee, neither Mike nor any of the other Ramblers was ever again asked to sign a loyalty oath. The group experienced only one additional instance of possible blacklisting. In April 1962 the San Diego superintendent of schools would cancel a Ramblers program ostensibly because of a reservation snafu. But Mike suspected political motivations, given his family ties to Pete. He complained bitterly to the press, which reported that the Ramblers had organized an alternative San Diego date.[14]

In early 1962 the Ramblers turned to Manny Greenhill and their old network of friends and acquaintances for work. Greenhill's progressive politics and deep appreciation for traditional music made for a comfortable relationship with the Ramblers, who by nature loathed the music business and its representatives. He would serve as the group's primary booking agent in subsequent years, although never with an exclusive arrangement.[15]

Mid-January found the Ramblers at the Second Fret in Philadelphia, where Peter Welding reviewed their show for *Down Beat*. Describing their music as "rollicking and delivered with authority and joy," he praised the Ramblers as "active crusaders for this [country string-band] music, but they let the music itself convert you." He went on to comment on their "relaxed, effortless stage manner. There is a good bit of badinage (which serves to divert one's attention while they tune and retune instruments between numbers). Seeger announces most of the numbers in a wry, half-mocking manner, with humorous asides from Cohen and Paley. The audience lapped it up."[16]

Welding closed his *Down Beat* review by weighing in on the questions of stylistic re-creation and imitation that John and Tom had attempted to address in the notes to their recently released *Volume 3* LP. "Apparently there is plenty of room for a good measure of improvisation within the form," he insisted, "for at no time did I get the impression that I was listening to any sort of slavish imitation. What the New Lost City Ramblers presented was alive, vigorous, and wholly convincing."[17] This was a recapitulation of a point he had made in a prior *Sing Out!* article, in which he hailed the Ramblers as "Crusaders for Old-Time Music." He commended the "intelligence and sensitivity" that they brought to their interpretation of traditional songs: "What they offer are not mere slavish imitations of what they've heard on old 78s, for this would inevitably lead them up a blind alley. No, they have succeeded—by dint of thoroughly steeping themselves in the music of the period—in capturing the spirit of old-timey music, not its letter."[18]

Welding attempted to move beyond the rhetoric of re-creation and emulation toward a deeper understanding of the creative process in which the Ramblers were engaged. So did another persuasive voice, that of jazz critic Nat Hentoff, who had previously commented positively on the group's *Songs from the Depression* album. In a review piece for the *Reporter* Hentoff noted the growing trend among "post-graduate citibillies" to successfully blend traditional songs and styles with their own creative sensibilities. He singled out two examples. First was the young Bob Dylan, whose just-released 1962 Columbia LP explored traditional blues, mountain songs, and Scottish ballads, "adapt[ing] his sound and phrasing to the varying needs of the material, but throughout he is unabashedly himself." The second was John Cohen and the Ramblers, who, Hentoff observed, "retain their respect and affection for the traditions but are also gradually finding ways to express their own particular skills and interests. They begin to realize that they legitimately bring their own background and personalities to various styles of folk music and get as much satisfaction from music making—in their city ways—as the 'ethnic' folk singers have done."[19]

In late January 1962 the Ramblers returned to the Midwest for an engagement in Minneapolis, followed by their second appearance at the University of Chicago Folk Festival. For the next two months they would play strictly college dates, visiting the campuses of Dartmouth, Colby, Clarke, Antioch, Oberlin, the University of Rochester, Columbia, Trinity, and Harvard. They briefly toured south to the University of North Carolina at Chapel Hill, then west to the University of Texas at Austin, and finally to the West Coast, where they arrived at the Ash Grove in early April.

While the college engagements were generally one-time concerts that did not pay terribly well, the students who attended were eager to listen and, in some cases, to play the music themselves. The Ramblers' performance at the University of Chicago Folk Festival particularly ingratiated them with their young audience. Following the precedents set in 1961, the second annual Chicago gathering turned the spotlight on the traditional performers. Clarence Ashley and his "band of farmers," which included fiddler Fred Price and guitar-banjo virtuoso Doc Watson, played unpolished mountain tunes and songs. Jean Ritchie and her sister Edna, a Kentucky schoolteacher, sang traditional Appalachian and Scottish ballads. Reverend Gary Davis, bluesman Big Joe Williams, and the soon to be nationally acclaimed Staple Singers provided a vital component of African American traditional music. A recording of the Ramblers' Friday evening performance captures the group at its best, moving through a lively set that included high-spirited renditions of the early bluegrass numbers "Feast Here Tonight" and "Foggy Mountain Top." John's performance of the Dock Boggs banjo piece "Country Blues" "brought the house down," reported Jon Pankake and Paul Nelson to their *Little Sandy Review* readers.[20] Following their enthusiastic rendition of Uncle Dave Macon's "Sail Away Ladies," the raucous audience refused to let them leave the stage.[21] Off the main concert stage Mike, John, and Tom each participated in banjo and guitar workshops, helping interpret the techniques of Ashley, Watson, and Davis. D. K. Wilgus lent an air of scholarly legitimacy to the proceedings with a well-received lecture on the relation of academic folklorists to the folk song revival.

In March the Ramblers were welcomed at Harvard, ground zero for traditional ballad (Francis Child) and cowboy folk song (John Lomax) scholarship. Inspired and perhaps a bit intimidated by playing at the nation's oldest and most prestigious institution of higher learning, the Ramblers shaped their patter into informative but sardonic minilectures. After introducing the group as coming from "New Lost City, Pennsyltucky," Mike joked, "We're making history here, folks. Actually, we're making it up as we go along. Creative folklore, yes, that's a course that was initiated at Harvard by one Alan Lomax," a knock at Lomax's brief time spent at Harvard. Mike's tone turned slightly more serious when he introduced a Carter Family song, but he managed to slip in a subtle dig at ballad scholars who prefer their folk songs to be old and dead:

Among the many people who recorded folk songs on commercial records—they were called "hillbilly" in those days—were the Carter Family. This music is now known as folk music because it's beginning to get died-outer and died-outer. But the Carter Family was one of the favorites, and they made about 350 sides of the old-time music done their own way with guitars and autoharps. And lately a lot of attention has been drawn to them. Flatt and Scruggs had made a record of their songs and were influenced by them. And there have been reissues on a couple of LPs of their old records. And I suppose we've been influenced by them too. So we thought we'd do a couple of Carter Family songs. This one is "Black Jack David."

John's introduction to "Country Blues" ended with a demonstration of banjo tuning:

We like to do some of these songs the way they were originally done back in somebody's home in the kitchen. . . . Here's a song called "The Country Blues." Now I learned it from a recording of a man named Dock Boggs. But I never could figure out how he did it on the banjo until I met this other old feller down in Kentucky named Roscoe Holcomb, and he showed me how to tune the banjo for this song. And I've done the best I can since then. It's not all the way there, but it's close. For you specialists in ethnomusicology in the audience here's the tuning [picks F#–D–G–A–D tuning on the banjo].

Mike offered a straightforward explanation on the evolution of bluegrass in the 1940s, crediting the innovations of Bill Monroe and Earl Scruggs. Next he and John delivered a brief tongue-and-cheek discussion on the relationship of bluegrass and Marxism before introducing "Feast Here Tonight":

JC: Well, to continue with our lecture here, the sixth in a series of anti-intellectualism in America. Mike has some kind of theory he's worked out about this music and where it stands.

MS: Well, I figure the New Lost City Ramblers are sort of a transitional phase, very much like the government in Russia, a transitional phase on the way to bluegrass, or acceptance of bluegrass music in the cities, which I consider utopia. We'll probably just wither away, shortly. . . . What's the use—I think that's an excellent bit of folklore right there.

JC: I think we've put it in college style, Mike.

Mike responded in a humorous and slightly self-deprecating tone that his grandfather, father, and half-brother John had all graduated from Harvard; that his other half-brother, Pete, only made it through two years; and that he, Mike, never bothered to try. "I didn't need intellectual activity very much. I was smart already."

Tom demonstrated his skill as a wordsmith in his snappy introduction to "Brown's Ferry Blues," managing to loop together a homophobic quip, a reference to McCarthyism, and an observation on whites playing the blues:

> Now here's a song that actually means a whole lot to us, all of us from New Lost City, because it does come from there. There was a fellow named Whitey Brown. He used to run a ferry out of New Lost City, and then after he run all of them out [laughter], he took the political persecutions and he fastened his baleful eye on this pink named Red Green who used to sit around in the dark of the purple evening and sing this white blues called the "Brown's Ferry Blues."

Late in the concert Mike took a satirical shot at banjo-picking college students in general, and perhaps John in particular, with his introduction to "Arkansas Traveler," set up by Tom:

> TP: And now as we get toward the end of things we have a moment of sublime, dramatic import called "Arkansas Traveler."
>
> MS: The idea is that I sit here and play the fiddle, this tune the "Arkansas Traveler." And then up steps this New York college boy [played by John], with an out-of-tune 5-string banjo—that's the way you can tell them these days, at least the ones who are flunking out of school. And he's got a Nikon camera on his other shoulder, and he's got a pretty, long-haired girl carrying their Nagra tape recorder. They're obviously on a collecting trip through Arkansas, showing the local people that they can play the songs better than the local people that they got on their last trip, last year. The only one trouble is that he's lost, like most New York college boys. And he asks a couple of questions, something a little like this [they play "Arkansas Traveler"].

The Ramblers did not hold back on their best barbs of self-deprecating humor. Their ability to simultaneously poke fun at academics, intellectuals, city folkniks, and themselves reflected a degree of sophistication that their Ivy League audience appreciated.[22]

The Ramblers left Cambridge and drove south for only the second time, arriving at the University of North Carolina at Chapel Hill on March 24. There they found a receptive audience for their music in a locale that, within the next few years, would emerge as the southern Mecca for the old-time music revival. Their next stop was the University of Texas at Austin, where they played for a crowd that included a history graduate student named Bill Malone. At the time Malone was finishing a dissertation that would become *Country Music U.S.A.* (1968), the first serious historical treatise on country music and a work that established the topic as a bona fide field of scholarly study. Malone, who hailed from east Texas working-class roots, personified the skepticism many young southerners felt toward northern folk revivalists: "When we heard the music of Mike Seeger and the New Lost City Ramblers, my friends and I scoffed at their pretensions and made fun of these northern city boys, these 'outsiders,' who had the gall to perform 'our' music, southern country music. But I must note that, not only did I attend their concert [at the University of Texas], I also faithfully bought their records, wore out their songbook, learned scores of their songs (which I still perform today), and shamelessly borrowed the recording data that they had compiled about their songs."[23]

Whatever he thought of the Ramblers' concert, Malone would later write in *Country Music U.S.A.* that "their instrumentation sounds almost like a carbon copy of the early hillbilly string band styles" but added the caveat, "Their vocal styles, also intended to be as accurate as possible, do not fare quite as well; in many cases, the New Lost City Ramblers give the impression of *trying* to sound country."[24]

A partial recording of the March 29, 1962, concert reveals that the Austin students, presumably including Malone, responded with tremendous enthusiasm to the Ramblers' presentation. Whatever internal tensions the group was experiencing at the time were not apparent from their stage performance. The trio seemed completely at ease with the audience, talking freely about the development of southern string-band and bluegrass styles as well as the hillbilly record sources of their songs. They dispensed their usual fare of puns, sardonic jokes, and mocking humor, which included Tom's obligatory shots at the Kingston Trio for copyrighting traditional songs and for wearing striped shirts and straw pants, Mike's hawking of "our six long-playing, short-selling Folkways records," and John's careful instructions to the audience to watch his banjo technique as, "amazingly, my fingers never leave my left hand." They did not miss a beat in introducing songs with specific southern references such as the "Dallas Rag," "Sweet Sunny South," and "Arkansas Traveler." Before their last number Mike unabashedly reminded his Texas audience of the Ramblers' mission to promote old-time southern music: "We hope that you'll be having more of the kind of people we like to listen to here to play for you. People like Mance Lipscomb, one of the best of the old-time country players, who lives right here in Texas. And maybe some of the mountain singers, and maybe some bluegrass. There's a great deal of this music still alive. We hope that you'll have some more of it down here soon. But until then it's the NLCR signing off. Here's a song called 'Foggy Mountain Top.'"[25]

Malone recalled that John and Tom later showed up to an informal song session at Threadgill's, an Austin watering hole where students mixed with working-class Texas folk and where one could hear "everything from hoary hillbilly material (like that of the Carter Family) to bluegrass, blues, traditional ballads, and Woody Guthrie and Bob Dylan songs."[26]

At both the Harvard and Texas programs Mike pitched their recently released *New Lost City Ramblers Volume 4* (Folkways FA 2399, 1962). Pankake and Nelson reviewed the album in their *Little Sandy Review*, declaring, "Those know-nothing critics who continually disparage the Ramblers as mimics and imitators (one even went so far as to label them *parodists* of country music) ought to listen to the sharp arrangement the boys have done on 'Crow Black Chicken,' transforming the faraway sound of the Leake County Revelers' original version into a real bust-up show-stopper of a performance."[27] In truth, the Revelers' and Ramblers' versions, separated by three decades, are nearly identical in key, tempo, basic melody, and harmonic accompaniment. The instrumentation is similar (the Revelers featured double banjos in addition to fiddle and guitar). But the Ramblers' version kicks with an energetic, rhythmic pulse that clearly distinguishes it from the more lilting Revelers' original.[28]

In the notes to *Volume 4* Mike offered a critical assessment of the different ways in which urban singers were approaching their material, and he did not hesitate to name names. He chided "art" folksingers like Richard Dyer-Bennett and William Clauson who, with their training in the Western classical tradition, embrace "non-dynamic antiquarian views of a peasant folk music," which led them to "scorn[ing] completely the authentic performance." Popularizers of folk song like the Kingston Trio, the Weavers, and Burl Ives were dismissed as profiteers who disregarded traditional styles and whose output was of "little lasting musical value." Not surprisingly, Mike advocated for a third group, those "using vocal styles and accompaniments from those already existing in authentic folk music in the belief that the traditional performance is important and exciting enough for an audience outside of its immediate culture." Mike credited his father along with Lomax and Wilgus for articulating the folk-performance-style paradigm and points to his brother Pete (especially his work in the 1940s), the Almanac Singers, Jack Elliott, the Greenbriar Boys, and the Ramblers as leading urban exponents of this approach. He underscored the seriousness of the work by noting, "Their (our) musical education consists of learning the rules by ear from watching and listening to performances and phonograph records of traditional folk musicians in order to play more or less within the tradition."

John picked up this theme, observing, "As we spend more and more time listening to old recordings, visiting old time country musicians, and singing and living with the songs, other qualities have revealed themselves through the music." At an abstract level he observed that these qualities "have to do with the definition of the country feeling, the experience of things coming from and dealing with the earth, and of things that grow." Musically, "it has to do with the expressive nature of the strident harmonies used, the skill in keeping the melody while elaborating on it and pushing it as far as it can go without losing its identity; of keeping the beat steady and regular while introducing extra beats or irregularities; of playing the music as straight as possible, playing it square without becoming square." He recounted his own cathartic experiences visiting Ashley amidst the hills and barns of his Tennessee home and listening to Bill Monroe at the country music parks where rural folks gathered to enjoy bluegrass. Through total immersion in the music via old recordings and through direct contact with rural traditional performers, John claimed the Ramblers were moving deeper into the artistic and cultural sensibilities of the original creators. Implicit in this narrative was the Ramblers' role in connecting rural performers and city players and "giving something in return to the country singer to whom we owe so much." The New York FOTM, the University of Chicago Folk Festival, and the Ash Grove were cited as examples of urban venues where "authentic traditional singers" had been presented. He concluded, "This has met with great audience response and some good jobs for the artists."

Tom also surveyed the contemporary revival, noting a "growth of interest in the authentic article" among city folkniks who "jumped from digging the slick, commercial arrangements to living real folk music." He reported on the enthusiastic response of college students to "genuine country musicians," adding that "everywhere we travel, each college campus has some sort of string band which plays old-time traditional music or the somewhat more modern bluegrass." In what would be his final statement as a member of the Ramblers, he observed with some pride that the group played an important role in bringing "a new lease on life" to music that was, in his view, "all but extinct."

Taken together, the three *Volume 4* commentaries provided a retrospective on the Ramblers' accomplishments during their initial three and a half years. Most important, they had managed to carve out a place for traditional mountain music amidst the boom in commercial folk music. They had nurtured a small but devoted following of urban and college fans who were eager to explore the perceived authentic roots of American folk music. The Ramblers' performances and early recordings provided a road map for the uninitiated to navigate the complex terrain of hillbilly and prebluegrass music, offering background on sources, instrumentation, and style. To complete the project the Ramblers and their associates had helped arrange for a select group of "genuine country musicians" to come north to play at colleges, clubs, and festival workshops. With this model the Ramblers could maintain their position as the premiere urban arbiters of southern mountain music. They performed the music with great accuracy, documented the originators of the traditions, and brought these "real folk" to eager concert and workshop audiences. And finally, the Ramblers measured their success as cultural liaisons not only by the numbers of followers who attended their concerts and bought their records but by the growing legions of young people who, upon hearing them play, were actually taking up the music themselves.

Despite their overall success at promoting old-time music, all was not well with the band. When the Ramblers reached the West Coast in early April 1962 for a two-week stint at the Ash Grove, it was clear that tensions had reached a breaking point. Tom's refusal to make a long-term, full-time commitment to the Ramblers, on top of myriad personality squabbles and musical disagreements, finally led Mike and John to seriously consider replacing him. In a bitter statement he penned to Moe Asch the following year, Tom claimed he had taken a leave of absence from teaching and agreed to tour with the Ramblers for a year "with the clear understanding that I refused to continue the full-time aspect past the autumn of 1962." He went on to explain, "Mike and John wanted the group to go full-time, but I was unwilling. I did not wish to be a full-time entertainer. They were determined and said they would replace me (as if the group was theirs and I was just a hired hand). . . . An essential thing is that I did not just decide that I was leaving the NLCR, but that I was forced out of the group."[29] Mike had a different perspective, which he expressed in a letter to the British magazine Folk Music in 1964:

> [We] played part-time on weekends until the summer of 1961 when we all decided to go full time for one year or longer depending on our success. After about six months we were not doing particularly well at getting jobs, but John Cohen and I felt that we should continue. Tom did not agree and in January of 1962 said he wanted to leave the group, his sole reason being that he did not want to play full-time. Furthermore, he wanted a cash settlement for his share of the NLCR name. John and I felt that there was no reason to give Tom a large settlement when he was leaving.[30]

Whether Tom actually expressed his intentions to leave, as John and Mike contended, or was forced out against his wishes, as he maintained, will never be known for sure. Either way, it is clear he did not share Mike's and John's commitment to full-time work with the Ramblers, a reality that made the trio's demise inevitable. For Tom, becoming a "full-time entertainer" somehow tainted the mission of promoting grassroots music, which by nature did not lend itself to commoditization or to the conventions of the formal stage. The battle that would soon unfold over the rights to the New Lost City Ramblers name would last for several years and leave lasting scars.

Shortly after the Ash Grove engagement a nasty incident occurred that underscored just how far the situation had deteriorated. According to Tom:

> We played in a bookstore in San Diego, and we had some sort of argument. John and Mike were having an argument, and John turned to me to back him up, and I didn't back him up. I don't remember what the question was. But I said I think whatever Mike is suggesting makes perfect sense. So John said, "Well, you can just get up to Sacramento yourself. I'm not taking you!" So I got up to Sacramento myself. And we were trying to hear Sara Carter at Angel Camp, I think. And John wouldn't take me, so I didn't get to meet Sara Carter. And I wasn't even the one having the argument with Mike![31]

Tom did manage to get to Sacramento to play with the Ramblers, but he refused to travel back east with Mike and John. Marge Seeger had to sit in on guitar at engagements in Fort Collins, Colorado; Wichita, Kansas; and the University of the South in Sewanee, Tennessee. Fences were temporarily mended, and Tom did play several more jobs with the Ramblers that summer, including two weeks at Philadelphia's Second Fret. He also recorded material for their two final Seeger-Cohen-Paley Ramblers albums, *American Moonshine and Prohibition Songs* (Folkways Records FH 5263, 1962) and *New Lost City Ramblers Volume 5* (Folkways Records FA 2395, 1963). An engagement at a Homesdale, Pennsylvania, summer camp with Pete Seeger in late July 1962 would be the last time Tom played with Mike and John as a member of the Ramblers.

In the meantime Mike and John were actively seeking a replacement. They first approached Arthel "Doc" Watson, the blind North Carolina banjo player and guitarist who played with Ashley's band. Watson's extraordinary talents as a guitarist had come to the attention of Ralph Rinzler when he traveled to eastern Tennessee in the summer of 1960 to record Ashley. Rinzler befriended Watson and coaxed him to lay aside his electric guitar and revive his old family repertoire. He arranged for Ashley and Watson to perform at the second FOTM concert in March 1961 and again at the February 1962 University of Chicago Folk Festival, where they shared the stage with the Ramblers. Pearl had booked the Ashley band for the Ash Grove that spring, and just before the Ramblers arrived in mid-April an event unfolded that dramatically changed the course of Watson's career. Ashley had developed a severe case of laryngitis, leading Rinzler to suggest that Watson take center stage as host and band leader. Watson's down-home demeanor and homespun humor made him a natural, and Rinzler immediately realized he would be even more appealing to city audiences as a soloist without Ashley's band.[32] On hearing this news John had a brief conversation with Watson about joining the Ramblers before the latter returned to North Carolina.

The prospects of a traditional southern mountain musician like Watson joining forces with urban revivalists like John and Mike were intriguing. Watson was a phenomenal guitar player, equally adept at flat-picking a blazing dance tune and fingerpicking an intricate accompaniment to a mountain ballad or blues. His virtuosity on guitar as well as his warm baritone voice, charming stage presence, and prodigious repertoire of traditional songs made him a favorite with the urban coffeehouse and college crowds. Like Tom, he could play guitar or banjo and lead or harmonize on a wide variety of songs. But unlike Tom (or Mike or John), he spoke and sang in the natural southern drawl native to his home in rural North Carolina. Although his tastes were broad and included a genuine love for honky-tonk and rockabilly music, Watson was able with Rinzler's coaching to present himself to urban audiences as the essence of the down-home country picker and singer whose style and repertoire dovetailed perfectly with those of the Ramblers.

Doc Watson, with Rinzler's support, would go on to become a star of the folk revival, but not as a member of the Ramblers. In a letter dated June 12, 1962, Watson graciously turned down Mike and John's offer to join the group: "As far as I can figure now practicing with you all enough to play with you regularly would present too many problems; that is unless we lived closer together. However, if there are times when you have big concerts where I could take a small part of the show it would be a pleasure and a privilege to work with you."[33] In retrospect, this was probably a wise decision for both parties. Watson would go on to shine as a soloist with a talent and charisma so immense that he might have overshadowed Mike and John (or anyone else, for that matter) in a group situation. Though disappointed, Mike and John moved quickly to another candidate, a young fiddler and country singer who, like themselves, was born in the city and reared in the suburbs before gravitating toward traditional country and bluegrass music.

Daniel Tracy Schwarz was born on November 13, 1938, in New York City's St. Clair Hospital. He spent his childhood in the suburban town of Montclair, New Jersey. His father, Hamilton D. Schwarz, was an investment banker who hailed from a central Pennsylvania family of German stock. His mother, Constance Loraine Harrigan, was a classically trained pianist who grew up in New Hampshire. Tracy's great-grandfather on his mother's side was a wagon builder from Ireland and his grandfather was a lawyer who played fiddle as a hobby. Hamilton was not fond of city or suburban living and in 1950 moved his family to the small town of New Canaan, Connecticut, which offered easy train access to Manhattan.

Tracy completed junior high school in New Canaan and was shipped off to the Portsmith Priory School in Rhode Island. During the summers the family spent time in southern Vermont, where they had an old farmhouse. "My brother and I spent a lot of time next door, at the neighboring farm," Tracy recalled. "It was almost Appalachian, very low level, poverty almost, the standard of living. There were still workhorses and that old system. So we would follow these guys around, ask questions; they were very patient. We were underfoot most of time. It was a wonderful place to be when you were a kid." The summers in Vermont "were a real country experience for me, and I think that predisposed me in one way or another to do this rural music. I accepted some things that other people had to think about—country folklife or whatever, what was on the musicians' minds. I know there is a bit of difference between northern Appalachians and southern Appalachians, but I'm not sure there is a whole lot."[34]

As a youngster Tracy had a few years of both piano and guitar lessons, but he resisted learning to read music, preferring to play by ear, and eventually lessons on both instruments were dropped. Meanwhile, he became fascinated with the country music that occasionally made it onto the New Jersey airways in the late 1940s. He listened to the nationally syndicated Gene Autry show and to a local Patterson disc jockey who spun the popular honky-tonk sounds of Hank Williams, Ernest Tubb, and Merle Travis. Shortly after moving to Connecticut in 1950, Tracy responded to a radio ad and ordered an Osborne Brothers record from the Jimmie Skinner Music Company in Cincinnati. Fascinated by the exotic-sounding instruments, he convinced his father to take him to the city, where he bought a 5-string banjo. Knowing no better, he tuned the banjo like a guitar, and, after failing to duplicate anything that sounded vaguely like the bluegrass banjo he heard on records, he set the instrument aside.

It was not until 1957, when Tracy entered Georgetown University to study Russian, that his musical interest in country music was rekindled. Sometime in the spring of 1958 he stumbled onto a group of bluegrass musicians, including Tom Gray of the Country Gentlemen, who were jamming in an apartment above the DC cafeteria where he often ate dinner. Gray and his friends introduced Tracy to Washington's thriving bluegrass scene. He finally figured out how to tune his banjo to an open chord, taught himself the rudiments of mandolin, and worked on his guitar playing and singing. As he grew more confident in his guitar and mandolin playing, Tracy began attending bluegrass sessions in various DC bars. Then, in late 1958 or early 1959 he joined Bill Baily's Melody Mountain Boys, a local bluegrass band that played every Friday night at a bar called the Mel-Al in Manassas, Virginia. Tracy played mandolin and string bass and sang solo lead and tenor harmonies. The banjo player, Lamar Grier, would go on to play with Bill

Monroe, and a decade later he would join Tracy as a member of the Strange Creek Singers. From the mandolin Tracy began dabbling with the fiddle but progressed slowly. He was told in no uncertain terms to go back to mandolin the first night he tried to fiddle with the Baily band at the Manassas bar.[35]

In addition to playing with bluegrass bands Tracy also attended John Dildine's informal hoots at Cabin John. There he first met Mike, who was playing banjo and Dobro at bluegrass sessions: "Mike was able to play old-time and bluegrass, as he chose, which is the way I wanted to go."[36] Encountering Mike at the hoots pricked his interest in the roots of bluegrass, and he began to buy old hillbilly records in a neighborhood junk shop. In the summer of 1959 seeing Mike and the Ramblers play at the 1959 Newport Folk Festival was a revelation for Tracy: "It was so exciting, seeing these guys [the Ramblers] up there playing and knowing that, like me, they were not from the tradition or from the South; that they were crossing over from one culture to another when they played the music. That sort of boosted my energy in that direction. It was nice to have more validation, that I could be part of this, that I could play this music too. When I was entering into this sort of different world, it was nice to have a path to follow."[37]

Shortly after Newport, in the fall of 1959, Mike and Marge moved into an apartment next door to Tracy on M Street in Washington, and for a brief period the three became close friends. Mike introduced Tracy to Hazel Dickens and her family and to various other bluegrass musicians who occasionally dropped by his place for informal singing and picking sessions. Eventually, Tracy's infatuation for music eclipsed his interest in language studies, and he dropped out of Georgetown and ended up "in a bar listening to bluegrass, down at 8th and H Street, following that bluegrass, following my heart."[38]

With the draft in full swing, many employers were reluctant to hire a twenty-one-year-old who might be called into military service at any time. Tracy had a hard time finding a serious job and finally, in frustration, faced the inevitable and signed up for the United States Army Reserve. He was inducted in August 1960 and sent to Fort Dix for basic training and then to Fort Gordon, Georgia, for radio teletype training. Finally, at his request, he was assigned to active duty in Germany. What happened next turned out to be a surprising stroke of good fortune, or, as he later put it, "I really fell into an outhouse and came out smelling like a rose." He continued:

> They flew us over to Germany, where I was stationed in Neu-Ulm, a really
> nice area of Germany. It was only an hour and a half from Munich, Lake
> Constance, and the Alps. It was a great area, and a cushy job. The only
> battle I was ever in was to get my pass to get off post. By coincidence I had

found this little Gasthaus about twelve kilometers away, in a factory town. There were like country people there, and factory people and Italians. So for me this was great, and we played a lot of music there. What happened was when we got stationed there I met one guy from Kansas, one guy from Alabama, and another one from Georgia who were interested in playing music, in making a little country band. So we hadn't been there but two weeks, and already we were starting to play.[39]

Tracy's band played acoustic country music, a combination of honky-tonk, bluegrass, and gospel. Tracy sang, played guitar, and, most important, developed his fiddling skills. Fortunately, he had a lot of downtime between his maintenance duties on the military base. Since he had access to bluegrass and country recordings he was able to spend hours each day practicing. After a year things were going so well that Tracy and his buddies from Alabama and Kansas agreed to start a band back in the States when their service time was up.

Tracy was contacted by Mike in the spring of 1962 about joining the Ramblers. He initially turned them down, thinking he would join a band in Alabama when he and his fellow soldier-musicians were discharged that summer. But when one of them decided he wanted to go back home to Kansas, Tracy got back to Mike immediately: "You see, I was a radio teletype operator. And just as soon as the guy from Kansas finally blurted it out that he didn't want to go to Alabama, I knew it was over with those guys. I knew the Ramblers were already going . . . so the next morning I didn't have to think much about it, I just sent this flash message—there's been a change! Is the offer still open? Apparently it was."[40]

In a letter dated June 16, only four days after receiving Watson's note, Mike wrote back enthusiastically to Tracy, confirming his invitation to join the Ramblers and welcoming him to stay with Marge and his family in Roosevelt, New Jersey, when Tracy arrived back in the States. He estimated that Tracy "should be able to clear $150–200 a week from the NLCR, and I hope we can make a record (NLCR that is) after a couple of months of working together."[41] Mike's financial predictions were reasonable, based on the Ramblers' income for the first half of 1962, which amounted to approximately $4,000 per man (before expenses) for twenty appearances plus a week at the Second Fret and two weeks at the Ash Grove.

At first glance Tracy was not an obvious choice to replace Tom as a Rambler. The about-to-be-discharged veteran was relatively unknown in the folk revival and bluegrass scenes, and he certainly did not carry Tom's reputation as a crack guitarist and banjo player. Mike knew Tracy was a competent guitarist and mandolin player from their experience jamming together at Dildine's hoots, and he liked the way their voices blended when they sang bluegrass duets. But Mike had never heard Tracy fiddle or play banjo, nor had he heard him play or sing for nearly two years when he invited Tracy to become a Rambler.

Shared taste and temperament rather than an analytical assessment of pure musical skill probably lay at the heart of Mike's desire to have Tracy join the group. Despite their relatively limited experiences actually playing music together, in Mike's mind Tracy was a fellow traveler, another suburban kid who, like him, had developed a sublime love for old-time country and bluegrass music. The prospects that Tracy could take over some of the fiddling and thereby free Mike up for other instrumental possibilities and that the Ramblers would now play more bluegrass were tremendously appealing. But the most important factor, Mike would later reflect, was the "gut feeling" he had about Tracy as a person and musician: "There was just something that was down-to-earth country about Tracy. He just kind of has a feeling for the music, it was in his bones. And I loved that about him when we played at the hoots in Washington, and we sometimes got together at music parties."[42]

For John, Tracy was an unknown entity whom he recalled meeting once or twice but whom he had never heard play. After the bruising disputes with Tom, John had a clearer sense of just how essential personality dynamics were in holding a group together. Tom's replacement would need to be someone with an easygoing manner who could cool down, instead of stir up, the stubborn attitudes that sometimes put Mike and him at loggerheads. John went along with Mike, figuring that Tracy might be such a person, and, for the immediate future, both Mike and he were right.

SEEGER, COHEN, AND SCHWARZ PERFORM THE FOLK, 1962-1964

News of Tom Paley's departure was not well received by all fans of the Ramblers. *Little Sandy Review* editors Jon Pankake and Paul Nelson, in a review titled "The Old and the New Lost City Ramblers," recounted Tom's immense contributions to the group: "Paley, the most extroverted and exuberant of the New Lost, takes with him a good deal of the group's image, for in retrospect, the familiar tuning frenzy larded with quips and fantastic, corny word play that seemed so much of the Ramblers' presence can be seen to have originated primarily in this personality. The sophistication of the puns, alien to but oddly complementing the nature of the group's material, was also largely Paley-produced, and is no more." They went on to praise "his genius with the guitar," singling out his stellar performances on "Road to Austin" and "Johnson City Blues" from *New Lost City Ramblers Volume 5* (Folkways Records FA 2395, 1963), his final recordings as a Rambler. "In the pleasure, range, and esthetic success of his performances, we are tempted to feel that we can discern the secret of the model city folksinger of our time."[1] Although later in the review they spoke highly of Tracy and would continue their unflagging support for the new Ramblers, Pankake and Nelson reflected the sentiments of many fans who lamented the loss of Tom. His services to the group were described as "inestimable" by Izzy Young, who reminded *Sing Out!* readers that Tom "never really wished to be a full time performer." Young joined Pankake and Nelson in welcoming Tracy to the group, noting: "He plays five instruments, just about par for the course [for the Ramblers]."[2]

While Tracy settled in and the Ramblers opened up for a two-week stint at Gerde's Folk City in Greenwich Village in September 1962, Tom did not fade quietly from the scene. Angered that he felt forced out of a group he helped found, he claimed rights to a share of the Ramblers' name. In a September 10, 1962, letter to Mike and John, copied to Moe Asch and promoter Manny Greenhill, Tom threatened legal action if a settlement over use of the group's name could not be reached.[3] In a handwritten personal note Tom tried to reason with Mike as to why he was due some financial compensation:

> Through the time that we worked together in the New Lost City Ramblers we all earned some money, but part of our labor was going toward building the value of the name (monetary value, as well as other things). The name now has some value, which is only partly financial—there are other compensations in being in the NLCR. That value is the result of efforts the three of us put in. We have disagreed on how to continue the group and are separating, but if you two expect to keep the name and the value that goes with it, then you must expect to pay me for my share.[4]

Meanwhile, Tom formed a new band with Artie Rose and Roy Berkeley and threatened to record under the New Lost City Ramblers name.

On October 25 Mike and John received another letter, this time from the law firm of Benson and Israelson, ordering them to stop using the New Lost City Ramblers name and to resume negotiations over Tom's share in the group.[5] A similar letter was sent to Greenhill, demanding he cease any promotional activities for the Ramblers until the name issue was cleared up.[6] Mike and John finally agreed to negotiations, and on November 23 Russell Karp drew up an agreement that would pay Tom $500 cash and a portion of the Ramblers' 1963 earnings, not to exceed $500. In return Tom would give up all interests in the New Lost City Ramblers.[7]

The agreement appeared to be sealed, and Tom went ahead with his recording project with Rose and Berkeley using another name, the Old Reliable String Band. But events transpired that prevented closure of the dispute. Tom had decided not to go back to teaching immediately, and he and Claudia planned an extended trip to Europe. They departed in early December, apparently before Karp had executed a final copy of the agreement. When the written agreement finally reached him several months later in Sweden, Tom claimed that "it had been altered in such a way that I could not sign it. Apparently, once I was out of the country, it didn't seem worth going through with the deal we had made."[8] The snag evidently regarded the exact wording of the parameters for determining the additional $500 payment. The legal disposition of the group's name remained in limbo as Mike,

John, and Tracy continued to tour in the fall of 1962 and planned their first album as a trio. With Tom's departure to Europe they incorrectly surmised that the issue was behind them, and they turned to the business of building their audience for the new New Lost City Ramblers.

Tracy's first appearance as a member of the Ramblers was appropriately enough in Galax, Virginia, at the annual Old-Time Fiddlers Convention in August 1962. After a brief period of getting reacquainted and beginning to work up a repertoire at Mike's place in Roosevelt, the two headed south to rendezvous with John, who had spent the month of August filming in east Kentucky for what would become his acclaimed documentary, *The High Lonesome Sound*. John's 1962 return trip to Kentucky was his first attempt to record mountain culture with moving image technology and marked the beginning of his career as a filmmaker.

The trio did not win the old-time-band contest, but they reveled in the ambience of a real southern fiddle contest. The choice of Galax for the premiere public performance of the new New Lost City Ramblers was probably a conscious effort by the group to pay homage to the source of their music, the southern Appalachians. But it was a region they would rarely revisit. The reconstituted Ramblers, like the original group with Tom, would play the vast majority of their engagements north of the Mason-Dixon Line and on the West Coast.

The Ramblers returned north and, following several weeks of rehearsing, were ready to begin their two-week engagement at Gerde's Folk City. No recording or review of the new Ramblers' debut exists, but according to Tracy it took a bit of adjusting for him to keep up with all the new songs and instrument changes and to find a way to fit in with Mike and John's sardonic humor, wrought from four years of stage experience with quick-witted Tom. One audience member who seemed to appreciate the group was a young singer named Bob Dylan, whose star was on the rise following his signing with Columbia Records and the release of his first album in March 1962. Dylan was a regular at Gerde's, and Tracy remembered the Ramblers joining him for jam sessions in the bar's basement room.[9] Of the Ramblers Dylan would later recall: "I took to them immediately. Everything about them appealed to me—their style, their singing, and their sound. . . . All their songs vibrated with some dizzy, portentous truth. I'd stay with the Ramblers for days. . . . For me they had originality in spades, were men of mystery on all counts. I couldn't get enough of them."[10]

The Ramblers spent the rest of the fall touring East Coast and midwestern colleges. A review of their November appearance at Harvard's Jordan Hall suggested that although the trio's sound had yet to gel, Tracy's singing and fiddling were starting to win over audiences: "The group still does not have the unity it did when Tom Paley was present, but we suspect that this is only a matter of time. Tracy stole the show with his solo 'That Tickled Me,' however, and with the encore 'Orange Blossom Special,' which was by far their best number of the evening."[11] The Ramblers' December appearance at the University of Michigan at Ann Arbor generated the headline "Folk Trio Shows Authenticity." The review opened with the wry observation that "southern mountain music is invading urban and collegiate America through the medium of three witty New Yorkers known as the New Lost City Ramblers." Tracy's a cappella singing was singled out for its "tonal virtuosity." But Mike reported that the group was still having trouble finding enough work, and their first six albums were not selling well: "Our press has been phenomenally good, better than our audiences."[12]

College bookings remained the Ramblers' bread and butter, bringing in anywhere from $200 to $250 per program (at Rutgers and Shimer College, respectively) to $700 to $800 per program (at McGill and the University of Illinois, respectively). A week at Chicago's Gate of Horn, where they appeared with Josh White in December, netted the group a total of $900. Their fall pre-expense income totals were in keeping with Mike's estimates to Tracy, as each band member earned approximately $2,100. John and Mike saw their 1962 royalties for the first six Folkways records rise to about $320 for the sale of just over three thousand records.

The question of group unity was on the mind of a reviewer who attended the Ramblers' January 25, 1963, concert for the Minnesota Folksong Society: "The Group lost a very fine performer, Tom Paley, last year; and the performance of his replacement, Tracy Schwarz, does not seem quite up to Paley's standards. Schwarz is nonetheless a very capable musician in his own right, and the main problem with the trio seems to be a very noticeable lack of integration. This difficulty will no doubt work to resolve itself in the future, and one can look forward to considerable improvements over Saturday's performance, which was noticeably ragged in spots."[13]

Live concert recordings made in the winter and early spring of 1963 attest to that improvement and to Tracy's successful integration into the group. Their set at the University of Chicago Folk Festival began with two pieces from their previous repertoire with Tom, "Up Jumped the Devil" and "New River Train," but this time with Tracy fiddling and Mike playing banjo. "Pretty Little Miss Out in the Garden" was done in a classic bluegrass style, pairing Tracy's fiddling and Mike's mandolin. Their vocal harmonies were tight, with Tracy's tense tenor consciously echoing the high lonesome sound of the Monroe Brothers and the Stanley Brothers. Mike introduced the piece, noting, "Lately we've been doing some songs in the bluegrass style; we heard an old song and we decided to change it around a little bit. We sang it for the Stanley Brothers, and they liked it pretty well. You'll probably find it on their next LP [audience laughter]. We don't mind things going the other way once in a while, because we usually steal all their songs first." Another new instrumental configuration, featuring Tracy and Mike playing double fiddles, was introduced on a lively version of the Carter Brothers and Son's "Liza Jane." Tracy sang the crowd-pleasing and slightly suggestive ditty, "She Tickles Me," and led the night's finale, "Orange Blossom Special," demonstrating his mastery of the bluegrass-fiddle classic. Though some members of the festival audience undoubtedly missed Tom, their response to Tracy and the new Ramblers that evening was unabashedly enthusiastic.[14] In a festival preview piece a writer for the *Chicago Maroon* commented on the group's recent turn toward bluegrass. He reported that Tracy sang the high harmony in "a clear but unaggressive voice" and that his fiddling "gave Mike more of a chance to use his talents on the banjo."[15]

A concert recording made two months later at the Ash Grove revealed the Ramblers' renewed interest in early bluegrass. More than a third of the trio numbers were arranged in early bluegrass style, with Tracy fiddling and Mike picking Scruggs-style banjo. In terms of staging, the long interludes of tuning had disappeared. Tracy did not attempt to ape Tom's stage presence, and the humorous repartee, handled mostly by Mike and John, at times fell flat. But Tracy's easygoing manner created a more laid-back feel to their overall stage presentation. Musically, they appeared to be jelling in the way Mike had hoped—Tracy's fiddling had allowed him to play more banjo, their voices blended well on tight harmony numbers, and bluegrass was playing a more prominent role in their repertoire.[16]

During the transitional period of Tom's departure and Tracy's apprenticeship the terrain of the folk music revival continued to shift. In 1962 *Time* magazine ran a series of articles on the revival, culminating with a cover story on Joan Baez in its November 23 issue that included an exposé of the rising fortunes of urban folksingers. As the commercial revival continued to ramp up in 1962 and early 1963, the Ramblers' income seemed a pittance compared with the substantial fees that more commercial groups could command. In February 1963 *Business Week* reported that the Kingston Trio was paid between $8,000 and $12,000 per concert and earned an additional $300,000 a year in record royalties.[17] Pete Seeger, who had signed with Columbia Records in 1961, saw his annual income break into six figures, an impressive number for any musician at that time.[18] Two of his songs, "Where Have All the Flowers Gone?" and "The Hammer Song," charted in the Top 40 in 1962, sung by the new folk supergroup, Peter, Paul and Mary. Assembled by promoter Albert Grossman in late 1961, Peter Yarrow, Noel Stuckey (who would become Paul), and Mary Travers signed with Warner Records in early 1962 for an advance of $30,000. Their first album had reached the top of the pop charts by the fall and went gold by year's end.[19] Another pop-folk group, the Rooftop Singers, scored a number-one hit with the old Gus Cannon jug-band song "Walk Right In" in early 1963. When ABC television announced in March 1963 its intention of producing the weekly national network show *Hootenanny*, folk music was approaching the apex of its national popularity. Despite their disdain for such developments, the Ramblers rode the coattails of the commercial folk boom, benefiting from the national network of folk music concert promoters and venues that catered to the tastes of the burgeoning youth audiences who hungered for folk music.

Of course, the revival remained more than a one-dimensional pop phenomenon. While loyal supporters of traditional music, including Izzy Young, Ed Pearl, the organizers of the University of Chicago Folk Festival, and the editors of the *Little Sandy Review*, maintained an important presence, new currents were developing that the Ramblers would have to navigate. The topical-song movement resurged with the February 1962 publication of *Broadside*, a magazine devoted to, as the subtitle read, "A Handful of Songs About Our Times." Edited by Sis Cunningham and Gordon Friesen, veterans of the Almanac Singers and People's Songs, the mimeographed publication provided a forum for folk songs that addressed contemporary issues, particularly the surging civil rights and nascent antiwar movements. Pete Seeger, Bob Dylan, Malvina Reynolds, Phil Ochs, Tom Paxton, and Len Chandler were among the early contributors.[20] The sixth issue featured Dylan's "Blowin' in the Wind," destined to become a 1960s anthem. Its provocative lyrics addressed both issues of civil rights ("How many years can some people exist / Before they're allowed to be free?") and war ("How many times must the cannon balls fly / Before they're forever banned?").

Dylan's first album, released in March 1962, was a potpourri of southern blues, ballads, country, and gospel songs delivered with a hard-edged, Guthrie-influenced voice that certainly placed him stylistically closer to the Ramblers than to the sweet-singing folk popularizers. But with his second release in early 1963, *The Freewheelin' Bob Dylan*, he emerged as the preeminent topical songwriter of the period. In addition to a hauntingly spare rendition of "Blowin' in the Wind," the LP included his Cuban missile crisis–inspired "A Hard Rain's A-Gonna Fall," his spiteful "Masters of War," and his powerful antisegregation ballad "Oxford Town." "Blowin' in the Wind" would climb to the top of the pop charts by August, but with a smooth arrangement sung by Peter, Paul and Mary. Meanwhile, the freedom-song movement gathered steam. Guy Carawan worked through the Highlander Folk School to encourage the use of folk songs in the civil rights movement, Pete Seeger traveled south to sing at black churches, and Bernice Johnson and the Freedom Singers of the Student Nonviolent Coordinating Committee began touring the country. The marriage of the folk revival and civil rights reached a zenith at the 1963 Newport Folk Festival, when, during the first evening concert, Johnson and her Freedom Singers came on stage, linked arms with Dylan, Baez, Seeger, and Peter, Paul and Mary, and sang "We Shall Overcome" and "Blowin' in the Wind."[21]

The Ramblers were not scheduled to sing until Sunday evening at Newport, but their absence from the impromptu Friday-night finale underscored yet another fissure that would divide urban folksingers along the fault line between tradition and social activism. The Ramblers sang neither freedom nor peace songs, nor any contemporary topical pieces, for that matter. With the exception of the Spanish American War satire "The Battleship Maine" and a handful of Depression songs, their antiquated mountain music appeared to be at best irrelevant and at worst "white sheet" and "lynching" music to those who increasingly sought to enlist folk song in support of progressive social causes. The Ramblers, deploying humor that was at once parody and self-deprecation, began announcing the comical farce "There Ain't No Bugs on Me" as "a song of social significance." Their satirical prelude alluded to the song's references to the Ku Klux Klan ("The old man joined the Ku Klux, and Ma she lost her sheet") and to the 1926 *Scopes* trial ("Oh, there may be monkey in some of you guys, but there ain't no monkey in me"). The subtext was clear—for the Ramblers there was no easy fit between protest songs and old-time mountain music.

Questions of politics would directly confront the Ramblers in March 1963, when they received an invitation to perform on ABC's *Hootenanny* program. At first the promise of a national television program devoted to folk music was eagerly greeted from all corners of the revival. But enthusiasm waned as it became clear that the focus would be on slick commercial groups like the Limeliters, the Tarriers, the Brothers Four, and the Chad Mitchell Trio. Indifference quickly begot outrage when it was discovered that ABC would blacklist Pete Seeger and the Weavers from the show because of their prior leftist affiliations. Pete, whose charges of contempt of Congress for refusing to answer questions put to him by the House Committee on Un-American Activities had been thrown out in March 1962, was still considered a contemptible proponent of the old Left by certain factions of the American Right.[22] Joan Baez refused to appear unless an invitation was extended to Seeger, and soon the Folksingers Committee to End the Blacklist was organized in New York. As a result of the ensuing boycott, a number of big-named acts, including Baez, Dylan, and Peter, Paul and Mary, never sang on the program.[23]

The *Hootenanny* boycott presented a crisis of consciousness for the Ramblers, especially for Mike, whose own half brother was the center of the controversy. Before reaching a decision Mike consulted with Pete, who was ambivalent toward the show. He predicted it would compromise its promise to bring traditional folk music to a national audience.[24] Empathizing with Mike's mission to promote traditional music, Pete encouraged his younger brother to follow his instincts, and the Ramblers finally decided to go ahead with the appearance. Mike later recalled, "I just felt that the issue was also musical. And that our music, that is, traditional music, had been blacklisted from the commercial airways. And I thought that being on a nationally broadcast television show might be a change."[25] John further explained:

> It was quite amazing to us that we [the Ramblers] were even considered for the show, and we went through a great deal of soul searching to arrive at our decision. Central to our argument was to balance our repugnance at the blacklist industry with the opportunity to bring traditional music, played in a traditional style, to the widest possible audience. However, there was another type of blacklist at the time, a musical blacklist. It manifested itself in our conflict with the commercial folk singers, their driving desires for exposure, and their total disinterest in traditional music or traditional musicians. From our point of view, they were our enemies.[26]

The *Hootenanny* episode left a bitter taste, beginning with a humiliating audition. Lou Gottlieb of the Limeliters, who had been placed in charge of selecting the show's repertoire, turned his back on the Ramblers to greet a friend, Bob Gibson, while the trio was in the middle of playing a song for him.[27] The Ramblers eventually played an Ernest Stoneman–inspired version of "New River Train" to an enthusiastic Ann Arbor audience that included several zealous Ramblers fans positioned close to the stage. But in the aftermath Mike was disappointed, realizing that one old-time song in a sea of pop arrangements "didn't make a blip" in terms of exposing the country to traditional music.[28] They were paid $750 for the initial shooting and broadcast and an additional $350 when the show was rebroadcast in September. By Ramblers standards this was high remuneration but hardly a windfall, considering they were performing for national broadcast television. Nor did the appearance make a significant difference in the band's long-term fortunes. That summer and fall the Ramblers continued to accept a steady stream of low-paying engagements at colleges and clubs.

The folk music community remained divided on the merits of *Hootenanny*, which was dropped from ABC's fall 1964 programming. Writing in *Sing Out!* Irwin Silber cynically bid "Madison Avenue's Answer to Folk Music" a fond farewell. Meanwhile, an outraged Tom Paley denounced the Ramblers to the British folk press for participating in the show.[29] But worth noting is that in addition to the Ramblers a handful of traditional performers of some notoriety, including Doc

Watson, the Carter Family, and Flatt and Scruggs, did make it onto the program. This led historian Ronald Cohen to conclude that despite its menu of predominantly "slick" and "packaged" performers, *Hootenanny* did succeed in allowing "numerous musicians to reach an audience previously unimagined. Once hooked, many in the audience went out to purchase records, and some may even have discovered the music's rural roots and traditional performers."[30]

During the spring of 1963 the Ramblers stepped up their efforts to locate and work with traditional artists, collaborating with three rural musicians whose early recordings had appeared on Harry Smith's 1952 *Anthology* collection. In March, following a performance at Austin College, several of Roger Abrahams's folklore students mentioned that the legendary hillbilly musician Eck Robertson was still alive and fiddling just to the north in Amarillo, Texas. Robertson, born in 1887 in Delaney, Arkansas, had worked in medicine shows before gaining a reputation as a champion old-time fiddler. In June 1922, after playing at a Civil War veterans' reunion in Virginia, he and fellow fiddler Henry Gilliland decided on the spur of the moment to drive to New York to make a record, showing up unannounced at the Victor Studios. Country music historian Bill Malone recounted what happened next: "The Victor recording people, who to this point had shown no interest in rural talent, must have been taken aback when Gilliland and Robertson, dressed in Confederate uniform and cowboy suit respectively, marched into the Victor offices and asked for auditions. We don't know what went on in the minds of the Victor directors—they may very well have been charmed by the music they heard (or by the romantic symbols of the Old South and Old West being displayed before them)—but they did permit the tests [recordings], and several selections were subsequently released."[31] Robertson's rendition of the fiddle tune "Sallie Gooden" became a hillbilly classic after its release in 1922, and his superb 1930 recording of "Brilliance Medley," reissued on the *Anthology*, was well known by urban connoisseurs of folk fiddling like the Ramblers.

Mike and his family drove on to California while John and Tracy traveled north to Amarillo, where they pulled into a motel on the main road. Tracy recalled:

> So as we were registering, the lady asked, "Oh, are you on vacation?" So we said, "No, we're here to visit an old fiddler named Eck Robertson." She said, "Oh, his instrument shop is just across the street and down there about a block." Wow, talk about good luck! So after we had breakfast we went over there, and he took us right into his shop. It was a small place where he lived by himself, no family. Think he was around seventy five. And he was loquacious, talked for about an hour, about his career and all. And then he picked up the fiddle and started playing "Leather Britches," in the place where

people usually play it, in first position. And then he switches up to second position, no open strings. And he lifts his eyes up at us with this little sly grin like saying, Don't you know this is a good fiddler here, I'm one of the best. It's not easy to do this, and he had all the notes right. He didn't have to hunt for them like most fiddlers had to do—he knew right where to go.[32]

John and Tracy recorded Robertson's stories and tunes, and later that summer Mike returned to make further recordings that would eventually be issued on County Records. The Ramblers arranged for Robertson to perform at the 1964 UCLA Folk Festival and the 1965 Newport Festival, where they served as his accompanists.[33]

Following their successful encounter with Robertson, Tracy and John headed west, where the Ramblers had a two-week engagement at the Ash Grove with the legendary hillbilly singer Maybelle Carter. The Carter Family, from Scott County, Virginia, was perhaps the most popular of all the early hillbilly groups, having recorded over three hundred sides from the late 1920s through 1940 for the Victor, Decca, American, and Columbia record companies. Musically, the group was best known for Maybelle's much-emulated thumb-brush guitar style, where the melody is picked on the bass and a chord strummed on the treble strings, and the impeccably executed harmonies by Maybelle and her sister-in-law Sara. The family sang the gamut of traditional ballads, love songs, and gospel numbers, often rearranging folk melodies and verses into their own original songs. They sang of hearth and home, as Malone noted, "evok[ing] images of the old country church, Mama and Daddy, the family fireside, and 'the green fields of Virginia far away.'"[34] Such imagery was appealing, although probably for different reasons, to prewar southern rural audiences and later to northern revivalists who were familiar with the Carter songs that were included on John Lomax's 1941 Smoky Mountain Ballads and Smith's Anthology collections.

Mike had first heard Maybelle Carter in the early 1950s, when she sang live on the Richmond radio station WRZA, which he could pick up at night in DC. In 1957 he saw her live at the Grand Ole Opry and was amazed to learn that she played the autoharp and sang standing up (as opposed to sitting with the instrument on the lap, as he was used to). He was finally able to make contact with her through the Briar Record Company in Nashville, and, with the prompting of Pearl, she was booked at the Ash Grove with the Ramblers. But when John and Tracy finally joined Mike in Los Angeles, the specter of Hootenanny again raised its head, this time with an unexpected result. John remembered:

> And at the last moment, the weekend before, the Ash Grove was told,
> Maybelle's not going to come because she and her daughters had been
> invited to play on the ABC-TV Hootenanny show, and her management thinks

this is more important than playing in a coffeehouse. We were devastated because we had worked so hard to set the stage so that she could make her triumphant entry into the folk revival. But she couldn't give in to her management. And she was at the time on tour throughout the Northwest with Johnny Cash. She was apparently quite upset that she had to turn us down, and at the last moment Johnny Cash came and sat in for her. So it was the Ramblers and Johnny Cash for the first weekend at the Ash Grove. . . . He played his own set, just by himself with no band. And he would stand up there big and broad and tall—because he would play in these huge stadiums—with this big Johnny Cash swagger. But then he would say, "Now I know you have all come to hear Maybelle Carter, but she couldn't make it, but she's lovely and she plays the autoharp." He'd take out an autoharp and put it on a stool and hunch over it like a little boy, and play the autoharp and sing Carter Family songs. It was so amazing, he'd say stuff like, "Well, here's a song—as Mike Seeger would say—learned off an old phonograph record." Cash was listening to us, parodying us a little. It was a nice, warm relationship that weekend. And then Maybelle came for the second week. And we'd back her up. We'd take turns, depending if she was playing the guitar or autoharp—it was a great privilege.[35]

In late April the Ramblers toured with Carter to Riverside, Tuscan, and Victorville, opening for her and then accompanying her on her own set.[36] They returned to Los Angeles for the first annual UCLA Folk Music Festival, produced by the university with advisement from D. K. Wilgus and in conjunction with Pearl. By 1963 UCLA was becoming a center for folk music research. Folklorist Wayland Hand had been joined by Charles Seeger and folk music specialist Wilgus. The latter's 1959 tome, *Anglo-American Folk Song Scholarship since 1898*, historicized the field and advocated more serious study of folk song function and style to complement older historical and comparative approaches. Wilgus's interest in the traditional roots of hillbilly music and the folk music revival made him a natural ally for Charles and the Ramblers.[37] The UCLA festival made the most concerted effort to date to mix performance, workshops, and academic presentations, as suggested in the festival brochure, which posited three purposes for the event:

1. To present traditional lore (particularly of the United States and at this stage largely song) in traditional form—by traditional performers or by performers using traditional styles.
2. To provide occasions for discussion and further understanding of traditional material in its form, substance, presentation, and social context.

FIGURE 10. John Cohen and Tracy Schwarz with Maybelle Carter, 1963 Newport Folk Festival. Photograph by John Byrne Cooke.

3. To bring together scholars, students, laymen, and traditional performers in as relaxed an atmosphere as is possible in an organized program.[38]

The first goal was amply realized with an impressive lineup of traditional performers, including Maybelle Carter, Clarence Ashley and Doc Watson, Roscoe Holcomb, Bill Monroe, the Dillards, Bessie Jones, Mance Lipscomb, and Lightning Hopkins. The Ramblers and the Greenbriar Boys filled the slot of city singers "using traditional styles," and Pete Seeger and Sam Hinton served as host-performers. Discussion took the form of instrumental and vocal workshops led by Mike, John, Tracy, Ralph Rinzler, Pete Seeger, and others and a series of lecture-demonstrations by folk song scholars Archie Green ("Topical Songs"), Wayland Hand ("The Folklore of Folk Song"), and Charles Seeger ("Music and Society"). Wilgus, Ed Kahn, and Ralph Rinzler led a session on collecting folk music. The UCLA festival reflected the next stage in a trend initiated at the University of Chicago and Berkeley festivals—the serious commingling of traditional performers, city singers, and folk music scholars. Wilgus, Green, and Charles Seeger had emerged as strong advocates for the traditional wing of the folk music revival, although their views were not shared by most folklore scholars of the period, who were skeptical of any intrusion of urban performers into their domain.

Following several more dates in California, including an appearance with Bill Monroe in Berkeley, the Ramblers headed east in late May 1963. Mike, traveling with Marge and their three young children, first stopped in Amarillo to meet and record Eck Robertson. He then made another stunning discovery as they wended their way east through the Appalachians. During a conversation with folklorist Guthrie Meade at Antioch College, Mike got wind that the Virginia coal miner and banjoist Dock Boggs was still alive, living somewhere in eastern Kentucky. Boggs's archaic banjo blues pieces were among the most haunting tunes on the Smith *Anthology*, making him something of a celebrity with urban musicians like Mike and John who had carefully studied his tunings and picking techniques. After rumbling across rutted roads around the hamlets of Mayking, Eolia, and Neon, Kentucky, the Seegers were directed over the state line to Norton in south-western Virginia, where they found Boggs's name in the telephone book. In the liner notes to the *Dock Boggs* Folkways LP he would produce the following year Mike wrote:

After a call, we went up to visit him and his wife at their home, a small meticulously clean and bright four room house over-looking Norton. Our meeting was one of mutual disbelief: we couldn't believe that this was the Dock Boggs and he, though he was pleased that someone remembered his records was not certain what I was up to. We talked awhile and he warmed quickly to the kids and later that evening after getting the family settled in a motel I returned. That evening he recorded about eight songs, largely unrecorded by him heretofore and an interview in which he related a good deal of his history, talked about his early years, learning to play his first recordings and so on. He also expressed the desire to play and record again.[39]

Mike was accommodating, immediately calling Bill Clifton of the newly constituted Newport Folk Festival board with the exciting news that Dock Boggs was alive and ready to play. Boggs was booked for the Newport festival the following month. Next, Mike called his contacts in Asheville, North Carolina, and arranged for Boggs and the Ramblers to appear at the Mountain Dance and Folk Festival in late June. Over the following months Mike would assist Boggs in securing engagements at the University of Chicago Folk Festival, the FOTM series in New York City, and numerous colleges.

Mike recorded three volumes of Boggs's music for Folkways Records, occasionally accompanying him on guitar.[40] Although he had done little public performing over the past thirty years, Boggs had not lost his arcane and highly individualistic manner of singing or playing. Strongly influenced by traditional singers in his community and by African American race records, his voice is an amalgamation of mountain and blues styles. He maintained the tense, nasal sound typical of Kentucky singers like Holcomb but also bent and slurred his notes like a bluesman, often hanging on the minor thirds and sevenths of the scale. His raspy, melismatic moans led one critic to describe him as "singing with a sour, nagging irascibility, as if singing for him were like paying taxes."[41] His banjo playing was also unorthodox, employing unusual modal tunings, a unique up-pick/brush stroke, and dissonant intervals resulting from playing and singing the melodic line in a minor modality while introducing the major third of the scale on the fifth drone string (e.g., in the key of D Minor, using an F-natural in the sung melodic line while occasionally thumbing an F-sharp on the fifth string to create a dissonant half-step interval).[42]

While there is no documentation of Boggs at the Ashville festival, a full recording of him accompanied by Mike at the December 1963 FOTM concert in New York provides a window into his interaction with an urban audience. Mike began by recounting his efforts to locate Boggs in southwestern Virginia earlier that spring. With tremendous reverence for the artist he was about to introduce, Mike briefly sketched Boggs's upbringing, his rough work in the coal mines, and his early career as a banjo player and recording artist for Brunswick Records. He then turned the program over to Boggs, who addressed his listeners:

> Well, folks, I'm very pleased to be here tonight. This is the first time I've had an opportunity to play music for an audience in New York—the last time I was in New York to play music I recorded for the Brunswick Talent Company, like Mike here was telling you. I went back home, and they gave me a couple of contracts, for twenty-four songs. And my wife didn't approve of me making music, and of course I wouldn't give up more than the king of England did if I gave my wife up. But I wanted her and I kept her, and I just went back to the coal mine. I laid down my banjo and let my music go for twenty-five years. Not many people could lay it down and play again after that long. . . . And Mike came along five or six months ago and got me interested in playing again and made these appointments for me. So I'm glad to be here to try and play something and give a little of myself. I have a lot of old pieces; some of them I guess are a hundred and fifty years old, and hardly any of them are under fifty years old. And there are a lot of young people in the country who would like to learn these pieces. I don't know if they want to learn the method and the way I play. I've taken up my way of playing just my own self. And I don't play hardly like anybody else. And I tune my banjo different keys to fit the song I'm playing. There are many banjo players that are better than I am, but I have some pieces they

FIGURE 11. Mike Seeger with Dock Boggs, 1963 Newport Folk Festival. Photograph by John Byrne Cooke.

don't play. The first piece I'm going to give you all is a piece I recorded for the Brunswick Recording Company, "Down South Blues." I put it on record back in 1927.

Boggs moved through nine selections, including "Down South Blues" and "The Country Blues" from his early recordings, drawing an enthusiastic response from the audience. A natural storyteller, he was relaxed and chatty, spinning anecdotes about each song. Mike maintained a strictly supportive role in the program, playing simple guitar progressions to anchor Boggs's banjo melodies when necessary and occasionally making song suggestions. In keeping with the Ramblers' approach to presenting traditional musicians, Boggs was the center of attention, while Mike remained in the background throughout the program.[43]

When the Ramblers reached Newport in July 1963 they found the event transformed, much to their liking. Now run by the nonprofit Newport Folk Foundation with a seven-member advisory board made up of performers that included Pete Seeger and Jean Ritchie, the reconstituted festival strove to strike a balance between the popular commercial acts and grassroots artists. As the directors put it in their festival booklet "Welcome" statement, "We would like to repay in some measure what we owe to the raw materials upon which we draw in our work." All performers, from the popular artists "normally commanding huge salaries" to the "unknown country fiddler," would work for the same union scale, and any profits from the festival would go toward folk music research and education.[44] The lineup ran the full spectrum, from the chart-busting Peter, Paul and Mary and Rooftop Singers, to topical songsters Bob Dylan, Joan Baez, Judy Collins, and the Freedom Singers, to traditional southern artists Dock Boggs, Maybelle Carter, Doc Watson, Clarence Ashley, Bessie Jones, Mississippi John Hurt, John Lee Hooker, Bill Monroe, and the Dillards. In addition to playing in the final Sunday-night concert, Mike, John, and Tracy led workshops in fiddle, banjo, and autoharp technique, and John screened footage from his spring field trip to eastern Kentucky. Although the Ramblers did not join in the topical-song workshop or the Friday-night "We Shall Overcome" finale, they surely took comfort in seeing the proliferation of traditional artists and the respect they now commanded.

In the festival booklet Ralph Rinzler linked the mission of the recently organized FOTM with the reconstituted Newport festival: "Across the country there has been a growing interest, mainly among college students, in the origins of folk song and folk-song style: this interest leads to a desire to see and hear traditional folk singers deliver their songs. . . . It is hoped that by making performers available for appearances and arranging for their transport and accommodations, the society [FOTM] will stimulate interest among students, coffeehouse, and club owners to present traditional musicians of high caliber on their folk music programs thereby bringing the folk into the folk music revival."[45] Rinzler would soon be hired by the Newport Foundation to conduct fieldwork. In the ensuing years he would develop models for locating, documenting, and presenting traditional performers to urban audiences that would form the foundation of the Smithsonian Festival of American Folklife that he would organize in 1967.

Just prior to the Ramblers' appearances at the Newport and Ashville festivals, two important events took place. In mid-June 1963 the Seeger and Cohen clans gathered at Pete's home in Beacon to celebrate the wedding of John Cohen and Penny Seeger, Mike's youngest sister. Their courting had begun several years prior when they first met at California's Camp Idyllwild. Twenty-year-old Penny, who played dulcimer and guitar and as a youngster had recorded with Mike and Peggy, was a student at UCLA and living at home with Charles when the two decided to wed. John's marriage into the Seeger family added yet another dimension to his complex relationship with Mike. The following week Mike and John, now brothers-in-law, entered the studio with Tracy for the new trio's initial recording session.

THE
NEW LOST CITY RAMBLERS
JOHN COHEN. MIKE SEEGER. TRACY SCHWARZ

Folkways

FA 2491

Gone To The Country

PHOTO: LAURENCE SIEGEL

FIGURE 12. Cover of *Gone to the Country* Folkways LP (1963).
Photograph by John Cohen. Image courtesy of the Ralph Rinzler
Folklife Archives and Collections, Smithsonian Institution.

The Folkways LP *Gone to the Country* (FA 2491), released in the fall of 1963, gave fans their first chance to hear the new Ramblers on disc. The cover photograph featured the trio in their hallmark vests and ties but not in their familiar urban environs. In keeping with the album's title, they were posed quite literally in the country, dwarfed by the woods, appearing as three hillbilly leprechauns who just popped out of thin air to entertain a weary wanderer with guitar, fiddle, and banjo (figure 12). That the photograph was not taken in some deep Appalachian mountain holler but rather in the New Jersey Palisades woods just north of the George Washington Bridge was not mentioned in the notes. The title, according to John, came from a tall tale told by Clint Howard and Fred Price of Clarence

Ashley's band. After driving up a remote mountain road, riding a horse through the woods, swinging across a stream, and finally crawling up a cliff to the cabin where he hoped to visit some friends, the protagonist of the story is greeted by a note tacked to the door proclaiming, "Gone to the Country."

In the liner notes John introduced Tracy by observing that his addition had expanded the group's repertoire at least ten years back and forward to include a cappella ballad singing and more bluegrass material. Tracy explained that his love for early country music went beyond bluegrass to include fiddle-based "straight hillbilly," which was popular up through the 1940s and into the early 1950s, before the emergence of rock and roll. He left no question about his commitment to the Ramblers' mission, commenting, "It's gratifying to see how hillbilly, old time and bluegrass music is becoming so well appreciated in the cities."

In the remainder of the notes John recounted the Ramblers' recent collaborations with Dock Boggs, Maybelle Carter, and Eck Robertson, once known to them only as "voices from the past" on scratchy 78 rpm recordings. Playing alongside these traditional performers and introducing them to urban audiences had been a revelation for the Ramblers. Connecting old commercial and field recordings to bona fide living artists provided concrete evidence that southern folk music was indeed an animate, dynamic tradition. Old attitudes defining folk music as antiquated survivals that informed previous academic scholarship must be discarded, John continued, to make way for "new tools" of study that include "record catalogues, collectors, discographies, master numbers and interviews with country musicians." Though not accepted by most folklorists at the time, the study of old recordings, combined with oral histories provided by elder practitioners, would become common practice among the young folk music scholars and ethnomusicologists who were coming of age in the early 1960s and who would go on to transform those disciplines in the ensuing decades.

Tracy's musical debut on *Gone to the Country* was somewhat inconsistent. His high, slightly gritty voice was clearly better suited for southern mountain-style singing than was Tom's discernibly warmer tenor. He demonstrated the ability to sing with what *Little Sandy Review* critics Pankake and Nelson identified as a "nasal bite" suggestive of "the hard, near-falsetto of Bill Monroe and Ralph Stanley" on bluegrass classics like "Little Glass of Wine" and "Pretty Little Miss."[46] His high harmonies on the Carter Family tunes "Sinking in the Lonesome Sea" and "Wild and Western Hobo" were well executed, and his a cappella version of "Tom Sherman's Bar Room" (a variant of "The Unfortunate Rake") unaffectedly captured the tension of the older mountain balladeers. But his lead vocal on the Stanley Brothers' "Rambler's Blues" clearly faltered in the higher register. Likewise, Tracy's fiddling was uneven. His bluegrass technique on "Little Glass of

Wine" and "Pretty Little Miss" was tentative at best, and his interpretation of Wade Mainer's prebluegrass fiddling on "Riding That Train 45" sounded formulaic and stiff. But his twin fiddling with Mike on the old-time tunes "Hello, John D" and "Liza Jane" was more relaxed and flowing, bringing a vital new dimension to the group's sound. In the former the two fiddles played in unison, melding perfectly with John's frailing banjo to re-create the feel of a nineteenth-century square-dance trio. The latter piece, from the Carter Brothers of Mississippi, featured the fiddles pitched in octaves, feverishly bowing against John's punchy guitar runs and nonsense vocalizing.

Surprisingly, Mike played banjo only once, and that in a supportive role on "Train 45." He opted to play mandolin on the three most identifiable bluegrass numbers, "Little Glass of Wine," "Pretty Little Miss," and "Rambler's Blues." For whatever reasons, Mike's flashy Scruggs-style banjo picking, which had become a prominent part of the group's live performances, was absent from the recording. John provided the most interesting banjo work, using a variety of two- and three-finger styles on Boggs's songs "Danville Girl" and "Down South Blues," the fiddle-banjo numbers "Hello, John D." and "The Little Carpenter," and the lilting Uncle Dave Macon song "Grey Cat on the Tennessee Farm." Pankake and Nelson described his renditions of Boggs's material as "labored and somewhat uncomfortable" but lauded "his attempts to get inside the difficult and private art of another experience." They invoked John Updike's pronouncement that "the willingness to risk excess on behalf of one's obsessions is what distinguishes artists from entertainers, and what makes some artists adventurers on behalf of us all."[47] John admitted that comparing his version of the tunes to the Boggs originals is "sobering" but views the exercise as a necessary component of an ongoing self-reflection on personal identity and creative fulfillment, or, as he put it in his opening statement on the first Ramblers album, "where one searches to encounter his own image in the world."

The best music by the new Ramblers was yet to come, but *Gone to the Country* demonstrated that Tracy had integrated comfortably into the group. While the trio's overall repertoire had shifted slightly in the direction of early bluegrass material, they remained firmly anchored in the old-time mountain style, and their overall sound had not changed dramatically. If Pankake and Nelson were accurate barometers of the traditionalist wing of the urban folk scene, Tracy had passed the test and proven himself to be a suitable replacement for Tom. Noting the subtle change in Gid Tanner's Skillet Lickers with the addition of guitarist-singer Riley Puckett in the late 1920s, they concluded: "So it is with the Ramblers: A different group with the same aims; the same songs with a new sound; a reawakened absorption with technique, coupled with a new approach to humor; a new combination of voices and instruments. Like the bourbon drinker changing over to Scotch, the listener who has been with the Ramblers since their formation in 1958 will need to acquire a new taste. But the intoxication is still there."[48] Further proof of Tracy's acceptance by Ramblers fans were the relatively brisk—at least by Folkways standards—sales of *Gone to the Country*. Six hundred copies were sold in the fall of 1963, and an additional thousand would be sold in 1964.

It is tempting to interpret the Ramblers' *Gone to the Country* title as a reference to something more than simply their collective infatuation with rural music and culture. The album title, in tandem with a cover photograph physically situating them for the first time in a rural setting, could be read as a literal announcement of a planned change in lifestyle, an actual relocation back to the land. In the fall of 1963, when the album was released, however, no such move had occurred. John and Penny were still living in a small apartment in Greenwich Village and soon would move to a loft on Dye Street in lower Manhattan. Mike and Marge had settled into small-town Roosevelt, New Jersey, located just off the New Jersey Turnpike, halfway between New York and Philadelphia. Tracy was living just outside Freehold, New Jersey, about thirty miles south of New York. But Tracy's and John's situation would soon change. By year's end Tracy would relocate to a farm in southeastern Pennsylvania. In early 1965 John would buy an old farmhouse in the upstate New York hamlet of Tompkins Corners. Mike's move to Pennsylvania farm country would come a few years later. In the summer of 1963 neither Mike nor John nor Tracy had literally "gone to the country," but they were certainly contemplating the move.

In September 1963 the Ramblers played Toronto's Purple Onion for a week before making a quick trip to El Paso. The remainder of the fall was spent performing small concert hall and college shows in the Northeast and a three-week tour of midwestern colleges. The final numbers for 1963—the new Ramblers' first complete year as a touring folk ensemble—were encouraging although hardly spectacular. The group had played roughly eighty engagements: forty individual shows, five multiday folk festivals, and a handful of week- and two-week-long engagements at the Ash Grove (two weeks), Philadelphia's Second Fret (two weeks), Toronto's Purple Onion (one week), and Dallas's PM Club (one week). Twenty of the individual shows were at colleges, and two of the five folk festivals were college sponsored. While folk festivals provided them with opportunities to work more closely with traditional performers and to foster their educational mission through instructional workshops, engagements at colleges and extended stays at urban folk clubs remained their primary source of income. Of the eighty shows they performed that year, only those at the Asheville Folk Festival, the PM Club and Texas Christian University in Dallas, and Austin College in Sherman, Texas, were in the South.

While the work was steady, the pay remained stagnant, ranging between $300 and $600 for an individual performance and $750 and $1,000 for four to five nights' work at a club. John's before-expense Ramblers performance income for 1963 was just under $8,000. In addition, he and Mike earned just over $500 in royalties from the sale of approximately seven thousand Ramblers LPs.[49] These income figures, which sound reasonable by middle-class standards of the time, must be weighed against the economic realities of life on the road. The Ramblers were generally responsible for their own transportation, room, and board. Most traveling was done in one or two cramped cars; rarely did they stay in hotels, usually crashing on the couches and floors of folk music enthusiast acquaintances who formed a national network in cities and college towns; and food expenses were out-of-pocket unless meals were provided by their hosts. Mike, who was attempting to support a family with three small children, felt the pinch most acutely and continued to augment his income through individual performances. In December 1963 Tracy married Eloise Smith and took on the additional responsibility of three young stepchildren.

The Ramblers began 1964 with a week at Philadelphia's Second Fret, followed by a concert at the Walker Arts Center in Minneapolis organized by *Little Sandy Review* editors Jon Pankake and Paul Nelson. The Ramblers brought along Holcomb and Boggs, leading critic Thomas Scanlan to remind readers of the *Minnesota Daily* that the concert would not be a commercial hootenanny but rather "a magnificent opportunity for those interested in traditional American music to come into contact with authentic performers of southern rural music styles. For many it will be the only chance to hear in person performers whose music and recordings reach the highest and most profound level of folk artistry."[50]

From Minneapolis the Ramblers traveled to the fourth annual University of Chicago Folk Festival, where they joined a now-familiar lineup of traditional performers, including Dock Boggs, Doc Watson, and Maybelle Carter. In addition to playing on the evening concert, the three Ramblers participated in banjo and guitar workshops. John screened his *High Lonesome Sound*, and all listened with interest to Archie Green's lecture on the relationship between commercial hillbilly and folk music. In a letter to festival organizer Dan Auerbach, Green—then a librarian at the University of Illinois, Urbana—was especially laudatory of the performance by Boggs and the "blend of knowledge and flair" that Ralph Rinzler demonstrated in emceeing the Saturday-evening string-band concert. He encouraged the University of Chicago Folk Song Society to invite more folk music scholars to visit the campus during the semester and to include as many as four talks on case studies of hillbilly and blues music at its 1965 festival.[51] Green, who would soon enter the University of Pennsylvania to earn a PhD in folklife studies, was fast becoming an important link between the academic folklore world and the revival.

The Ramblers appeared at the second annual UCLA Folk Festival in March 1964 and then traveled to the Bay Area, where they were scheduled to play with Kentucky banjoist Cynthia May Carver, better known as Cousin Emmy. She was well known to the Ramblers and aficionados of southern traditional music from her 1947 Decca album, *Kentucky Mountain Ballads*, edited by Alan Lomax. Mike and John had stumbled across Carver in 1961 at a concert of country music at Disneyland, where she was performing with Roger Miller. A veteran of Kentucky country radio and country music clubs in Los Angeles, where she played after moving to southern California in the 1950s, Carver welcomed the opportunity to sing for the young revival audiences who heard her at the Ash Grove. John would later recall that her Kentucky ballads and flamboyant stage presentation came across as an exotic mix of Hollywood and hillbilly: "Her music was as we knew it, but instead of coming from a farm kitchen it was coming from a spangled jukebox."[52] The Ramblers arranged for her to perform with them at the Newport Folk Festival in 1965, tour with them to Europe in 1966, and record a Folkways record with them in 1968 (Folkways FT 1015).

In mid-May the Ramblers returned to the Pequot, Connecticut, library with Peter Bartok to record their second LP with Tracy, *String Band Instrumentals* (Folkways Records FT 9802, 1964). For the first time the liner notes include no introductory statements but rather consist of lengthy commentary and sources for each tune. To assist listeners who want to learn the pieces, each selection has information on the tonic key, banjo-playing technique (e.g., "frailing," "three finger roll," "thumb and two fingers with pick," and "index finger picking upwards throughout"), and alternative tunings for banjo, fiddle, and guitar where necessary.

Musically, *String Band Instrumentals* was a step up from *Gone to the Country*. The LP opened with the wild breakdown "Saddle Up the Grey" from the Carter Brothers and Son, featuring Tracy fiddling in standard G–D–A–E classical tuning and Mike in the alternative G–D–G–D tuning. While both played roughly the same melody in the key of G, the sound was enriched by Mike's open-drone strings and enlivened by John's guitar runs and whooping "da-di-da-di" scat singing. Tight twin fiddles were also heard on another Carter Brothers and Sons piece, "Jenny on the Railroad," but this time with no guitar accompaniment and occasional octave harmonies. On "Black Eyed Suzie" the shuffling twin fiddles melded with John's crisp banjo in one of the trio's more energetic dance numbers. Tracy's lead fiddling on the dance tunes "Take Me Back to Georgia" and "Bill Chetham" exhibited a stronger command of the subtle rhythmic phrasing and melodic ornamentations of the tradition than his previous playing on *Gone to the Country*.

His rendition of the ragtime-influenced "Going to Jail" swung with skillfully executed melodic slurs and syncopations. Mike's robust banjo playing, all but absent on *Gone to the Country*, is featured on several selections. Most impressive is "Chinese Breakdown," a Scruggs-style tune he learned from Earl's older brother Junie. Against the hard-shuffling rhythmic accompaniment of Tracy's fiddle and John's guitar, Mike rolled the melody up and down the neck with his fanciest banjo picking heard on record to date. Mike's thumb-and-two-finger guitar picking is featured on the arrangement of "Smoketown Strut." Based on a recording by the black guitarist Sylvester Weaver, the performance demonstrated Mike's mastery of the lilting, slightly syncopated style of his guitar mentor, Elizabeth Cotten. John contributed several of his finest banjo efforts to the project. "Soldier's Joy," a breakdown he learned form Hobart Smith at the University of Chicago Folk Festival the previous year, was becoming one of the most popular (and overplayed) dance tunes of the revival. But John's rendition was frailed with precise accents, subtle melodic variation, and a surprising interpretation of the A strain of the tune in the upper-high register of the banjo heard midway through the piece. Likewise, his arrangement of "Shout Lulu," a composite borrowing from versions by Kentucky banjoists Rufus Crisp and Roscoe Holcomb and city pickers Woody Wachtell and Pete Steele, exploited the drive and drone of the frailing banjo style. "The New Lost Train Blues," the Wade Mainer tune that inspired the Ramblers' name, combined Mike's blues-inflected fiddling with John's precise three-finger guitar work. The piece's asymmetrical form, built on an AA (eight bars + eight bars), B (twelve bars), C (eighteen bars) structure, along with its rhythmic interplay of shuffling fiddle and syncopated guitar picking on the C section, produced one of the Ramblers' most novel and satisfying arrangements.

In addition to the notable individual efforts, *String Band Instrumentals* was enhanced by the introduction of unusual instrumental combinations, such as the autoharp and guitar on the ragtime piece "Victory Rag," mouth harp and banjo on "My Wife Died on Saturday Night," and mouth harp and fiddle on "Stone's Rag." The overall sequencing of pieces, smoothly segueing among a variety of fiddle-driven dance tunes, ragtime numbers, waltzes, and lighter parlor ditties, provided a well-balanced listening experience despite the paucity of vocal material. Pankake and Nelson stress this point in their *Little Sandy Review*, characterizing *String Band Instrumentals* as "a dozer of an album devoted to reviving some of the finest, rarest, most beautiful, and (in at least one instance) weirdest of the old sting-band instrumental styles and performances." They aptly point out that because instrumental style is easier to emulate than vocal technique, "the NLCR performances here are exceptionally true and well done." In learning from another person, they continue, "it is less difficult to penetrate his mind than his heart, and this is what the Ramblers have chosen to do here."[53] While their 1959 *Songs from the Depression* album contained their most impressive vocal material, *String Band Instrumentals* was unquestionably the Ramblers' strongest instrumental effort to date.

The cover photograph of *String Band Instrumentals* offers a window into the Ramblers' world in 1964 (figure 13). The image has the feel of an old-time family portrait. Tracy, Mike, and John, dressed in vests and ties, are posed with fiddle, banjo, and guitar standing in front of an old log barn. Seated in front of them are their wives, Eloise, Marge, and Penny, holding six disgruntled-looking children in their laps. The message is unambiguous: the Ramblers and their respective broods appeared to have literally gone to the country, the source of the string-band instrumentals heard on the record. Indeed, the photograph was taken in front of a barn that was just up the hill from a farmhouse Tracy and Eloise had rented in late 1963 near the rural hamlet of Delta, located in York County, Pennsylvania, about fifty miles west of Philadelphia, just north of the Maryland state line. By this time John and Penny had decided to leave the city to raise a family and were actively looking for a house in rural upstate New York. John, who conceived the photograph, later recalled: "Part of the inclination was the want to live in the country. . . . This was rural music and home music; the photographs supposedly conveyed the home setting of the music rather than the stage setting."[54]

The same photograph would appear on the title page of *The New Lost City Ramblers Songbook*, a volume Mike and John had been working on for several years that was finally published by Oak Publications in late 1964.[55] The book's cover, a photograph of a group of Galax musicians taken by Eck Dunford around 1910 (figure 14), was clearly the source of inspiration for John's Pennsylvania barn image. Burton Stoneman, holding a fiddle and dressed in his best Sunday church clothes, stands stiffly next to banjo player William Frost in front of a log house. Seated in the foreground are three very proper looking women, hair up in nineteenth-century style, holding two autoharps and a guitar.[56] In both photographs the men are posed as patriarchs, lording it over the seated women. But in the Dunford image the latter hold instruments and are presumably part of the band, while in John's Pennsylvania barn shot the women clutch children, not guitars and autoharps. The choice of this configuration is curious, for Marge, Eloise, and Penny were all musicians and singers in their own right. But, unlike Dunford's women, they were not part of the band, nor are they presented as possible participants in John's vision of "home music."

Oak Publications was a subsidiary of Folkways Records, launched by Moe Asch and Irwin Silber in 1960 to issue folk music songbooks. John and Mike had approached Silber with the idea of a songbook in 1961, but it took three years to

STRING BAND
INSTRUMENTALS

THE NEW LOST
CITY RAMBLERS

MIKE SEEGER
TRACY SCHWARZ
JOHN COHEN

FOLKWAYS RECORD FA 2492
DESIGN & PHOTO BY JOHN COHEN

FIGURE 13. Cover of *String Band Instrumentals* Folkways LP (1964).
Photograph by John Cohen. Image Courtesy of the Ralph Rinzler Folklife
Archives and Collections, Smithsonian Institution.

assemble the essays, 83 visuals, and 126 transcribed songs and tunes that would compose the collection. Visually, the work is a striking document of southern Appalachian culture. John included FSA photographs by Walker Evans, Ben Shahn, Dorothea Lange, and Russell Lee and photographs of hillbilly performers from the John Edwards Memorial Collection. He added his own photographs from his 1959 trip to eastern Kentucky. There is little of the romanticism often associated with popular depictions of southern mountain life. Rather, the images depict tough people living through hard times and harsh conditions but always clinging to music as a means of cultural identity and survival.

John's "Introduction to Styles in Old-Time Music" surveyed the fiddle, banjo, guitar, and singing styles associated with southern mountain music, including detailed information on tuning and playing techniques. He reiterated the

FIGURE 14. Photograph of Galax musicians taken by Eck Dunford around 1910. Standing (left to right): Burton Stoneman, J. William Frost; seated (left to right): Sophinnia Leonard, Myrtle Stoneman Hawks, Betty Leonard. This photograph appeared on the cover of the *New Lost City Ramblers Songbook* (Oak Publications, 1964).

Ramblers' mission to "preserve style" and asserted that "song and style cannot be divorced—if the aim is to present rather than interpret."[57] Mike offered his own history of the music, emphasizing the role of industrialization, the automobile, and the expanding recording and broadcast industries in shaping the contours of the earliest commercial recordings of mountain music up through the advent of bluegrass in the 1940s. The final section of his essay, drawn from his 1962 interview with artists and repertoire man Frank Walker, who recorded southern folk music for the Columbia 15000 series, presented fresh insights into the role early commercial record companies played in documenting and packaging rural music.

A final essay by John wrestled with the thorny issue of copyrighting oral folk songs, a practice the Ramblers had been denouncing for years. With record companies and professional entertainers rushing to cash in on the commercial folk boom, the situation had "reached the point where everyone feels obligated to copyright something before someone else does, even though the claim may be questionable in the first place. Fear begets fear, money begets only money, and the question of morality is left behind."[58] John claimed that most of the material in the current collection is or was at one time in the public domain and is derived from an expression of community aesthetics and style, thereby justifying the editors' decision not to include copyright notices on any of the songs. "It is our desire to see this material return to its public domain (PD) status," to "offer some kind of bypass to the muddled copyright situation," and ultimately "to arouse interest and appreciation for the music."[59] Implicit, though never stated in the essay, is the rationale for not paying fees to organizations like Peer International that claimed to hold copyright on the fifteen Carter Family songs included in The New Lost City Ramblers Songbook.

The songs and tunes included in The New Lost City Ramblers Songbook reflected the broad repertoires of the Ramblers and the traditional performers who inspired them. The material was arranged into categories reminiscent of early Lomax songbooks: "Old Love Songs," "News and Occupational Hazards," "Lonesome Blues," "Wild Men & Murder," "Whoop 'em Up," and so forth. The header to each song cites an original hillbilly or LOC recording as its source and in about two-thirds of the cases a specific Ramblers recording. There is usually a sentence or two on the source recording, followed by references to the original key, instrumentation, and tuning and playing technique. For example, the header for Roscoe Holcomb's "Across the Rocky Mountains" from the Folkways record Mountain Music of Kentucky (FA 2317, 1960) reads: "Guitar is tuned GGDGBC, similar to banjo tuning. It is played in a two-finger style, with the thumb leading, and the index finger seldom leaving the first string."[60] Below each header the main melody and additional tenor and bass vocal lines are scored out in standard Western notation, with the words for the chorus and all verses.

The musical transcriptions for *The New Lost City Ramblers Songbook* were done by Hally Wood, a folksinger and acquaintance of Silber who was knowledgeable about both folk and Western classical music. Her thorough transcriptions include a series of signs to designate tonal variations common to folk music, such as "drop in pitch," "scoop attack," "sliding attack," "fiddle slides," and so forth. Occasionally, banjo and guitar tablature appear alongside standard notation. In a brief "Music Note" Wood echoed the earlier concerns of Charles Seeger and Ruth Crawford Seeger regarding the limitations of transcription: "At its best, notation is a crude method of setting down what voices and instruments immediately convey to the practical listener." She urged folk music enthusiasts to go back to the original recordings "and listen to them over and over again until you can hear them in your head. Treat the book as a jog to memory, a source of detail, a help in working out particular passages."[61] In a letter to John she laid out the argument for learning by listening and admitted that her transcription efforts were basically "setting the notes down, for a record of what happened, a record that can be studied, preserved, and so on—a necessary and useful companion to the recordings of the actual sounds."[62]

Wood's hope that the transcriptions would be both descriptive (an accurate representation of the actual sounds that occur) and prescriptive (a blueprint to aid the performer in reproducing the actual sounds) was undermined by her decision to set the transcriptions in keys that "generally [place] the [main] melody in the usual singer's range" instead of in the specific key in which the Ramblers performed the piece or the key of the original source recording. What she means by "usual singer's range" (later described as an "ordinary singer's range") is not clear, and there is certainly nothing unusual about Mike's, John's, Tom's, or Tracy's vocal ranges. Her parameter seems to have been that no lead vocal line should stray far below or above the octave between middle C and the C above middle C. The result is confusing. For example, "Don't Let Your Deal Go Down" (page 182) was originally played in the key of G by both the Ramblers (*New Lost City Ramblers*) and Charlie Poole (Columbia 15038), but Wood chose to set the piece in the key of D (including the fiddle line) to avoid the lead vocal jumping to the E above the C above middle C.[63] But both John and Poole—neither of whom possesses an exceptionally high vocal range—easily hit the high E on their respective recordings. Moreover, a violinist, wishing to use notation as a guide to Mike's fiddle part, would have to learn the piece in the written key of D and then transpose it back to the original key of G. Similarly, "There'll Be No Distinction There" (page 232, from *Songs of the Depression*), "Ain't No Bugs on Me" (page 226, from *Gone to the Country*), and "Hopalong Peter" (page 104, from *Old Timey Songs for Children*) are originally played in D, C, and G, respectively, but Wood placed them in E, a key with four sharps that might be difficult for a novice reader to negotiate. Nearly half the transcriptions in *The New Lost City Ramblers Songbook* do not coincide with the original keys, diminishing the usefulness of the collection for scholars and performers alike.

Despite these problems, *The New Lost City Ramblers Songbook* received a glowing review in the *Saturday Review*; the popular magazine praised the scholarly integrity of the volume, calling it "an invaluable reference piece devoted to 'old-time' music."[64] Robert Shelton, writing for *Sing Out!* lauded the collection as "conceivably one of the half-dozen most important works recently published on American folk music."[65] *The New Lost City Ramblers Songbook* sold well, and in 1976 Music Sales Limited, the company to which Asch and Silber sold Oak Publications in 1967, republished the work under the title *Old-Time String Band Songbook*.

The Ramblers were caught by surprise in the summer of 1964, when the question of ownership of the New Lost City Ramblers name resurfaced. While Mike was negotiating with his British contacts to organize a Ramblers European tour for the fall, an announcement appeared in the British newsletter *Folk Weekly* that Tom Paley's New Lost City Ramblers would be opening in August at Edinburgh's Palladium. Inside the newsletter a short article entitled "Will the Real NLCR Stand Up Please" announced the Palladium engagement and noted that the Seeger-Cohen-Schwarz trio, also known as the New Lost City Ramblers, were considering a British tour that fall. Promoter Roy Guest, *Folk Weekly* reported, was concerned that "the appearance of two New Lost City Ramblers groups in Britain within a couple of months could cause confusion." The article ended by repeating charges Tom had made in an earlier edition of the magazine *Folk Music*. There he had claimed: "Among the principal reasons for the break-up of the New Lost City Ramblers were: 1. My refusal to perform for segregated audiences (John and Mike wished to be free to do so), and 2. My refusal to sign an NBC Loyalty oath (resulting in our being blacklisted on TV). . . . I have nothing to do with any performances under the name New Lost City Ramblers before segregated audience or on the American TV show *Hootenanny* which banned Pete Seeger."[66] Guest's concerns were serious, and in a September letter to Mike he explained: "It is now impossible to bring to England a group called the New Lost City Ramblers since there is already a group touring the clubs under that name (Tom Paley's group)."[67] Several months later another British publication, *Combo Musical Weekly*, ran a similar article entitled "Who Are the Real New City Ramblers?" with an accompanying picture of Tom, Stan Bloom, and Joel Latner decked out in familiar Ramblers vests and ties.[68]

Mike and John were outraged that their English tour had been torpedoed and at Tom's accusations that they were insensitive to segregation and McCarthy blacklisting. Mike shot off a letter to Folk Music, in which the original charges had been made, recounting that in 1962 Tom's sole reason for leaving the group was his reluctance to become a full-time musician. He characterized Tom's comments as "reckless" and "reminiscent of our McCarthy scare in the U.S.," since they "insinuate that we are pro-segregation and blacklist. Such reasons are first and most emphatically untrue, but also absurd and odious, and are issues that had nothing to do with the NLCR." The ABC Hootenanny show, he pointed out, had no effect on Tom's departure, since it occurred almost a year after he left the group.[69] Mike's letter was never published, but he did send a copy to Asch, asking his advice. On November 2 Russell Karp, again representing the Ramblers, sent a threatening letter to Asch, demanding he stop paying royalties to Tom until he discontinued "his unauthorized use of the name New Lost City Ramblers" in England.[70] Asch apparently refused but was growing weary of the quarrel between members of a group who had made a dozen recordings for Folkways and who he hoped would make more.

The dispute would drag on into the following year, when the Ramblers tried once more to organize a British tour. In an August 11, 1965, letter to Mike, Tom reiterated his desire for a settlement, this time offering a series of options involving approximately $500 in cash plus a vintage guitar, banjo, or Dobro or cash and thirty quarter-inch tapes of old-time music. He closed the letter by noting that he hoped he and Mike could continue to communicate reasonably but that relations between him and John had "deteriorated long ago to the point where a really civil exchange might be impossible."[71] Apparently, Mike did not respond, and it would finally be up to Asch to pose a solution. Later that month, on a visit to London, Asch met with Tom and offered him a payment of $750. In return Tom would relinquish all rights to the New Lost City Ramblers name and any future assets earned by the group while retaining his royalties for the prior Folkways recordings he made with the Ramblers.[72] Tom wrote Mike on September 5, notifying him that he agreed to Asch's terms, and the Ramblers would encounter no future objections from him regarding use of the name in England or the United States. While clearly relieved that the ordeal was finally settled, Tom expressed his bitterness over the affair in his closing line to Mike. After wishing him good luck on the upcoming tour, he scoffed, "I'm in such a habit of opposing your use of the NLCR name that I can't avoid a feeling of outrage whenever I see a reference to you three as the NLCR."[73]

The Ramblers took off the summer of 1964 while John and Penny traveled to Peru to photograph and record indigenous music, a project that would eventually yield the Folkways recording *Mountain Music of Peru*. The band's fall touring began with a week at Philadelphia's Second Fret, followed by an extended West Coast tour that included two weeks at the Ash Grove and a series of college engagements that included California Tech, Fresno State, the University of California campuses at Riverside and Los Angeles, and a brief stint at Berkeley's Cabal coffeehouse. Their overall numbers for 1964 were slightly down from those of the previous year. They played approximately seventy dates, including six week-long engagements at the Ash Grove, the Second Fret, and Boston's Someplace Else; three multiday festivals; and thirty additional individual shows, twenty of which were at colleges. In terms of income, John estimates his Ramblers earnings before expenses had dropped to about $6,000 and his Folkways royalties to around $550, despite the fact that *String Band Instrumentals* had sold eleven hundred copies since its release that summer.

In the waning weeks of 1964 the Ramblers came face-to-face with elements of the burgeoning 1960s counterculture that gave them pause. On November 30, after playing a gig at the Off Stage coffeehouse in San Jose, their hosts arranged for them to spend the night at the home of author Ken Kesey in La Honda, a small community located in the nearby Santa Cruz Mountains. Kesey and his bohemian gang of merry pranksters, which included Beat author Neal Cassady and archetype hippy earth-mother Carolyn "Mountain Girl" Adams, had just returned from their LSD-laced cross-country bus odyssey. Collectively, they were engaged in a radical social experiment based on the consumption of hallucinogenics at a time when no one outside a small group of government scientists had ever heard of LSD.[74] John was more receptive to the scene than were Mike and Tracy, who he recalled were at first perplexed and then indifferent to Kesey's psychedelic commune. He was intrigued by the stoned hipsters: "The people were out there; they were doing it, living it, going someplace I'd never seen before. It was a real adventure. It was not back to nature, it was not back to the land, but it was back to something!"[75] But, exhausted from their day-long drive from southern California and earlier engagement that evening, the Ramblers went to sleep without meeting Kesey, Cassady, or Adams and apparently without realizing the magnitude of the social revolution that was simmering around them.

The next day, December 1, the Ramblers came down from the mountains and played at Berkeley's Cabal coffeehouse. When they arrived news was spreading about a student strike called by leaders of the Berkeley Free Speech Movement (FSM) in response to the University of California's suspension of students who had been involved in the unlawful distribution of civil rights movement and related political materials in front of the campus earlier that fall. Just two weeks prior Joan Baez had given a free concert in support of the FSM. Meanwhile, through the combination of a communication breakdown and the drama that was gripping the city over the potential FSM student strike, the owner of the Cabal had forgotten to advertise the Ramblers' appearance. The opening night audience was slim. John recalled a young teenager entering the Cabal and "marching around with a sign that said 'Revolt! Revolt! Revolt!' He was going around in circles—it was really bizarre!" On Wednesday, December 2, more than five thousand protesters and spectators converged on the university's Sproul Plaza. Roused by student organizer Mario Savio's call to action, between a thousand and fifteen hundred students and their supporters took over Sproul Hall, reportedly singing "We Shall Overcome" and Dylan's "The Times They Are A-Changin'" as they entered the building.[76] That night the police removed and arrested nearly eight hundred students while the Ramblers played several blocks away to another empty house at the Cabal. John recalled that someone at the club approached them about singing at Sproul Plaza, but nothing came of it. "It was a complicated thing, and we didn't really feel part of it," he later reflected, adding, "It was some kind of war zone, but it wasn't our war."[77] The next day, on the outskirts of the Bay Area as they drove to Fresno State College, the Ramblers witnessed the bizarre sight of hundreds of young people, undoubtedly students who had been arrested the night before, herded into an outdoor prison facility. The Ramblers kept driving, seemingly oblivious to the social tremors that were shaking all around them. The times were indeed changing, but the Ramblers apparently were not. Or were they?

Back on the East Coast Mike, John, and Tracy regrouped just before Christmas to record their third album, *Rural Delivery No. 1* (Folkways Records FA 2496, 1964; Verve/Folkways FV 9003, 1965). Perhaps in response to questions concerning the Ramblers' relevancy amidst the new wave of topical folk material, Mike commented in the liner notes: "It is unfortunate today that many believe the urban folksinger must create a new song or style, bad or good, or else be branded an imitator. This mania for wanton change is similar to that of tearing down fine old buildings to put up faceless new ones under the rationale of progress." Then, trying to strike a balance, he concluded, "[We must] preserve and create among the old forms and make room for the best of the evolving forms."[78] Although Mike made no mention of it, the album did contain the Ramblers' first original piece, a fiddle tune by Tracy called "Fish Creek Blues," inspired by the creek running near his house in rural Pennsylvania.

John's observations revealed further the Ramblers' struggle to find a place in the rapidly evolving folk revival and volatile social milieu of the mid-1960s. He opened with an announcement that by the spring of 1965 all three Ramblers would be living in the country, a reference to the Putnam County, New York, farmhouse he and Penny were about to purchase. He commented on the proliferation of old-time string bands around the country that play "in an honestly homey atmosphere—without the pressures of the commercial music scene, and with no ambition about the music other than to enjoy it, make it heard, and get it better. None of the bands who play old time music have any idea that they might make a 'hit.'" Perhaps with recent political developments on his mind he speculated, "More likely this music serves many of them as a means of social criticism—as an indication of real values which are within easy reach in an oftimes [sic] frantic urban society. This distance from modern society is the only controversial aspect of our music." John concluded that old-time music for each individual Rambler had become "a personal and handmade statement in the midst of mass produced mass culture. It is a way of dealing with the past and present, a connection with people faced with similar problems—a simple statement of human needs, or a highly sophisticated and stylized expression of an old tradition which is still at work."[79] By invoking the rhetoric of folk romanticism and mass-culture criticism, John was beginning to articulate a position of cultural politics based on the embrace of a simpler lifestyle that rejected urban consumerism, suburban sprawl, and commercial entertainment. Adherents to this philosophy did not take to the streets in behest of a specific political cause or sing songs of social protest but rather looked for ways to create their own communities, ideally away from the frenetic pace of city life. Years before the appearance of the first *Whole Earth Catalogue* in 1968 and the publication of the first issue of *Mother Earth News* in 1970, John was struggling to imagine a space outside mainstream urban culture where homemade music might flourish, untarnished by commercial and material concerns. Whether that homey, handmade music could continue to provide the Ramblers with a means of making a living was uncertain, but one thing was for sure: although he still lived on Dye Street in lower Manhattan, a part of John had already gone to the country.

7

GONE TO THE COUNTRY, 1965–1968

In the late fall of 1964, when Penny Seeger Cohen realized she was pregnant with their first child, she and John discussed their reservations about raising a family in New York. The city wouldn't do, but neither would the sterile suburbs of John's youth, so the couple began to scour the countryside north of New York. They initially hoped to find a place near Pete's log house outside Beacon, overlooking the Hudson River. But real estate prices near the river proved too high, so they focused their search to the east in Putnam County, not far from Lake Oscawana, where John and his family had summered in his youth. When they pulled into Tompkins Corners they met a general-store proprietor who remembered John's mother and cordially directed them to a local realtor. John recalled what happened next, when they were shown a ramshackle property that had been on the market for some time: "When we first drove in this place was covered with wrecked cars, and the roofs of the buildings were all full of holes, and it was patched together—it was a big mess. And it reminded me of Eastern Kentucky. I had just done the *High Lonesome Sound* film—it looked like a scene out of that! And nobody wanted it—it was very reasonable. And I saw all these buildings—there were at least four outbuildings. And I said we can have a studio here, an editing room there, a something else here—da, da, da, da."[1]

They purchased the land and buildings for around $11,000 and that spring began renovating the farmhouse and converting an old barn into a studio. In July 1965, following the birth of their daughter Sonya, the family moved in. For John, Tompkins Corners was a reasonable compromise, far enough away from the grind of city life but close enough to the art galleries, museums, and music scenes that continued to inspire him. Despite his occasional diatribes against consumer culture and the commercial music industry, John maintained an essential urban sensibility. Unlike Mike and Tracy, he never lost his affections for New York and its cultural amenities. Tompkins Corners, located in a bucolic valley but only minutes from the Taconic State Parkway, was just fifty miles from Times Square, a fact that John was quick to share with visitors.

Tracy chose a different sort of rural experience. In early 1963, not long after he joined the Ramblers, he rented a small house adjacent to a farm outside Freehold, New Jersey. But this location proved too close to the state's expanding suburbs, so following his marriage to Eloise Smith, a singer he had met through folk music circles in Washington, he decided to move farther west. The newlyweds, along with three young children from Eloise's first marriage, found an old country house near Delta, Pennsylvania, about fifty miles southwest of Philadelphia in York County, just north of the Maryland state line. Nestled in a hollow next to a creek and an old mill, their new home provided a pastoral setting but lacked sufficient land for the couple to pursue their ambitions of farming and horse ranching. In the spring of 1965, with Eloise pregnant with Tracy's daughter Sallyann, the family moved farther west in York County near Glen Rock, where they purchased a fifty-acre farm for about $10,000. With the help of a neighboring Pennsylvania Dutch dairy farmer with whom he traded labor, Tracy began to fulfill his childhood dreams of farming. He and Eloise raised hogs, hay, and feed corn; kept a large vegetable garden; and trained horses. "The idea was subsistence, not a commercial farm," Tracy later recalled. "We wanted a great place to raise kids and all. But music was still the main income."[2] In their self-conscious rejection of city life and its excessive materialism in favor of a simpler rural lifestyle based on ecosustainability, Tracy and Eloise were at the forefront of the nascent back-to-the-land movement that would proliferate in the late 1960s and early 1970s. As much as Mike and John savored country music and the country experience, Tracy was the one truly committed to emulating something closer to the agrarian lifestyle that had spawned Appalachian folk music.

In the spring of 1965 Mike was living with Marge and their three small sons, Kim, Chris, and Jeremy, in the small town of Roosevelt, New Jersey, where they had moved in late 1961. The town, originally established as Jersey Homesteads, was a New Deal experiment in cooperative farming and manufacturing that was renamed Roosevelt following FDR's death in 1945. In the early 1960s it had evolved into a quiet hamlet with a population of around 750. Mike viewed Roosevelt as "kind of a little country town, but with lots of urban people living there; it was something like an artist colony."[3] In addition to the small-town ambience, Roosevelt was ideally located just east of the New Jersey Turnpike and only about an hour's drive from New York.

By the mid-1960s all three Ramblers had left behind the urban and suburban environs of their youth, but each individual had different motivations and expectations in doing so. Mike simply wanted nothing to do with city life; although Roosevelt was not exactly country living, it offered him a slower pace that fit his temperament. Tracy, who was never comfortable in cities or suburbs, longed for the rural lifestyle he had experienced during his boyhood summers in Vermont and was not afraid to get his hands dirty in the process. John, like many urban artists, found the natural beauty and tranquility of the countryside reinvigorating for his creative muse.

The Ramblers' urban exodus was in part a self-conscious move to distance themselves socially as well as musically from modern life and mass culture, points John alluded to in his notes to their *Rural Delivery No. 1* album. That all three Ramblers now had families to support added a pragmatic incentive to their choice of locale. By the mid-1960s New York and other Northeast cities were experiencing what appeared to many as out-of-control crime, drugs, and crumbling infrastructure; rural and small-town living offered the promise of a simpler, safer, and cheaper environment for raising a family. Their embrace of country living did not, however, reflect the utopian idealism that characterized Pete Seeger's Beacon homestead or the communal counterculture aspirations of soon-to-be-realized projects like Stephen Gaskin's Tennessee Farm. In 1965 each Rambler wanted his own space with his respective nuclear family; the idea of communal rural living, a configuration some musicians would experiment with in the later 1960s, was never considered, nor was there an effort to settle in close proximity to one another.

Abandoning the city for the farm was totally congruous with the group's aspirations to make "handmade" music in a "homey atmosphere" that stood in stark opposition to mass-produced entertainment. But living in the country only made sense if each Rambler stayed close to the network of urban clubs, colleges, and recording facilities that provided the band's livelihood. Thus, John, Mike, and Tracy remained in the Northeast, in relatively close proximity to New York City. The idea of actually living in the southern Appalachians, the wellspring of their music, was simply impractical and perhaps not altogether desirable, particularly for John. It would be decades later, and years after the Ramblers ceased to work as a touring and recording band, that Mike and Tracy would make their respective moves to southern Appalachian communities in Virginia and West Virginia.

Meanwhile, Moe Asch, frustrated over stagnant Folkways sales figures, reached an agreement with Verve Records, a subsidiary of the record giant MGM. Beginning in early 1965, select Folkways albums would be repackaged under the Verve/ Folkways label and marketed and distributed by MGM. New material, with Asch's approval, could also be released under the arrangement.[4] The risk for artists like the Ramblers was that they would give up the total control of cover art and notes that they had enjoyed on their earlier Folkways LPs. That risk was balanced by the hope that MGM's superior distribution networks would result in a significant uptick in record sales.

One of the first Verve/Folkways LPs released that spring was the Ramblers' *Rural Delivery No. 1* (FV 9003, 1965). The cover featured one of John's most contemplative Kentucky photographs—a shot of two rural mailboxes, backgrounded by a farmer with his workhorse traversing a field bordered by an empty coal train (the same photograph appeared on the original Folkways issue of *Rural Delivery No. 1*, FA 2496, which carried a 1964 release date; see figure 15). On the back cover each individual Rambler was allotted a brief personal statement, but, unlike their previous releases, the notes to the songs are thin, listing only personnel and (often incomplete) instrumentation for each number. Fans used to the Ramblers' informative comments on song sources and tuning information, along with their quirky musical and cultural observations, were undoubtedly disappointed with the new format.

Musically, *Rural Delivery No. 1* was uneven, with the instrumental work generally outshining the singing. "Durham's Bull" and "Train on the Island" were rollicking dance tunes, and the unusual harmonica-fiddle unison lead on "Going Down the River" produced a striking sonority. Mike and Tracy's energetic mandolin and guitar interplay on "Rosa Lee McFall" and Mike's guitar work on "The Days of My Childhood Plays" were crisp and compelling. While much of the solo singing was undistinguished at best, Mike and Tracy's bluegrass-tinged duets on "Soldier and the Lady" and "Twenty-one Years" demonstrated a maturing vocal blend, and the tight trio singing on the Carter Family's "Gold Watch and Chain" was perhaps the group's best effort to date. Gauging the record's reception is difficult, since Asch did not include the Verve/Folkways sales figures on the annual Folkways royalty statements that he sent to each of the Ramblers. But a December 1965 statement suggests that under the new Verve distribution scheme approximately 2,500 copies were sold by year's end, a modest improvement over previous releases, which rarely sold more than 1,000 copies per year.[5] Even so, each Rambler received only $130 in royalties for *Rural Delivery No. 1* sales that year, dispelling any expectations that Verve/Folkways sales would bring the group significant financial gain.

On January 30, 1965, the Ramblers played Town Hall with Elizabeth Cotten in a show billed as "Honest-to-Goodness String Music of the Hills."[6] The engage-

THE NEW LOST
CITY RAMBLERS

Rural Delivery Number One

Folkways Records FA 2496

FIGURE 15. Cover to *Rural Delivery No. 1* Folkways LP (1965).
Photograph by John Cohen. Image courtesy of the Ralph Rinzler
Folklife Archives and Collections, Smithsonian Institution.

ment, their first New York City appearance since their fall 1962 stint at Gerde's
Folk City, caught the attention of Robert Shelton, who touted the Ramblers as
the "leading revivers" of southern mountain music in a complimentary *New York
Times* review. But he went on to characterize their arrangements as "musical antiques" from a "golden age of country music" and their sound as reminiscent of
"a scratchy, cherished old 78-r.p.m. disc."[7] While the Ramblers probably chortled
at Shelton's reference to old 78 recordings, they did not appreciate his implication
that they were first and foremost antiquated cultural archaeologists rather than
artists who creatively reinterpreted a particular oeuvre of music. Shelton's *Times*
review reinforced the image of the Ramblers as imitators rather than artists, a
characterization that would haunt them throughout their career. The concert also

underscored the Ramblers' continued economic frustrations; although they could command headline status at a prestigious 1,500-seat New York City venue, ticket prices were a mere two to three dollars. They had agreed to give a portion of the door-income profits to support Oak Publications' production of their recently released songbook, and once Cotten was paid and expenses for promotion and the hall were deducted, each Rambler was left with only $68.

In early February the Ramblers performed with Johnny Cash in Boston's Symphony Hall, continuing to foster one of their few connections to the contemporary Nashville country music scene. They played another dozen engagements at northeastern and midwestern colleges that spring, but tensions between Mike and John were festering. In a letter to Archie Green dated April 30, 1965, John expressed surprise and aggravation at learning that Mike, with help from Tracy, was assembling an album of southern industrial folk songs for Folkways Records and that Green had agreed to write the notes for the collection. John went on to explain that this was a project the Ramblers had been collectively talking about for several years, but now Mike was moving ahead with it on his own. John further complained that Mike had told him flatly, "We are each in business for ourselves," and John worried that this "solo vs group" mentality might well "tear us apart." Green wrote back several weeks later, apologizing for contributing to any group friction. He vowed that on completing the notes for Mike's Folkways album he would refrain from future work with the Ramblers as individuals or as a group in order to "avoid conflicting situations. . . . If possible I wish to concentrate my energy on projects where I can get through the day without tearing myself apart." Green's frustration over John and Mike's inability to resolve their differences was painfully clear.[8]

Tipple, Loom and Rail: Songs of the Industrialization of the South Sung and Played by Mike Seeger, was released on Folkways (FH 5273, 1966) the following year, with Tracy backing Mike on four of the album's sixteen cuts. Mike's well-crafted arrangements of songs documenting the hardships of southern factory, mining, railroad, and cotton mill work, accompanied by Green's engaging historical notes, resulted in an album reminiscent of the Ramblers' earlier *Songs from the Depression* release. Given the subject matter and Tracy's participation, John's objection that the project should have been a Ramblers album was not surprising.

Tipple, Loom and Rail was not, as John was well aware, Mike's first solo endeavor. Since he began playing music full time in 1960, Mike had pursued an active career as a soloist, playing several dozen engagements a year, in between Ramblers tours. In late 1962 Folkways released Mike's first solo album, *Oldtime Country Music* (FA 2325, 1962), featuring him singing and playing the fiddle, banjo, dulcimer, guitar, harmonica, mandolin, and autoharp, with overdubbed instrumental and harmony tracks. The album reflected the typical Ramblers repertoire of southern dance tunes, ballads, and mountain blues, several arranged with unusual instrumental and vocal combinations. A second solo LP entitled *Mike Seeger* was released on Vanguard Records in 1964. Mike played a similar selection of southern dance tunes and traditional songs accompanied on guitar by his wife, Marge, but this time with no additional instrumental or vocal overdubbing. In the liner notes folk song scholar D. K. Wilgus praised Mike's "fidelity to tradition," noting that he "has mastered a range of variations within the tradition, without slavishly imitating individual performances."[9] Commenting in *Sing Out!* on Mike's two solo albums, Jon Pankake concluded that Mike's music was a synthesis of his studied devotion to traditional vocal and instrumental techniques and his own creative sensibilities: "It is now impossible to distinguish in a Seeger performance just where the influence of a Fiddlin' John Carson or an Ernest Stoneman leave and Mike's own interpretive genius takes over; the total effect is that of a smoothly expressive musical whole, and the individual guiding touch is Seeger's alone."[10]

Mike's decision to pursue his dual careers as a member of the Ramblers and a solo artist was motivated by aesthetic and financial concerns. He enjoyed playing old-time music in an ensemble situation rooted in the traditional mountain string band of fiddle, banjo, and guitar with two- or three-part harmony singing. But he also appreciated the solo tradition of singing and playing, which had strong currency among mountain musicians. Playing with the Ramblers and playing as a soloist allowed him to participate in both traditions. On the more practical side, his solo tours and recordings augmented his income and by the mid-1960s accounted for nearly half his annual earnings.

Tensions over artistic and financial competition stemming from Mike's solo career had been a source of friction with John for several years. With Manny Greenhill now serving as the booking agent for both the Ramblers and Mike, John feared that some jobs the Ramblers might have landed if Greenhill had held out for a larger fee ended up going to Mike, who offered struggling promoters a less-expensive solo act. Although Mike maintained the Ramblers always took priority, John saw the former's personal touring commitments occasionally interfering with potential Ramblers engagements.

Mike thought John's concerns were overblown, in part because both John and Tracy were also pursuing their own creative projects apart from the Ramblers. Intrigued by the large numbers of young people he encountered on tour who were trying to take up fiddling, Tracy had approached Moe Asch the previous year about putting together an instructional record for Folkways. Asch agreed, and in 1965 *Learn to Fiddle Country Style with Tracy Schwarz* (Folkways Records FI 8359) was released with an accompanying booklet outlining the rudiments of old-time and bluegrass fiddling. On the record Tracy demonstrated various tunings as well as bowing, double stops, slides, trills, and vibrato technique on simple tunes like "Cripple Creek," "Old Joe Clark," "Soldier's Joy," and "Bonaparte's Retreat." The record moved slowly, but it would continue to sell several hundred copies a year well into the 1970s and fit well with the Ramblers' pedagogical mission of spreading instrumental folk styles. Aside from his fiddle album Tracy was too busy with the Ramblers and with trying to establish his farm to pursue a solo career. As a result, he limited his outside playing to informal sessions with old friends from the Washington folk scene and with local Pennsylvania fiddlers and bluegrass acquaintances.

John, for his part, was constantly juggling a variety of photography and writing projects. Like Mike, he was an avid documenter of traditional music. His extensive fieldwork in eastern Kentucky resulted in several projects focusing on the region's music cultures. His 1959 Folkways album *Mountain Music of Kentucky* (Folkways Records FA 2317, 1960) captured the varied traditional banjo styles of Roscoe Holcomb, Lee Sexton, Willie Chapman, and Granville Bowlin as well as local ballad and church singing. Nat Hentoff, writing for the *Reporter*, commended John's musical choices and informative notes and compared his portfolio of accompanying photographs to Walker Evans's work in *Let Us Now Praise Famous Men*.[11] Wilgus's review in the *Journal of American Folklore* called the recording "excellent" and noted John's "understanding and sympathy in dealing with the folk of the depressed areas around Hazard."[12] In 1962 John recorded and produced a second Folkways album with Holcomb and Virginia banjoist Wade Ward and in 1965 an additional album of Holcomb's music.[13] In the summer of 1964 he and Penny traveled to Peru to photograph and record indigenous musicians, a project that culminated in the Folkways LP *Mountain Music of Peru* (FW 3459, 1966). All John's Folkways productions included extensive liner notes on the musicians, culture, and music featured on the album as well as a sampling of his striking photographs.

In 1962 John returned to Kentucky to shoot black-and-white footage that would eventually become the acclaimed documentary film *The High Lonesome Sound*. A second film, *The End of an Old Song*, captured the life and music of the enigmatic North Carolina balladeer Dillard Chandler. Filmmaking became an increasing preoccupation, and he would eventually produce a dozen films on traditional music.

Sometime in 1964 or early 1965 John was approached by Paul Rothchild of Elektra Records to help assemble two albums of urban old-time musicians. The resulting albums, *Old Time Banjo Project* (EKL 276, 1965) and *String Band Project* (EKL 292, 1965) offer a fascinating glimpse into the escalating urban old-time music scene in the mid-1960s. Six banjoists living at the time in New York (John Cohen,

Peter Siegel, and Winnie Winston), Baltimore (Hank Schwartz), Philadelphia (Bill Vanaver), and Boston (Bob Siggins) were featured on the banjo collection. The string-band compilation casts a wider net to include bands from Minneapolis (Uncle Willie's Brandy Snifters), Los Angeles (Stu Jamieson's Boys and the Dry City Scat Band), Boston (the Mother State Entertainers), and New York (the Spontaneous String Band). The performances were uneven and tended to lack creative arrangements, but the music was generally spirited and certainly demonstrated an attempt to emulate traditional mountain vocal and instrumental styles, modeled after the Ramblers. John characterized the players as relatively young, city-bred individuals who, like the Ramblers in their early days, were dependent on old recordings as sources for their music. Typical were Allan Block, Peter Siegel, Bob Siggins, Eric Thompson, and others who jammed regularly at Block's sandal shop in the Village, an important nexus of old-time music in New York since the late 1950s. John is heard playing banjo and singing on both albums, the second release pairing him with Penny Seeger Cohen on guitar and Bob Mamis, an old friend from the Yale hoots, on fiddle. The Cohen-Cohen-Mamis trio, he noted, had performed at Club 47 in Cambridge between sets of a Roscoe Holcomb show.[14]

In addition to undertaking these record and film projects, John continued to work as a photographer, and occasionally he designed album covers for Folkways Records. Most of John's ventures were related in one way or another to the promotion of old-time music, but because he was not pursuing a separate career as a performer he rationalized that these outside activities did not compete or interfere with his commitment to the Ramblers. He remained the most committed of the three Ramblers to keeping the group together as a full-time recording and performing enterprise.

John's resentment over Mike's solo career was an ongoing tension that would become a factor in the group's eventual demise, but in 1965 their relationship was still manageable. In early May the trio looked forward to their first international tour, which would take them halfway around the world to Australia. Organized through Greenhill's contacts with Australian promoters Brian Nebenzal and Asch's Folkways distributor in Melbourne, Peter Mann, the itinerary called for six performances in Adelaide, Brisbane, Melbourne, and Sydney between May 21 and June 1, 1965. The Ramblers' arrival was touted by Edgar Waters of the *Australian* as "the first contingent in the main wave of the great American Folk singing invasion" to reach Australia. The story went on to explain that in addition to the Ramblers, a second group of American folksingers that included Judy Collins and Josh White had simultaneously landed for a tour. The Ramblers' "remarkable skill and fidelity" in presenting American hillbilly music, surmised Waters, may have accounted for their surprising popularity among Australian university students.[15] After hearing the Ramblers perform, Waters penned a second article for the *Australian*, praising them as "most skillful, versatile musicians" and taking note of their exceptional ability to interpret traditional country music: "It is a marvel of showmanship for these young, highly educated city musicians to put across the unsophisticated country humor of their songs; showing themselves aware of its limitations and lack of sophistication, but not patronizing or sending up the original makers of the songs. . . . The New Lost City Ramblers are in fact ideal folk-song revivalists."[16] A review of their Melbourne concert was equally laudatory, remarking how "their good-natured humor throughout belies a seriousness of the musicians for their music" and noting how they easily adapted to "the vast, half-filled Town Hall, all the more remarkable because they are used to performing in small theaters on university campuses in the United States."[17]

At the suggestion of Mann, the organizer of the Melbourne concert, the four-city tour headlining the Ramblers also included a contingency of Australian folksingers who had recently performed at Sydney's Newport Folk Festival. Gary Shearston, Marian Henderson, and Margaret Kitamura were among the local singers who played traditional British and Australian folk material, which complemented the Ramblers' repertoire of mountain ballads, blues, and string-band music.

Mike recalled that the Ramblers' tour was in marked contrast to the more commercial American entourage led by Judy Collins, which predictably garnered the lion's share of publicity. "It was an echo of what was going on in the American folk revival back home!" he observed. "And we were definitely the underdogs; I believe the other tour just outsold us." According to Tracy, the two tours, often appearing on consecutive nights, simply "killed each other. . . . The natural result was our show suffered, enough to inspire the promoters to cancel the final concert at the Trocadero Theater in Sidney. We protested. They finally relented by tacking a handwritten sign on the concert-hall door directing the audience to the TV studio, our last venue. We then did a live show to the audience in the studio, drinking beer from tea cups, as it was against the law there to drink on camera."

The Ramblers were warmly received by their hosts, reveled in the beer-in-teacups Sydney TV show hosted by ex–Kingston Trio singer David Guard, and enjoyed a back-country tour on the dirt roads between Sydney and Melbourne with Gary Shearston, but Mike concluded that the trip was an "ill-fated adventure" conceived of by naive entrepreneurs like Nebenzal who hoped to jump on the folk music bandwagon. John was more sanguine, recalling the challenge and excitement of playing American folk music in a foreign country. He believed the tour "helped plant the seeds for performing traditional music in Australia." The Ramblers were introduced to the sounds of indigenous Aboriginal singing and didgeridoo music, and John returned with a large primitive bark painting for his collection. The finances were adequate, with each man netting about $1,300 for the two-week excursion.[18]

Following their return to the states in early June, the Ramblers played on two large folk music shows at Lewisohn Stadium and Carnegie Hall in New York, both conceived as overtures to the upcoming Newport Folk Festival. Their appearance at Carnegie Hall was part of the weeklong New York Folk Festival, which featured a variety of contemporary and traditional singers as well as a series of panels led by Archie Green and Sam Charters. The inclusion of electric bluesman Muddy Waters and rock-and-roll pioneer Chuck Berry in the Carnegie Hall extravaganza was a harbinger of things to come in Rhode Island.[19]

Penny Seeger Cohen gave birth to a baby girl on July 18, 1965, at New York University Hospital in Manhattan. Three days later, the couple tucked Sonya Cohen in a basket, placed her in the back seat of their Volkswagen Bug, and headed north to Newport. The Newport Folk Foundation, which now included Mike as a board member and his old friend Ralph Rinzler as field researcher and program coordinator, continued to successfully expand the festival's traditional music component. In 1964 Rinzler claimed to have traveled some 12,000 miles across the United States and Canada, documenting and recruiting Cajun fiddlers, the Alabama Sacred Harp Singers, Nova Scotia fiddlers, and a host of Appalachian banjoists, fiddlers, and ballad singers.[20] The 1965 lineup of roots performers was equally impressive. Kentucky banjoists Roscoe Holcomb and Cousin Emmy, country music legend Maybelle Carter, Texas fiddler Eck Robertson, Appalachian balladeer Horton Barker, Tennessee string-band favorites Kirk and Sam McGee with Fiddling Arthur Smith, and bluegrass pioneer Bill Monroe were among the traditional country artists that the Ramblers had helped locate and/or promote over the past five years. The African American contingent was no less striking, with a Texas work gang, a Mississippi fife and drum ensemble, a South Carolina spiritual group, and a host of influential country bluesmen and songsters, including Mississippi John Hurt, Son House, Mance Lipscomb, and John's old acquaintance, Reverend Gary Davis.

As a board member, Mike had lobbied for more workshops that would provide intimate settings where festival attendees could mingle with traditional artists and experience their music close up.[21] The 1965 festival featured twenty-five daytime workshops spread over Friday and Saturday, covering a plethora of traditional singing and playing styles. Shelton lauded this effort, choosing to devote his entire July 24 *New York Times* review to the workshop activities instead of the main-stage headliners Bob Dylan, Pete Seeger, Joan Baez, Peter, Paul and Mary, Donovan, and Odetta. Noteworthy was the "Blues Origins and Offshoots" session hosted by

Alan Lomax, whom Shelton described as "an articulate, illuminating, fluent, but sometimes maddeningly pedantic host narrator." The workshop, featuring such seemingly disparate participants as Ed Young's Mississippi fife and drum band, Son House, Bill Monroe, Willie Dixon, and Paul Butterfield, "took the listener from primitive African survivals in Mississippi to the electronic razzle-dazzle of big-beat modernity." Shelton chose not to comment on the tussle between Lomax and Albert Grossman, Bob Dylan's manager, who took umbrage at Lomax's snide introduction to the white blues harmonica player Paul Butterfield and his band. Instead, Shelton closed his review commenting that the Butterfield group "proved themselves an exciting present-day link in the long chain of the blues."[22] Lomax's qualms about the inclusion of an electric blues band led by a young white man foreshadowed the storm that would erupt on the Sunday evening main stage, when some members of the Butterfield band would serve as Dylan's accompanists.

Newport proved to be a whirlwind for the Ramblers. They performed a full set at the Thursday evening opening concert, participated in the Friday afternoon string-band workshop, and sang at the Sunday morning performance of religious music. They also accompanied their mentors Carter, Holcomb, Robertson, Cousin Emmy, and Kirk McGee on workshop and concert stages throughout the festival.[23] Individually, Mike led workshops on traditional autoharp, country guitar, and old-time and bluegrass banjo styles; John hosted sessions on ballad swapping and banjo accompaniment; and Tracy oversaw a demonstration of country fiddle and mandolin techniques. A portion of Mike's banjo-style workshop that was captured on tape demonstrated the Ramblers' approach to workshop teaching: "We're going to develop this more or less hysterically—historically," he quipped, then sketched the development of the nineteenth-century frailing (knocking or thumping) and up-picking styles that had currency among white and black southern banjoists. He demonstrated both and played an extended frailing version of "Leather Britches." Following Mike's introduction, Kentucky banjoist Cousin Emmy frailed "Free Little Bird" at breakneck speed. Over the next half hour Mike, Cousin Emmy, and Kirk McGee demonstrated various old-time picking and frailing techniques, interspersed with Mike's commentary. The second half of the workshop, led by Mike and Bob Siggins, focused on the more modern Scruggs-style picking.[24]

The 1965 Newport Folk Festival is best remembered for Dylan's Sunday-night appearance with an electric band featuring Mike Bloomfield and other members of the Butterfield Blues Band. His high-voltage arrangements of "Maggie's Farm" and "Like a Rolling Stone" elicited a kaleidoscope of audience emotions, ranging from fascination and delight to shock and outrage. Supporters of traditional music shouted "Bring back Cousin Emmy," who, accompanied by the Ramblers, had appeared prior to Dylan. Accounts vary, but there is consensus that Pete Seeger, Alan Lomax, and Theo Bikel were fuming at the high decibel level, and a backstage brawl between Seeger and Peter Yarrow was narrowly avoided. The main problem, recalled Mike, who was in the audience, was that the sound system was not properly adjusted to accommodate Dylan's vocals, which were lost in the mix of heavy electric guitars, keyboards, and drums.[25] Pete was particularly vexed, since he had high hopes of Dylan leading the next generation of serious folk songwriters. For him, his young protégé's flamboyant display at Newport was a betrayal, signaling a radical shift not only away from acoustic folk music to an amplified rock-based sound but toward the dark world of the corrupt music industry.

Pete, Lomax, Bikel, and other traditionalists had valid concerns, for by mid-1965 the folk revival as a national movement was showing signs of decline. The days of acoustic folk-styled groups reaching the pop charts were all but over, and national media attention was beginning to dwindle. Many young talents who cut their musical teeth in the folk revival—Roger McGuinn, Gene Clark, and David Crosby of the Byrds; Jerry Garcia and Bob Weir of the Grateful Dead; Grace Slick, Marty Balin, and Jorma Kaukonen of the Jefferson Airplane; Cass Elliot and Denny Doherty of the Mamas and the Papas; John Sebastian of the Lovin' Spoonful; and Janis Joplin, to name but a few—would soon plug in and shape the contours of the 1960s pop and alternative-rock scenes. But laying the blame at Dylan's feet was misguided, for young Americans' appetite for rock music had been growing steadily at the expense of folk music since the Beatles' invasion the previous year. Moreover, as Benjamin Filene has persuasively argued, Dylan's electric style, beginning with his 1965 LP *Bringing It All Back Home* and stretching through his 1997 CD *Time Out of Mind*, remained deeply infused with elements of traditional blues, gospel, and country music.[26] Dylan would never abandon folk music, although the movement's most strident supporters would turn their backs on him.

The Ramblers shared little of Pete's despair over Dylan's performance that night, for they championed the music of hillbilly performers who, in their heyday, were considered stylistic innovators with serious commercial aspirations. Yet the Dylan controversy surely gave them pause, for by mid-1965 Mike, John, and Tracy must have realized that as urban practitioners of a style now considered antiquated to contemporary listeners they would face an uncertain future with the ascendancy of folk rock. They had no more interest in going electric than they had in writing topical folk songs, and they were confident that their small cadre of loyal fans—the ones who shouted "Bring back Cousin Emmy" when Dylan hit his first amplified chord—were not about to abandon them. And, with no aspirations of recording a "hit" tune or playing for arena audiences, they showed little concern that acoustic folk music was no longer topping the record charts or that stylized folk ensembles were no longer able to command large venues. But the national decline of the folk boom might certainly threaten the viability of folk festivals, urban coffeehouses, and college folk clubs, which had been the bread and butter of the Ramblers' livelihood for years. Although specific interest in old-time and bluegrass music showed no signs of abating, whether the infrastructure to support a touring band like the Ramblers could be sustained was far from clear. John, as recently as a few months before Newport, remained optimistic, writing to Archie Green that even though "the folk boom is sort of finished . . . we have more jobs ahead for the next year than we have ever had before."[27]

On another front, the Ramblers could also take pride in the new face of Newport. The folk festival had evolved from a commercial extravaganza to a national showcase for dozens of traditional performers whose music could be experienced in small, interactive settings as well as on formal concert stages. The model of locating, documenting, and preparing traditional artists for festival performance as well as the dignified presentation of those artists in a setting that mixed education and entertainment was the culmination of years of work by the Ramblers, Lomax, and Rinzler. With the addition of traditional craftspeople in 1966, the Newport festival would become, in producer George Wein's words, "a massive organic workshop of folk life."[28] Rinzler would use this model and many Newport veteran performers to stage the first federally supported Smithsonian Festival of American Folklife on the National Mall in Washington in 1967. The event would grow into an annual summer celebration of folk music, dance, and crafts from around America and the world and serve as the prototype for state- and locally funded folk festivals in the ensuing decades. The Ramblers had helped create the modern folk festival, yet their place in the new world of government-funded folk arts was yet to be determined.

While folk music enthusiasts were reeling from Dylan's electrified Newport performance, many folk music scholars were probably surprised when they received their summer issue of the *Journal of American Folklore*. The entire volume was devoted to hillbilly music, a genre that traditional ballad specialists had previously scorned as a commercial bastardization of genuine folk music. In his introduction to the volume, coeditor D. K. Wilgus chided folk music scholars for their myopic vision and underscored the connections between southern oral folk ballads and the songs heard on hillbilly recordings: "We can discover in the professional hillbilly tradition itself a microcosm of at least Southern, Southwestern, and Midland folk tradition—the materials, backgrounds, and experiences of the performers beckon a larger army of folklorists than we are likely to produce in another generation."[29] Among the volume's offerings were provocative articles deconstructing the origins of the paradoxical term hillbilly by Archie Green; a study of the Skillet Lickers' repertoire by Norm Cohen; an introduction to bluegrass by L. Mayne Smith; and a lengthy review of hillbilly recordings by Wilgus.

The Ramblers, longtime champions of hillbilly music, relished academic folklorists' recognition of the music's traditional roots. But Wilgus's record review presented them with something of a conundrum. Since taking the position as the journal's official record review editor in 1959, Wilgus had reviewed hundreds of folk music recordings, including a growing number of reissues of vintage 1920s and 1930s hillbilly and race records. In the 1965 JAF hillbilly issue he reviewed dozens of reissues, including material by Jimmie Rodgers, the Carter Family, Uncle Dave Macon, Grayson and Whitter, and Charlie Poole on small labels like County, Cumberland, and Old-Timey Records. The 1941 *Smoky Mountain Ballads* reissue of recordings that had mesmerized a young John Cohen had been pressed and rereleased as an LP by Victor, bringing back the original sounds by Gid Tanner and Riley Puckett, the Carter Family, Uncle Dave Macon, and J. E. Mainer's Mountaineers.[30] These reissues, along with the dozens of field recordings being produced by Mike, John, Alan Lomax, and others, were reaching the growing legions of urban and college string-band music fans, many of whom had been originally introduced to mountain music through the Ramblers' performances and early Folkways recordings.

Among the small independent labels specializing in old-time and bluegrass music, none was more important than County Records. The company was founded in 1963 by Dave Freeman, a New York City postal worker and avid collector of old 78 records. Freeman's first release, *A Collection of Mountain Fiddle Music* (County 501, 1964), was an anthology of 1920s and 1930s hillbilly recordings made by Charlie Poole, Crockett's Mountaineers, the Leake County Revelers, and numerous other mountain musicians familiar to Ramblers fans. In addition to his historic reissue 500 Series, Freeman's County 700 Series featured newer field recordings of traditional Appalachian fiddle and banjo players, including Tommy Jarrell, Fred Cockerham, Oscar Jenkins, and Kyle Creed. In 1965 Freeman began his successful County Sales mail-order operation, which reached a broad audience of urban and college listeners as well as southern old-time and bluegrass fans.[31]

When the Ramblers started their work in the 1950s, they had to rummage through junk shops and the closets of eccentric record collectors to find old hillbilly 78s or search through libraries for field recordings of traditional mountain music. But by the mid-1960s an abundance of hillbilly and mountain-folk music had become available on LP records that were easily found in many city and college-town record stores or from mail-order companies like County. In their initial years the Ramblers had been the primary conduit between urban audiences and the southern country music of the 1920s and 1930s, but now, with many of the original sources back in print, their Folkways recordings had become one among many choices younger players could turn to. These developments in the record industry, along with the proliferation of traditional mountain performers at folk festivals like Newport and on the coffeehouse circuits, begged the inevitable question: was a city-bred group like the Ramblers still necessary to "interpret" southern mountain music to northern audiences, who were increasingly experiencing the real thing live and on records? Had their hard work sown the seeds of their eventual demise?

The Ramblers pressed on undaunted for the remainder of the summer, presenting a program at the Shakespeare Theater in Stratford, Connecticut, in early August, followed by a brief West Coast stint that ended with two nights at the Ash Grove. In the Bay Area they performed in late August as part of the month-long Marin County Summer Festival of the Arts, a series that included presentations of ballet, modern dance, contemporary composers, mime, modern drama, and jazz. The idea that folk music and jazz might be programmed as part of an elite arts festival in Marin County at Lewisohn Stadium (presented in conjunction with the Metropolitan Opera) and in the affluent suburban town of Stratford (presented in conjunction with the Shakespeare Theater) seemed to signal a loosening of cultural boundaries that had traditionally drawn sharp distinctions between cultivated and vernacular arts. In this new environment the Ramblers hoped to be received as a chamberlike ensemble that could accurately reproduce the repertoire and performance practices of late-nineteenth- and early-twentieth-century Appalachian folk music. The concept was intriguing and the pay reasonable ($600 for the group per program that summer), but such opportunities still proved to be few and far between in the mid-1960s.

While Mike was in England in January 1965, performing solo, he again approached promoter Roy Guest about bringing the Ramblers over later in the year. In August, when Moe Asch finally reached an agreement with Tom Paley over rights to the New Lost City Ramblers name, the way was clear for a three-week tour, which began in late September 1965. Guest, working through local folk song clubs, was able to set up eighteen engagements over three weeks, including shows at the Cecil Sharp House in London; at halls in Manchester, Cambridge, Norwich, Leeds, and Kensington; and at a number of small-town venues. Mike's January tour, his sister Peggy's popularity in English folk music circles, and Dylan's much-ballyhooed spring 1965 tour helped generate interest. The Ramblers' opening concert was in Romsford, where they played with Bill Clifton, a Baltimore-born bluegrass singer and promoter who had been an important link between the folk revival and bluegrass before relocating in England. The British fan magazine *Country & Western*

Roundup touted the Romsford show as "an evening of pure old-time country music and bluegrass, without any modern trimmings" that ended with "thunderous applause for the audience and shouts of 'More.'"[32] In Norwich a reviewer admired the Ramblers' "mixture of racy, uninhibited American bluegrass and country music," praised their "relaxed and entertaining stage presence," and proclaimed their first England tour a smashing success that warranted another visit.[33] The Ramblers were well received on the rest of the tour, often playing for folk clubs in small towns like Birtly, Redcar, and Matluck. "Small halls were what England was about," recalled John. "Little tiny towns and a pub, and everybody was starting a folk club, . . . people standing around in their overcoats, drinking their pints and singing—that was the ambience . . . that was the grassroots nature of the English folk revival."[34] Mike was so impressed that he reported back to *Sing Out!* readers, "We need more informal (less show-biz like) outlets such as the very popular community folk clubs in Britain."[35] But the small venues meant modest remuneration, and several times John and Tracy were irked to find posters advertising the group as "Mike Seeger and the New Lost City Ramblers." Mirroring their experience in the States, the Ramblers found small but enthusiastic British audiences for the music but minimal financial return. After travel expenses each Rambler netted only $570.

After returning to the States the Ramblers spent a relatively quiet fall as John and Tracy worked to prepare their new country homes for the winter. The Ramblers ended 1965 in a New Jersey studio recording an episode for the educational television folk music series *Rainbow Quest*, hosted by Pete Seeger. A single camera panned in on the three Ramblers, dressed in their familiar vests and ties, sitting around an old wooden table at the center of an austere set apparently designed to evoke the ambience of a simple country kitchen. While the Ramblers played "Stone Mountain Rag," Pete looked on approvingly from his old-timey rocking chair, eyeing a very wholesome-looking bottle of milk prominently displayed at the center of the table. The Ramblers ran through seven pieces, each prefaced with a low-key introduction apparently meant to educate listeners about Appalachian music and instruments. Pete rocked away, occasionally interjecting an inquisitive comment, and finally poured some milk into an old-fashioned tin cup. The program ended with the elder Seeger joining the Ramblers to sing "I Never Will Marry" and then to play mandolin on a medley of jaunty fiddle tunes. While the instrumental work was well executed and the harmony singing tight, the spoken interludes were stiff and self-conscious, with all three Ramblers occasionally lapsing into slightly affected folky accents. With the exception of the final fiddle tune, the show failed to capture the spirit of down-home, informal music making that Pete hoped would set it apart from the Hollywood production values of the *Hootenanny* show. Clearly, it would take more than an antique rocking chair and a bottle of milk on a farm-kitchen table to create a television environment conducive to the spontaneity of traditional music making. Despite Pete's good intentions, with no live audience the *Rainbow Quest* episode simply fell flat. The Ramblers did not appear on television again for years.[36]

John's earlier letter to Archie Green expressing optimism that the Ramblers had more work than ever was not quite accurate. They performed approximately sixty shows in 1965, as opposed to seventy the previous year. But John's before-expenses Ramblers performance income was up from $6,000 in 1964 to approximately $8,000 in 1965. Mike's Folkways royalties from sales of Ramblers albums increased slightly from $500 in 1964 to $550 in 1965, as *Rural Delivery No. 1* sold over 2,500 copies (for which each Rambler received only five cents a record). In addition to his Ramblers touring income, Mike grossed nearly $5,000 in 1964 and $6,000 in 1965 from his solo performances.

In early 1966, perhaps to make sense of the ongoing role of tradition in the urban revival shaken by Dylan's folk rock transformation, Mike wrote a critical essay for *Sing Out!* titled "A Contemporary Folk Esthetic." Refining ideas introduced in the liner notes of earlier Ramblers recordings, Mike encouraged urban folksingers to pay attention to the elements of textual composition (lyrics), musical composition (folk tunes), and performance or arrangement style. According to his narrative, the urban revival of the 1940s, dominated by political causes, and the current scene so preoccupied with commercial gain had lost touch with traditional folk aesthetics, particularly performance style. He acknowledged that American folk music was part of a living, dynamic process in which the composition of new folk material has always been the norm. Thus, he viewed portions of the current singer-songwriter trend as healthy and natural extensions of a centuries-old process. Dylan, who early in his career had immersed himself in many styles of traditional music, initially "wrote songs that are not only good but are virtually folk in identity." But much of Dylan's new material—"now part of the Urban Electrification Program"—was dismissed by Mike as "pop-rock" that was "simply no longer even folk-based." Mike expressed his preference for contemporary songwriters like Ewan MacColl (now the husband of his sister Peggy), whose knowledge of folk idioms resulted in new pieces that were natural "extension[s] of tradition." Even popular country singers Johnny Cash, Roger Miller, Buck Owens, and Jim Nesbitt had produced admirable "folk-based" songs. Mike closed on an ominous note, warning that the corrosive forces of popular entertainment would prevail if urban performers (like the Ramblers) faltered in their mission to foster awareness for diverse traditional styles and if informal hoots, coffeehouses, and folk clubs did not continue to provide a strong community base for the music.[37]

Mike's discussion of folk aesthetics was based heavily on performance style while ignoring the question of cultural context, a concept that was rapidly coming to redefine the parameter of folk authenticity for a new generation of academically trained folklorists and folk music scholars. One of the first to clearly articulate the context issue was folklorist Alan Dundes. In 1964 he called for a fresh way of conceptualizing folklore in an article appropriately titled "Texture, Text, and Context." Dundes proposed three levels of analysis: "texture"—linguistic and stylistic features (similar to what Charles Seeger and Lomax had referred to as "style" with regard to folk song); "text"—the item of lore itself (what Mike referred to as the lyrics and tune with regard to folk song); and "context"—the social situation in which an item of lore is actually performed.[38] As Neil Rosenberg later observed, this new approach to folklore, with its emphasis on the social context of performance and the cultural background of the performers, would prove problematic for urban folk revivalists who were geographically and culturally disconnected from the music they played.[39] Even groups like the Ramblers, who had meticulously studied folk performance style, could hardly lay claim to folk authenticity if the new criteria defined genuine "folk" as those who grew up and learned their music in its original social setting. The middle-class suburbs of New York and Washington were simply not rural Appalachia.

The issue of context as a marker of authenticity was painfully clear in another 1966 essay on the folk revival written by folklorist Ellen Stekert. Once a folksinger herself, Stekert had pursued a scholarly career, initially studying folklore at Indiana University, where the patriarch of postwar academic folklore, Richard Dorson, routinely dismissed the revival as "fakelore."[40] In an attempt to clarify the increasingly heterogeneous city folk scene of the mid-1960s, Stekert devised a classification system clearly shaped by the new contextual sensibility, defining traditional singers as "those who have learned their songs and their style of presentation from oral tradition as they grew up." A second group of city singers, somewhat dismissively labeled as "imitators" by Stekert, carefully studied traditional styles and repertoires by "immersing themselves in the aesthetic of a culture different from their own." Such urban, middle-class, educated, and white imitators could not possibly be authentic, she explained: "Think twice, and nothing seems more incongruous than John Cohen of the posh suburbs of New York City's 'West Egg' [F. Scott Fitzgerald's fictitious name for Great Neck, Long Island, in The Great Gatsby] singing in old-time style with the New Lost City Ramblers."[41] Reflecting twenty-five years later on her piece, Stekert expressed regret at her use of the "unconsciously disparaging" term imitator but admitted that at the time (1966) she was genuinely "puzzled by people such as John Cohen and Mike Seeger, who were beginning to take on the mannerisms of the southern mountaineers whose music they were beginning to master," and that she still had trouble "see[ing] beyond imitation to the potentials for creativity in their approach."[42]

During their initial years the Ramblers had found strong advocates for their work among respected folklorists such as Charles Seeger, D. K. Wilgus, Alan Lomax, and Archie Green. But the new crop of academically trained folklorists, many of whom, like Stekert, had come to the study of folklore through the folk music revival, privileged context and performance and thus were wary of city-bred folk performers who learned their music from recordings and performed primarily at urban coffeehouses and college hoots. While the Ramblers would continue to play for college audiences, they received little attention or support from members of the expanding ranks of academic folklorists and ethnomusicologists with whom they had hoped to form alliances. Dorson's disdain for the 1960s folk revival cast a long shadow—in 1976 another of his students, Jan Brunvand, pronounced that folk song revivalists were "largely irrelevant to the study of folklore" in his widely read *Folklore: A Study and Research Guide*.[43]

Sometime in 1965 the Ramblers met with Chris Strachwitz, an Austrian-born record collector and founder of the Bay Area–based Arhoolie Records, and Horst Lippmann, a German music promoter. In 1962 Lippmann and his associate Fritz Rau had brought American bluesmen Muddy Waters, Memphis Slim, Sonny Terry, and Brownie McGhee to Germany. Strachwitz had convinced the Germans to host a tour of traditional American country music and with the help of the Ramblers wanted to assemble an entourage that would include the Stanley Brothers, Roscoe Holcomb, Cousin Emmy, and Cyp Landreneau's Cajun band. A deal was reached for a February–March 1966 tour in Germany, Switzerland, Sweden, Denmark, and England. John, who was enthusiastic about the tour, was asked by Strachwitz to attend to the details of contacting artists, signing contracts, and procuring passports for those artists who had never been out of the country.

In February 1966 the Ramblers made a junket to the University of Chicago Folk Festival and several midwestern colleges before returning east for two warm-up shows with the tour participants at New York's Fashion Institute and the Boston Winter Festival. Between the two engagements the entire touring cast was taped for Pete's *Rainbow Quest*. On February 27 the musicians flew to Germany and began their tour in Baden-Baden by taping the television show *Volksmusik der Welt*, which Tracy narrated as best he could using the broken German he had learned during his military stint. During the next twenty days the group traveled by chartered bus and plane through five countries. On the long bus rides the Ramblers deepened their acquaintances with the artists they had revered for years, reveling in magical moments like the time Ralph Stanley and Roscoe Holcomb sang old Baptist hymns together. For Mike, who had borrowed a portable tape recorder to capture reminiscences of the Stanley Brothers, the tour resembled "a great three-week working party."

John recalled that it was a challenge to present "a rough-edge spectrum of American down-home [country] music" to German audiences who were more familiar with African American blues than mountain or hillbilly music. Mike remembered that the European audiences were "probably perplexed" by some of their music; the crowds did not always know what to make of Cousin Emmy's flamboyant stage behavior and may have heard the Cajun music as slightly "out of tune and a little dissonant." The March 11 show at London's Royal Albert Hall drew several thousand British folk music fans and generally positive reviews. One observer who characterized the show as a "solid" musical success did complain about the "bumpkin brand of humor" that the audience had to endure. Another slightly more cynical critic praised the "genuine feeling about real life" conveyed by the music but sniped that the program was "essentially a museum piece which can endure even in its native Appalachia only so long as President Johnson's war on poverty is unsuccessful there."[44]

A compilation documenting the tour, released by the Bear Family label in 2007, presents a sampling of live performances and an audio window into the staging of the program, which presented a breadth of traditions, from backwoods hymn singing and banjo tunes to the stage-savvy routines of the Stanley Brothers and Cousin Emmy. John opened the show with a brief welcome to what he identified as "a concert of traditional country music," lamenting that much of this music was not well known in America because it was no longer a part of our mass culture. "It's people who are holding on to their own way of life, their own way of living, and their own ideas of music. It's music from the country, from the south, or the mountains, or a farm somewhere." He introduced the Stanley Brothers and about fifteen minutes later returned to invite Holcomb to the stage to line a haunting Baptist hymn. John consciously presented Holcomb as a genuine tradition bearer from the hills who "doesn't consider himself to be a musician at all. He considers himself to be a working man first, he works with his hands. . . . He says that he just plays music to help pass the time. And when you hear his music you'll understand that it's a very different kind of time that we're talking about. His name is Roscoe Holcomb, and he comes from way back in the mountains of Kentucky." Following Holcomb's set of solo banjo tunes, Carter Stanley returned John's favor by introducing the Ramblers, identifying them as "city boys, but they play country music and play it well, that's the truth." The Ramblers played a lively set, interspersing their songs with snippets of historical background and jokes, including a pitch for their "thirteen long-playing short-selling Folkways records." Just how much the German audience understood lines like "Here's a song called 'Our Cow Gave No Milk So We Had to Sell Him'" or "Here's another one called 'I'm So Lonesome in the Saddle since My Horse Died'" was not clear. John brought on Cyp Landreneau's Cajun Band, comparing the joys of a Louisiana "Bal du Maison" to the Garden of Eden, followed by Mike's introduction of Cousin Emmy as a "star of hillbilly radio." The finale featured the entire entourage playing "Chicken Reel" while Chick Stripling of the Stanley Brothers, Cousin Emmy, and Landreneau took turns showing off their fancy country flat-foot dancing to the delight of the audience, who responded with enthusiastic applause.

The travel arrangements and accommodations were superior to what the Ramblers were used to in the States, where they continued to do a good deal of traveling by car and often stayed with friends or in cheap hotels. All airfare, hotels, and food expenses were included in the original agreement, so each Rambler cleared just over $1,000 for the three-week commitment. But perhaps more important, as John later recalled, "for the New Lost City Ramblers this tour was a dream-fulfilling trip, surrounded by so many of the musicians who had inspired us. It was a way of getting the message out . . . and although the tour was probably not a financial and audience-packed success, once again we were ahead of the curve, a prophetic moment and remembrance of things to come." John's recollections were accurate, for it would still be several years before this sort of "roots music" tour would be organized in the States.[45]

After returning to the States the Ramblers spent a busy spring and summer touring colleges in the Northeast and Midwest, stopping on the East Coast long enough to play at the Brandeis Folk Festival, Princeton, and a May 4 Boston antiwar benefit organized by the Students for a Democratic Society. In search of an appropriate song for such a political event, John dusted off "Battleship Maine," introducing it as a song about "America's first imperialist war."[46] In late June and early July a California tour was sandwiched around a pair of week-long stints at the Ash Grove. In July only Mike attended the 1966 Newport Folk Festival, where he hosted workshops on folk guitar, country music, and steel guitar and sang in a "ballad topping" competition.

In early August 1966 the Ramblers regrouped in Pequot, Connecticut, to work on material for their fourth album with Tracy. The resulting LP, *Remembrance of Things to Come*, appeared in early 1967 as a Verve/Folkways release (FT/FTS 3018). As with *Rural Delivery No. 1*, no program notes were inserted; commentary on songs and sources was limited to the back cover. While *Sing Out!* characterized *Remembrance of Things to Come* as "uneven" and "mostly unexciting," a close listen suggests otherwise.[47] The album opened with an unusual rendition of "Soldier's

FIGURE 16. German tour, 1966. Standing (left to right): Cyprien Landreneau, Adam Landreneau, Mike Seeger, Carter Stanley, Roscoe Holcomb, George Shuffler, Ralph Stanley, Cousin Emmy, Donny Miller, Revon Reed, Tracy Schwarz. Kneeling in front: John Cohen. Photograph by John Cohen.

Joy" borrowed from the Crook Brothers, whose early recording doubled the fiddle and mouth harp on the melodic line. Tracy's shuffling fiddle melded with Mike's chugging mouth harp and John's hammering banjo to propel the tune forward, while the perfectly balanced stereo mix maintained the distinctive timbre and subtle melodic variations of each of the three instruments. The result was an extraordinarily fresh arrangement of an old standard. The vocal trio on the Carter Family's tragic ballad "Titanic" was relaxed and flawlessly blended, absent the self-conscious oversinging that occasionally plagued earlier recordings. A bluesy version of "Single Girl" attributed to Roscoe Holcomb featured Mike's intricate three-finger banjo picking and high, tense singing reminiscent of early bluegrass styles. Mike and Tracy sang the British ballad "Lord Bateman," learned from an LOC recording of Kentucky singer Pleaz Mobley, as a close-harmony duet. "We hope in our phrasing we have retained some of the weird old-time qualities of the original performances," observed Mike in the liner notes.[48] Tracy contributed a haunting a cappella rendition of "The Sioux Indians," a modal cowboy ballad recounting a bloody battle between a westward-bound wagon train and a band of Native Americans. The album also included the Ramblers' first foray into Cajun music, with double fiddles and triangle accompanying Mike's singing on "Parlez-Nous [sic] a Boire," learned from the Louisiana fiddler Dewey Balfa. Mike was far from mastering the vocal nuances of Cajun singing, but the piece reveals the group's ongoing search for new styles and sounds. Cajun music was relatively unknown outside the South at the time, and the Ramblers' recording of "Parlez-Nous a Boire" helped to introduce the music to urban and college audiences.[49]

Remembrance of Things to Come reflected a further maturing of the Ramblers' sound in the four years since Tracy joined the group. Their voices blended increasingly well, especially on Tracy and Mike's duets. Peter Bartok's recording and sequencing of the tracks were superb. The variety of vocal styles and instrumental configurations flows seamlessly from cut to cut, creating a satisfying wholeness that had not been achieved on the earlier LPs with Tracy.

Following the recording session for *Remembrance of Things to Come* the Ramblers were off to perform at the Mariposa Folk Festival in Canada. Their next stop was Washington, DC, where on August 10, 1966, they joined their old friend Archie Green on the terrace steps of the Smithsonian Institution's Museum of History and Technology. The program, titled "Old-Time Music, 1880–1945," was part of the outdoor summer-concert series Making Music—American Style sponsored by the Smithsonian. The series had grown out of a new initiative by Smithsonian secretary S. Dillon Ripley to make the National Mall more accessible to the public in hopes of increasing visitation to the museums. In 1966 Ripley hired James Morris to develop a series of public performances on the National Mall, which in addition to the Ramblers' folk music presentation would include programs on American military band music, New Orleans jazz, and eighteenth-century American music.[50] The gathering was well publicized, and Mike would recall during an interview the following year with a British journalist that about two thousand people turned out to hear "this illustrated lecture on American country music."[51]

Green's plainspoken, folksy delivery coupled with his astounding knowledge of folk and country music made him the perfect choice to introduce the program to the large audience that gathered that summer evening. His opening remarks connected hillbilly recordings, American folk music, and the urban folk music revival with the emerging movement for government preservation of American folklife. Green began with background on the semantically complex term *hillbilly*, explaining its paradoxical usage as both a pejorative and a humorous expression among poor southern whites. He invited the audience not only to experience the deep emotions evoked by the hillbilly music they were about to hear but also to consider the role such music might play in contemporary urban society:

> As America moves in the direction of airports, launching pads, and concrete highways, we have a tendency to get away from lawns and fields. We either hang onto rural folkways and rural music to remind us of a very beautiful past—here there is a lot of nostalgia in our approach—or we modify the music. I would submit that Nashville feels the necessity to bring country music into contemporary life. Many people from rural cultures do not want to be reminded of their rural past. Folk fans, folk song enthusiasts, the New Lost City Ramblers, and the folks at the Library of Congress, in contrast, want to preserve old forms. And this beautiful building behind me is dedicated to preserving portions of the past. As you listen to hillbilly music, think, what does it mean to you? Is it simply nostalgia? Or is it a reminder that there are many values in rural life that we need today.[52]

Green pointed out that American folk music in general and hillbilly music in particular are not "pure" Anglo-American forms but rather an amalgamation of diverse cultural influences. He challenged listeners to hear strains of Irish, Scottish, African, and Latin materials in the Ramblers' songs and proudly concluded that "[folk] music is probably the most integrated aspect of American life." Later he asked Mike to do a hillbilly blues song and talked more about the interchange between black and white southern musicians. Green deftly contextualized the Ramblers' work within the rhetoric of cultural preservation and cultural diversity, the ideological cornerstones that would undergird the soon-to-be-realized Smithsonian Festival of American Folklife and the expansion of government-sponsored folk arts programming over the next decade.

The Ramblers opened with a snappy rendition of the aforementioned fiddle-harmonica arrangement of "Soldier's Joy" and moved into their illustrated lecture on mountain music. Tracy prefaced his rendition of "The Sioux Indians" with a brief explanation of a cappella balladry; Mike reviewed the importance of the folk fiddle and played a drowning version of "Bonaparte's Retreat"; John recounted the history of the banjo among mountain musicians before performing "Black Jack Daisy." Tracy and Mike displayed the early fiddle-banjo sound on the dance piece "Sally Anne," followed by a demonstration of thumbpicked guitar melody on the Carter Family tune "Rambling Boy." Next, Mike delivered a brief history of the autoharp, which he used to accompany the ballad "Fair and Tender Ladies." The program eased into a more standard Ramblers set with shorter introductions and sarcastic puns interjected between a variety of mountain material, including pieces heavily influenced by blues, gospel, and ragtime as well as several early bluegrass songs.

A moment of potential tension occurred when John introduced the song "Battleship Maine":

> It's not too often we get to sing between the White House and the Capitol. So we'd like to do a song that's kind of ripe with history, almost rank. . . . We found it on an old record from the 1920s, maybe the early 1930s—the name of the song is "The Battleship Maine." And it's all about how people were still singing in those days about the sinking of the ship in Cuba Harbor. That was a fightin' event, and America went to war over it. Nobody ever figured out who sunk the ship or how it got sunk, but everybody had to fight. It was a historic moment in American foreign policy. It marked a change; it was the first time America was seeking peace on foreign shores. And this song was more or less from the point of view of a mountain fella who didn't want to go to fightin' in a war he didn't understand anything about. Sound kind of contemporary, doesn't it? Here's "The Battleship Maine."

While John never mentions Vietnam, the implications of his historical narrative, delivered on the National Mall in the summer of 1966 as the antiwar movement was ramping up, were clear. The Smithsonian organizers undoubtedly did not appreciate John's interjection of the politically sensitive topic, given their goal of presenting folk music to the public as a fragile vessel brimming with American heritage and in need of preservation rather than as a vehicle for contemporary social protest. Fortunately for the organizers, the remark was not mentioned by Library of Congress worker Joseph Hickerson, who covered the concert for the *Washington Evening Star*. Hickerson commended Green and the Ramblers for offering an alternative perspective to that of the commercial country music business, one that "seek[s] to preserve, study, and perform the music in its own terms, often as a reminder of an otherwise disappearing past." He closed his review by calling for more programs of this sort, "especially when the participants are as successful for combining erudition and talent as were Archie Green and the New Lost City Ramblers last night at the Smithsonian Institution."[53]

In retrospect, the 1966 Smithsonian "Old-Time Music" program was a warm-up for the first Festival of American Folklife, which would take place the following summer after Rinzler was hired by the Smithsonian in the spring of 1967 to organize the event. But the Ramblers would not be invited to the first great celebration on the Mall; only Mike would participate under the guise of a consultant-presenter, not a performer. Rinzler's reluctance to program city-bred folk musicians like the Ramblers foreshadowed a contentious debate over authenticity and the folk music revival that will be returned to in the next chapter.

The Ramblers spent the remainder of 1966 playing a dozen engagements around the Northeast at colleges and coffeehouses. In early 1967 they embarked on their fourth international tour in three years, one that would turn out to be their last for several decades. Eric Winter, writing for the British publication *Music Maker*, described a flourishing country music scene that would welcome the Ramblers. They arrived in February for a three-week tour of the United Kingdom that opened at the prestigious five-thousand-seat Royal Albert Hall. Picking up on the earlier rhetoric of American reviewers, Winter characterized the Ramblers as "re-creators of old-timey music" whose greatest achievement was "a mammoth rescue operation, snatching from the jaws of a jukebox society and the swamp of banality some of the finest music in the US tradition." While noting that the Ramblers "re-create with meticulous care" the hillbilly styles of a bygone era, he added, "It was not mere copying of the style, but a breathing of new life into [it]."[54] Tony Wilson, writing for *Melody Maker*, explained to his British readers that the Ramblers had not jumped on the folk-rock bandwagon. Unlike the legions of "folkniks" who "swapped their banjos for electric guitars," the Ramblers remained part of "a small band of dedicated musicians who refuse to compromise at any price." Mike told Wilson that after eight years of playing together the Ramblers sometimes felt like "old-timers" themselves who "stand out on the American folk scene" because of their commitment to traditional music. In response to Wilson's query about U.S. government support for folk music, Mike mentioned the previous year's Smithsonian presentation, and John opined, "We need someone to encourage cultural organizations to represent American traditional music."[55]

Reviews of the winter 1967 tour were consistently positive. Peter Coulston of *Country News and Views* attended the opening Albert Hall show and reported a well-balanced set that concluded with a spirited rendition of "Orange Blossom Special," "complete with train noise, etc, all coming from Tracy's fiddle."[56] The Ramblers' final March 1 concert at Leeds Town Hall was touted as "superb" by Mike Stott, who lauded the Ramblers' multi-instrumental prowess, describing them as "technically brilliant." He indicated that the Ramblers were quite comfortable with their British audiences and praised them for "presenting such a spontaneous act, and creating such an informal atmosphere even among an audience as large as this."[57] Between the London and Leeds dates the Ramblers played nine shows, including engagements at large halls in Birmingham, Manchester, and Worcester; at the latter two they shared the stage with the popular

British folk group the Watersons. Drawing on archetypal rural American imagery, a reviewer at one of the Watersons' concerts described the Ramblers as "reviv[ing] epoch-making performances given long ago in crowded Western kitchens and barns, whose memory is still intensely alive."[58] Audiences were larger than those during the Ramblers' 1965 tour and no less enthusiastic, but pay remained modest. After travel and housing expenses each Rambler netted slightly under $600 for the three weeks of work.

The Ramblers told Coulston that they hoped to record an LP in London during their stay, leading him to report to his *Country New and Views* readers that a deal "was almost definite."[59] The group's frustration had been growing for several years over Asch's lackluster efforts to distribute Ramblers recordings in the States and abroad. Before their departure for England, John had written to Asch, complaining, "I think I realize how your energies have been going toward Verve and the other arrangements you have with Scholastic, but I don't think that our sales on Folkways should stop on account of this. I know that this is not intentional on your part, or that you desire it; yet faced with the prospects of no returns for our records I don't know what to do."[60] On arriving in England, the group was further disturbed to find that Ramblers albums were more readily available on the bootleg Ember label, which paid no royalties to the Transatlantic label with whom Asch had made arrangements for Folkways U.K. distribution. While in London the Ramblers contacted Fontana Records, a company that had expressed an interest in signing the group to make a U.K. recording. But after apprising Asch of the potential deal they received a stern reproach. Asch dashed off a letter to John in London, reminding him that the Ramblers had an exclusive contract with Folkways and that a lawsuit against Fontana would ensue unless he approved any agreement. "Don't do anything rash. . . . I fight for you as long as you play fair with me," Asch warned.[61] The Ramblers reluctantly turned down the Fontana offer.

While the exact sales numbers of Ramblers records on Verve/Folkways and Scholastic/Folkways are difficult to chart, the Ramblers' respective ledger books reveal that their income from Folkways royalties had indeed been steadily declining since 1965 and would remain relatively insignificant in comparison with the money they made as a touring band. The Ramblers' decision to remain with Folkways over the years in the face of disappointing record sales had little to do with contractual agreements and much to do with the freedom that Asch had given them in recording, producing, and designing their albums. John, always the artist, conceived of each Ramblers album as a total creative project and would later reflect that "working with Folkways was like having a show in a gallery. Moe gave us a place, a venue to display our work and to distribute our work and to get it to people. And for us to articulate our ideas about music and of course to capture our performances. It was all part of a system, and we were lucky to have Folkways, which allowed us to do it."[62]

Upon returning to the States the Ramblers resumed their regular schedule of club and college engagements and at folk festivals in Ft. Lauderdale, Philadelphia, and Newport. Their July 1967 performance at the Newport folk festival was their last at the venue that helped launch their career in 1959. Several months earlier the Ramblers made one of their rare southern appearances when they returned to the University of Virginia at Charlottesville. The program, billed as the Southern Folk Festival, was organized by Student Nonviolent Coordinating Committee activists and singers Anne Romaine and Bernice Johnson Reagon. The biracial concert featured blueswoman Mabel Hillary, spiritual singers Reverend Pearly Brown and Reagon, mountain balladeer Esther Lefever, and the Ramblers. "A large crowd greeted the ethnic freshness and diversity with sustained enthusiasm," reported the *Virginia Weekly* under a large picture of the Ramblers, who prior to the concert led a workshop in southern mountain music.[63] The early-April concert was a benefit to kick off a tour of southern folk music sponsored by Romaine and Reagon's Southern Folk Culture Revival Project, and the Ramblers' contribution would earn them an invitation to join the tour the following spring.

In the summer of 1967 the group made a few ventures into the political arena. In late July they performed at a benefit for striking textile workers in Wilmington, North Carolina. Although the strike was ultimately unsuccessful, the experience was memorable. The Ramblers played for a spirited, racially mixed crowd of union workers in a hall in the black section of Wilmington. This audience, unlike the bemused city listeners for whom the Ramblers usually performed Dorsey Dixon's "Weave Room Blues," understood the textile-mill references in the song:

> With your looms a-slamming, shuttles bouncing on the floor,
> When you flag your fixer, you can see that he is sore;
> Trying to make a living, but I'm thinking I will lose,
> For I'm sent a-dying with them weave-room blues.

Another southern industrial song by Dave McCarn, "Cotton Mill Colic," brought a tumultuous response when Mike sang:

> No use to colic, no use to rave,
> We'll never rest till we're in our grave.
> I'm a-gonna starve, and everybody will,
> 'Cause you can't make a living at a cotton mill.

The experience was exhilarating for the Ramblers. The songs they had been singing for years seemed instantaneously authenticated when performed for striking southern mill workers, the very sorts of people whose miseries had inspired the original Depression era pieces.

A month later the trio appeared at the Conference for New Politics in Chicago, a gathering of antiwar, civil rights, and feminist activists that included Martin Luther King, Jr., Dr. Benjamin Spock, and Dick Gregory. Tracy recalled that the gathering was strained by internal disputes among the organizers and that the Ramblers' music did not seem particularly "useful" in the context of such a political event.[64] John, for his part, saw nothing incongruent about the Ramblers playing at an antiwar rally, since their general status as folksingers seemed to automatically presuppose leftist sentiments and their reputation as the gurus of old-time mountain music placed them outside the mainstream "establishment."[65] That said, apart from a few novelty songs like "Battleship Maine" and Roger Miller's "Private John Q.," there was little in the Ramblers' repertoire that spoke directly to the issues of the mounting antiwar movement. In general, the Ramblers continued to resist the incursion of overt political messages into their performances. Too much ideological rhetoric, as Mike put it, compromised folk music "without regard for tradition or art."[66] Their ambivalence toward political protest music was evident at a 1965 concert where they appeared immediately following the antiwar songster Phil Ochs. In response to Ochs's closing polemical song, "Here's to the State of Mississippi" ("Here's to the land you've torn out the heart of / Mississippi, find yourself another country to be part of!"), John convinced the Ramblers to open their set with the traditional fiddle tune "Mississippi Sawyer." John realized that few, if any, in the audience would know the tune's name or make the connection back to the Ochs song. The exercise was, at least for John, a subtly ironic critique of a naive northern folksinger who was too quick to condemn a culture he knew little about.[67] The Ramblers never voiced open criticism of Ochs or other political folksingers; personally, they remained committed to a progressive political philosophy and certainly would never want to be put in a position of allying themselves with Mississippi's segregationists. Rather, they strove to keep their art and politics separate, as John noted during an interview with the popular magazine *Woman's Day*: "Sometimes we raise questions in our singing, but these are always about the city life as opposed to the country life. We don't extend our message to politics or the international situation."[68] But avoiding politics would prove increasingly difficult as the atmosphere of the late 1960s grew more volatile.

There were other adventures with the emerging counterculture. Just prior to their show at Reed College in Portland, Oregon, in April 1967, the Ramblers were invited to a huge meal prepared by an enthusiastic fan. John recalled what happened next: "So at the end of the meal she said, 'Oh, would you like to go upstairs and turn on before the show?' That was the first time. We had missed that—it was everywhere, and it was the conventional thing to do, turn on before the show. . . . So we might have had a puff or two."⁶⁹ In the spring of 1968 Tracy was surprised to be offered marijuana at a postconcert party of Allegheny College students who had gathered at a professor's home to watch live coverage of urban race riots. "We didn't inhale," he claimed.⁷⁰ Although drugs were becoming increasingly prevalent on college campuses and at coffeehouses, the Ramblers maintained that they generally steered clear of mixing pot and performance.

While 1967 continued to be a busy year for the Ramblers, the number of domestic shows dropped from sixty-five in 1966 to approximately fifty for 1967, and John's gross Ramblers touring income diminished from $7,000 to $5,500 over the same period. The situation would slowly decline in 1968, with the number of domestic shows dropping to about forty-five (this year with no international tours) and gross touring income to just over $5,000. John had certainly been justified in his earlier letter to Asch regarding the precipitous drop in the Ramblers' Folkways royalties. In 1966 and 1967 Mike and John barely broke $100 on their early recordings.⁷¹ Mike continued to pursue his solo touring career. In the fall John was invited to lecture on photography and design at the Silver Mine College in western Connecticut, a move that would eventually lead him back to academia and a full-time career as a teacher.

The Ramblers began 1968 on an encouraging note, playing at the University of Chicago Folk Festival, which continued to focus exclusively on traditional performers. Trying to allay folk enthusiasts' anxieties over the growing hegemony of rock music, John wrote in Sing Out! "At the conclusion of last year's [1967 University of Chicago] festival, several of us held the dim view that since most everything else is going rock, we might just turn around and find that there was no more festival. This year [1968] we all left believing that the festival and its music will continue as an institution of America's non-conforming traditions."⁷² In retrospect there was veracity to John's optimistic appraisal. The University of Chicago festival and the folk music world's appetite for traditional music would continue into the 1970s, although the Ramblers' role in that world would soon diminish. His choice of language is noteworthy. Coupling the seemingly contradictory notions of tradition and nonconformity was a clever semantic maneuver that allowed John to position folk music as an alternative to modern mass society. This was certainly not a new idea, having been a core value of the traditionalist wing of the urban folk revival for at least a decade. But as the 1960s wore on and rebellion from the mainstream became the siren song for a new generation of young Americans, "nonconforming traditions" might take on fresh dimensions.

The Ramblers had another chance to ally themselves with a progressive cause in the spring of 1968, when they agreed to spend a week touring for Anne Romaine and Bernice Johnson Reagon's Southern Folk Festival. Like the 1967 Charlottesville festival at which the Ramblers had appeared, this tour was sponsored by the Southern Folk Culture Revival Project, a grassroots organization dedicated to promoting racial unity by presenting traditional black and white folk musicians to southern audiences. In the tour's program book Romaine and Reagon unabashedly proclaimed their cultural mission of cross- racial exchange and respect:

> Tonight we hope to show that in the South our grassroots music, as a part of our history and culture, is a common bond we share. In spite of the fact that for years, we have existed at opposite poles on many issues, when it comes to music we draw freely from one another. . . . We are concerned with the South recognizing and utilizing its own resources. We want to focus on the common experiences of its people and the various forms of its musical expressions which make the South the greatest source of folk music in America. . . . We are also concerned with building a South in which black people and white people can live together in mutual respect. Our feeling is that this goal can be reached by each recognizing the worth of his own grassroots tradition as well as the value of the underlying cultural exchange that has existed in the South for several centuries.[73]

On April 7, three days after the assassination of civil rights leader Martin Luther King, Jr., the Ramblers joined Romaine's tour during its appearances on college campuses in Chapel Hill, North Carolina; Johnson City, Greenville, and Swanee, Tennessee; Davidson, North Carolina; and Lynchburg, Virginia. John recalled experiencing "a moment of risk" when he boarded the plane to head south, given the heated political climate. But the tour proceeded without incident, and while the college crowds were not large, they were enthusiastic. The Ramblers performed alongside New Orleans bluesman Babe Stovall, African American spiritual singer Bessie Jones, Kentucky balladeer Jean Ritchie, and West Coast banjoist and topical singer Michael Cooney. Romaine encouraged an interactive program; she would clog dance when the Ramblers played breakdowns and encouraged the audience to join in. Tracy remembered grabbing his fiddle and John his banjo to join Stovall for an onstage impromptu blues jam. While each Rambler was paid only $100 for the six performances, all three were adamant that the effort to promote southern music in southern communities and to present the racially mixed roots of southern folk music in the wake of the King tragedy was well worth it.

Following the final concert in Lynchburg, several members of the tour made a stop at the Union Grove Fiddlers Convention. With motorcycles zipping around,

Bessie Jones was afraid to get out of the car until Babe Stovall pulled out his guitar and began entertaining the all-white, rowdy crowd. According to Tracy, the mixed entourage was refused service in one North Carolina restaurant and had to endure muttered racial slurs at an auto repair shop when live coverage of the King funeral suddenly cut into the regular daytime television programming. "It was a heady time for doing this," reflected Mike, who, like John and Tracy, had tremendous admiration for Romaine's efforts. Indeed, the southern folk music tour provided the Ramblers the perfect vehicle to express their attitudes toward southern cultural politics. By appearing with a troupe of traditional black and white musicians and acknowledging the biracial origins of the southern music they championed, the Ramblers positioned themselves as ardent supporters of integration and equality without having to demonize Mississippians or any other white southerners.[74]

In the spring of 1968 the Ramblers released *Modern Times* (Folkways Records FTS 31027). Whether the album's title was a reference to the 1936 Charlie Chaplin film or was meant as an ironic commentary on the fate of old-time music in contemporary urban America was not at once clear. The LP's cover was a Robert Frank photograph of the three Ramblers posed by an old Chrysler that appears to have been abandoned in the woods (figure 17). John and Mike, holding guitar and banjo, stood poised to jump in, while Tracy's head protruded through the windshieldless chassis. The grinning Ramblers looked look ready to travel, but obviously they were going nowhere in this car. John's brief notes clarified the group's intentions: "This album might be subtitled 'Rural Songs from an Industrial Society.'" After quoting Charles Seeger on the role of folk songs in maintaining identity among uprooted rural migrants, he continued: "This record documents precisely such a change—the movement of Southern mountaineers and farmers during the first half of the 20th century, as they went into the coal mines and weaving mills. The same period saw the horse and wagon replaced by the automobile, and the steam locomotive by the diesel." Like many of the songs on their earlier album with Tom, *Songs from the Depression*, the materials on *Modern Times* "come from commercially conceived recordings. They were intended as popular songs (not traditional folk songs), and were sold in the popular marketplace." Noting that many of the pieces on *Modern Times* were topical in nature, John suggested they were a continuation of older folk song traditions that sought "not simply to preserve the past, but to make the present comprehensible."[75]

Musically, *Modern Times* extended the Ramblers' repertoire forward in time to include country songs written and recorded during the postwar years. Roger Miller's 1965 single was the source for "Private John Q.," the tale of an unemployed country boy who worries about being drafted into World War III. Terry Fell's "Truck Driving Man," Hobo Jack Adkins's "Union Man," the Masters Family's "From 40

THE NEW LOST CITY RAMBLERS
MODERN TIMES

FIGURE 17. Cover to *Modern Times* Folkways LP (1968).
Photograph by Robert Frank. Image courtesy of the Ralph Rinzler
Folklife Archives and Collections, Smithsonian Institution.

to 60," and Arthur Smith and Don Reno's "Bye, Bye Black Smoke Choo Choo" all came from 1950s recordings. The first three chronicled the hardships of working-class men, while the fourth bemoaned the disappearance of the steam engine. Rudy Sooter and Doyle O'Dell's "Dear Okie" from 1948 offered a slightly updated version of the Steinbeck-Guthrie narrative of California dreams gone bad. The Smith Family's "The Death of Ellenton" recounted the story of the razing of a small South Carolina farm town in 1950 to make way for a hydrogen bomb production facility. "Ellenton" and "Private John Q." provided the Ramblers with two topical country songs that criticized the military industrial complex from a distinctive southern perspective. In 1968, as the antiwar movement ramped up in the wake of the Tet Offensive, it would be hard for listeners to miss this connection.

Although chronologically nearly half of the repertoire would be considered more "modern" than previous Ramblers recordings, there was nothing contemporary about the instrumentation or style on any of the *Modern Times* performances. Absent were the twangy electric guitars, whining pedal steel, sweet fiddles, steady bass lines, and drum accompaniment that became the hallmarks of the postwar honky-tonk sound. The Ramblers still sounded like a 1930s hillbilly string band, crafting tasteful arrangements with various combinations of acoustic fiddle, guitar, Hawaiian slide, banjo, autoharp, harmonica, and vocal harmonies. In terms of subject matter—the industrialization of the rural South—*Modern Times* covered much of the same ground as Mike's 1966 *Tipple, Loom and Rail* LP. But overall the *Modern Times* songs were not as strong and the album was not as well conceived and sequenced, leaving Ramblers fans to suspect that the choicest offerings ended up on the earlier album. Nor is *Modern Times* as musically consistent as the previous *String Band Instrumentals* and *Remembrance of Things to Come* releases. The Ramblers simply did not sound as comfortable with the 1950s country songs as they did with the older hillbilly and early bluegrass repertoire. *Modern Times* also marked the end of a steady string of Ramblers Folkways releases—the group would not produce another album for seven years.

In November 1968 the Ramblers marked their ten-year anniversary with a concert at Columbia University's McMillan Theater. The folk revival's most esteemed critic, Robert Shelton, described the Ramblers' performance as "fresh, witty, and musically adroit," informing *New York Times* readers that their "sophisticated form of self burlesquing wit keeps them evergreen."[76] But it was a lengthy piece written by the longtime Ramblers observer Jon Pankake for *Sing Out!* that viewed the Ramblers' first decade through a broader historical lens. Subtitling the article "Random Observations of the Decennial of the New Lost City Ramblers," Pankake pondered the lasting contributions of a group who spent a decade "Not Making It" in the commercial world of folk music. His opening diatribe against the commercial folk revival concluded that the Ramblers' ten-year tenure stood as a "triumph for the aging Loyalists of the defunct Folk Revival." Their longevity underscored that the revival "was more than simply another pop music fad" and no less than "the discovery of a forgotten corner of the American soul." Comparing the Ramblers with the French film collector and curator Henri Langlois, who "labored in love and with integrity and in a cause against the limiting effects of established taste," Pankake cast the Ramblers not only as artists but also as dedicated curators of American music who "may well be remembered more for their workshops than their actual concerts." Those concerts "cannot be understood apart from their workshops, their collecting trips, their friendships." His comments on the personal dynamics of the group were insightful. Tracy's replacement of Tom resulted in more than simply an expansion of the Ramblers' repertoire into bluegrass and a cappella balladry. In addition, "the Ramblers moved away from vaudeville popular appeal towards a chamber music concept; toward art, away from entertainment. Not the Mechanics of Making It." Next, invoking a Hegelian dialectic, he postulated that the dynamic tension between Mike's and John's seemingly opposite personalities was central to the group's achievements. John possessed a deep sense of social consciousness, a profound "concern for the community and human context," while Mike gravitated toward a "preoccupation with the relationship between the music and the self, with what it means to be a musician deeply involved in a tradition, with finding personal expression in an old song." It was the synthesis of these two imaginations, accordingly, that allowed the Ramblers to flourish in their multiple roles as collectors, interpretive artists, and educators. Pankake underscored the triumphs and tribulations of the Ramblers' first decade as urban pioneers of old-time music. He wisely predicted that while traditional music would continue to endure among a segment of modern urban listeners, the chances of Mike, John, and Tracy holding it together for another ten years of "Not Making It" was at best uncertain.[77]

A SECOND DECADE,
1969–1979

The Ramblers were not among the half million young people who gathered on Max Yasgur's farm outside Bethel, New York, for three days of peace and music. In mid-August 1969 Mike, John, and Tracy found themselves on the other side of the continent, starting a three-week West Coast tour. Coincidentally, their opening shows were at the Family Dog, a San Francisco skating rink turned dance hall that had become a favorite hangout for the Bay Area counterculture crowd. Perched on a cliff overlooking the Pacific, the hall advertised itself as "Magic at the Edge of the Western World." The Ramblers had been invited to play at the Family Dog by San Francisco rock promoter Chet Helms, who had first heard them perform in Austin in 1963. The gig was his way of thanking the group, he later confided in John, for turning him on to old-time music. That weekend they would share the stage with Taj Mahal, Mike Bloomfield, and the bluegrass band Southern Comfort.

The Ramblers arrived a day early and decided to check out the Family Dog's Thursday evening show, which featured San Francisco's quintessential acid rock band, the Grateful Dead (who the next day would fly east to perform at the Woodstock Festival on Saturday, August 16). At the time the Ramblers were not aware that the Dead's lead guitarist, Jerry Garcia, had seen them play in Palo Alto in 1960, probably the eighteen-year-old's first brush with live old-time music. His wife, Sara Katz, later told John that Garcia and his friends listened to early Ramblers Folkways LPs around the time he was learning banjo and beginning to play folk and bluegrass music. Garcia's band, Mother McCree's Uptown Jug Champions, eventually morphed into the rock-oriented War Locks and finally into the Grateful Dead. Even though he plugged in and became one of the most influential rock guitarists of the era, Garcia continued to play banjo and pedal steel with the bluegrass group Old and in the Way and the country rock band New Riders of the Purple Sage. Decades later John chronicled Garcia's brush with the folk revival in the liner notes to the CD *Shady Grove*, a bluegrass collaboration between Garcia and mandolin player David Grisman.[1]

If the Ramblers felt slightly out of place the following night, bathed in a psychedelic light show and surrounded by a crowd of stoned, tie-dyed longhairs, they did not let on. They played a lively set as the crowd stomped and howled to the breakdowns "Old Joe Clark," "Run Mountain," and "Wild Bill Jones." Particularly well received was their arrangement of Don Bowman's satirical Nashville song "Wildwood Weed," which Mike dedicated to "all of you who are involved in the current revival of interest in farming." Played to the music of the Carter Family's famous "Wildwood Flower," the song tells the story of a naive hillbilly family who find a bumper crop of marijuana accidentally growing in their field. They have a high time until they are busted by the Feds but get the last laugh when the crop-burning authorities forget to confiscate the sacks of seeds on which the narrator sits. Taking advantage of the large dance space, the Ramblers ended the evening with a Virginia reel called by Mike and accompanied by a medley of fiddle-banjo tunes played by John and Tracy.[2]

Things took an interesting twist three nights later when the Ramblers returned to the Family Dog to play a benefit square dance promoted to the flower-power patrons as a "Hoe-Down . . . S.F. Hayride" with an admission of "98 Cents or Best Offer, Girls with Box Lunches Free." While he was tuning up John was approached by a young man with a bushy beard. "He asked me if I want some apple cider, and I said, 'Sure.' I drank it, and he said, 'Have you ever tripped?' I said, 'No.' He laughed and said, 'Well, you're going to now!' So I told Mike and Tracy because I didn't know what would happen. They were terrified that it might have happened to them." Having recently read Aldous Huxley's *Doors of Perception* and Carlos Castaneda's *Teachings of Don Juan*, John was familiar with the potential effects of hallucinogenic drugs:

> So I asked for a chair—I didn't know if I would fall down or writhe on the ground or what. And as the music went on and the dancing went on I would focus on this and that. But the music was interesting, because I was reducing what I was doing on the banjo to fewer and fewer notes, but they were so amplified with this sound system that they sounded gigantic! You played the basic part of a square dance tune, but hearing it very big. . . . Eventually, I obsessed on this girl's bright red shoes—like from *The Wizard of Oz*—and

I'm just kind of "Whooo!" So I'm playing music, looking at the red dancing shoes, and this whole scene is around me. And I was hanging on, I wasn't falling behind, and the music certainly had interesting qualities.[3]

Somehow John was able to play through the square-dance set. "Then afterwards the colors and everything happened, and they took me upstairs. There was another bluegrass band playing in the dressing room, and I was astounded by their precision—it was overwhelming."[4]

Acid and square dancing may have seemed totally copasetic to the Family Dog hippies, but not to the Ramblers. While John found the LSD experience fascinating, he certainly was in no condition for serious musical performance. Mike's and Tracy's anger at John's unsolicited drug trip underscored their own reservations about the burgeoning drug culture and its compatibility with playing old-time music.

The Family Dog was not the Ramblers' first brush with a West Coast rock audience. In May 1969 they had performed at the Northern California Folk Rock Festival in San Jose, a three-day event that included rock notorieties Jefferson Airplane, Big Brother and the Holding Company, Quicksilver Messenger Service, Canned Heat, and the Youngbloods (Jimi Hendrix and Led Zeppelin were advertised but evidently did not show). The previous August they had appeared at the Sky River Rock Festival, a multiday outdoor event that took place on an organic raspberry farm in Sultan, Washington, about thirty miles northeast of Seattle. Santana, Country Joe and the Fish, It's a Beautiful Day, and an unscheduled appearance by the Grateful Dead entertained an audience John characterized as "a bunch of drug-crazed hippies. . . . There was a lot of dancing and arm waving and tie-dyes!" Following a brief stint at Berkeley's Freight and Salvage coffeehouse in late August 1969, the Ramblers traveled north to appear on the second annual Sky River Festival, this time held in Tenino, Washington, outside Olympia. Along with Steve Miller, Country Joe, and the Flying Burrito Brothers, they shared the stage with kindred spirits from the Berkeley old-time music scene, Dr. Humbead's New Tranquility String Band. On the final day the Ramblers were scheduled to perform at 9:30 A.M. for a field of sleeping, hungover festivalgoers. Toward the end of their set a medley of twin fiddle tunes finally roused the crowd, prompting Mac Benford, Eric Thompson, and other members of the Berkeley Humbead band to join them onstage for an extended fiddle-tune jam. "Suddenly, the whole place was roaring to this Sunday morning old-time music," John recalled. "They were all dancing, some with clothes and some without clothes."[5] Rolling Stone magazine reported that "subcultures blended together well; in fact the most beautiful sight of the three days was seeing a hundred longhairs enthusiastically square-dancing to the New Lost City Ramblers backed up by Dr. Humbead's New Tranquility String Band."[6]

Such magic moments aside, the intersection of old-time and rock music at large concerts and outdoor festivals was generally not a comfortable fit. While West Coast rock luminaries Grace Slick, Marty Balin, Jerry Garcia, Bob Weir, Janis Joplin, and Joe McDonald had begun their careers within the folk revival, their new electric bands, driven by booming rhythm sections and piercing electric guitars, simply overwhelmed acoustic folk acts like the Ramblers. Audiences increasingly seemed more interested in getting high and dancing (or at least jumping around) to pounding drums and throbbing bass lines than in listening to close-harmony singing or grasping the arcane beauty of a modal banjo tune. The new rock festivals did not include intimate workshops where the Ramblers were in their element as demonstrators and educators. Their self-conscious concerns with preservation and heritage did not resonate with young rockers, nor did their appearance. Dressed in matching old-timey vests and ties and sporting (relatively) neatly cropped hair and clean-shaven faces, they undoubtedly appeared "old" to youthful audiences who embraced the contemporary adage "trust no one over thirty." By those standards the Ramblers were clearly suspect—in 1969 John turned thirty-seven, Mike thirty-six, and Tracy thirty-one. In retrospect the Ramblers were probably as out of place at Sky River and the Northern California Folk Rock Festival as Dylan had been at Newport with his electric band in 1965. Not surprisingly, the 1969 Sky River gathering would be the Ramblers' final excursion into the world of rock festivals.

The first half of 1969 turned out to be a busy time for the Ramblers as they logged approximately forty-five engagements by summer's end. But suddenly the work dried up in the fall. The demise of the commercial folk revival, combined with the rise of folk rock and alternative rock in the late 1960s, was finally catching up with the Ramblers. These larger social and economic forces, coupled with shifting personal circumstances and internal tensions in the group, led to a precipitous drop in the trio's touring schedule. The Ramblers played only eighteen engagements in 1970, sixteen in 1971, fifteen in 1972, and again fifteen in 1973 compared to approximately seventy engagements in 1966, sixty in 1967, and forty-five in 1968. Their only public appearance in 1974 was at the University of Chicago Folk Festival. Over the following five years, up until they disbanded in 1979, they averaged only six engagements a year. Perhaps seeing the writing on the wall, in May 1969 Mike told a reporter from the *Virginia Pilot* that the group was "not a full-time occupation for any of us," citing his own solo career, John's photography teaching, and Tracy's farming activities as occupying their additional time.[7]

By the late 1960s rock had completely eclipsed folk music on the pop charts, and many middle-class young people and college students saw folk rock and alternative rock as viable art forms capable of conveying their generational concerns the way folk music had during the earlier years of the decade. The college folk music circuit, which for nearly a decade had been the staple of the Ramblers' bookings, was contracting and no longer able to provide them with steady work. Likewise, venerable venues like Club 47 in Cambridge, the Second Fret in Philadelphia, the Gate of Horn in Chicago, and the Purple Onion in San Francisco had closed or would soon close down, and a series of fires forced Ed Pearl to curtail his bookings at Hollywood's Ash Grove. The UCLA Folk Festival had folded in 1965, Newport's final festival had come and gone in the summer of 1969, and after 1970 the Berkeley Folk Festival dwindled to a local one-day event. While pockets of Americans remained devoted to folk music, as the 1960s moved on "the record industry, the media, and the broader public shifted their attention, creativity, and money away from folk music and toward the British Invasion and rock in general," observed cultural historian Michael Scully.[8]

Folk music, of course, had not disappeared. In a late 1969 issue of Sing Out! editor Happy Traum reported with some relief that the commercial folk boom was over while optimistically recounting that diverse local folk scenes were enduring and even flourishing across the country.[9] A small but devoted number of clubs, coffeehouses, and college groups continued to sponsor less commercial acts; multiday gatherings like the University of Chicago, Fox Hollow, and Philadelphia folk festivals maintained an emphasis on traditional performers and instructional workshops; and southern fiddling conventions and bluegrass festivals were on the rise. These developments were good and bad news for the Ramblers. On the one hand, thanks in part to their efforts, more people than ever were aware of and actually playing old-time music. On the other, the commercial infrastructure to support a touring band specializing in such a narrow genre of folk music had grown increasingly shaky.

Contemporaneous to the decline of the folk music boom was an increase in government support for folk culture. Government-sponsored research and programming would result in a significant shift in the way folk music would be perceived and consumed by urban audiences for decades to come, which in turn had profound ramifications for urban performers like the Ramblers. Most important was the initial success of the Smithsonian-sponsored Festival of American Folklife, which by the late 1960s had developed into a weeklong, multistage event held annually on Washington's National Mall. Organized by Ralph Rinzler in 1967, the Smithsonian festival aimed to "deepen and advance public appreciation of the richness and viability of American grass-roots creativity."[10] The focus was on traditional, community-based practitioners of American music, dance, storytelling, crafts, and occupational practices presented onstage and in workshop settings with an emcee-interpreter who could add an educational dimension to the proceedings. Key to Rinzler's concept of "folklife" and "grassroots" was a strong anchor in local community culture. Rinzler and his people were committed to presenting artists who had learned their craft in their home communities, with an emphasis on rural and urban-ethnic communities, not middle-class revivalists who learned from recordings or other city singers of similar ilk. Despite their years of intensive study of mountain vocal and instrumental styles and the scores of traditional artists whom they had visited, recorded, and promoted, the Ramblers were still viewed as urban revivalists, not grassroots practitioners of community-based folk music. Their close relationship with Rinzler notwithstanding, the Ramblers were not invited to appear as performers at the early festivals. Mike was asked to emcee a concert and lead a workshop in ballad singing at the 1968 festival, and the following year he and John served as emcees and advisors. When the Ramblers were finally invited to perform in the summer of 1970, Rinzler's stage introduction reflected his uneasiness about their status as nontraditional musicians:

> This evening's program is kind of a departure for us—it's a mixture of different types of music. But the departure derives from the fact that we've got three groups of musicians on the festival who are different from most of the musicians we've had in the past. This festival has been dedicated to trying to give people a feeling for grassroots music and crafts, urban and rural style—the way people do things, sing 'em and cook 'em all over the country. Some people are Americans as of three hundred years ago and some as a few months ago. And we have both kinds of musicians on tonight's festival. But we also have some musicians who perhaps didn't grow up singing and playing the kind of music they're playing tonight. But they heard that kind of music all their lives and happened to choose it. It wasn't the only music they could have chosen, but they decided that they liked this style, and they really learned the traditional style. We have three such groups tonight, the Pennywhistlers, the New Lost City Ramblers, and Norman Kennedy, who have really deeply studied and immersed themselves in tradition. So without any further delay let's bring them on, the people that you really know well. They've been appearing throughout the week at the festival as emcees and performers: the New Lost City Ramblers![11]

Rinzler's remarks foreshadowed attitudes that would shape funding priorities for government-supported documentation, festival, and media projects that would proliferate in the 1970s and 1980s with the establishment of the Folk Arts Program of the National Endowment for the Arts in 1973 and the American Folklife Center in 1976.[12] Projects receiving funding would focus on traditional and grassroots artists rather than urban revivalists. This sort of thinking was clearly shaped by the contextual theories of folk culture discussed in the previous chapter. Under this paradigm urban revivalists were automatically judged to lack cultural authenticity because they did not grow up and learn their musical craft in a traditional community. Thus, the logic followed, a city-bred group like the Ramblers could never fully grasp and re-create the deep-seated, unconscious essence of rural Appalachian music—they could never be native speakers, only practitioners of a second language. In order to justify the use of federal and state tax dollars for folklore programming, government-based folklorists would have to carefully distinguish between those artists who were actually community-based tradition bearers and those who had come to the music through the urban folk revival.

One of the key figures in establishing the criteria for what would constitute authentic (and thus fundable) folk culture was Alan Jabbour, himself an accomplished fiddler who became the director of the NEA Folk Arts Program in 1974 and the head of the American Folklife Center in 1976. At the time, Jabbour would later explain in a letter published in the *Old-Time Herald*, he and his coworkers "were conscious of the smallness of our budget" and "the largeness of the cultural needs our program represented. . . . It would have been unseemly for us, the lovers and learners [that is, the revivalists] to focus on ourselves" or "to have seemed anxious to be—first at the trough."[13] While Jabbour would later recant his hard line on the authentic-imitator dichotomy, in 1974 he saw to it that the bulk of the Folk Arts Program's support went to older, traditional musicians instead of younger urban players like himself or the Ramblers.[14]

Under the new guidelines the Ramblers might work in the capacity of workshop leaders or apply for funds for their documentation projects, but they were clearly not eligible for support as traditional performers or even to play at festivals primarily funded by the new NEA program. Not surprisingly, they viewed such developments with a degree of resentment, feeling like victims of their own success who were suddenly on the outside looking in. After a decade of documenting and promoting traditional musicians, they found themselves more often than not disqualified from performing as equals with their mentors at festivals and concerts that received government support. Ironically, at least in their view, the rigid criteria defining folk in such a narrow and exclusionary terms had been developed and implemented by Rinzler, Jabbour, Bess Lomax Hawes (Alan Lomax's sister and Jabbour's successor at the NEA Folk Arts Program), and other folklorists who, like the Ramblers, had discovered folk music through the urban revival. The Ramblers would appear once more on the 1971 Festival of American Folklife, but not again as a trio until they were honored at a reunion concert in 1997.

A similar situation developed with the National Folk Festival, the country's longest-running folk festival, founded by Sarah Gertrude Knott in 1934. In the early 1970s the festival partnered with the National Parks Service and began staging its annual festival in Wolf Trap, a bucolic outdoor-park venue in northern Virginia. By this time the National Folk Festival was attracting a large number of revivalists, and in 1971 the Ramblers were invited to perform. But in 1976 the festival's new director, Joe Wilson, sided with board members—one of whom was Mike—who wanted to emphasize traditional musicians and began weeding out the city revivalists in favor of those born and reared in rural and ethnic communities. Over a decade later banjoist Mac Benford complained to readers of the *Old-Time Herald* that "the folklore establishment" who ran large festivals and government-sponsored tours was unfairly biased against city revivalists like his own Highwoods Stringband. Like the Ramblers, the Highwoods had played the Smithsonian and the National Folk festivals in the early 1970s but were not invited back, allegedly because of their status as revivalists. Wilson's National Council for the Traditional Arts, Benford sniped, would become "the National Council for the Dying Arts" if it continued to exclude younger city musicians like himself who had embraced traditional styles and repertoires. Wilson shot back a vitriolic response, excoriating revivalists in general and Benford in particular for being naive romantics with no genuine connection to tradition and who just wanted government-affiliated organizations like the NCTA to serve as their booking agents. The testy 1989 exchange underscored the tensions that had been simmering between revival musicians and professional folklore administrators for over two decades regarding the question of what constituted authentic and fundable folk art.[15]

Throughout the 1960s folk boom the Ramblers reigned as the sole touring stage band specializing in old-time mountain music. By middecade other old-time bands were springing up in cities and on college campuses, but their activity was mostly local, with occasional jaunts to southern fiddle contests and festivals. The terrain would shift in the early 1970s with the emergence of the above-mentioned Highwoods Stringband from Trumansburg, New York, and the Red Clay Ramblers from Durham, North Carolina. The Highwoods' roots can be traced back to the Bay Area's growing old-time music scene in the late 1960s. John recalls that when the Ramblers would visit the Bay Area they were often invited to jam at a large house on Colby Street on the Berkeley-Oakland city line. There they met a group of young musicians who, to their delight, shared their infatuation with southern mountain music: "They were all independent musicians, full-time exploring old time music, busking and lifestyles. . . . They produced a musical high, a meeting of minds and excellent musicianship."[16] The Freight and Salvage coffeehouse on San Pablo Avenue in Berkeley was another favorite gathering spot where the new old-time musicians would play, sometimes under the quirky moniker Dr. Humbead's New Tranquility String Band, some of whose members had joined the Ramblers onstage at the 1969 Sky River Festival. Mike and John were so impressed with the scene that they both set about recording various configurations of what they saw as the next generation of old-time urban musicians. Walt Koken, Sue Draheim, Hank Bradley, Will Spires, Mac Benford, Eric Thompson, and Jody Stecher were among the best known. In 1972 Mike produced the Folkways LP *Berkeley Farms* (FA 2436), and decades later John's recordings were issued on a Field Recorder's Collective CD entitled *Berkeley in the 60's* (FRC 609, 2008). In his liner notes to the former Mike wrote, "This recording to me outlines the creativity and joy in the true maturation of rural music played by (mostly) city folk. . . . We were fortunate in recording during a time of great musical ferment when the best musicians were in town playing in a variety of combinations."[17]

One of those combinations was a double fiddle-banjo trio that called themselves the Fat City String Band when they busked on the streets of Berkeley and San Francisco. Fiddlers Walt Koken (from Missouri) and Bob Potts (from San Francisco) and banjoist Mac Benford (from New Jersey) had all gravitated to the Berkeley old-time scene in the late 1960s. In 1971 Koken returned east to Ithaca, New York, and began playing with an old acquaintance, Doug Dorschug, a Cornell student who picked guitar and banjo. Dorschug introduced Koken to another Cornell student, bassist Jenny Cleveland, who had recently discovered old-time music through her interest in square dancing. Sometime in early 1972 Koken convinced Potts and Benford to join them in Trumansburg, a small hamlet outside Ithaca. Snatching their name from a line in the Charlie Poole song "Gonna go to the high woods when I die," the Highwoods Stringband took to the road playing fiddle conventions, festivals, coffeehouses, and colleges across the country. They found their way to the stages of the Smithsonian and National Folk festivals and in 1974 participated in a State Department tour of nine Latin American countries.[18] Their influence was further extended through the three superb albums they released on Rounder Records between 1973 and 1976, all of which received favorable reviews in *Bluegrass Unlimited*.[19]

The Highwoods took inspiration from the Ramblers. Just before leaving Berkeley to return east, Benford reminisced about a friend at summer camp who "had a guitar and also a tape recorder and also tapes of the New Lost City Ramblers. They just blew my mind. I'd never heard anything like that before. I decided I'd start out with the banjo and stick with it."[20] Years later Koken would credit the Ramblers' reinterpretations of classic hillbilly records as one of the key sources that turned him and his bandmates on to old-time music.[21] Like the Ramblers, the Highwoods drew much of their material from early country records by groups like Uncle Dave Macon, the Skillet Lickers, J. E. Mainer's Mountaineers, Grayson and Whitter, and Charlie Poole as well as from musicians, old and young, whom they encountered at southern fiddle conventions. But unlike the Ramblers, who included bluegrass as well as old-time tunes in their presentations, the Highwoods were strictly an old-time band, reflecting the increased fissure between the two music cultures by the 1970s. Nor did they rotate their instruments; the twin-unison fiddles, banjo, guitar, and bass configuration remained a constant despite the multi-instrumental talents of the five band members. Switching instruments made it difficult to achieve cohesion, Benford reflected. "We wanted a band sound, one that could be readily recognized as our own."[22]

Whatever they borrowed musically from the Ramblers, the Highwoods did craft a distinctive sound that was unmistakably their own. Mike would later comment: "He [Walt Koken] was the first of the younger urban fiddle players I heard that really got that old-time rhythmic bow lick, and it worked with Mac's particular banjo style which is also rhythmic. Bob added some sort of rough and ragged, whimsical bowing, which I still can't figure what he's doing. The first time I heard the trio I thought it was the most amazing thing I'd ever heard, rhythmically."[23] The driving twin fiddles and percussive banjo formed a pulsing beat accentuated by Dorschug's crisp guitar runs and Cleveland's booming bass. The bass fiddle had become a mainstay in bluegrass bands but was rarely adopted by old-time revival groups, perhaps due to its absence on most early hillbilly records and field recordings. The Highwoods used the bass to their advantage, creating a raucous sound that throbbed with the exuberance of a rock band and that was capable of transforming their young audiences into dancing throngs. While they adopted a wisecracking stage persona reminiscent of Tom Paley, the Highwoods avoided the didactic song introductions and history lessons that had become part and parcel of the Ramblers' shows. When they played and sang, their listeners simply danced.

In concert the Highwoods presented a youthful counterculture image that was more in keeping with the early 1970s than the Ramblers' antiquated matching vests and ties. The Highwoods balked at the idea of matching stage outfits, choosing rather to dress like their blue-jeaned and flannel-shirted audiences. With long hair, bushy mustaches, and battered cowboy hats they looked like a cross between old-time mountain men and young hippies, with Cleveland appearing as the cheery farmer's daughter–earth mother hybrid. Although they preached no overt political message, members of the Highwoods did not hesitate to hide their disdain for mainstream culture: "City life and City music are failing us," they collectively wrote on the liner notes of their first album, *Fire on the Mountain*. "A good laugh, a good tune, and a good time are what we need to get through these crazy times." Their embrace of the back-to-the-land ethos was clear in the album cover photograph of the group standing around a recording microphone in a field, surrounded by woods and hills. "Most of the tunes were recorded out of doors, where we feel most comfortable, and if you listen you can hear the crickets."[24] Their subsequent albums were recorded in Dorschug's specially outfitted chicken barn.

The Highwoods' appeal to younger, college-aged audiences may explain in part why they found more work in the 1970s than did the Ramblers. But instead of distancing themselves from the Highwoods, who had clearly emerged as their main rivals, the Ramblers embraced the younger group, holding them up as proof that the seeds they had sown for old-time music in the 1960s were coming to fruition. Years later Mike told readers of the *Old-Time Herald* that the Highwoods were unquestionably "the most important old-time string band of the 1970s in terms of spreading the old-time style of music. . . . They encouraged and inspired their generation and younger, to take up old-time music. The five of them presented a loose, rhythmic music that was really compatible to the rock and roll music that people were listening to then. And they presented a visual image that was perfectly in tune with the contemporary alternative party life style." He differentiated the Highwoods' "band sound" from the Ramblers, which he described as "more a repertoire type group which did a lot of different styles."[25] In 1978 the Ramblers honored the Highwoods with an invitation to appear as special guests at their twentieth-anniversary concert at Carnegie Hall. Sixteen years later Mike and John would write glowing tributes to the Highwoods when Rounder Records reissued their early 1970s recordings in a CD package. "They provided an unprecedented musical force that energized string bands and opened up new ways to partake in this vibrant music," pronounced John.[26]

Despite their popularity among old-time music fans, the Highwoods struggled to make a living at their trade. "We're too traditional to appeal to a side commercial audience, but the folklorists say we're outside the tradition because we weren't born into it," complained Benford to Mike Greenstein of *Bluegrass Unlimited* in 1979. He went on to explain that, despite their gypsy lifestyle, band members were barely able to eke out a subsistence-level income. They had settled around Ithaca because the area offered them cheap land where they could maintain homes and raise much of their own food. As the 1970s drew to a close, individual members of the Highwoods had grown weary and disillusioned with life on the road. In the fall of 1978 the decade's most popular string band disbanded.[27]

Outside of New York and California's Bay Area, the most important center of the old-time music revival was in and around Durham and Chapel Hill, North Carolina. The aforementioned folklorist and fiddler Alan Jabbour, a native Floridian who had studied classical violin as a youngster, was a graduate student in Duke University's English Department when he met Tommy Thompson in 1966. Thompson, a West Virginia native who was studying philosophy next door at the University of North Carolina at Chapel Hill, was a superb banjoist. Jabbour started attending the weekly music session hosted by Thompson and his wife, Bobbie, a guitarist and visual designer. One of the many old-time musicians who frequented the Thompsons' gatherings was mandolin player Bert Levy, a Long Islander studying medicine at Duke. From these sessions Jabbour, the two Thompsons, and Levy formed their own group, taking the name Hollow Rock from a nearby community.

The Hollow Rock String Band specialized in regional fiddle tunes, many collected by Jabbour from Henry Reed, an octogenarian fiddler from Glen Lyn, Virginia. Jabbour maintained that the Ramblers, whom he did not meet until the spring of 1968 when they played in Chapel Hill, were not a direct influence on his Hollow Rock band.[28] Their repertoire was not gleaned from old hillbilly recordings or Ramblers Folkways albums but learned directly from rural fiddlers like Reed. Like Mike and John, Jabbour relished combing mountain communities in North Carolina and Virginia, locating and documenting old fiddlers and learning new tunes. And as the Ramblers had done with their early Folkways recordings, he rigorously annotated the fifteen tunes appearing on the group's first album, appropriately titled *Traditional Dance Tunes*. The LP was released on the Kanawha label in early 1968, just months after Reed passed away. With no singing, the band's emphasis was on the melodic interpretation of the tunes; Jabbour stayed close to Reed's original fiddle style, with Thompson's clawhammer banjo and Levy's mandolin seconding his lead fiddle line. A number of Hollow Rock tunes, most notably "Over the Waterfall," would become standards among revival fiddlers.[29]

One close observer of the Chapel Hill scene, folklorist and fiddler Thomas Carter, drew clear distinctions between the styles of the Ramblers and the Hollow Rock String Band. Members of the latter never changed instruments (as the Ramblers often did) or engaged in solo breaks (as the Ramblers occasionally did). Rather, Hollow Rock forged a tight-unison style that Carter argued would be emulated by revivalist string bands in the 1970s. This latter point is well taken; when a thorough history of the instrumental dimensions of the folk music revival is compiled, Hollow Rock will surely be recognized as a pioneering fiddle band. But also worth noting is Carter's admission that his initial exposure to old-time music came at a 1964 Ramblers concert at the University of Utah. A 1966 photograph of Carter's own Hippo Choral String Band locates the group in front of a barn, decked out in Ramblers-style vests and ties.[30]

The Hollow Rock band dissolved in 1968, when Jabbour and Levy moved on, the former to teach and eventually to direct the American Folklife Center. Meanwhile, a second band had emerged from the weekly Thompson sessions. Dubbed the Fuzzy Mountain String Band, the group consisted of a rotating cast of players that included fiddlers Bill Hicks and Malcolm Owen, banjoists Blanton Owen and Eric Olson, guitarist Bobbie Thompson, and dulcimer player Vickie Owen. Often using multiple fiddles and banjos along with mandolin, guitar, and dulcimer, the group developed a loose unison sound where the basic melodic line was shared among the various string instruments, with only the guitar providing harmonic accompaniment. Tunes were played over and over and sometimes looped into extended medleys, leading Hicks to describe the band as "a controlled jam session."[31] Much of their repertoire was based on regional fiddle tunes, and like Hollow Rock they were never a touring stage band. Fuzzy Mountain rarely traveled except for annual trips to southern fiddle conventions such as Union Grove, where they won the Best Old-Time Band competition in 1972. At their core they were an informal kitchen, porch, and festival band whose primary purpose was celebrating the music and creating a sense of community among a circle of like-minded musicians and friends. Their two Rounder Records albums, The Fuzzy Mountain String Band (0010, 1972) and Summer Oak and Porch (0035, 1973), reached a broad audience and brought them notoriety among string-band fans across the country, many of whom had never seen Fuzzy Mountain perform.[32]

By the early 1970s two distinct, though occasionally overlapping, strands of the old-time music revival were developing. One, exemplified by the Hollow Rock and Fuzzy Mountain groups, included the fiddle-driven jam session bands that played strictly instrumental tunes for informal home, dance, and festival gatherings. A second, represented by the Ramblers and Highwoods, consisted of the repertoire stage bands that played a broader range of material, including songs, for more formal performance situations.[33]

Another influential repertoire stage band emerged from the Durham/Chapel Hill milieu around this time. In the fall of 1972 Tommy Thompson and Bill Hicks began playing with guitarist and mandolin player Jim Watson. The following year they joined forces with multi-instrumentalist Mike Craver to form a more serious stage band that became known as the Red Clay Ramblers (RCR). After playing local Chapel Hill cafes the band began to tour in the summer of 1973. In late 1974 they relocated to New York to provide the music for Bland Simpson and Jim Wann's two-act show, Diamond Studs: A Saloon Musical, based loosely on the life of Jesse James. New York Times critic Clive Barnes was impressed with the music, noting that the RCR and Southern States Fidelity Choir were "authentic almost to the point of musicology and beyond."[34] The RCR left New York after *Diamond Studs* closed its eight-month off-Broadway run and continued to tour and record, releasing six albums before Hicks left the group in 1981.[35]

The group's first album, *The Red Clay Ramblers with Fiddlin' Al McCanless* (Folkways Records FTS 31039, 1974), was a transition from the Hollow Rock String Band that offered glimpses of things to come. In addition to fiddle-banjo tunes (several from Henry Reed) the band dabbled in bluegrass, vaudeville blues, and ragtime-influenced country material. Their later albums on the Flying Fish label were eclectic mixes of old-time string band, blues, jazz, ragtime, and gospel as well as original numbers. Their overall sound maintained a traditional flavor, particularly when they played fiddle-banjo dance tunes or sang Carter Family numbers. But many of their arrangements reflected an air of self-conscious sophistication, often involving individual solo breaks on fiddle, banjo, and guitar, piano, organ, and even trumpet. Tempos changed, keys modulated, jazzy chords flashed by, and vocal and instrumental pieces were joined in unexpected medleys. Their 1976 album *Twisted Laurel* (Flying Fish FF-030) opened with a haunting unaccompanied vocal duet of the song "Blue Jay" and flowed right into the rousing dance tune "The Girl I Left Behind Me," featuring solos on banjo, piano, and pipe organ. Instead of emulating Charlie Poole's lilting mountain chamber style, as the Ramblers did, the RCR's arrangement of Poole's "Milwaukee Blues" on *Merchants Lunch* (Flying Fish FF-055, 1977) chugged along to a groove of electric piano and strumming banjo and featured jazzy improvisations, stop-time figures, and a rock-inflected vocal by Watson. Unlike the Hollow Rock and Fuzzy Mountain bands but similar to the Ramblers, the RCR emphasized songs, many of which they gleaned from old hillbilly recordings. Their harmony singing was always tight, with Thompson's soulful baritone supplying just enough West Virginia twang to make the group sound genuinely southern.

Although the RCR sounded nothing like the Ramblers, Thompson acknowledged the latter's influence in his 1974 liner notes to the first RCR Folkways LP: "The New Lost City Ramblers have done incalculable service to those of us who value old-time string music. It was the Ramblers, for example, who more than anyone else developed the audience which makes the present flood of reissues feasible. This could not have been accomplished without the loving attention to detail which characterizes their recreations of the classic performances. But the Ramblers seemed destined to remain unique as a band which can make their brand of creative imitation work." Eager to differentiate his own band from creative imitators like the Ramblers, Thompson characterizes the RCR as "experimental," never hesitating to "alter instrumentation and harmony nor to combine originally divergent music styles." Their sound had evolved naturally through their playing together, not as "the result of emulating, as a group, other bands, past or present." Whether Thompson's remarks were meant as an indirect criticism of the New Lost City Ramblers is not certain, but clearly he viewed the RCR as undertaking a very different sort of creative work. Yet despite the RCR's eclectic repertoire and progressive arrangements, Thompson maintained, "We persist in calling ourselves an 'old-timey' band" whose respect for tradition and admiration for innovation "attests to the essential continuity of the string band tradition and to its persistent vitality."[36] This view is not dissimilar to the one expressed by the Ramblers on their own inaugural Folkways liner notes sixteen years earlier, where Mike argued that the pioneer hillbilly performers they emulated were innovators in their time.

Mike, John, and Tracy certainly did not appreciate the "imitator" label rearing its head once more, but they respected the RCR's ability to take old-time music in new directions and to new audiences. Sometime during the *Diamond Studs* run Tommy Thompson visited John in Tompkins Corner and asked to see the ledger book containing the Ramblers' financials. "Tommy wanted to know if they could really make a living as a touring band," John recalled.[37] Although the early 1970s had been lean years for the Ramblers, Thompson evidently took some solace from what he saw in John's ledger book, and his band soon embarked on a period of intensive touring and recording. The new paths the RCR and Highwoods blazed for old-time music in the 1970s were made possible in part by the Ramblers' initial efforts in the 1960s, which nurtured audiences for the music and demonstrated the possibilities for a touring old-time band.

While other old-timey bands were springing up in the late 1960s, Mike, John, and Tracy were each being drawn into music spheres apart from the Ramblers. After Mike and Marge divorced in early 1967, Mike moved back to the DC area and began to see Alice Gerrard, a guitarist and singer he had met at Antioch in the mid-1950s. Mike and Alice, who shared similar tastes in old-time and bluegrass music, started playing informally with a circle of acquaintances that included Mike's old friend and Alice's singing partner Hazel Dickens, bluegrass banjoist Lamar Grier, and Tracy Schwarz. By the fall of 1968 the group had jelled musically and decided to make an album. During a visit with Tracy in Glen Rock, Pennsylvania, Mike used a portable Nagra to record the four singing the unaccompanied Primitive Baptist hymn "When I Can Read My Titles Clear." The following January the group went into a Silver Spring, Maryland, studio and recorded material that would be issued on an Arhoolie Records LP entitled *Strange Creek Singers* (CD 9003, 1972). The name came from a small North Carolina community Mike and Alice had once passed through. David Axler informed *Sing Out!* readers that the album was one of the best he had ever heard: "Although there is considerable instrumental ability here, it's the singing that really makes the album—solos, duets, trios, and quartets that are just terrific."[38]

Musically, the *Strange Creek* release was a diverse mix of bluegrass, old-time, and contemporary country. The band's repertoire included original pieces done in traditional style, like Tracy's humorous "Poor Old Dirt Farmer" and Dickens's haunting a cappella "Black Lung," written and sung in commemoration of her West Virginia coal-mining brothers. Mike and Tracy traded around fiddle, guitar, banjo, mandolin, Dobro, and autoharp, while Grier provided imaginative bluegrass banjo leads and accompaniment. The singing was the most distinguishing element, with Gerrard and Dickens delivering edgy lead lines and high harmonies that the Ramblers could never approach. Their duet singing on the woeful ballad "No Never No" and the rollicking bluegrass arrangement of "New River Train" is some of the best female harmonizing by any folk or country group of the era. Richard Spottswood, who wrote the liner notes for the LP, was tremendously impressed by Hazel. "She sings country by heritage," he noted, as opposed to the other group members, who sang "by choice." "More than any one person it is Hazel who gives this collection its feeling and depth. Her mournful country voice has influenced the singing of the others to a remarkable degree."[39] Spottswood was correct—Mike and Tracy contributed some of their most impressive vocal efforts to date, and Gerrard had clearly picked up the nuances of mountain singing from her years of performing with Dickens.

Mike would later describe the Strange Creek Singers as something of a "dream group," given its high level of musicianship, spectacular vocal possibilities, and broad repertoire. But Grier's and Dickens's work schedules, Mike's solo career and duet appearances with Alice, and Mike and Tracy's commitment to the Ramblers prevented the band from becoming a full-time operation. The group's touring was limited to festivals, several West Coast swings, and a six-week trip to Europe in 1975.[40] The Strange Creek Singers further solidified Mike and Tracy's personal and musical alliance, and in 1970 the two became neighbors after Mike and Alice married and bought a farm near New Freedom, about ten miles from Tracy's spread near Glen Rock in southern York County, Pennsylvania.

Meanwhile, Mike continued his solo recording and touring career. The late 1960s had been a relatively slow period, but the release of two solo albums on the Mercury Records label brought him national attention. In 1972 Mercury put out *Music from the True Vine* (SRM 1–627, 1972). While *Sing Out!* reviewer David Axler carped that Mike's "weird style of singing" was becoming increasingly "idiosyncratic," he praised his versatility and "his constant efforts to unearth good old songs and to find new instrumental and vocal combinations with idiom he knows so well."[41] Jon Pankake was more laudatory in a review that appeared in the widely circulated rock magazine *Rolling Stone*. Pankake touted Mike as a soul-searching, latter-day Emerson, praising his arrangements for "the newness of their conceptions" and for being "as clean and crisp as any acoustic music now being played."[42] Although the album did not sell well, Mike received a one-thousand-dollar advance for making the recording—a sizable sum in comparison with the negligible recording fees and small royalty checks he garnered from Folkways.

A second Mercury release, *Second Annual Farewell Reunion* (SRM 1–685, 1973), presented a retrospective on Mike's fifteen-year recording career. With a five-thousand-dollar budget—an amount Moe Asch would never muster—Mike was able to bring together friends and family. He chose to pair himself with brother Pete, sisters Peggy and Penny, the Ramblers, the Strange Creek Singers, the Highwoods Stringband, Ry Cooder, and traditional musicians Elizabeth Cotten, Kilby Snow, Leslie Riddle, and Roscoe Holcomb. *Sing Out!* reviewer Bob Norman was surprised but elated that a major label like Mercury Records would put out an album devoted to such grassroots, noncommercial music. He praised Mike as a "catalyst" for traditional musicians and called *Farewell Reunion* "one of the finest folk music albums of recent years."[43] As with the first Mercury release, sales were not significant, but Mike considered the recording to be one of his most successful artistic projects.

By the mid-1970s Mike was increasingly mixing performance with education and tour administration. He spent the spring of 1974 as a resident at California State University in Fresno, teaching classes in American folk music and demonstrating traditional Appalachian playing and singing techniques. That year he received an NEA Folk Arts Program grant to organize the American Old-Time Music Festival, which would tour traditional musicians around the West Coast. The 1975 tour included Cajun musicians Sady Courville, Dennis McGee, and Marc Savoy; the African American string band Bogan, Martin, and Armstrong; and Mike and banjoist Blanton Owen (from the Fuzzy Mountain String Band) accompanying North Carolina old-time fiddler Tommy Jarrell. Mike organized the tour and served as presenter as well as Jarrell's musical accompanist. While the NEA Folk Arts Program was not comfortable funding a city group like the Ramblers, it was willing to support someone like Mike in the role of organizer and presenter. The touring festival would continue for three years with a rotating cast of traditional musicians.[44]

Mike and Tracy's involvement with the Strange Creek Singers inevitably caused tensions with John, who, not surprisingly, resented seeing two-thirds of the Ramblers performing without him. He also feared that the Strange Creek Singers, along with Mike's availability as a soloist, might siphon off work opportunities that otherwise would have come to the more established and pricier Ramblers. Neither the Strange Creek Singers nor Mike alone could command a fee comparable to that of the Ramblers, making the former more affordable alternatives for producers with tight budgets. But John had little time to brood over these developments—his own life as a musician and visual artist was taking new and unexpected turns. Sometime in 1971 John and Penny were playing at one of Pete Seeger's informal Hudson River Sloop Festivals in Nyack when they ran into fiddler Jay Unger and guitarist Lyn Unger, who had recently moved to Lincolndale in neighboring Westchester County. Eventually, the Ungers, John, and another neighbor, celloist Abby Newton, began holding weekly late-night music sessions at John and Penny's home. By the fall of 1971 they had cobbled together a repertoire of old-time tunes and original songs and began playing publicly at festivals and coffeehouses. The quartet took the name Putnam String County Band (PSCB).[45]

The idea, mused John on the liner notes to the PSCB's first (and only) album (Rounder Records 303, 1973), was not to form another touring band but rather to "return to the local communities," or, to quote Voltaire's message to Candide, to "cultivate our own gardens." Describing himself as "a travel-weary musician (currently 15 years with the New Lost City Ramblers)," John presented a list of reasons to stick closer to home that sounded like the mission statement for a back-to-the-land commune: "to fix the barn, to prevent a highway from going through our back yard, to locate other people sympathetic to a new lifestyle in the beautiful wilderness of Putnam County, to help Pete Seeger in his effort to clean up the Hudson and Bring the Community Together and, not least, to plant our own garden."[46] PSCB kept busy, logging in thirty engagements in 1972 and another twenty-five in 1973. Staying true to their "community-first" ethos, nearly all their playing was local or at venues within a day's drive of Putnam County. Remuneration was thin, often between $25 and $50 a person, topping out at $100 each only on rare occasions.

Musically, PSCB was a cross between an old-time and a modern folk ensemble, with a classical cello thrown in for good measure. Their repertoire included southern hillbilly songs learned from the likes of Uncle Dave Macon, Charlie Poole, and Arthur Smith as well as traditional ballads arranged for two female voices and cello accompaniment. But nearly half of their songs were original pieces composed by Jay and carefully arranged for country-flavored vocals and instrumentation. "Come to the Mountain," for example, begins with droning cello and fiddle, which are eventually joined by light guitar and banjo. Lyn sings a modal, rhythmically irregular verse with lyrics "Come to the mountain, we can sing together / Time flying by, light as a feather" before breaking into an Aquarian chorus "Our spirit shall be as one / And shine bright as the sun." A minute and a half into the piece the vocals drop out, the tempo picks up, and Jay and John trade fiddle and banjo leads on what has become a spirited mountain breakdown.

PSCB continued to play together until the mid-1970s, when Jay and Lyn moved on to other projects. Meanwhile, John's Yale training as a visual artist had opened up another world of possibilities. In the fall of 1967 an old Yale acquaintance contacted John about teaching photography at the Silvermine College of Art in New Canaan, Connecticut, about thirty minutes from his home in Tompkins Corner. An agreement was worked out whereby he would teach once a week, and if a Ramblers tour took him out of the area, he would miss the class without pay. The arrangement worked well for both parties, and by 1970 John was teaching photography and design two days a week, schedule permitting. In the early 1970s Silvermine lost its accreditation and returned to its status as a community arts guild center, just at the time the State University of New York was opening up a new campus in Purchase that would emphasize visual and performing arts. In 1971 John was hired to teach in the Continuing Education program and to help screen prospective art students. The following year he was offered a full-time teaching position at SUNY Purchase based on his experience at Silvermine and a portfolio of published work that included a recent spread in the prestigious photography magazine *Aperture*. He was tenured in 1978 and would continue to teach photography, design, and drawing at Purchase until he retired in 1997. SUNY Purchase provided John with something the other Ramblers did not and never would have—a steady paycheck from a day job he was passionate about.

In addition to his new teaching responsibilities, John kept busy working on several documentary film and audio-recording projects. Encouraged by his successful 1963 documentary shot in eastern Kentucky, *The High Lonesome Sound*, he had begun filming North Carolina ballad singer Dillard Chandler in 1967. *The End of an Old Song*, released in 1972, chronicled the life of the traditional songster in a rapidly changing southern community. Writing for *Rolling Stone*, Michael Goodwin called the film a "superbly conceived, masterfully executed work of art. The black and white images are stunning in their simplicity and evocative power. . . . Cohen builds a universe in his film and hands it to us complete."[47] In 1975 John edited and produced *Musical Holdouts*, featuring miniportraits of noncommercial roots musicians, ranging from bluegrass bands and balladeers to cowboy and Native American songsters and culminating with a rollicking performance by the Highwoods Stringband. His audio recordings of Chandler were released in 1975 on the Folkways LP *Dillard Chandler: The End of an Old Song* (Folkways Records FA 2418, 1975). The previous year he produced *High Atmosphere: Ballads and Banjo Tunes from Virginia and North Carolina* for Rounder Records (rereleased as Rounder CD 0028, 1995), a collection of his field recordings that included the music of

Frank Proffitt, Gaither Carlton, Wade Ward, Fred Cockerham, Dellie Norton, Dillard Chandler, and others.

Tracy also found himself drifting away from the Ramblers by the late 1960s. Like Mike, he was intrigued with the new musical possibilities offered by the Strange Creek Singers. When he was not working with one group or the other, most of his time was spent trying to farm. His Glen Rock land was hilly and hard to work, at best providing only subsistence living. With two young children of his own, Sally Anne and Peter, and three stepchildren to care for, Tracy felt the need for additional income, so in 1969 he decided to go back to college to become certified as a teacher. In 1972 he graduated with a bachelor of arts in education and German from Millersville State College (now Millersville University) but was unsuccessful at finding a teaching job in the area. In 1973 Tracy and Eloise bought a farm near Brodbecks, Pennsylvania, where the flatter land was easier to work and better suited for Eloise's aspirations to raise horses.[48]

Throughout this period Tracy took advantage of southern Pennsylvania's local music scene, playing with various area bluegrass bands and old-time fiddlers. In 1969 he discovered that one of his Glen Rock neighbors was the guitarist and singer Del McCoury, a North Carolina native and veteran of Bill Monroe's Blue Grass Boys. Tracy occasionally played bass and fiddle with McCoury, who for several years had a steady job at a small club called the Stonewall Inn just outside Baltimore and less than an hour from Glen Rock. Tracy also attended local festivals, fiddlers' picnics, and jam sessions in and around York County where he met the old-time fiddlers Bill Gipe and Bill Grey. Gipe hosted a weekly music session and square dance in his converted chicken shed near Red Line, gatherings known to the locals as the "chicken-house sessions." Tracy picked up new bowing techniques and ornamentations from Gipe and the other fiddlers and added Pennsylvania tunes to his repertoire.[49]

Playing with the bluegrass bands brought in needed income, but, taking a cue from Mike, Tracy realized that performing as a soloist was his best chance at earning additional money at a time when work with the Ramblers was seriously ebbing. By the early 1970s he had begun booking himself—sometimes as a duet act backed by Eloise Schwarz on guitar—at small clubs, colleges, and festivals around Pennsylvania and nearby Maryland and Virginia. By the mid-1970s the couple was playing as many as twenty engagements a year, occasionally venturing out of the region to places like the Mariposa Folk Festival and the Ark in Ann Arbor, Michigan. In 1975 he convinced Moe Asch to put out his first solo album on Folkways, *Look Out! Here It Comes!* (FA 2419). Drawing from sources familiar to Ramblers fans (Cousin Emmy, Arthur Smith, Tom Ashley, Roscoe Holcomb, and Charlie Monroe), Tracy offered a potpourri of Appalachian songs and tunes, occasionally accompanied by Eloise on guitar. Like Mike, Tracy had developed impressive skills on the fiddle, banjo, and guitar. His voice had matured into a strong, clear tenor that had just enough bite to sound country without seeming affected, no small accomplishment for a northern-born singer.

Any doubts concerning Tracy's commitment to agrarian life were assuaged by the cover of *Look Out!* magazine. There was Tracy, perched on his John Deere 1020 tractor, hauling a wagon piled high with hay bales. An insert photo has Tracy and Eloise standing in a field, fiddle and guitar in hand (figure 18). In keeping with a DIY approach, he recorded the music in a friend's basement with a Sony portable tape machine: "No splicing, no echo, no 16 tracks. What you hear is the real thing."[50] Two additional Folkways albums, *Down Home with Tracy and Eloise Schwarz* (FTS 31052) and *Dancing Bow and Singing Strings* (FTS 6524), featuring the couple playing with neighboring bluegrass musicians, would follow in 1978 and 1979. *Down Home* included a medley of Pennsylvania dance tunes learned from local fiddlers as well as a Cajun song, "Madeleine." The latter was Tracy's debut on Cajun-style accordion and signaled a new direction in his musical interests.

Between playing with the Ramblers, Strange Creek, and Eloise, minding the farm, and trying to finish his college degree, Tracy had little time for the sorts of documentation projects that Mike and John pursued. He enjoyed playing informally with the older fiddlers in his community and working with traditional musicians at folk festival workshops, but it was not until the mid-1970s that he became seriously involved in fieldwork. At the 1974 University of Chicago Folk Festival Tracy was asked to play second fiddle for the legendary Balfa Brothers Cajun band. The group's leader, Dewey Balfa, who had first met Tracy at the 1964 Newport Folk Festival, was so pleased with Tracy's playing that he approached him about collaborating on a Cajun fiddling project. Moe Asch, whose Folkways catalog was low on Cajun material, was supportive of the venture, and Mike arranged for Tracy to borrow a Nagra portable tape recorder from the Smithsonian. In February 1975 Tracy visited Balfa in Basile, Louisiana, to play and record. Two instructional albums resulted: *Traditional Cajun Fiddle: Instruction by Dewey Balfa & Tracy Schwarz* (Folkways Records FM 8361, 1976) and *Cajun Fiddle Old & New with Dewey Balfa* (Folkways Records FM 8362, 1977). The second LP included a full side of live performances by the Balfa Brothers recorded by Tracy at Cajun dances and radio broadcasts. Tracy described the scene he came upon in Basile: "The establishment, C.C.'s Lounge, looks quite ordinary from the outside and at 4:45pm is almost empty. However, by 5pm it was jam-packed with happy, noisy listeners, and dancers. Most of the selections are intended to be for dancing and the band is set up that way—electric pickups on all instruments and drums for a heavy beat. The tempo is either waltz or two-step, with waltzes favored 2 to 1."[51]

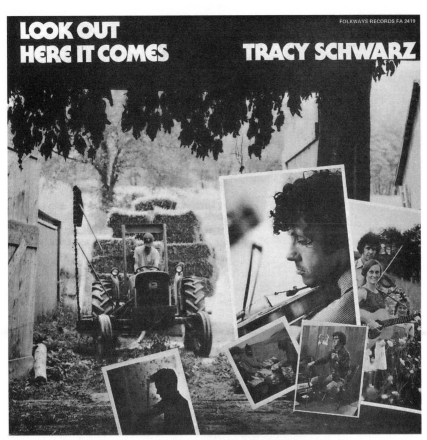

LOOK OUT
HERE IT COMES   TRACY SCHWARZ

FIGURE 18. Cover of *Look Out! Here It Comes* Folkways LP (1975).
Image courtesy of the Ralph Rinzler Folklife Archives
and Collections, Smithsonian Institution.

Tracy was deeply moved by the music and people he found in Louisiana. As work with the Ramblers and Strange Creek continued to dry up, he immersed himself in Cajun music, mastering the rhythmic bowing and high-keening singing characteristic of the tradition. He would eventually record a third Cajun LP, *Les Quatre Vieux Garçons* (Folkways Records FW 02626, 1984), featuring himself playing and singing with Dewey and Tony Balfa and Tracy's son, Peter Schwarz. Tracy's three Folkways Cajun albums introduced many northern players to the music.

As the three Ramblers ventured off on new musical excursions and tried to manage the stress of family life, internal personality tensions between John and Mike increasingly plagued the group. The depth of the problem became evident in a series of letters between the two in 1975 following what was apparently a difficult weeklong tour of New York and Connecticut in late February of that year. In a May 9 letter to John, Mike talked about the allocation of jobs between the Strange Creek Singers and the Ramblers, mentioning that he and Tracy had recently decided to have Strange Creek take an engagement at the Middletown, New Jersey, Folk Festival, that did not pay enough for the Ramblers. "It is Tracy's feeling that the NLCR should command a certain fee, about $1500 or so I gather. I feel that way also as I explained at Wesleyan in February." A fee of $1,500 was high for that time, one the Ramblers only received for multiday festivals or multinight runs at a club (the group fee for a one-night engagement continued to fluctuate between $300 and $750). Establishing such a high fee ceiling may have been Mike's indirect way of expressing his lack of interest in future touring with the group. He also reported rebuffing a recent inquiry about a Japanese tour, citing scheduling problems resulting from John's teaching. But he went on to conclude: "In addition of course I know we just wouldn't be able to do a tour for 10 days." The implication was that scheduling issues were not the only obstacles to touring. In Mike's view the trio could no longer get along together for an extended period of time.[52]

Following a Fourth of July appearance at the Castleton Bluegrass Festival in Vermont (for which the Ramblers were paid $1,500), Mike, John, and Tracy had a lengthy discussion regarding the future of the group. Reflecting on that meeting several weeks later, Mike wrote to John, "I have given considerable thought to the talk we had on 5/July and the way that you and I have not been able to resolve continuing problems and hassles." In a moment of stark honesty he admitted, "It makes things so miserable and difficult for all concerned that I have decided from my point of view that the NLCR can not continue with both you and I in the group." But Mike immediately backed off from demanding a complete dissolution of the Ramblers, noting, "I would like to continue but for the constant hassles so it is not simply a matter of my wanting to stop. I consider that the most I would want to do would be a couple of retrospective concerts or perhaps a festival (such as the UCFF) each year, but no tours of coffeehouses." The rest of the letter considered various possibilities for the future: retiring the Ramblers completely; either he or John leaving the group; maintaining the Ramblers name but forming rotating personnel configurations for different job situations. He closed by reiterating: "As far as I'm concerned it's not feasible for the group to go on tours."[53]

John wrote back to Mike on August 12 regarding "the recent confusion about the continued existence of the New Lost City Ramblers." Ignoring Mike's comments about their personal clashes, he underscored his commitment to keeping the group together: "I have a considerable investment in the NLCR. I am determined to continue the existence of the band under any circumstances." John proposed a solution under which, if all members of the band did not want to take a particular job, "the other two would be free to accept it by replacing the missing original member with a substitute acceptable to them, and notifying the prospective employer of the substitution." Under such circumstances the modified band might be called something like "The New Lost City Ramblers #2."[54]

In early October Mike responded to John, explaining that he did not want to use the Ramblers name unless all three members were present: "I think we have something very special as a group when all 3 of us are there and that substituting one member in a stopgap fashion would be weakening the whole thing." He had considered calling some alternative configuration "The Renewed Lost City Ramblers" but concluded that it would be best to call any new group by a completely different name. Grappling with his aggravation over the situation, he reflected: "All of our needs have been changing constantly over the past 6 years and I'm sure they will change again—and perhaps the time will come when we'll be able to function as a growing, operating group."[55] But that time was clearly not then. In an October 25 letter to Manny Greenhill, Mike stated, "I have decided to remove myself from the extended 3 days or more NLCR jobs and isolated others as well," and added he would only "work with NLCR for occasional special events." He cited John's insistence on having a New Lost City Ramblers #2 and continued bickering between the two of them as the reasons for his decision.[56] In the end, no New Lost City Ramblers #2 or Renewed Lost City Ramblers ever materialized, and Mike, John, and Tracy's joint appearances as the New Lost City Ramblers dwindled to a handful of engagements over the next three years. Because the Ramblers had always been dependent on a high degree of self-promotion and self-booking, Mike's growing dissatisfaction with the group and John's intensifying focus on teaching and filmmaking proved crippling for the ensemble's future. Yet neither one could completely let go.

Whatever demons beset Mike and John's personal relationship did not appear to affect the Ramblers' musicianship or their ability to perform together in public. During what would be their last California tour in September 1973, the Ramblers were recorded live at the Boarding House, a club in San Francisco. Reviews in the *San Francisco Examiner* and the *San Francisco Chronicle* confirmed that after fifteen years the Ramblers were still a commanding stage show. Under the headline "Folk 'Authentics' from the Big City," Philip Elwood of the *Examiner* proclaimed: "As instrumentalists, Seeger, Cohen, and Schwarz are now 'authentic,' in fact they even talk and sing more like old recording artists (such as Gid Tanner's Skillet Lickers) than they do like New Yorkers." "The Ramblers' singing is charming in its way," opined Joel Selvin for the *Chronicle*, "but it is the instrumental work that astounds."[57]

In 1975 the Boarding House recordings were released as *On the Great Divide*

THE NEW LOST CITY RAMBLERS

On The Great Divide

FSA PHOTO   RUSSELL LEE

Folkways Records FTS 31041

FIGURE 19. Front cover of *On the Great Divide* Folkways LP (1975).
Farm Security Administration photograph by Russell Lee. Image courtesy
of the Ralph Rinzler Folklife Archives and Collections, Smithsonian Institution.

(Folkways Records FTS 31041). The album was the Ramblers' first LP since 1968
and would be their last Folkways recording for more than two decades. Perhaps in
homage to their early albums, the cover of *Great Divide* featured a Russell Lee FSA
photograph of a rural couple sitting at home—a grizzled man in overalls casually
frails a banjo while his gaunt-looking wife reads from an open Bible or hymnal.
Two small American flags atop a small corner table behind the couple complete
a stark portrait of poverty and patriotism (figure 19). The image on the back of
the LP looked suspiciously like the Ben Shahn photograph from the Ramblers'
1959 *Songs from the Depression* LP. But this time the three musicians perched on the
running board of an old car are Mike, John, and Tracy, all sporting long, bushy
heads of hair (figure 20).

FIGURE 20. Photograph from *On the Great Divide* Folkways LP (1975). Photograph by Chris Strachwitz. Image courtesy of the Ralph Rinzler Folklife Archives and Collections, Smithsonian Institution.

With the exception of one 1950s Carter Stanley song, *Great Divide* was a return to the older, prewar repertoire. The superb editing and sequencing combined with imaginative instrumental and vocal arrangements to yield one of the Ramblers' most pleasing LPs. The recording's opening number was an unusual rendition of Tommy Jarrell's "John Brown's Dream," propelled by Tracy and John's interlocking fiddle and banjo lines backed by Mike's droning dulcimer. Sara Carter's "Railroading on the Great Divide," with its majestic, anthemlike chorus, was sung in rich three-part harmony. "La Valse des Bamboucheurs" showcased Tracy's budding proficiency at Cajun fiddling and singing. The album ended with John recounting a bizarre tall tale of the hillbilly band Carter Family and Son getting lost on their way to the Okeh studios (which did not exist), where they would have recorded "Cotton-Eyed Joe." The Ramblers launched into the breakdown, a frenzied flow of shuffling double fiddles and nonsense lyrics that John characterized as "an exercise in improvisation within the limits of great consistency and madness."[58]

From its Depression era imagery to its repertoire drawn from hillbilly discs and field recordings, *Great Divide* looked back, not forward. On the one hand, it was a testimony to the Ramblers' greatest strength—the group's ability to creatively reinterpret choice traditional tunes and songs while staying true to the stylistic spirit of the original material. On the other hand, there was little new here, with the exception of Tracy's Cajun number. In the rapidly evolving music environment of the mid-1970s the Ramblers probably sounded out of step to younger audiences. For those old-time and bluegrass enthusiasts looking for new directions, the Ramblers were not pointing the way.

As the 1970s rolled on the Ramblers' engagements were limited to festivals and an occasional college venue. Press coverage began to take on a nostalgic tone, emphasizing the Ramblers' historical accomplishments and cultural efficacy rather than their current musicianship. The group's appearance at the New York University Loeb Student Center in March 1977 prompted reflections from the *Village Voice* and the *New York Times*. In a *Voice* piece appropriately titled "Ramblers Still Wear Vests" Jerry Leichtling observed that the Ramblers had "scarcely changed at all" since their debut nineteen years ago, when they "helped usher in the era of the citybilly." Describing their presentation as almost "formal, classical in manner," he praised them for achieving "a subtle eminence; interpreters, they nonetheless have become synonymous with their field, almost primary sources themselves." Nearly misty-eyed, he concluded, "Even today the Ramblers function with an almost celestial cohesiveness. They are in touch with something old and precious and are still unsurpassed in their calm, smiling dignity." Writing for the *Times*, rock critic Robert Palmer noted that for nearly twenty years the Ramblers had paid "scrupulous attention to the historical accuracy in their arrangements." As a result, "the Ramblers have transcended the somewhat artificial idiom they helped spawn. They have swapped songs and stories with so many authentic folk performers for so many years that the question of authenticity doesn't really seem to matter. Their grasp of traditional materials is so sure that they can improvise plausibly." A similar theme appeared in Billy Altman's *Voice* review of the Ramblers' twentieth-anniversary concert, which was held in Carnegie Hall the following year. Lauding them for keeping traditional music "fresh and challenging," Altman continued: "Although they have started out as young men carrying on a tradition, they have become—and not only by dint of their long existence as a band—part of that tradition."[59] Journalists like Palmer and Altman were ahead of most scholars and government folklorists in challenging the validity of the terms *authenticity* and *tradition* when applied to urban folk musicians like the Ramblers. This issue will be returned to shortly.

On the evening of September 30, 1978, the Ramblers returned to Carnegie Hall to celebrate their twentieth anniversary. The concert was an attempt to look back over two decades of musical advocacy and forward to the future of old-time music.

Acknowledging their roots, they invited the two traditional musicians, Elizabeth Cotten and Roscoe Holcomb (who had to cancel at the last minute), who had served as Mike's and John's earliest inspirations. Pete Seeger, who had supported Mike and the trio since the group's inception, joined them onstage and performed a brief solo set. With a nod to the next generation of old-timey musicians, the Ramblers introduced the Highwoods Stringband and the North Carolina Green Grass Cloggers. The final number, a medley of fiddle tunes played by the whole cast, brought down the house when Mike and Tracy put down their fiddles and joined the cloggers to show off their own flat-foot steps.[60] Mark Greenberg described a vibrant evening of music making in his *Vermont Vanguard Press* review, which went beyond the predictable superlatives to laud the Ramblers' efforts to bring traditional musicians like Cotten and Holcomb to new audiences. Perhaps sensing the group's internal tensions and hoping to bring historical context to what he realized might be one of the Ramblers' final major concerts, Greenberg tactfully noted, "From the very start, the Ramblers have been a surprisingly loose collection of individuals trying to behave like a group. That's a difficult balance to maintain, and the boys have had their rough moments." But when that balance worked, as he asserted it did at the anniversary concert, "it's what gives the Ramblers their special character and what makes the music so accessible despite its—and their—eccentricities." Most important, that evening they emanated "a sense of shared purpose, expressed most simply by each of the Ramblers as love for the music and commitment to its living preservation."[61]

As too often was the case for the Ramblers, the occasion of their twentieth-anniversary concert was a resounding artistic success but a financial flop. With the *New York Times* on strike that week, the Carnegie show got little publicity, and producer Harold Leventhal had to paper the house to attract a respectable audience. A week later Leventhal wrote to the Ramblers, thanking them for "a memorable evening" of music. Acknowledging that the program had suffered with no *Times* preview, he remained upbeat in his final assessment: "The house looked good, and the audience loved it, and that's what counts." His attached financial report told another story; the show had lost $2,815 even before calculating in any artist fees. Pete Seeger played for gratis, as did the Ramblers, who took it upon themselves to pay the expenses for Elizabeth Cotten and the Highwoods out of their own pockets. Hopes of generating extra income from sales of their recently released album, *The New Lost City Ramblers: Twenty Years of Concert Performances* (Flying Fish 102, 1978), proved to be wishful thinking—less than $50 was realized in profit.[62]

As the Carnegie Hall curtain closed on their anniversary concert, the Ramblers surely realized that their days as a touring band were numbered. Mike, John, and

Tracy would not appear again as a trio until the following summer, when they performed at several folk festivals, the last being the Brandywine Friends of Old Time Music Festival held on July 21 and 22, 1979. A week before Brandywine Tracy sent a letter to Mike and John, announcing: "This is to serve notice that after the last obligation that the New Lost City Ramblers are presently committed to, I will no longer be available for appearances with the New Lost City Ramblers . . . Two major reasons for this are the escalating feud and my growing dissatisfaction with the music and approach of the New Lost City Ramblers."[63] On August 1 Mike sent out a general mailing to his Ramblers contacts that read: "The New Lost City Ramblers disbanded as a performing group as of 1/August, 1979. All members of the group are accepting engagements in their respective fields and we suggest that you contact any individual that you may be interested in."[64] Under the July 21–22 Brandywine date in his ledger book John had carefully sketched the word "END."

THINKING LEGACY
AND MOVING ON

In the fall of 1979, no doubt inspired by his experience at the Ramblers' twentieth-anniversary concert, Mark Greenberg penned a thoughtful minihistory of the Ramblers for *Frets Magazine*. But just before the publication went to press the editors must have received Mike's mailing, prompting the following addendum to Greenberg's article: "We learned that the New Lost City Ramblers had decided to make their 'unofficial semi-retirement' both official and permanent. The Ramblers formally closed the book on their music partnership August 1." What followed was nothing short of a eulogy: "Though the trio is now part of history, its unique spirit and enriching musical heritage will live on in its recordings, in the performances of its former members, and of those of the many groups and individual artists inspired by its infectious energy, its remarkable musicianship, its dedication, and its monumental achievements."

Looking back over two decades of accomplishments, Greenberg opened his piece by declaring that "the evidence of the Ramblers' influence is everywhere: from the numerous old-time bands, both amateur and professional, scattered across the country, to the recognition received by such traditional artists as Elizabeth Cotten, Dock Boggs, and Roscoe Holcomb, to widespread interest in many kinds of ethnic music and the growth of independent folk music record companies." He continued: "The terms 'old-time music' and 'traditional music' may not be household words, but they are now commonplace in a music world that can credit the New Lost City Ramblers for much of the expansion it has undergone over the past couple of decades."[1]

Such accolades positioning the Ramblers as the forefathers of the revival of old-time music had been part of the fan magazine discourse for several years prior to the trio's announced retirement. A review of *On the Great Divide*, appearing in the July 1975 edition of *Bluegrass Unlimited*, began: "It is difficult to imagine anyone interested in bluegrass or old-time music who has not, at least in some small way, been influenced by the efforts of the New Lost City Ramblers . . . [They] were the first practitioners of revived old-time music and they are still the best." Perhaps in hopes of allaying growing tensions between the old-time and bluegrass crowds, the reviewer went on to credit the Ramblers with "reintroduc[ing] many bluegrass and country listeners to the sources of the music they love so much."[2] In a lengthy 1975 interview with the Ramblers for *Pickin' Magazine*, editor Doug Tuchman introduced them as the group who "led the way back in time" for fans to "discover" the golden era of old-time music.[3] The reviewers of *Sing Out!* were among the first to champion the Ramblers as "crusaders for old-time," and the magazine had not lost enthusiasm for them or their cause. Near the occasion of the Ramblers' twentieth anniversary, Rhonda Mattern acknowledged the group's success in igniting a "Country Music Renaissance" among urban folk. "The revival and the Ramblers were childhood sweethearts," she reminisced. "Like chickens and eggs, it's hard to say which came first."[4]

These sorts of tributes, along with the aforementioned *Village Voice* and *New York Times* reviews of the Ramblers' New York University and twentieth-anniversary concerts, reflected a growing consensus. First, the Ramblers were the progenitors of the old-time music revival who had served as the essential bridge between traditional country styles and modern urban audiences from the late 1950s on. Second, they had seemingly transcended the old urban/rural, revival/traditional dichotomies to become synonymous with tradition itself. The Ramblers could not have agreed more—they hoped to be remembered as a vital link in an ongoing folk music process rather than a blip in the faddish folk boom or some sort of exotic cover band specializing in the re-creation of arcane hillbilly recordings. Yet as obvious as all this seemed to the Ramblers and their supporters at the time, their role as originators of the old-time music revival, their prowess as artists, and their status as bona-fide tradition bearers would be called into question.

While journalists and popular writers were quick to grasp the magnitude of the Ramblers' contributions to American folk music, academic folklorists and cultural historians were slow to join in the chorus. D. K. Wilgus and others had occasionally reviewed Ramblers recordings in scholarly journals, but most academics (and nearly all academically trained folklorists) still viewed the revival with a degree of skepticism. Wilgus himself bemoaned this situation in a 1968 *Journal of American Folklore* review, pointing out that although the Ramblers had "presented and taught to countless numbers the materials and styles of Southern folk tradition," they "have not been integrated into academic study, and both sides are poorer for the separation."[5] The previously discussed 1966 comments by Ellen Stekert regarding the "incongruous" nature of a city group like the Ramblers playing mountain music (chapter 7) and Bill Malone's 1968 observation that the Ramblers' slightly affected singing couldn't match their "carbon copy" instrumentals (chapter 5) had raised troubling issues of authenticity while bypassing any attempt to historicize the group within the context of postwar American society.

A 1971 article in the *Journal of American Folklore* exploring the relation of the folk revival to the so-called counterculture of the 1960s was the first scholarly piece to seriously acknowledge the contributions of the Ramblers. Coauthors Jens Lund and R. Serge Denisoff surveyed the various segments of the folk revival, identifying, in addition to faddish commercial singers and proponents of political-protest music, a third stream. This "so-called 'ethnic' or 'purist' strain" consisted of musicians "who advocated the ideal of 'traditional' music." Lund and Denisoff pointed to the Ramblers as prime examples of the ethnic strain, recognizing them as "the first performing group in the urban 'folk' scene to specialize in material of traditional rural origins." A brief group history praised the Ramblers for their instrumental versatility, their "careful imitation of the early Southern recording artists," and their disciplined efforts to carefully credit the sources of their songs.[6] While none of this came as news to Ramblers fans, the fact that the scholarly publication of the American Folklore Society had finally recognized the Ramblers as serious students and interpreters of traditional folk music was not insignificant.

In 1979 ethnomusicologist David Evans, the record reviewer for the *Journal of American Folklore*, wrote a lengthy piece on folk-revival releases. Tracing the evolution of folk revivals back to the nineteenth-century efforts of the Fisk University Jubilee Singers, Evans proposed a new stage made possible by the expansion of reissued recordings in the 1960s that put listeners in touch with the actual sounds of rural folk music. This in turn, he reasoned, resulted in "a new wave of revivalism spurred on by performers like the New Lost City Ramblers, who strove for authenticity in re-creating folk music styles." The Ramblers and their followers were responsible, according to Evans, for helping usher in a new stage of the urban folk revival, which was "characterized by an increasing competence and authenticity in the re-creation of folk style and a strong tendency toward conscious specialization and regionalism or ethnicity." Bucking the tide of folklorists who still dismissed the revival as "fakelore," Evans staked out more progressive ground: "Good new pieces are being created in traditional styles, while at the same time old styles are undergoing development and experimentation. These are processes that have always taken place in healthy folk traditions, and it is gratifying to witness them once again."[7]

By the mid-1980s the history of bluegrass and its relation to the folk revival was finally being charted by scholars, and the Ramblers were part of the story. In *Bluegrass Breakdown* cultural historian Robert Cantwell touted the Ramblers as "the first and most important of the postwar revival string bands" and credited them for bringing early bluegrass material by Bill Monroe and the Stanley Brothers to northern audiences. But Cantwell realized that the Ramblers' contributions went well beyond bluegrass, noting that they "pioneered the revival of old-time string-band music and continued its dissemination for nearly twenty years without a rival." Indeed, the band "warrants a book of its own," he aptly observed.[8] Neil Rosenberg, in *Bluegrass: A History*, acknowledged the Ramblers for introducing Lomax's concept of performance style into the revival at a time when song texts and tunes were the main focus of urban singers. The Ramblers not only emphasized regional styles but also offered choice source material to their listeners: "Like reissue records, their performances had the effect of providing repertoire for revivalists, as well as other bluegrass bands." As evidence Rosenberg pointed to the inclusion of Ramblers arrangements on the early 1960s recordings of bluegrass legends Flatt and Scruggs and the Stanley Brothers. Rosenberg also emphasized the important role Mike's Folkways bluegrass LPs and John's *High Lonesome Sound* documentary played in introducing bluegrass to city audiences. (The latter was the first documentary film to include bluegrass and led to the association of Bill Monroe with the phrase "high lonesome sound.") The Ramblers, he concluded, "more than any other group created an interest in southern rural string-band music among urban listeners."[9]

Cantwell's and Rosenberg's studies focused on the history of bluegrass, acknowledging the old-time music revival only in passing. At some point in the 1970s practitioners of old-time music had drifted away from their bluegrass counterparts, and by the decade's end a full-blown old-time music renaissance had burgeoned into a national network of players and fans. A fascinating 1985 double-LP release, titled appropriately *The Young Fogies* (Heritage Records 056), documented a vibrant scene that stretched from coast to coast. Produced by record collector and banjoist Ray Alden, the double album featured cuts by some forty revivalist bands. The set showcased not only the Ramblers and the aforementioned Highwoods, Hollow Rock, Dr. Humbead's New Tranquility String Band, and the Hot Mud Family but also groups that had achieved some notoriety through recordings and intermittent touring, including the Plank Road String Band (from Lexington, Virginia), Agents of Terra (from Ithaca, New York), the Deseret Stringband (from Salt Lake City, Utah), the Chicken Chokers (from Boston), and the Canebreak Rattlers (from New York City). Most of the featured bands were informal, nontouring operations that played primarily at local venues and occasional festivals.

Like the Fuzzy Mountain and Putnam String County bands, they tended to view themselves as participants in homegrown music making, occasionally hooking up with kindred spirits during their travels. Collectively, they formed, Alden wrote, "a family of 'fogies' sharing the old fashioned notion that we can play our own style of music using traditional instruments." What was most important for these players was "a sense of community and celebration when we do get together. All night jam and clogging sessions. String band contests which have a delicate balance of fun and competition. The sharing of food and drink and putting someone up for the night are all part of the hospitality and celebration."[10]

An eighteen-page insert titled *The Young Fogies Gazette* featured over a hundred autobiographies of these new old-time musicians. Most of the older musicians (born before 1950) claimed to have discovered folk music through the initial folk boom of the 1950s, old 78s collected from junk shops or friends, collections like the 1952 Folkways *Anthology of American Folk Music*, Pete Seeger's recordings and banjo book, and the Ramblers' early Folkways recordings. Those born after 1950 were more likely to cite younger bands like the Highwoods, anthology reissues and field recordings of traditional musicians released in the 1960s (a number of the latter produced by Mike or John), and trips to southern festivals and fiddle conventions. A few like Alan Jabbour, Bert Levy, Bill Dillof, and Art Rosenbaum admitted pursuing professional careers (government arts administration, medicine, law, and arts education, respectively) while continuing their music as a pastime. Others presented themselves as wandering troubadours, playing in various bands and moving from one scene to the next. As a musician identifying himself as Jumalh aka Dr. Bubba narrated, "[I] was kidnapped in 1979 by the Gypsy Gyppo String Band and dragged off to Galax. This experience seriously warped my reality, firmly placing both feet on that bum American road."[11] Many noted their ongoing involvement in record collecting, research and field documentation, writing, and record production. If old-time music was a part-time hobby for these young fogies, they certainly pursued it with unbridled enthusiasm.

The autobiographies also reveal that the scope of the old-time music movement was far broader than the forty bands presented on the two *Fogies* LPs. Many of the musicians had played with multiple bands, many of which had constantly rotating personnel. Influential bands like the Delaware Water Gap (New York City), the Wretched Refuse String Band (New York City), the Correct Tones (Ithaca, New York), and the Gypsy Gyppo String Band (Seattle) did not make it onto the compilation, nor did scores of lesser-known groups mentioned in the autobiographies. A thorough history of the old-time music renaissance remains to be written, but Alden's collection makes it clear that by the mid-1980s scores of bands and hundreds of musicians were scattered in communities across the country.

The Ramblers were crucial players in the scene Alden described. The original group (with Tom) was honored with the initial track on the compilation. Tracy, backed by Eloise and his son, Peter, had the second track. Alden identified Mike, John, and Tom as "the primogenitors of the young string bands." *The Young Fogies Gazette* insert included an Alden cartoon of a caveman discovering a banjo. The cartoon was labeled "before n.l.c.r." (figure 21). Many of the musicians credited Ramblers records and the traditional artists recorded and brought to festivals by Mike and John as their initial contact with old-time music.

In retrospect, just how much of the 1980s musical activity documented on Alden's *Young Fogies* project could be directly attributed to the Ramblers is open for debate. A decade later Mark Greenberg would suggest that the Ramblers "gave birth to a new, transnational (and even international) community of old-time music lovers."[12] Evoking the birthing function or using hyperbolic language like "primogenitors" in reference to the Ramblers or, for that matter, to any musical group is suspect. It is always dangerous to lay the monogenesis for any musical style or movement at the feet of any single artist or ensemble. No one would challenge the fact that the Ramblers were the first postwar northern band specializing in old-time music to extensively record and tour or that their emphasis on traditional sources and style represented a radical alternative to urban folk music during the commercial boom. But, as Alan Jabbour has pointed out, tracing a strict ancestral lineage from the Ramblers to all that followed in the later 1960s belies a more complex historical record.[13] By the mid-1960s there were groups of old-time music enthusiasts who, completely independent of the Ramblers, were gathering to play in places like Alan Block's sandal shop in Greenwich Village, Tommy and Bobbie Thompson's house outside of Durham, North Carolina, and the Colby Street house in Berkeley. Bands like Hollow Rock, Fuzzy Mountain, Dr. Humbead, and Fat City would have emerged from these communities to play at festivals and busk in the streets whether or not there had ever been a New Lost City Ramblers. Several of these groups, particularly Hollow Rock and Fuzzy Mountain, drew their repertoire from local sources and developed styles completely independent of any Ramblers influence.

While acknowledging that a good deal of old-time music making that sprang up in the 1960s and 1970s had no direct link to the Ramblers, all the old-time bands that recorded and toured during the period benefited in one way or another from the Ramblers' earlier work. Rounder Records' decision to take a chance and record Hollow Rock and Highwoods as well as Flying Fish Records' choice to take on the Red Clay Ramblers and the Hot Mud Family in the 1970s were undoubtedly influenced by the Ramblers' demonstration that there was a small but devoted niche market for old-time music. Likewise, the second-generation touring bands

FIGURE 21. Ray Alden, "before n.l.c.r." cartoon (1985) from
The Young Fogies Gazette, part of the double-LP release
The Young Fogies (Heritage Records 056).

of the 1970s, particularly the Highwoods and the Red Clay Ramblers, played to
audiences the Ramblers had nurtured over the previous decade. Had there been
no Ramblers, it is not at all certain that these bands would (or could) have taken
to the road when they did or that they would have survived as long as they did.
The old-time music movement would undoubtedly have happened whether or not
Mike, John, and Tom had stepped into John Dildine's radio station in May 1958
and gone on (with Tracy) to promote old-time music over the next two decades.
But the scope and shape of the scene Alden documented in the mid-1980s would
have been immeasurably different, and presumably not as rich, without them.

Worth noting is that nearly all of the young fogies on Alden's compilation
were born outside the rural South and grew up in northeastern or midwestern
cities and suburbs. By the mid-1980s a handful (including Mike) reported relocating to the Southeast, primarily to small communities in Virginia and North
Carolina, presumably to be closer to the sources of the music. The fact that most

of the old-time musicians documented by Alden were based in urban centers and colleges outside the Southeast (with the notable exceptions of the college-oriented Durham/Chapel Hill, North Carolina, and Lexington, Virginia, scenes begs the question of just how much revitalization was going on within the rural communities that were the actual sources of the music. By the early 1960s most young southerners had moved beyond old-time and early hillbilly music in what they perceived to be a natural progression toward more contemporary bluegrass, rockabilly, and Nashville country-and-western styles. Perhaps the South was not ready at that time for a serious revival of older styles, especially a revival spear-headed by a group of young Yankees. This lack of interest probably explains why the Ramblers played the lion's share of their live performances for urban and college audiences outside the Southeast; when they did venture below the Mason-Dixon Line, it was to progressive college towns like Chapel Hill, Charlottesville, and Austin. With the exception of the 1962 Galax Old-Time Fiddlers Convention, the 1963 Mountain Dance and Folk Festival in Ashville, and Anne Romaine's 1968 Southern Folk Festival tour of five college venues, the trio never played in small southern towns, nor did they appear at the bluegrass festivals or outdoor country music parks that were frequented by the working-class southerners who were the historical heirs to the music. The Ramblers' impact as "crusaders for old-time music" during their heyday as a touring band in the 1960s was felt primarily outside, rather than within, those southern source communities.

Just how much influence the Ramblers' documentation and promotion of southern folk artists like Holcomb, Boggs, Carter, Robertson, Watson, and Ashley had on the musical practices of their respective home communities is difficult to assess. To what degree did the Ramblers' work in those rural communities, along with the efforts of other outside documenters and cultural activists like Rinzler and Jabbour, actually result in a rekindling of interest in older styles among younger musicians? This question and the broader issue regarding how those senior traditional musicians felt about being "discovered" and "revived" for urban audiences deserve a thorough study of their own. At this juncture all we know is that the old-time music revival gained momentum in the South during the two decades following the release of Alden's *Young Fogies* collection and that Mike and Tracy, who relocated to Virginia (in 1981) and West Virginia (in 1989), respectively, served as strong advocates for the music in their adopted home locales.

Scholarly treatments of the folk music revival that appeared in the 1990s and early 2000s continued to historicize the Ramblers as the originators and unrivaled champions of the old-time music revival, "setting the pattern for the hundreds of amateur bands that followed them."[14] These narratives tended to position the Ramblers as the traditional alternative to commercial folk music, but the details

of how they accomplished their work and the breadth of their contributions remained sketchy at best. With the in-depth study Robert Cantwell had called for
a decade earlier nowhere in sight, again it fell to writers in the popular arena to
flesh out the Ramblers' legacy. In the early 1990s longtime revival observer Jon
Pankake compiled two "best of" volumes of Ramblers material drawn from their
early Folkways recordings. His notes to both are insightful. In the 1991 volume
he underscored the historical importance of the electronic recordings that put
musicians like the Ramblers in direct touch with sounds from the past and allowed
them to dig deep into regional performance style. He went on to sweep aside
the persistent myth that the Ramblers were "scholarly imitators" of old records,
arguing that through their mastery of traditional musical syntax they were able
"to recreate in their own voices new performances" that captured the spirit of
the old hillbilly bands.[15] His essay accompanying the 1993 volume emphasized
the Ramblers' accomplishments as documenters and presenters of traditional
southern musicians: "When the final history of the Ramblers is written, their
role as interpretive intermediaries between the Folk Music Revival and traditional
musicians who would otherwise have never been known to contemporary audiences may well overshadow their importance as performers."[16]

These points were not lost to cultural historian Philip Gura, who in 1999 wrote
the most thorough history of the Ramblers to date. He did so not for a scholarly
publication but for the *Old-Time Herald* fan magazine. Gura stressed that in addition to playing traditional music from traditional sources, "one of the NLCR's
most significant innovations was to bring on stage with them living exemplars of
the folk tradition."[17] Their role as "interpretive intermediaries," to use Pankake's
term, was clear in their advocacy for traditional musicians in venues like the University of Chicago Folk Festival and New York City's Friends of Old Time Music.
With the founding of the Smithsonian Festival of American Folklife in 1967 and
the NEA Folk Arts Program in 1973, Gura observed, "What the NLCR had begun
in the early 1960s on their own initiative—bringing traditional performers to new
audiences—now was federal policy."[18] Perhaps Gura indulged in a bit of hyperbole
when he pronounced that the Ramblers had "ignite[d] a cultural movement in
which music became the marker for a renewal of interest in the oldest kinds of
communities, those built on respect for tradition," but his larger point is well
taken. The Ramblers were not the sole progenitors, but they certainly played an
indispensable role in laying the foundations for the broader ethnic music movement that would explode in the post-Bicentennial era and lead to a resurgence in
Cajun, Yiddish, and Irish traditions, to name but a few.

One renowned observer of the postwar folk revival expressed similar sentiments. Archie Green, during a 2008 interview, told Mike and John he was "one of

your number one intellectual fans." He then went on to unabashedly explain: "You see I don't value you guys as musicians, I value you as educators. Wherever you went on a college campus, from Cambridge to Berkeley, six months later there was a hillbilly band imitating the Ramblers. You guys were teachers and pioneers."[19]

No history is ever final, but from our present vantage point Green's, Gura's, and Pankake's observations pose an intriguing question: Did the Ramblers' accomplishments as cultural conduits, educators, and instigators of an ongoing roots music movement perhaps outweigh their musical achievements? Put another way, will they be remembered first and foremost as cultural workers or as creative artists?

Recognition of the Ramblers' work as preservationists and advocates for traditional musicians has expanded over time. Their efforts to connect city audiences with what they perceived to be authentic rural folk expression have taken on fresh significance as contemporary cultural historians shed light on the importance of twentieth-century American cultural revivals and the notions of tradition and heritage they purvey. Consider, for example, Cantwell's argument that the folk music revival of the 1960s was a complex social and political response by young (mostly college) students to the stifling conformity of middle-class suburban life—a movement marked by a rejection of authority and rigid structure, nostalgia for an imagined past inhabited by an idealized folk, and the search for community and self-transformation.[20] While the Ramblers never espoused the utopian romanticism or overt political rhetoric of a Pete Seeger, they did self-consciously present their listeners with alternatives to commercial folk music that involved the embrace of neglected musical styles of a bygone era when people supposedly made informal music with friends, family, and neighbors. Mike's, John's, and Tracy's choices to live in the country and to announce their moves with LPs titled Gone to the Country and Rural Delivery No. 1 further clarified their discontent with modern urban and suburban lifestyles.

Cantwell's observations are central to the way cultural historians have come to understand the interrelated roles of tradition, authenticity, and revival in the modern world. Increasingly, the notion of tradition has come to be seen as "a construction rather than an inheritance," as folklorist Barbara Kirshenblatt-Gimblett succinctly put it.[21] That construction of tradition, argued folklorist and fiddler Burt Feintuch, is a hallmark of revivals that involves "an ongoing process of interpreting and reinterpreting the past" through a kind of cultural editing. As a result, "each of the revivals achieved its own momentum with its own preferred repertoire, its own sanctioned styles, and its own selective view of the past."[22] In other words, a musical revival becomes, according to ethnomusicologist Philip Bohlman, "an overt and explicit act of authentication."[23] The Ramblers personify the revivalist impulse Feintuch and Bohlman describe. For more than two decades they were about the business of selecting and defining what constituted authentic Appalachian repertoires and styles and presenting them to urban listeners. They aimed to establish canons of preferred artists (living and deceased) and favorite songs and tunes as well as explicating the correct ways of playing and tuning mountain stringed instruments. They were the sorts of "cultural middlemen" described by Benjamin Filene, individuals who "made judgments about what constituted America's true musical traditions" and "helped shape what 'mainstream' audiences recognized as authentic, and inevitably, transformed the music that the folk performers offered."[24]

The idea that such self-conscious intervention with folk musicians may lead to some sort of manipulation or a "sentimentalizing [of] them [the folk] as Other," as Filene has suggested, does not necessarily hold sway for the Ramblers.[25] From the beginning the Ramblers made it clear that many of the early hillbilly bands they venerated aspired to be popular entertainers, not purveyors of pure folk tradition. Indeed, a few, most notably, the Carter Family and Uncle Dave Macon, were among the first stars of commercial country music. Perhaps more importantly, a number of the traditional musicians with whom the Ramblers worked most closely in the 1960s—Maybelle Carter, Cousin Emmy, Eck Robertson, Clarence Ashley, the Stanley Brothers, and Dewy Balfa—were semiprofessional entertainers with ample recording and touring experience. Elizabeth Cotten and Doc Watson, who had little prior professional experience outside their home communities before meeting the Ramblers and Ralph Rinzler (who promoted the latter), would go on to successful musical careers performing primarily for urban folk music fans. Watson, whose music so deeply embodied southern tradition that Mike and John invited him to become a Rambler, was well versed in popular music, from rockabilly to Gershwin. Roscoe Holcomb and Dock Boggs perhaps came closest to the image of true backwoods folk for whom music had been strictly a pastime (although Boggs had made several commercial recordings for the Brunswick label in the late 1920s), yet each had developed his own highly individualistic, esoteric style and was eager to play for city and college audiences. The Ramblers spent enough time working and playing with their mentors to not mistake them for idealized repositories of untainted tradition. They refrained from presenting them to urban audiences as exotics or primitives the way the Lomaxes, according to Filene, did with Lead Belly when they initially brought him to New York in the 1930s.[26] While perhaps overusing loaded terms like *authentic* and *genuine* when differentiating rural musicians from urban revivalists, the Ramblers viewed individuals like Carter, Watson, Robertson, Holcomb, and Boggs first and foremost as great artists and exemplars of southern regional styles that could not compete with contemporary

FIGURE 22. Workshop, University of Chicago, ca. 1964–65.
Left to right, seated: Mike Seeger, Roscoe Holcomb, Dock Boggs,
Caither Carlton, John Cohen, Dock Watson, Arnold Watson.
Photograph courtesy of John Cohen.

commercial folk or country music. To the Ramblers they were fellow travelers, not sentimentalized others, who loved the older music and would help keep it alive.

Filene offered convincing evidence that culture brokers like the Lomaxes manipulated the repertoires and styles of the folk musicians (particularly Lead Belly) they promoted to make them more palatable to city listeners.[27] Just how much influence the Ramblers exerted on the repertoire choices of the traditional artists they recorded and promoted is difficult to say. Undoubtedly, the Ramblers encouraged them to emphasize older material at the expense of better-known pop tunes they might have learned from the radio or commercial recordings, and they certainly advised them against performing potentially offensive black-face material (as Clarence Ashley was evidently prone to do). But most were savvy enough to not need the Ramblers to tell them what their new city and college listeners wanted to hear. The most talented, like Doc Watson, found ways to seamlessly weave more popular material into their performances—over the years Watson would include nontraditional songs such as "Summertime," "St. Louis Blues," and "Nights in White Satin" in his repertoire.

The Ramblers' own eclectic tastes in southern music may explain in part their reluctance to intervene too heavily into how or what their mentors performed for revival audiences. Mike, John, Tom, and Tracy had always painted with a broad brush, drawing materials from both commercial hillbilly records and field recordings while emphasizing a variety of genres, styles, and instrumental combinations. Far from advocating a restrictive pure stream, they celebrated the diversity of white southern folk music—string-band dance tunes, hillbilly love and novelty songs, bluegrass duets, ballads, blues, gospel, and ragtime-influenced songs and instrumental pieces. By the early 1970s they were one of the few northern bands capable of moving comfortably between old-time and bluegrass styles. Their efforts undoubtedly helped set the precedent for the musical diversity that continues to characterize the ongoing old-time music scene.

Returning to Filene's broader concerns, it is useful to consider just how far down the road of romanticism the Ramblers ventured in their role as interpreters of southern rural music. If romanticism represents, as intellectual historians Michael Lowy and Robert Sayre suggest, "a critique of modernity, that is of modern capitalist civilization, in the name of values and ideals drawn from the past," then surely the Ramblers indulged.[28] Through their choice of music and lifestyles the Ramblers, along with those kindred spirits who comprised the traditional wing of the folk music revival, expressed their deep discontent with midcentury American life and its homogenizing media. They did not hesitate to wax nostalgic for the old days (witness their famous Blue Eagle logo fan card, which read: "I am lost. Please return me to 1932") and in general tended to look back, rather than forward, for inspiration. In keeping with the basic tenets of romanticism, they valued the creative muse over pure reason, the logic of the market, and the bureaucratic structures that had come to characterize the modern world they grew up in. This acknowledged, whatever romanticism the Ramblers practiced did not turn them into antiquarians, Luddites, or folk exoticizers; nor did it leave them lost in an idealized past and out of touch with contemporary life. As Lowy and Sayre point out, romanticism is a complex and often contradictory concept that itself is grounded in the critical modernist enterprise; that is, romanticism is in part "a modern critique of modernity."[29] From this perspective the Ramblers could only undertake their cultural and artistic work because they were modern men who were well educated, well traveled, politically progressive, and cosmopolitan in temperament. While Tracy and Mike moved deeper into the country, John and Tom maintained stronger connections to urban culture and consciousness. John was equally at home with backwoods banjo tunes and mountain ballads as he was with the avant-garde art of de Kooning, Pollack, Kline, and Grooms, all of which he perceived as alternatives to mass-produced culture.[30] All four Ramblers recognized the modernist paradigm of newness, especially when it came to folk music, which they viewed as a dynamic process rather than a stagnant body of antiquated tunes and songs. Unlike purist folk song scholars and many urban folk singers of the 1950s, they avoided the trap of becoming mired in centuries-old, supposedly orally transmitted folk songs and tunes, turning rather to hillbilly and bluegrass music, expressions they rightly identified as traditionally rooted modern styles. While they were dismissive of most midcentury mass culture, the Ramblers unashamedly embraced technology, using the latest advances in recording equipment and the burgeoning independent record industry to capture old sounds and disseminate them to new audiences. They succeeded in channeling their own brand of progressive romanticism into their larger mission of cultural advocacy as they sought to convince their contemporaries of the value of maintaining traditional folk practices in the modern world.

Turning to the question of artistry, the Ramblers' musical legacy has been a mixed bag. Mike's stage quip about "our six long-playing, short-selling Folkways records" always resonated with an uncomfortable veracity—their Folkways recordings never did sell well. The group maintained a core following of old-time music enthusiasts as well as a broader audience of listeners who appreciated the distinctive sonorities of acoustic Appalachian instruments and singing rendered in elegant and often unusual arrangements. Creative interpretation rather than original composition or stylistic innovation was always at the heart of their artistic prowess. Their ability to imaginatively choose and recombine a broad constellation of traditional performance practices, choice regional repertoire, and fresh instrumental configurations made them unique among city performers of their time.

But not all folk music enthusiasts were Ramblers fans. Those who clung to an orthodox purist doctrine had a hard time accepting the possibility that any group of northern-bred musicians could capture the full range of nuanced instrumental and vocal styles that characterize southern mountain music. Many critics felt that the Ramblers' instrumental work outshone their vocal efforts, and Bill Malone was not alone in his assessment that too often the Ramblers were "trying to sound country" when they sang. Additional criticism came from those folk aficionados who dismissed the Ramblers' music as overly derivative and lacking in virtuosic technique and innovative arrangement. Moreover, by the mid-1960s the explosion of reissue anthologies and field collections that became available on LP from small independent labels allowed fans to bypass the Ramblers and go straight to the original sources of the music. More recent technological developments beg the question: Will the next generation of folk and old-time enthusiasts bother with the Ramblers' Folkways recordings when digitally remastered Uncle Dave Macon, Carter Family, Charlie Poole, and the Skillet Lickers (to name but a few) are only a click away on downloading services like iTunes, Amazon, and Rhapsody?

More time must elapse before these broad questions of cultural activism and artistic creativity can be fully sorted out. But at this juncture attempting to separately evaluate the artistic and cultural dimensions of the Ramblers' legacy is simply not productive. The musical and cultural aspects of their mission were too inexorably intertwined—performance, preservation, and presentation all flowed out of and back into one another. Mike's and John's respective "discoveries" of Boggs and Holcomb led to extensive audio and film documentary projects. Arrangements were soon made for them to appear at northern folk clubs and festivals, where the Ramblers served as their interpreters and musical accompanists. During recording sessions, stage performances, educational workshops, and informal music sessions the Ramblers absorbed additional stylistic practices and repertoire from their mentors, which they in turn integrated into their own stage performances, workshops, and recordings.

Surveying the state of various American ethnic music cultures in the 1980s, ethnomusicologist Mark Slobin observed that three sorts of individuals were necessary for a successful folk revival: historian-researchers, elder statesmen–repositories, and performance acolytes–band creators.[31] The Ramblers, at different points in their careers, excelled in all three capacities. They located and documented elder statesmen of the tradition through their research, created a recording and touring band to spread the music to new audiences, and eventually themselves became living repositories of style and tradition. Indeed, in their multiple roles as performers-documenters-educators the Ramblers were unique in the postwar revival. To put this in perspective, consider the widely acclaimed accomplishments of Pete Seeger, Alan Lomax, and Ralph Rinzler. Most folk music historians would agree that these three were unsurpassed in their respective efforts to perform, document, and present American folk music to urban audiences during the 1950s and 1960s. No one could get a crowd singing like the elder Seeger, but he rarely dabbled in fieldwork with traditional musicians. No one was more prolific at capturing American (and world) folk music on tape and film than Lomax, but he never distinguished himself as a performer of the music. And no one could match Rinzler's vision and administrative skills, which gave birth to the Smithsonian folk festival, but the effort forced him to lay down his mandolin and curtail his own field and record production projects. None of these influential figures, or anyone else for that matter, could match the Ramblers' versatility in all three domains. They were consummate musicians, meticulous documentarians, and innovative presenters of traditional music and of the musicians who created that music. They carried out their mission with impeccable skill, a steadfast respect for the originators of the music, and an unwavering commitment to foreground the accomplishments of their traditional mentors over their own. And they served as models for playing homegrown music and for taking that music to the stage and on the road.

When asked when and why the Ramblers broke up, John bristles, and his aggravation goes beyond what he sees as the literal inaccuracy of the query. The Ramblers, in his mind, never totally broke up, occasionally regrouping for festivals and special events. More important, he contends that each individual remained deeply committed to the original Ramblers mission: to keep old-time music alive and flourishing in a musical universe that continues to be dominated by commercial mass media. In their post-Ramblers careers Mike, John, Tom, and Tracy each maintained a vigorous advocacy for traditional music. The breadth of their efforts would fill a separate volume, one that will have to wait for students of the post-1970s folk music scene. The brief sketches that follow are guideposts for that journey.

Mike and Alice decided to move to less isolated environs in 1976, leaving rural Pennsylvania for the Washington, DC, suburb of Garrett Park, Maryland. But their marriage did not last, and by 1980 they had separated. While visiting a friend in Lexington, Virginia, the following year, Mike decided to fulfill a longtime dream of actually living in the southern Appalachians. In early 1981 he purchased a run-down, sprawling country house nestled on a pastoral hillside several miles outside of Lexington. Surrounded by the Allegheny and Blue Ridge mountains but not too far from Interstate 81 and Lexington's college-town amenities, the setting proved ideal. Mike went to work converting a section of his home into a recording and editing studio and plunged into a seemingly endless stream of projects. In 1995 he married Alexia Smith, a California native and environmental activist who was an old friend of his sister Penny. Mike and Alexia lived in Lexington until he passed away from multiple myeloma, a form of blood cancer, in August 2009.

Right up to the time of his death Mike maintained an astonishingly productive career as a solo performer, record producer, and educator. His main source of income came from his solo touring as an artist and lecturer. He recorded over a dozen solo albums, singing and playing traditional instruments ranging from fiddle, banjo, mandolin, and guitar to panpipes, Jew's harp, mouth organ, and autoharp (often combining two at once). He received Grammy nominations for *Solo—Old Time Country Music* (Rounder Records CD 0278, 1991) and *Southern Banjo Sounds* (Smithsonian Folkways SFW CD 40107, 1998), the latter featuring him playing over two dozen banjos for a guided tour of a century and a half of traditional African and Anglo-American banjo styles. With his sisters Peggy and Penny he has recorded three CDs of children's and Christmas music drawn from their mother's 1940s and 1950s song collections. Peggy and Penny joined him on the Grammy-nominated *Third Annual Farewell Reunion* (Rounder Records CD 0313,

1994). The album's stellar cast includes Bob Dylan, Pete Seeger, David Grisman, Ralph Stanley, Hazel Dickens, Jean Ritchie, Tommy Jarrell, and Michael Doucet. Another collaborative project, this time with David Grisman and John Harford, produced the Grammy-nominated CD *Retrograss* (Acoustic Disc, 1999).

Beside his own recordings Mike worked with Smithsonian Folkways to reissue a number of his vintage fieldwork LPs on CD with additional selections and updated notes. CDs of Elizabeth Cotten, Dock Boggs, the Country Gentlemen, and the Lilly Brothers as well as Mike's two 1950s bluegrass banjo collections and an updated country autoharp compilation became available in the 1990s and 2000s. The content of the collection *Close to Home: Old Time Music from Mike Seeger's Collection 1952–1967* (Smithsonian Folkways SFCD 40097, 1997) is self-explanatory.[32]

In addition to his Grammy nominations Mike was awarded the prestigious Rex Foundation Ralph J. Gleason Award in 1995, given to "a major figure in the advancement of music in America in the 1960s, whose openness to new music and ideas transcended differences between generations and styles."[33] He was also honored for his musical and documentary achievements with a Society for American Music's Honorary Membership Award in 2003 and for his work in cultural preservation with a National Endowment for the Arts Bess Lomax Hawes Award in 2009.

While Mike was the consummate musician and documentarian, John saw his work as a Rambler and beyond as "one giant painting that I just kept on doing. It's my work as an artist. It was the music and all the creative work that went into the photographing, filming, editing, album-cover design, and writing notes—they were all tied together."[34] In the post-Ramblers years John and Penny remained in Tompkins Corner, where they raised their two children, Sonya and Rufus. The couple eventually separated and divorced, and in 1993 Penny was struck down by cancer at nearly the same age that her mother had succumbed to the disease. John stayed on in Tompkins Corner in the farmhouse he and Penny bought in 1965.

John's position at SUNY Purchase allowed him to continue his creative and documentary work in photography and film. Encouraged by the success of his earlier eastern Kentucky and North Carolina films, he went on to produce another dozen documentaries that took him from Scotland to Peru to Virginia. During the 1980s and early 1990s his films explored the music of Sara and Maybelle Carter, British and Scottish ballad singing, Peruvian mountain music, textiles, Carnival traditions, Huayno music of the Andes, and Epirot-Greek music in Queens, New York. His photographs were shown across the United States and Europe and are in the permanent collections of the Metropolitan Museum of Art, the Museum of Modern Art, the Brooklyn Museum, the Corcoran Gallery, and the National

Portrait Gallery. In 2002 a retrospective show of his photographs of New York Beat writers and painters, city folk musicians, Harlem churches, and the music and culture of Appalachia and Peru toured a dozen museum venues nationwide. The accompanying catalog, titled *There Is No Eye* and published by Powerhouse Books in 2001, presented a sampling of his best photographs alongside thoughtful commentary.

As John's teaching career wound down toward his retirement in 1997 he threw himself back into audio-recording production. Like Mike, he worked with Smithsonian Folkways to reissue and expand his earlier Folkways field recordings by traditional artists, including Roscoe Holcomb, Dillard Chandler, and Reverend Gary Davis. The songs and tunes on his compilation *Back Roads to Cold Mountain* (SFW 40149, 2004), drawn from his field recordings and those by Ralph Rinzler, Alan Lomax, and others, provided the sound track for the movie *Cold Mountain*, based on Charles Frazier's critically acclaimed novel.

In addition to occasional Ramblers performances, John continued to play banjo and guitar informally with friends and neighbors, occasionally appearing at local concerts and town meetings in Putnam County. In 1999 he released his only solo album, *Stories the Crow Told Me* (Acoustic Disc 34). The collection included collaborations with guest performers David Grisman, Jody Stecher, and Sue Draheim. More recently, he has been playing with Peter Stampfel of the old Holy Modal Ramblers in a loosely organized outfit called the Velocity Ramblers.[35]

What began as a trip to Europe in the fall of 1962 led to a life as an expatriate for Tom. He and Claudia lived in Sweden for three years before settling in London in 1965. Claudia gave birth to their son, Ben, in March 1967, but the couple split up the next year. Although he taught for short stretches at Uppsala University in Sweden and later at Birkbeck College in London, Tom never seriously returned to his career as a mathematics lecturer, and, despite his earlier desire not to become a full-time musician, he did just that. In 1963 Folkways released *The Old Reliable String Band*, recordings Tom made with Roy Berkeley and Artie Rose before he left for Europe. In 1966 he formed the New Deal String Band with New York guitar and banjo player Joe Locker and fiddler Janet Kerr. The New Deal String Band played together throughout the 1970s and into the 1980s, and, following a brief hiatus, the group was revived in the 1990s with Tom's twenty-five-year-old son, Ben, as the primary fiddler. Sometime in the mid-1970s Tom began playing fiddle. In addition to Appalachian dance tunes he and Ben became deeply interested in the Swedish fiddle tradition. Tom's intense involvement in the music won him a Zornmärke (musician's medal) from the Swedish government.[36]

In 1969 Tom returned to the States to perform for the first time since he left the Ramblers in 1962. He began making annual American tours, playing as a soloist and occasionally with friends (but not with the Ramblers). In 2003 a New Lost City Ramblers reunion concert was held in London featuring Tom, Mike, John, and Tracy.

Like Mike and Tom, Tracy remained reliant on music for his livelihood in the post-Ramblers years. He and Eloise continued to tour and record in the late 1970s and into the 1980s until their marriage broke up in 1984. They sold their Brodbecks farm, and Tracy moved to Louisiana for a brief period before relocating to northeastern Vermont, where he lived for the next five years. In the summer of 1988, while teaching at the Ashokan Fiddle and Dance camp near Woodstock, New York, he met Ginny Hawker. A Virginia native, Hawker learned to sing bluegrass harmonies and old Primitive Baptist hymns from her father, Ben Hawker. Tracy and Ginny formed a musical alliance and moved to the small village of Tanner in Gilmer County, West Virginia, in 1989. They married in 1993. Since then they have toured, taught, and recorded a number of CDs of traditional southern music.

Tracy also remained active in the Cajun arena, playing fiddle and button accordion on occasional tours with Dewey Balfa. In 1990 he formed the Tracy Schwarz Cajun Trio with guitarist Lee Blackwell and fiddler Matt Haney. The group's two Swallow Records releases were both awarded the Prix Dehors de Nous by the Cajun French Music Association for best Cajun recording made outside Louisiana.[37]

Tracy recently received national notoriety when Levon Helm, formerly of the rock group the Band, recorded a Cajun-style version of "Poor Old Dirt Farmer" for Vanguard Records. The CD, Dirt Farmer, won a 2008 Grammy for Best Traditional Folk Album. Helm unwittingly cited the piece as traditional on the Vanguard CD, but a settlement was amicably worked out crediting Tracy with the song's authorship and assigning him an appropriate royalty. For Tracy the episode was bittersweet. He finally won recognition for his song, but it took a rock star like Helm (under the guise of "tradition") to attract the media spotlight.

The Ramblers never won a Grammy, either collectively or as individual artists. Throughout the post-Ramblers years they continued to operate under the mass-media radar as advocates and (for some) heroes of the ongoing old-time music movement. In 1998 they did manage a glimmer of national recognition with a Grammy nomination for their last joint venture. The previous year they had returned to the recording studio after a twenty-three-year hiatus to produce There Ain't No Way Out for Smithsonian Folkways (SFCD 40098, 1997). Mike explained that when the group got together several times a year they always seemed to come up with a few new songs that fit the Ramblers' unique sound and style: "So even though we're kind of ragged at times, perhaps we're worth one more recording."[38]

The trio had slowed down during the quarter century that had elapsed since they recorded *On the Great Divide*, but their overall sound had matured: "The hell-for-leather renditions of youth become the more thoughtful, circumspect performances of middle age," proclaimed Lyle Lofgren for the *Old-Time Herald*. The instrumentals were tight and crisp, at times featuring novel sounds such as Tracy feverishly beating fiddle sticks against John and Mike's interlocking banjo-mandolin lines on "Buck Creek Girls." Mike's quill-rack (panpipes), gut-string banjo, and cello, along with Tracy's button accordion, reflected new interests picked up in the post-Ramblers years. The group harmonizing on Carter Family and early bluegrass arrangements was superbly rendered, and Mike and Tracy delivered "some of the strongest vocal performances of their careers," pronounced a review in *Bluegrass Unlimited*. Tracy's singing on the bluesy "Jolie Petite Blond" and the Roscoe Holcomb–influenced rendition of "Oh Death" demonstrated a total mastery of Cajun and mountain-style singing. Mike's throaty vocal on the enigmatic "Brown Skin Girl" was at once eerie and evocative.[39]

A quick scan of the CD might lead the undiscerning listener to conclude that the Ramblers' approach hadn't changed much in forty years—they were still sourcing old 78s and field recordings while striving to balance innovation and tradition in a manner similar to that of the original trio. But to *Sing Out!* editor Mark Greenberg's ear, Mike, John, and Tracy had gone way beyond imitating the originals: "The Ramblers now take more liberties with their sources—without ever failing to honor them." John's revamping of Banjo Bill Cornett's "Buck Creek Girls," Tracy's fusing of Holcomb's and Boggs's styles on "Oh Death," and Mike's wild arrangement of "Free Little Bird," complete with quill and gut-stringed banjo accompaniment, are offered as compelling evidence of those liberties.[40] In what John playfully referred to as "retrohistory," the old Bill Monroe song "I'm on My Way to the Old Home" is refashioned into a Carter Family arrangement. Other pieces, like the Uncle Dave Macon and Carter Family numbers, are closer to the originals. Indeed, the group's respect for sources led them to revisit the classic "Colored Aristocracy," originally recorded on their first 1958 Folkways LP. The Ramblers' updated arrangement dropped the extra II (A) and IV chords (C) that John and Tom had added in 1958 and changed the VI chord (E) from a major back to a minor in keeping with the lead melodic line of the fiddle. In addition, John played mandolin to restore the original sound and spirit of the Rich Family source recording from 1936.

The cover of *There Ain't No Way Out* (figure 23) reprised the image on the Ramblers' first 1958 Folkways LP—the WPA Russell Lee photograph of the Depression era man sitting on a picnic blanket, strumming his guitar and serenading his reclusive wife (see chapter 3 and figure 4). But this time a small picture of a

there ain't no way out

New Lost City Ramblers

Smithsonian Folkways

FIGURE 23. Cover of *There Ain't No Way Out* Folkways LP (1997).
Reprise of the Ramblers' first 1958 Folkways LP with the Farm Security
Administration photograph by Russell Lee. Image courtesy of the
Ralph Rinzler Folklife Archives and Collections, Smithsonian Institution.

young Mike, John, and Tracy has been carefully inserted into the background. The three Ramblers sit attentively listening to the mystery man, seamlessly integrated into the scene. The booklet notes, again keeping with the tradition of no collaborative statements, consist of three miniessays under separate bylines. Predictably, Mike's comments were the most inwardly reflective. Musing on the tremendous "tactile, emotional, and aural pleasure" he gets from hearing and playing the music, he acknowledged his pedigree by waxing poetic: "The words are my Shakespeare and my mysteries, the music is my Bach." A common theme emerging from all three statements is a high degree of pride in the growth of southern string-band music over the past forty years. John identified the Ramblers as the presumptive font of that movement: "Our real achievement has not been in the number of records we sold, but in the proliferation of string bands who have found their own ways to enjoy and perpetuate this music." Such commentary might be read by some as self-serving, but as always John proved to be a complex admixture of ego, humility, and humor. In the same breath he acknowledged that many of the younger players the Ramblers presumably inspired had surpassed them in musical proficiency: "There are an overwhelming number of musicians who can polish off performances better than we ever could. To quote the banjo player Stringbean on the Grand Ole Opry, 'I feel so unnecessary.'"[41]

Looking back over four decades of work, Mike, John, and Tracy seem to have individually reached a common conclusion. Their legacy rested on their efforts to revitalize old-time music at a time when the tradition was on the wane in the South. Beyond their initial contributions as performers and promoters, they took great satisfaction in seeing old-time music flourish into the new millennium as a roots music subculture whose network extended from coast to coast and back into southern mountain communities where the music began.

10

PASSING FOR TRADITIONAL AND RETHINKING FOLK REVIVALISM

Tracy Schwarz is one of the most affable people you will ever meet, but he gets a little hot if you refer to him or his fellow Ramblers as folk music revivalists. "I left the city and suburbs forty years ago," he will remind you, "and country music and country living are in my blood."[1] In a 1989 letter published in the *Old-Time Herald* he commented on tensions between "folklorists and so-called folk revivalists." He complained that the latter suffered "discrimination, based on origin of birth," noting somewhat sarcastically, "If only I'd lied back in '57 [when he first started to play] I bet you a month's supply of old strings I could have passed for traditional."[2]

Tracy likes to tell the story of how he and his son, Peter, applied for NEA Folk Arts Apprenticeship Grants to study Cajun music with Dewey Balfa and Marc Savoy in 1984. Peter got the grant, but Tracy did not. "They told me I was already a master," Tracy scoffed. But the real reasons for his rejection, he suspected, were the funding guidelines that cast him as a "revivalist" instead of a community-based traditionalist. Two years later Dewey Balfa was invited to perform at the Smithsonian Festival of American Folklife. The festival programmers permitted Peter to appear as part of Dewey's band, but not Tracy. The elder Schwarz came along anyway, and the three plotted smuggling him onstage, wondering if security—"the folk music police"—would cart him away. In the end cool heads prevailed and Tracy played (but was not paid). While the two episodes probably had as much to do with tight funds as they did restrictive regulations, for Tracy they were a reminder that the folklore establishment still refused to recognize his legitimacy as a traditional musician.

Tracy's and Peter's experiences with the Folk Arts Program and the Smithsonian festival provoke intriguing questions about what constitutes a revivalist musician. Should Tracy and other city musicians who moved to rural communities to pursue the music at some point be considered bona-fide tradition bearers? What about their children and grandchildren? Can Peter, as the son of a revivalist, now be considered part of a linear heritage that connects him to some genuine line of tradition? Did he really come to the music in some way that was demonstratively more natural than his father's self-conscious discovery of a tradition foreign to his upbringing?

These questions do not lend themselves to easy answers, and one might wonder if today they are even worth asking. After all, if there is a general consensus that terms like *revival*, *tradition*, and *authenticity* are at best fuzzy cultural constructions rather than hard-wired realities, then what is all the fuss? Peter Schwarz and younger generations of old-time players draw from an astounding trove of American (and world) musics and tend to resist restrictive cultural labels such as folk, traditional, or revival. Peter does not see himself as a revivalist, or a second-generation revivalist, or even a first-generation genuine folk performer. He's a musician who loves and plays a wide variety of older country styles, including old-time, bluegrass, and Cajun, often performed in various combinations. Authenticity, the touchstone of the revivalist debate, is simply no longer an issue for him and his contemporaries.[3]

But for Tracy, Mike, John, and others of their generation, the question lingers. They cannot help but view the r word through a historical lens. From the beginning they were never comfortable being categorized as folk revivalists, a designation they found fraught with ambiguity and ripe with pejorative connotations. The linkage of the terms *folk* and *revival* during the Great Boom of the late 1950s and 1960s led to the popular (and persistent) misperception that the urban folk revival was all about commercial folk groups and the legions of amateur college kids who strummed guitars and sang along with them.[4] Although the Ramblers paralleled the popular boom and played to its college audiences, they were neither commercial singers nor enthusiastic amateurs, and they deeply resent any comparisons with the former, whom they viewed as the real imposters. "Back then we were antirevivalists," insisted John. "The 'revival' was about the Kingston Trio and the Limeliters, and we saw them as our enemies—all they cared about was popular entertainment and mass appeal."[5] Mike echoed these sentiments in 1997, when he wrote with pride about his years of involvement with "the revival of Southern string band music." He quickly qualified that by "revival" he meant "a restoration to life" of the songs and styles, not the folk song revival of the 1960s, which he dismissed as "urban popular songs and commercial music product."[6]

For the Ramblers the issue was more than simply semantics. To this day they are galled by those academics, government folklorists, and critics who continue to question their legitimacy because of their status as so-called folk revivalists. Their personal concerns illuminate the broader conceptual problems scholars and cultural workers have had dealing with folk revivals. Although academic folklorists and ethnomusicologists have developed sophisticated models for understanding the ebb and flow of cultural practice, they have remained loath to undertake the serious study of American folk music revivals, perhaps due to the commercial taint of the Great Boom. As one folklorist who was trained in the early 1970s reflected, "We learned, if only through subliminal suggestion, that revivals contaminated, spoiled, and distracted."[7] Likewise, a 1999 article in the journal Ethnomusicology noted "the reluctance of ethnomusicologists to enter into the revival arena . . . due to the ambiguous status of music revivals as 'legitimate' subjects of study."[8] On the few occasions that ethnomusicologists have studied the resurgence of traditional American styles, they have been more comfortable looking at movements instigated by community insiders, not cultural outsiders. The exemplary work done on the reinvigoration of Yiddish American klezmer and vocal music, for example, has focused primarily on Jewish American figures who revitalized the music from within.[9] Given the persistence of such attitudes, it is not surprising that the most thorough scholarly assessments of American folk revivals have come from historians and cultural studies critics and not from folklorists or ethnomusicologists.

Similar attitudes continue to inform funding entities like the NEA Folk Arts Program, whose 2010 guidelines clearly state the endowment supports "folk and traditional arts [that] are rooted in and reflective of the cultural life of a community. Community members may share a common ethnic heritage, language, religion, occupation, or geographic region."[10] Whether Mike and Tracy or, for that matter, the scores of other northern musicians who, like them, eventually relocated in the southern Appalachians would qualify as community members is unclear, but they are certainly not given priority. Many state arts councils follow the NEA model when it comes to funding folk arts projects. While exploring funding possibilities for a Ramblers fiftieth-anniversary concert in the spring of 2008, John was politely told by a state government folklorist that members of his review panel would probably not see the Ramblers' music as fitting the community-based criteria necessary to qualify as folk art. For the folklorist and the panel, limited funds meant tight restrictions on what constituted fundable folk art. For John, "plus ça change, plus c'est la même chose."

In the best of all worlds, support for traditional artists might be broadened to include those from outside source communities who chose to immerse themselves in local music cultures that were not theirs by birthright or cultural heritage. But present economic and political conditions are leveraged against such developments. What has become a perpetual funding crisis for NEA and other government granting sources may make their stringent eligibility criteria inevitable in order to survive. Moreover, free-market conservatives would argue that grassroots music activity in general and old-time music in particular have not dried up but rather flourished in recent decades in the absence of sustainable government support. These realities acknowledged, institutions devoted to cultural conservation have been slow to recognize the lifelong contributions of musicians and cultural workers like the Ramblers. The NEA awards National Heritage Fellowships to outstanding practitioners of the traditional arts, but they go almost exclusively to cultural insiders and rarely to individuals associated with the urban revival. NEA also supports an annual Bess Lomax Hawes Award in recognition of individual advocacy for the traditional arts through teaching and preservation. While Mike finally received the Lomax Hawes Award in 2009, the Ramblers as a group have received neither. Evidently, the band has slipped through the nominating cracks, in part because of members' residual association with the commercial revival and in part because of their diverse achievements as performers, preservationists, and promoters of traditional music. These factors make the Ramblers difficult to categorize for the purposes of such awards.

Returning to the question of semantics, the Ramblers were not the only ones bothered by the controversial terms *folk music* and *revival*. In recent years scholars have struggled to find more suitable, less loaded language. In place of the nebulous term *folk* Michael Scully used *vernacularity*, referring to musical forms that maintain "close connections between art and long-lived cultures" and that can encompass "a wide range of music derived, sometimes loosely, from the traditional folk forms of diverse ethnicities, races, regions, and occupations."[11] Benjamin Filene prefers *roots music*, by which he means "musical genres that, whether themselves are commercial or not, have been glorified as the 'pure' sources out of which the twentieth century's commercial popular music was created."[12] Another possible alternative to folk is *heritage music*. Barbara Kirshenblatt-Gimblett applies the concept to "music that has been singled out for preservation, protection, enshrinement, and revival." She views heritage music as "a mode of cultural production that gives the disappearing and gone a second life as an exhibition of itself."[13]

Folklorist Neil Rosenberg chose to focus on more specific genre-based terminology, or what he identifies as "named system revivals." Musicians interested in traditional regional and ethnic styles, he observed, tend to immerse themselves in "aggregates of shared repertoire, instrumentation, and performance style generally perceived as being historically and culturally bounded." Thus, he identified more circumscribed instances of revitalization such as the "blues revival," the "Cajun revival," or the "old-time revival" to differentiate them from the broader commercial "folk music revival." Cultural insiders and outsiders can interact within a named system, leading to integration and transformation, he argued, "because of agreement about the cultural values that the system is thought to embody."[14] Not surprisingly, the named system "old-time music" is particularly germane to describing the Ramblers' music, since they are architects of the current usage, which today encompasses a variety of vocal and instrumental substyles.

In place of revival, some musicians, such as those involved in the resurgence of Jewish klezmer and Cajun music, have embraced the term *renaissance*, referring to a period of vigorous artistic and intellectual activity. Anthropologists have spoken of *revitalization movements*, in which societies self-consciously attempted to revive past symbols and practices in response to high cultural stress—"revitalize" here meaning "to give new life or vigor."[15] The term *movement* itself has also been commonly used in reference to the rise and ongoing influence of a particular musical style or genre.

With such language one might describe artists and cultural workers like the Ramblers as heritage or roots musicians who played a leading role in the 1960s revitalization of old-time music and who helped usher in the old-time music renaissance of the 1970s and 1980s. Heritage, roots, revitalization, and renaissance emphasize history and preservation while connoting an ongoing process that is not necessarily wed to the strict cycle of life, death, and rebirth that revival implies.[16] While acknowledging the role of self-conscious perception and reinterpretation, these terms bypass the endless debates over authenticity while ascribing positive cultural value to such musics and their practitioners.

Jettisoning the term *folk revival* would undoubtedly please the Ramblers and others of their generation who have felt maligned by the revivalist albatross that folklorists hung around their collective necks in the 1960s and 1970s. But such a move is unlikely, given the strong currency the term maintains in our popular and scholarly discourse. If folk revival is to be retained as a useful concept for understanding the role of music in American life, it must be decoupled from its exclusive reference to the commercial folk music boom of the 1960s. As recent studies have suggested, interest in so-called folk music by urban, educated Americans goes back at least to the establishment of the American Folklore Society in 1888. The publication of folk song anthologies like Cecil Sharp's *English Folk Songs from the Southern Appalachians* in the late 1910s and 1920s, the founding of the Archive of American Folk Song in 1928 and the Lomaxes' subsequent field-collecting projects of the 1930s, the establishments of various Appalachian festivals and the National Folk Festival in the 1930s, and the singing union movements of the 1930s and early 1940s are but a few nodes of intensive activity that predated the postwar surge.[17] On the other side of the 1960s boom is what Scully has dubbed "the never-ending revival"—the complex of vibrant subcultures of American roots musics that has continued to thrive into the twenty-first century through a network of clubs, festivals, independent recording companies like Rounder Records, and promotional organizations like the Folk Alliance.[18] Broad interest in American roots music did not dissipate with the end of the Great Boom in the mid-1960s and certainly shows no signs of abating in the new millennium.

With this in mind, American folk music revivalism is best viewed as an ongoing process of revitalization and reinterpretation that is not limited to a single decade or to a small group of successful commercial performers. It is a process involving the self-conscious exchange of musical practices across the boundaries of region, social class, religion, and at times ethnic identity. Collaborations between cultural outsiders and local insiders are often essential components of folk music revivalism and should not be dismissed as unnatural or necessarily exploitive. Commerce and the national media have and will undoubtedly continue to play significant roles in such movements, but much of the activity has flourished below the mainstream radar at the local level. Moreover, folk music revivalism should be recognized as a multifaceted phenomenon that encompasses not only the fermenting of new wine in old bottles but also the savoring of the well-aged product. The creation of new songs and tunes based loosely on older musical practices has attracted the most attention and commercial success—hence the star status of singer-songwriters like Bob Dylan, Joni Mitchell, Paul Simon, and Bruce Springsteen. But as the Ramblers' story reveals, the powerful allure of tradition has been an essential component of America's broad embrace of folk music over the past fifty years. The discovery and reinterpretation of musical styles and repertoires of previous generations, in tandem with the desire to explore the constellation of extramusical values associated with those bygone cultures, be they real or imagined, have continued to attract new cohorts of young players with seemingly little interest in commercial gain or national notoriety.

Consider what has happened to the old-time music scene Ray Alden documented in the mid-1980s. As the new century unfolds yet another generation of young players has joined the legions of string-band musicians who can be heard in cities, college towns, and rural communities across the country. The pages of the Old-Time Herald and Bluegrass Unlimited chronicle scores of annual festivals and contests north and south as well as hundreds of independent releases of old-time and bluegrass music. Most of the activity is locally and community-based, with a handful of gifted players touring on national circuits. Occasionally, the music catches national attention on the sound tracks of Hollywood movies like *Oh Brother, Where Art Thou?* (2000) and *Cold Mountain* (2003) or when it pops up on a National Public Radio spot or on Garrison Keillor's *Prairie Home Companion* show. Of course, old-time and bluegrass music are only two pieces of a much larger pie. Performers of country swing, blues, jug band, Cajun, Irish, klezmer, polka, and Afro-Caribbean drum and dance ensembles as well as singer-songwriters of every stripe abound. They can be heard live at clubs, concerts halls, and heritage festivals and often on local radio broadcasts. Their music is circulated on independent (often self-produced) CDs or via various Internet streaming and downloading services, including iTunes, YouTube, Amazon, and Rhapsody.

This ongoing enthusiasm for American grassroots music is not so surprising when viewed through a wider historical lens. In the new millennium, as throughout the past century, Americans prefer to move into the future with at least one eye (and one ear) on the past. We are constantly engaged in a delicate dance of balancing the torrid pace of social and technological change with some sense of history and cultural heritage. We like to see ourselves as forward-looking, intrepid explorers of the frontier, space, and, most recently, cyberspace. But there is also a residual Jeffersonian agrarian spirit in us that draws us back to some imagined pastoral past. Likewise, we need to temper our rugged individualism with a sense of democratic communitarianism that binds us to one another in a broad array of kinship, ethnic, religious, neighborhood, and affinity groups. Oral-based music perceived to be rooted in an idealized past and imagined community has played and continues to play a vital role in this balancing act. The folk music revival associated with the postwar Great Boom is only one chapter in an ongoing story of the complex interaction of tradition and modernity in America.

How all this will play out in the postmodern landscape, where the sounds and sights of much of the world's music, dance, and ritual are a few clicks away, remains to be seen. But surveying the contemporary American folk scene, Scully observed "an appreciation of tradition, enthusiasm for the vernacular heritage of many cultures, an often tight-knit sense of community and an affinity for artistic forms that those who wield commercial power tend to marginalize."[19] These were certainly the values that the traditional wing of the postwar movement, and particularly the Ramblers, sought to propagate.

A quarter century ago Mark Slobin remarked that he did not think the term *revival* was applicable to most music situations because culture does not generally proceed in a linear fashion, where expressive forms completely die out and must be brought back to life on a regular basis. Rather, he viewed culture as "more of a spiral, changing, but dipping back along the way."[20] These are wise words, and ones that scholars of American vernacular music as well as government arts administrators should take to heart. The significance of Slobin's spirals of cultural revitalization will come into sharper focus when folklorists and ethnomusicologists abandon their orthodox notions of authenticity and cease constructing overly rigid insider-outsider dichotomies. Academic and government folklorists in particular should recognize that the very practices they once accused urban revivalists of perpetrating—romancing the folk, inventing tradition, and imagining community—are deeply inherent in their own discipline, whose roots spring from the romantic nationalism of the eighteenth and nineteenth century. Moving beyond these outmoded paradigms will be well worth it. Our knowledge of folk music's role in the modern world will be greatly enhanced, as will our appreciation of musicians and cultural activists like the Ramblers who sought to connect worlds that were eagerly waiting to discover one another. And maybe then Tracy can finally stop trying to pass for traditional.

DISCOGRAPHIC NOTES

Thanks to the wonders of digital technology, readers can easily locate and purchase most of the recordings referred to in this book through the Internet.

The Ramblers' twenty-plus Folkways LPs and EPs are available through Smithsonian Folkways at www.folkways.si.edu. Readers can listen to thirty-second samples of all songs and tunes and download liner notes for free. Individual songs and tunes can be purchased as downloads, and entire LPs and EPs can be purchased as custom-burned CDs.

The New Lost City Ramblers 20th Anniversary Concert (Flying Fish 70090, 1978) and *The New Lost City Ramblers: 40 Years of Concert Recordings* (Rounder Records CD 0481, 2001) are available through Rounder Records at www.rounder.com.

The Ramblers' live recordings at the Newport Folk Festival, issued as *The New Lost City Ramblers: Old Time Music* (Vanguard CD 77011–2, 1994), are available through Vanguard Records at www.vanguardrecords.com.

Mike Seeger's collection of unedited and unissued Ramblers concerts on quarter-inch tape is archived at the Southern Folklife Collection at the Wilson Library, University of North Carolina at Chapel Hill. CD copies of the recordings are available for research purposes by contacting the Wilson Library at www.lib.unc.edu.

Individual performance and documentary recordings by the four Ramblers are listed at their Web sites:

Mike Seeger: www.mikeseeger.info
John Cohen: www.johncohenworks.com
Tracy Schwarz: www.ginnyandtracy.com
Tom Paley: www.wirz.de/music/paleyfrm.htm

NOTES ON SOURCES

INTERVIEWS

Unless otherwise specified, all interviews were conducted by the author.

Cohen, John (all in Tompkins Corners, NY, unless otherwise specified)
    (A) October 3, 1991 (by Ronald Cohen)
    (B) December 13, 2005
    (C) January 26, 2006
    (D) July 7, 2006 (Brooklyn, NY)
    (E) July 24, 2006
    (F) November 17, 2006 (New York City)
    (G) March 12, 2007
    (H) January 22, 2008
    (I) June 13, 2008
    (J) July 25, 2008

Dildine, John, April 12, 2007 (New York City)

Paley, Tom
    (A) May 29, 1990 (Stockholm, Sweden, by Ronald Cohen)
    (B) September 15, 2006 (Brooklyn, NY)
    (C) August 24, 2007 (New Rochelle, NY)

Pearl, Ed, May 15, 2007 (phone)

Rinzler, Ralph, May 26, 1991 (Washington, DC, by Kate Rinzler and John Cohen; courtesy of the Moses and Frances Asch Collection, RRFAC)

Schwarz, Tracy
    (A) August 19, 2006 (Woodstock, NY)
    (B) November 17, 2006 (New York City)
    (C) June 21, 2007 (phone)
    (D) June 24, 2008 (phone)

Seeger, Mike (all in Lexington, VA, unless otherwise specified)
    (A) November 7, 1977 (by Matilda Gaume, Globe, AZ)
    (B) May 15, 2002 (Brooklyn, NY)
    (C) June 29, 2002 (Washington, DC)
    (D) July 21, 2002

(E) April 18, 2006

(F) November 17, 2006 (New York City)

(G) April 4, 2007

(H) May 22, 2007 (phone)

(I) June 18, 2007 (phone)

(J) December 31, 2007 (phone)

(K) February 1, 2008 (phone)

(L) June 8, 2008 (phone)

(M) June 21, 2008 (phone)

Spottswood, Richard

March 10, 2007 (phone)

COLLECTIONS

Many of the written and recorded sources for this work came from the personal collections of Mike Seeger, John Cohen, Tracy Schwarz, and Tom Paley. At the time of this writing John's collection is being organized for archiving at the Library of Congress. Mike's, Tracy's, and Tom's collections have yet to be fully organized and institutionally archived. In addition, written and recorded sources were drawn from the following archival collections:

RRFAC Ralph Rinzler Folklife Archives and Collections, Smithsonian Institution, www.folkways.si.edu

SFC Southern Folklife Collection, Wilson Library, University of North Carolina at Chapel Hill, www.lib.unc.edu/mss/sfc1/

NOTES

INTRODUCTION

1. Neil Rosenberg, ed., *Transforming Tradition: Folk Music Revivals Examined* (Urbana: University of Illinois Press, 1993); Robert Cantwell, *When We Were Good: The Folk Revival* (Cambridge, MA: Harvard University Press, 1996); Ronald Cohen, *Rainbow Quest: The Folk Music Revival and American Society, 1940–1970* (Amherst: University of Massachusetts Press, 2002); Benjamin Filene, *Romancing the Folk: Public Memory and American Roots Music* (Chapel Hill: University of North Carolina Press, 2000); Michael Scully, *The Never-Ending Revival: Rounder Records and the Folk Alliance* (Urbana: University of Illinois Press, 2008); and Thomas Grunning, *Millennium Folk* (Athens: University of Georgia Press, 2006). Recent memoirs include Bob Dylan, *Chronicles One* (New York: Simon and Schuster, 2004); Dave Van Ronk, with Elijah Wald, *The Mayor of MacDougal Street* (New York: Da Capo Press, 2005); George Wein with Nate Chinen, *Myself among Others: A Life in Music* (Cambridge, MA: Da Capo Press, 2003); Dick Weissman, *Which Side Are You On? An Inside History of the Folk Music Revival in America* (New York: Continuum, 2006); Bess Lomax Hawes, *Sing It Pretty: A Memoir* (Urbana: University of Illinois Press, 2008); and Hazel Dickens and Bill Malone, *Working Girl Blues: The Life and Music of Hazel Dickens* (Urbana: University of Illinois Press, 2008). See also David King Dunaway's updated biography of Pete Seeger, *How Can I Keep from Singing? The Ballad of Pete Seeger* (New York: Villard Books, 2008).

2. Alan Jabbour, foreword to Rosenberg, *Transforming Tradition*, xiii.

3. Eric Hobsbawm and Terence Ranger, eds., *The Invention of Tradition* (Cambridge, MA: Harvard University Press, 1983); Rosenberg, *Transforming Tradition*; Michael Ann Williams, *Staging Tradition: John Lair and Sarah Gertrude Knott* (Urbana: University of Illinois Press, 2006); Filene, *Romancing the Folk*; Regina Bendix, *In Search of Authenticity: The Formation of Folklore Studies* (Madison: University of Wisconsin Press, 1997); Simon Bronner, *Folk Nation: Folklore in the Creation of American Tradition* (Wilmington, DE: SR Books, 2002); Robert Cantwell, *Ethnomemesis: Folklife and the Representation of Culture* (Chapel Hill: University of North Carolina Press, 1993).

4. Filene, *Romancing the Folk*, 6.

CHAPTER 1. THE SEEGER FAMILY DISCOVERS THE FOLK

1. Charles Seeger's life is chronicled in Ann Pescatello, *Charles Seeger: A Life in American Music* (Pittsburgh: University of Pittsburgh Press, 1992). See also Judith Tick's discussion of Charles and Ruth's early relationship in *Ruth Crawford Seeger: A Composer's Search for American Music* (New York: Oxford University Press, 1997), 114–28.

2. Charles Seeger [Carl Sands], "A Program for Proletarian Composers," *Daily Worker*, January 16, 1934, 5. Quoted from Helen Rees, "'Temporary Bypaths?': Seeger and Folk Music Research," in *Understanding Charles Seeger*, ed. Bell Yung and Helen Rees (Urbana: University of Illinois Press, 1999), 92. For discussions of Seeger's thinking on the relation of folk music to proletarian music, see 92–94; see also Tick, *Ruth Crawford Seeger*, 194–96.

3. Charles and Ruth's discovery of folk music after moving to Washington in 1935 is examined in Tick, *Ruth Crawford Seeger*, 236–41.

4. Jerrold Hirsch, "'Cultural Strategy': The Seegers and B. A. Botkin as Friends and Allies," in *Ruth Crawford Seeger's Worlds: Innovation and Tradition in Twentieth-Century American Music*, ed. Ray Allen and Ellie Hisama (Rochester, NY: University of Rochester Press, 2007), 196.

5. See Rees's extensive review of Charles Seeger's contributions to the study of folk music in "Temporary Bypaths," 84–108. A number of Seeger's essays on folk music, including "The Folkness of the Nonfolk and the Nonfolkness of the Folk," are found in Charles Seeger, *Studies in Musicology, 1935–1975* (Berkeley: University of California Press, 1977).

6. Seeger, "The Folkness of the Nonfolk," 338.

7. Charles Seeger, "Reviews," *Journal of American Folklore* 61 (April–June 1948): 216.

8. The most comprehensive account of Ruth Crawford Seeger's life and music is found in Tick's biography, *Ruth Crawford Seeger*. Essays that explore her career as a composer, folk music scholar, and teacher/advocate for folk music are found in Allen and Hisama, *Ruth Crawford Seeger's Worlds*.

9. For more on Dane Rudhyar's influence on Crawford's early compositions see Carol Oja, *Making Music Modern: New York in the 1920s* (New York: Oxford University Press, 2000), 144–52. See 146–48 for her discussion of Crawford's Sonata for Violin and Piano and Preludes for Piano No. 6.

10. Carl Sandburg to Tome Stokes, December 26, 1947, in Tick, *Ruth Crawford Seeger*, 54.

11. Joseph Strauss, "Ruth Crawford's Precompositional Strategies," in Allen and Hisama, *Ruth Crawford Seeger's Worlds*, 33. The most thorough examination of Crawford as composer is found in Strauss's *The Music of Ruth Crawford Seeger* (Cambridge: Cambridge University Press, 1995).

12. Ellie Hisama, "In Pursuit of Proletarian Music: Ruth Crawford's Sacco, Vanzetti," in Allen and Hisama, *Ruth Crawford Seeger's Worlds*, 73–93.

13. Tick, *Ruth Crawford Seeger*, 241.

14. John A. Lomax and Alan Lomax, eds., *Our Singing Country* (New York: Macmillan, 1941; New York: Dover, 2000).

15. Ruth Crawford Seeger, *"The Music of American Folk Song" and Selected Other Writings on American Folk Music*, ed. Larry Polansky with Judith Tick (Rochester, NY: University of Rochester Press, 2001).

16. Robert Cantwell, *When We Were Good: The Folk Revival* (Chapel Hill: University of North Carolina Press, 1996), 278.

17. Accounts of Mike's childhood and the early Seeger household are found in Tick, *Ruth Crawford Seeger*, 247–67, 280–309. See also Mike Seeger, "Thoughts of Silver Spring, 1938," and Peggy Seeger, "About Dio," in *Ruth Crawford Seeger: Modernity, Tradition, and the Making of American Music*, ed. Ellie M. Hisama and Ray Allen (Brooklyn, NY: Institute for Studies in American Music, 2001), 12–13. Additional recollections concerning Mike's early years are drawn from Seeger interviews (A), (B), and (C).

18. Seeger interview (C).

19. Seeger, "Thoughts," 12.

20. Seeger, "Thoughts," 2–13.

21. Mike Seeger, "A Few Personal Words about Ruth Crawford Seeger's *The Music of American Folk Song*," in Crawford, *Selected Other Writings*, xvi.

22. Accounts of Mike's early musical instruction are drawn from Seeger interviews (B), (C), and (G).

23. Peggy Seeger remembers eighteen-year-old Mike learning to play banjo from Pete's manual while bedridden with a case of shingles. See her account in David King Dunaway, *How Can I Keep from Singing? The Ballad of Pete Seeger* (New York: Villard Books, 2008), 231. Mike recalls that he found the manual "hard to understand" and that he learned more watching Pete pick the banjo in Beacon (Seeger interview [G]).

24. Dunaway, *How Can I Keep from Singing*, 246.

25. Cantwell, *When We Were Good*, 190, 192.

26. John Cohen is quoted in Greil Marcus's essay "The Old, Weird America," found in *A Booklet of Essays, Appreciations, and Annotations Pertaining to the Anthology of American Folk Music Edited by Harry Smith*, 5. The booklet accompanies the 1997 reissue of the entire *Anthology of American Folk Music* by Smithsonian Folkways Recordings (FP 251–53, 1997).

27. Seeger interview (J). Folkways Records historian Peter Goldsmith reports that in return for cataloging information about Smith's donated records, Mike and Rinzler were allowed to borrow records for duplication. See Goldsmith, *Making People's Music: Moe Asch and Folkways Records* (Washington, DC: Smithsonian Institution Press, 1998), 259. Mike maintains that he and Rinzler had not received permission to borrow the records and had to smuggle them out.

28. Peter Goldsmith and Neil Rosenberg place the initial meeting between Ralph Rinzler and Mike at the 1953 Swarthmore Folk Festival. See Goldsmith, *Making People's Music*, 258; and Rosenberg, *Bluegrass: A History* (Urbana: University of Illinois Press, 1985, 2005), 148. Mike and Peggy, however, are sure they did not attend the 1953 Swarthmore festival because of Charles's reservations about having them participate in a public gathering with Pete, given their older brother's tenuous political situation in the early McCarthy era. Mike thought he first met Rinzler at Pete's house in Beacon, probably in the sum-

mer of 1954 (Seeger interview [E]). Rinzler recalled meeting both Mike and Peggy at the 1954 Swarthmore festival and subsequently being invited to Beacon that June (Rinzler interview).

29. Rinzler interview.

30. Rinzler interview.

31. "Christmas Early for Book Fair," *Washington Post*, November 12, 1953.

32. Seeger interview (G). For more on Mike's initial meeting and interactions with the Dickens family, see Hazel Dickens and Bill Malone, *Working Girl Blues: The Life and Music of Hazel Dickens* (Urbana: University of Illinois Press, 2008), 8–10.

33. Background on Sunset Park is found in Eddie Dean, "O Brother, Where Art the Sunsets of Yesteryear?" *Philadelphia Weekly*, October 31, 2001. See also Dean's essay in Eddie Dean and Robert Gordon, *Pure Country: The Leon Kagarise Archives, 1961–1971* (New York: Process Books, 2008), 115–17.

34. Background on New River Ranch is found in Dean and Gordon, *Pure Country*, 31–34.

35. Spottswood interview.

36. Seeger interview (C).

37. Richard Spottswood, "Mike Seeger," *Bluegrass Unlimited*, May 1985, 61.

38. The original 1957 *American Banjo* LP was reissued as a CD with additional tracks and updated notes under the title *American Banjo: Three-Finger and Scruggs Style* (Smithsonian Folkways CD 40037, 1990).

39. Charles Seeger, liner notes to *American Folk Songs Sung by the Seegers* (Folkways Records FA 2005, 1957).

CHAPTER 2. YALE HOOTS AND WASHINGTON SQUARE JAMS

1. Biographical information on John Cohen is drawn from Cohen interviews (A) and (B) and "John Cohen I," in *Wasn't That a Time!: First Hand Accounts of the Folk Music Revival*, ed. Ronald Cohen (Lanham, MD: Scarecrow Press, 1995), 25–56. Additional information on music in the Cohen family is found in John Cohen, *There Is No Eye: John Cohen Photographs* (New York: powerHouse Books, 2001), 18–20. For more on Margot Mayo and early New York City square dancing, see Margot Mayo, *The American Square Dance* (New York: Oak Publications, 1964).

2. Cohen, *There Is No Eye*, 19.

3. *Dust Bowl Ballads* (Victor Records P-27 and P-28), released in 1940 as two albums of ten-inch 78 rpm records, were Woody Guthrie's first commercial recordings. They consisted of twelve original Guthrie ballads chronicling the hardships of the Depression era Okies and their migration to California. See Ed Cray, *Ramblin' Man: The Life and Times of Woody Guthrie* (New York: Norton, 2004), 179–82. The original recordings were reissued in 2000 as *Dust Bowl Ballads* (Buddha CD B00004TY8S).

4. *Listen to Our Story: A Panorama of American Ballads* (Brunswick Album B-1024), edited by Alan Lomax, was released in 1947 as an album of 78 rpm records and an accompanying twenty-page booklet. *Mountain Frolic* (Brunswick Album B-1025) was also edited by Alan Lomax and released in 1947 as an album of 78 rpm records with an eighteen-page booklet. The two album sets received favorable reviews by Charles Seeger in "Reviews," *Journal of American Folklore* 61 (1948): 215–18.

5. Cohen interview (G).

6. *Smoky Mountain Ballads* (Victor P-79), edited by John Lomax, was released in 1941 as an album of 78 rpm records with liner notes. The record was reissued with additional material and notes by Ed Kahn in 1964 as Victor LPV-507.

7. Lomax, *Listen to Our Story* booklet, 4.

8. All quotes from Lomax, *Mountain Frolic* booklet, inside cover. His fictitious "Mountain Frolic" story and song lyrics are found on pages 3–10. Notated melody lines and chords to the songs and tunes are found on pages 11–18.

9. Cohen interview (G).

10. For a history of Camp Woodland, see Dale Johnson, "Camp Woodland: Progressive Education and Folklore in the Catskill Mountains of New York," *Voices: The Journal of New York Folklore* 28 (Spring–Summer 2002): 6–12.

11. Biographical information on Tom Paley is drawn from Paley interviews (A) and (B); and "Tom Paley Interviewed by Stephen Wade," *Banjo Newsletter*, March 1998, 14–20, and April 1998, 12–16.

12. Draft manuscript written by John Cohen, August 1960, John Cohen personal collection. Material in this draft was incorporated into a lengthy piece by Susan Montgomery, "The Folk Furor," *Mademoiselle*, December 1960, 98–100, 117–19.

13. Accounts of folk music in Washington Square during the 1950s are found in Arthur Jordan Field, "Notes on the History of Folksinging in New York City," *Caravan* (June–July 1959), 7–17; Barry Kornfeld, "Folksinging in Washington Square," *Caravan* (August–September 1959), 6–12; Michael James, "Free Show in Washington Square Is a Hit," *New York Times*, May 25, 1959; Ronald Cohen, *Rainbow Quest: The Folk Music Revival and American Society, 1940–1975* (Amherst: University of Massachusetts Press, 2002), 106–8, 137; and Dave Van Ronk, *The Mayor of MacDougal Street: A Memoir* (Cambridge: Da Capo Press, 2005), 24–25, 41–43.

14. Van Ronk, *Mayor of MacDougal Street*, 42–43.

15. Van Ronk, *Mayor of MacDougal Street*, 24.

16. Ronald Cohen (*Rainbow Quest*, 140) claims that around 1957 Roger Sprung was the first to introduce bluegrass banjo to the Washington Square scene. Sprung, accompanying guitarist-singers Bob Carey and Eric Darling, can be heard playing what producer Kenneth Goldstein characterized as a "galloping banjo" on *Folksay Ballads and Blues Volume 2* (Stinson Records 6, n.d.).

17. For more on the Greenbriar Boys and the northern bluegrass scene, see Neil Rosenberg, *Bluegrass: A History* (Urbana: University of Illinois Press, 1985, 2005), 148.

18. Harry and Jeanie West are heard accompanying themselves on guitars, banjo, and mandolin and singing traditional ballads, love songs, and gospel numbers on *Southern Mountain Folk Songs* (Stinson SLP 36) and *More Southern Mountain Folk Songs* (Stinson SLP 74), edited and with notes by Kenneth Goldstein. Neither record is dated, but both were probably released in the early 1950s.

19. Cohen interview (G).

20. Kornfeld, "Folksinging," 9.

21. *Folk Songs from the Southern Appalachian Mountains Sung by Tom Paley* (Elektra Records EKL-12, 1953), produced by Jac Holzman.

22. See John's description of the late 1950s Greenwich Village art and folk scene in "John Cohen II," in Cohen, *Wasn't That a Time*, 178–85.

23. For more on the impact of Young's Folklore Center see Cohen, *Rainbow Quest*, 120–22.

24. For more on the Folksingers Guild and the opening of the Village Gate, see Cohen, *Rainbow Quest*, 136–37.

25. Cohen, *Rainbow Quest*, 123.

26. Roger Lass, "Chronicle of the Urban Folksinger," *Caravan* (March 1958), 11–17, reprinted from *Columbia Review*, Autumn 1957. Lass's article prompted critical responses from Roger Abrahams and Ed Badeaux, who questioned Lass's categorizations of urban folksingers and his assertion that traditional music had all but disappeared in southern communities, respectively. See *Caravan* (April 1958), 7–9, 11.

27. Roger Lass, "The Art of the Urban Folk Singer," *Caravan* (October–November 1958), 20–23.

28. "The New York Scene," *Caravan* (August–September 1958), 46.

29. The Cohen-West-Glaser concert is noted in *Caravan* (December 1957), 24. Young's tribute to John appears in *Caravan* (June 1958), 5.

30. Seeger interview (G).

31. Dildine interview.

32. Dildine maintains that he initially invited Mike to perform on his show and that Tom and John were subsequently contacted (Dildine interview). Mike, John, and Tom are uncertain regarding exactly who initially suggested the idea and how the chain of phone calls unfolded. Mike thinks he may have asked either Tom or Dildine if he could join the program after Tom and John had been invited. See Mike Seeger, "Notes on the New Lost City Ramblers," *Gardyloo* 4 (1959), 5.

33. New Lost City Ramblers, WASH-FM radio show recording, May 25, 1958, tape FT-9786, Mike Seeger Collection, SFC.

34. Nearly fifty years later Dildine admitted his questions were prompted by idealistic

and in retrospect somewhat naive notions of "pure" folk music: "I was among those people who reacted badly to the commercialization of music. . . . Philosophically, I was an idealist about money and that money tainted things. What I was trying to do in a lot of ways was to say the stuff I was playing was not what you'd hear on a big record label. And there was this awareness in my mind of this stuff being pure somehow—people's music, what have you. This was music that wasn't being done as a performance for money" (Dildine interview).

CHAPTER 3. THE RAMBLERS TAKE THE STAGE

1. Mike Seeger, "Notes on the New Lost City Ramblers," *Gardyloo* (July 1959), 5.

2. Cohen interview (B). See also Goldsmith's account of the Cohen-Asch meeting in *Making People's Music: Moe Asch and Folkways Records* (Washington, DC: Smithsonian Institution Press, 1998), 261.

3. Mike Seeger to John Cohen, June 26, 1958, John Cohen personal collection.

4. Mike Seeger to John Cohen, August 8, 1958, John Cohen personal collection.

5. Seeger interview (F).

6. Seeger, "Notes," 6.

7. "Folk Music Scene," *Caravan* (October–November 1958), 47.

8. Quotes from Seeger interview (F) and Cohen interview (F).

9. Lee Shaw, "Concert Reviews," *Gardyloo* (April 1959), 18.

10. Cohen interview (B).

11. Cohen interview (B).

12. See Goldsmith's account of the Ramblers' first recording session in *Making People's Music*, 261–62.

13. See Mike's criticism of the September 1958 recording session with Asch in "Notes," 6.

14. Goldsmith, *Making People's Music*, 261–62.

15. The uncertain origins of the name New Lost City Ramblers are drawn from Seeger interview (F), Cohen interview (F), and Paley interview (B). Philip Gura, who interviewed Cohen and Seeger in 1991, came to a similar conclusion. See Gura, "Roots and Branches: Forty Years of the New Lost City Ramblers, Part 1," *Old Time Herald* (Winter 1999), 28.

16. Paley interview (B).

17. Cohen interview (B).

18. Seeger, "Notes," 5.

19. Mike Seeger, booklet accompanying *The New Lost City Ramblers* (Folkways LP F-2396, 1958). Additional quotes as attributed to each Rambler are from the booklet.

20. The only tune on the Ramblers' initial LP that was taken directly from a non-Anglo-American source was "Dallas Rag," which came from a recording by the African American Dallas String Band.

21. Jon Pankake, notes to *The New Lost City Ramblers: The Early Years, 1958–1962* (Smithsonian Folkways CD SF 40036, 1991).

22. The 1936 Rich Family LOC recording of "Colored Aristocracy" can be heard on *The New Lost City Ramblers: Where Do You Come From? Where Do You Go?* (Smithsonian Folkways CD SF 40180, 2009). The Rich Family recording is pitched closer to the key of F-sharp than the key of G, where the Ramblers play it. The discrepancy is probably due to variations in tape speed or the low tuning of the original instruments. The Rich Family undoubtedly played the tune in what they perceived to be the key of G. The Ramblers rerecorded "Colored Aristocracy" in 1997 on *The New Lost City Ramblers: There Ain't No Way Out* (Smithsonian Folkways CD SF 40098). In an effort to get closer to the original 1936 Rich Family arrangement John plays mandolin, and the additional IV (C) and II (A) chords are dropped.

23. *The New Lost City Ramblers* (Folkways FA 2396) carried a 1958 copyright date but to the best of everyone's memory was not released until early 1959. According to Mike Seeger's receipts from Folkways Records, the entire sales for 1959 were 333 pieces. Sales in 1960 were 297 and in 1961 jumped to 920.

24. D. K. Wilgus, "Record Reviews," *Journal of American Folklore* 72 (October–December 1959): 367.

25. Ed Cray, "Folk Song Discography," *Western Folklore* 17 (July 1959): 275.

26. See Rosenberg's discussion of the changing criteria for "authentic" folk songs in his introduction to Neil Rosenberg, ed., *Transforming Tradition: Folk Music Revivals Examined* (Urbana: University of Illinois Press, 1993), 10–17.

27. Alan Lomax, "A List of American Folk Songs on Commercial Records," in *Report of the Committee of the Conference on Inter-American Relations in the Field of Music* (Washington, DC: Department of State, 1940), quoted from Rosenberg, *Transforming Tradition*, 12.

28. Alan Lomax, "Folk Song Style," *American Anthropologist* 61 (1959): 930–31. This article as well as Lomax's 1956 note on folk song style in the *Journal of the International Folk Music Council* have been reprinted in *Alan Lomax: Selected Writings 1934–1997*, ed. Ronald Cohen (New York: Routledge, 2003). See also Alan Lomax, *Folk Song Style and Culture* (New Brunswick: Transaction Books, 1968).

29. Charles Seeger, "Folk Music in the Schools of a Highly Industrialized Society," *Journal of the International Folk Music Council* 5 (1953): 40–44, reprinted in and quoted from Charles Seeger, *Studies in Musicology, 1935–1975* (Berkeley: University of California Press, 1977), 333, 334.

30. Charles Seeger, "Singing Style," *Western Folklore* 17 (1958): 3–11.

31. Ruth Crawford Seeger, "Music Preface," in *Our Singing Country*, ed. John A. Lomax and Alan Lomax (New York: Macmillan, 1941; New York: Dover, 2000), xxxi–xxxii.

32. Ruth Crawford Seeger, *Animal Folk Songs for Children* (New York: Doubleday, 1950), 10.

33. Alan Lomax, "The Folkniks—and the Songs They Sing," *Sing Out!* 9 (Summer 1959): 30–31.

34. See John Cohen's response to Lomax, "In Defense of City Singers," *Sing Out!* 9 (Summer 1959): 32–33.

35. Lee Haring, "Concert Reviews," *Caravan* (April–May 1959), 27–28.

36. Shaw, "Concert Reviews," 18.

37. New Lost City Ramblers concert recording at PS 41 in New York City, February 28, 1959, tape from Elijah Wald's personal collection. The initial section of the concert, including the introduction and opening numbers, was not recorded.

38. See John Wilson's review of Folksong '59, "Program Given by Lomax," *New York Times*, April 4, 1959. Mike's short biography that identifies him as the leader of the New Lost City Ramblers is found in the booklet *Carnegie Hall Program—Season 1958–1959*, 11. Mike Seeger personal collection.

39. "New Lost City Ramblers and Elizabeth Cotten Invite You to Come to an Old Timey Program of Folk Songs and Tunes," press release prepared by Mike Seeger, April 1959, Mike Seeger personal collection.

40. *Negro Folk Songs and Tunes* (Folkways Records FG 5326, 1958).

41. Lee Shaw, "A New Lost City Ramblers Concert Is a Real Picnic," *Gardyloo* (mid-May 1959), 17–18.

42. Mike Seeger to John Cohen, n.d., John Cohen personal collection. Based on Mike's comments about John's forthcoming trip to Kentucky, the letter appears to have been dated just before John's departure in early May 1959.

43. John Cohen, booklet accompanying *Mountain Music of Kentucky* (Smithsonian Folkways SFW CD 40077, 1996), 22, 24.

44. Cohen, *Mountain Music of Kentucky* booklet, 29.

45. Mark Slobin, commenting upon the revival of Balkan traditions among American musicians from outside the culture, reported that the appeal of such "exotic heritage music" often initially manifests itself as a deeply visceral, "lightning-strike reaction" that emanates "entirely from within the individual's psyche." See Slobin's discussion of heritage music in *Fiddler on the Move: Exploring the Klezmer World* (New York: Oxford University Press, 2000), 11–18.

46. Scott Matthews, "John Cohen in Eastern Kentucky: Documenting Expression and the Image of Roscoe Holcomb during the Folk Revival," *Southern Spaces*, http://www.southernspaces.org/contents/2008/matthews/1h.htm, January 17, 2010. Pankake and Nelson's reflections on Holcomb as an existential folk poet focused on "the deep meaning of human experience" are found in *Little Sandy Review*, no. 12 (1961) and quoted by John Cohen in the booklet to *Roscoe Holcomb: The High Lonesome Sound* (Smithsonian Folkways SFW CD 40104, 1998), 11–12.

47. Winnie Winston, "New Lost City Ramblers," *Gardyloo* (late July 1959), 16–18.

48. Harriet Goodwin, "Concert Chronicles," *Caravan* (May–September 1959), 24.

49. New Lost City Ramblers concert recording at Mills College Theater in New York City, June 13, 1959, tape from Elijah Wald's personal collection.

50. Philip Gura, "Roots and Branches: Forty Years of the New Lost City Ramblers, Part 2," *Old-Time Herald* (Spring 2000), 23.

51. Roger Abrahams, *Caravan* (January 1960), 32.

52. Albert Grossman to Mike Seeger, June 11, 1959, Mike Seeger personal collection.

CHAPTER 4. SEEGER, COHEN, AND PALEY PERFORM THE FOLK

1. Robert Shelton, "Folk Joins Jazz at Newport," *New York Times*, July 19, 1959.

2. For more on the first Newport Festival, see Ronald Cohen, *A History of Folk Music Festivals in the United States: Feasts of Musical Celebration* (Lanham, MD: Scarecrow Press, 2009), 46–50; Ronald Cohen, *Rainbow Quest: The Folk Music Revival and American Society, 1940–1970* (Amherst: University of Massachusetts Press, 2002), 145–48; and Robert Cantwell, *When We Were Good: The Folk Revival* (Cambridge, MA: Harvard University Press, 1996), 293–98.

3. Seeger interview (F) and Cohen interview (F).

4. *The Folk Music of the Newport Folk Festival 1959–1960*, vol. 2 (Folkways Records FA 2432, 1961). Unfortunately, song introductions and applause were completely edited out of the final LP mix, making it impossible to accurately judge audience responses to the music.

5. Studs Terkel, liner notes to *Folk Festival at Newport Volume 2* (Vanguard VSD-2054, n.d.).

6. Billy Faier, "Folk Music Today," in the *First Annual Newport Folk Festival Booklet*, 1959, Mike Seeger personal collection.

7. See Cohen's account of the Sunday night concert, including remarks by Young and Morris, in *Rainbow Quest*, 147.

8. Robert Shelton, "Folk Music Festival," *Nation*, August 1, 1959, 59.

9. Shelton, "Folk Music Festival," 59.

10. Robert Shelton, "Folk Joins Jazz at Newport," *New York Times*, July 19, 1959.

11. Frederic Ramsey, Jr., "Newport Ho! The Folk Festival," *Saturday Review*, July 25, 1959, 27.

12. Cohen interview (F).

13. Robert Shelton, "Bluegrass Style: Mountain Music Gets Serious Consideration," *New York Times*, August 30, 1959.

14. John Wilson, "Hootenanny Fills Carnegie Hall as Eighteenth Season Begins," *New York Times*, September 21, 1959.

15. *Songs from the Depression* (Folkways Records FH 5264) carries a 1960 date on the record jacket. The accompanying booklet is copyrighted 1959, and John's notes are dated November 1959. Mike and John think that the record became available in January 1960.

16. The history of the urban folk revival and leftist politics is well chronicled in Richard Reuss and JoAnne Reuss, *American Folk Music and Left-Wing Politics, 1927–1957* (Lanham, MD: Scarecrow Press, 2000) and in Robbie Lieberman, *My Song Is My Weapon: People's Songs, American Communism, and the Politics of Culture, 1930–1950* (Urbana: University of Illinois Press, 1989).

17. Cohen interview (E).

18. John Cohen, comments from the album booklet accompanying *Songs from the Depression*. Additional comments from John and Mike are from the booklet.

19. Cohen interview (C).

20. Jens Lund and Serge Denisoff, "The Folk Music Revival and the Counter Culture: Contributions and Contradictions," *Journal of American Folklore* 84 (October 1971): 400.

21. Roger Abrahams, "Record Reviews," *Caravan* (June–July 1960), 42; Nat Hentoff, "Record Notes," *Reporter*, April 28, 1960, 43–44.

22. Jon Pankake, "The New Lost City Ramblers: Songs from the Depression," *Little Sandy Review* 1 (1960): 24–26. Pankake's later comments on his *Little Sandy Review* are found in "Jon Pankake," *Wasn't That a Time!: First Hand Accounts of the Folk Music Revival*, ed. Ronald Cohen (Lanham, MD: Scarecrow Press, 1995), 112–13.

23. J. Hollister Stein, "New Lost City Ramblers," *Yale Daily News*, March 21, 1960.

24. Robert Gustafson, "The New Lost City Ramblers," *Christian Science Monitor*, March 39, 1960. Gustafson wrongly equated bluegrass with early southern mountain music, which explains his claim that bluegrass, a style that did not emerge until the 1940s, was flowering in the 1920s.

25. New Lost City Ramblers Golden Vanity, concert recording, late March 1960, tape FT-9777, pts. 1 and 2, Mike Seeger Collection, SFC.

26. Cohen interview (C).

27. Mike Seeger, liner notes to *New Lost City Ramblers Volume II* (Folkways Records FA 2397, 1960).

28. "John Cohen I," 39–40.

29. Cohen, liner notes to *New Lost City Ramblers Volume II*.

30. John Cohen to Susan Montgomery, August 9, 1960.

31. D. K. Wilgus, "Record Reviews," *Journal of American Folklore* 74 (April–June 1961): 189; Jon Pankake, "The New Lost City Ramblers Volume II," *Little Sandy Review* 4 (n.d.): 13.

32. "John Cohen I," 36.

33. Selma Sawaya, "Trio Strums, Sings in Improbable Concert," *Michigan Daily*, May 21, 1960.

34. "John Cohen I," 36.

35. For background on the Gate of Horn, see Cohen, *Rainbow Quest*, 113–15.

36. Seeger interview (F).

37. Cohen interview (C).

38. "John Cohen I," 36.

39. Peter Desbarats, "New Lost City Ramblers Stars of Hootenanny '61," *Montreal Star*, December 18, 1961.

40. *Chicago Tribune*, June 12, 1960.

41. "Mountain Music," *Chicago Sun-Times*, June 26, 1960.

42. Robert Shelton, "40 Amateurs Join Hootenanny As Newport Folk Festival Ends," *New York Times*, June 27, 1960. See also Cohen, *Rainbow Quest*, 160–61.

43. Stacey Williams (aka Robert Shelton), liner notes to *The Newport Folk Festival 1960* (Vanguard VRS 9083/4, n.d.).

44. For Young's criticism of the 1960 Newport Festival, see "Frets and Frails," *Sing Out!* 10 (October–November 1960): 48.

45. Barry Olivier, "A Personal Beginning," Berkeley Folk Festival Artist Archive, n.d., quoted in Cohen, *Rainbow Quest*, 128.

46. Alfred Frankenstein, "The Question of Significance: UC's Folk Music Performers," *San Francisco Chronicle*, June 29, 1959.

47. Program flyer, 1960 Folk Music Festival at the Berkeley Campus of the University of California, Mike Seeger personal collection.

48. Alfred Frankenstein, "UC's Folk Festival Is Skillfully Shaped," *San Francisco Chronicle*, July 4, 1960.

49. "Folk Frenzy," *Time*, July 11, 1960, 81.

50. For further background on the Ash Grove, see Cohen, *Rainbow Quest*, 153–54; and Bill Oliver, "LA's Ash Grove Shelters Folk Music Beehive," *Sing Out!* 9 (Winter 1959–60): 36–37.

51. Pearl interview.

52. Cohen interview (C).

53. Michael Davenport, "Live and Legit," *Canyon Crier*, September 1, 1960.

54. According to Mike Seeger's 1960 Folkways Sales Statement, the annual sales for the four albums were as follows: *The New Lost City Ramblers*, 297 copies; *Old Timey Songs for Children*, 46 copies; *Songs from the Depression*, 340 copies; *New Lost City Ramblers Volume II*, 407 copies.

55. Seeger interview (I).

56. Susan Montgomery, "The Folk Furor," *Mademoiselle*, December 1960, 98–100, 117–19.

57. John Cohen, Israel Young, and Ralph Rinzler, "The Friends of Old Time Music," *Sing Out!* 11 (February–March 1961): 63.

58. Robert Shelton, "Students Import Folk Art to Chicago," *New York Times*, February 12, 1961.

59. Jon Pankake and Paul Nelson, "The First University of Chicago Folk Festival," *Little Sandy Review* 23 (ca. 1961): 49, 50–51.

60. Shelton, "Students Import Folk Art."

61. Sandy Paton, "Folk and the Folk Arrival," in *Dimensions of the Folk Song Revival*, ed. David De Turk and A. Poulin (New York: Dell Publishing, 1967), 41–42.

62. Studs Terkel, "The First Annual University of Chicago Folk Festival," *WFMT Chicago Fine Arts Guide*, May 1961, Mike Seeger personal collection.

63. John Cohen and Ralph Rinzler, "The University of Chicago Folk Festival," *Sing Out!* 13 (April–May 1963): 8.

64. John Cohen's comments are quoted from *Friends of Old Time Music: The Folk Arrival 1961–1965* (Smithsonian Folkways SFW CD 40160, 2006) CD booklet, 11. This CD includes a full recording of John's opening remarks; Holcomb's performances of "East Virginia Blues," "John Henry," and "Rising Sun Blues"; the Ramblers' performance of "Jordan Is a Hard Road to Travel"; and highlights of Friends of Old Time Music concerts.

65. Cohen interview (B).

66. Rinzler interview.

67. See John Herald's firsthand account of how he and Rinzler found Ashley at Union Grove in *The Friends of Old Time Music* booklet, 11–12.

68. Robert Shelton, "Folk Group Gives 'Village' Concert," *New York Times*, March 27, 1961.

69. For more on the role of the Friends of Old Time Music concerts in developing modes for presenting folk music to urban audiences, see Ray Allen, "Staging the Folk: New York City's Friends of Old Time Music," *Institute for Studies in American Music Newsletter* 35, no. 2 (2006): 1–2, 14–15.

70. Cohen interview (C).

71. Arthur Kyle Davis, Jr., "Carolyn Hester Charms Overflow Audience; Ramblers Also Please," *Daily Progress*, March 18, 1961.

72. Paley interview (B).

73. Cohen interview (F).

74. Seeger interview (F).

75. Cohen interview (F).

76. Cohen interview (F).

77. Paley interview (B).

78. Cohen interview (C).

79. New Lost City Ramblers Washington Theater Club, concert recording, March 18, 1961, tape FT-9786, Mike Seeger Collection, SFC.

80. John Cohen, liner notes to *The New Lost City Ramblers Volume 3* (Folkways Records FA 2398, 1961).

81. Mike Seeger, liner notes to *The New Lost City Ramblers Volume 4* (Folkways Records FA 2399, 1962).

82. D. K. Wilgus, "From the Record Review Editor," *Journal of American Folklore* 75 (January–March 1962): 88.

83. Cohen interview (F).

84. Seeger interview (F).

85. "Goings on About Town," *New Yorker*, June 24, 1961.

86. Robert Shelton, "Country Music Comes to Town: Blue Angel Is Host to the New Lost City Ramblers," *New York Times*, June 20, 1961.

CHAPTER 5. PALEY DEPARTS AND SCHWARZ ARRIVES

1. "Nightly Reviews: Ashgrove," *Variety*, August 3, 1961.

2. "Bluegrass Ramblers," *Daily Californian*, September 21, 1961; "Concert of Folk Song at UC," *Berkeley Daily Gazette*, September 20, 1961.

3. Cohen interview (C).

4. Howard Abrams, "The New Lost City Ramblers," *Folkways: A Magazine of International Folklore* 3 (1961): 14–15.

5. Cohen interview (C).

6. Paley interview (B).

7. Seeger interview (F).

8. Cohen interview (C).

9. Robert Gustafson, "Three Seegers in Symphony Hall," *Christian Science Monitor*, December 16, 1961.

10. Robert Shelton, "A Seeger Reunion at Carnegie Hall," *New York Times*, December 25, 1961.

11. Details on the recording and release dates of *Earth Is Earth: The New Lost City Bang Boys* EP are sketchy. Mike, John, and Tom agree that the recordings were made sometime in 1961, although the EP was probably not released until 1963 as Folkways Records FF 869. There may have been an earlier release under the same title with a different cover and catalog number (FF 369). The *Earth Is Earth* and *New Lost City Ramblers* EPs were re-released, probably in the late 1970s, as an eight-song compilation under the title *Earth Is Earth* and catalog number FF 869. Thanks to Mary Monseur and Jeff Place at Smithsonian Folkways for their help in identifying and dating these recordings.

12. Paley interview (B).

13. Paley interview (B).

14. "Balladeer Seeger Raps School Ban," *San Diego Evening Tribune*, April 28, 1962; "Ramblers Sing & Pick in Little Theatre Today," *San Diego Daily News*, May 3, 1962.

15. Manny Greenhill had been helping the Ramblers since 1960 and gradually took over the lion's share of their bookings. A Folkways Records flyer that came out just after the release of *Volume II* in the spring of 1960 lists both John and Greenhill as contacts for

concert arrangements. A 1962 flyer announcing the release of *Volume 4* only lists Greenhill. New Lost City Ramblers file, Moses and Francis Asch Collection, RRFAC.

16. Peter Welding, "The New Lost City Ramblers/Second Fret, Philadelphia," *Down Beat*, March 16, 1961, 34, 36.

17. Welding, "The New Lost City Ramblers," 36.

18. Peter Welding, "Crusaders for Old-Time Music: The New Lost City Ramblers," *Sing Out!* 11 (December–January 1961–62): 7.

19. Nat Hentoff, "The Citibillies," *Reporter*, May 24, 1962, 42–43.

20. Jon Pankake and Paul Nelson, "The Second Annual University of Chicago Folk Festival," *Little Sandy Review* 21 (ca. 1962): 5.

21. New Lost City Ramblers University of Chicago Folk Festival concert recording, February 4, 1962, tapes FT-9716 and FT-9717, Mike Seeger Collection, SFC.

22. New Lost City Ramblers Elliot House, Harvard University concert recording, March 22, 1962, tapes FT-9800 and FT-9801, Mike Seeger Collection, SFC.

23. Bill Malone, "Reaffirming Authenticity: Mike Seeger and the Rediscovery of Southern Roots Music," paper presented to the Southern Intellectual History Conference at Sewanee, Florida, December 2005, 20. Quoted with the permission of the author.

24. Bill Malone, *Country Music U.S.A.* (Austin: University of Texas Press, 1968), 339–40.

25. New Lost City Ramblers University of Texas at Austin concert recording, March 29, 1962, tape FT-9768, Mike Seeger Collection, SFC.

26. Malone, *Country Music U.S.A.*, 394.

27. Jon Pankake and Paul Nelson, "The New Lost City Ramblers Volume 4," *Little Sandy Review* 22 (ca. 1962): 30.

28. The original "Crow Black Chicken" can be heard on *The Leake County Revelers: Recorded Works in Chronological Order, Volume I, 1927–1928* (Document Records DOCD 8029, 1998).

29. Written statement by Tom Paley, ca. 1963, Tom Paley file, Moses and Frances Asch Collection, RRFAC.

30. Mike Seeger, "Regarding Tom Paley's Departure from the New Lost City Ramblers," statement sent to the British magazine *Folk Music*, August 25, 1964, and copied to Moe Asch, Mike Seeger file, Moses and Frances Asch Collection, RRFAC.

31. Paley interview (B).

32. Ralph Rinzler's recollections on meeting and recording Watson in 1960 and the subsequent 1962 Ash Grove performances are recounted in his liner note to *The Original Folkways Recordings of Doc Watson and Clarence Ashley, 1960–1962* (Folkways Records SFW 40029, 1994). See also Ronald Cohen's account of the 1962 Ashley-Watson Ash Grove performance in *Rainbow Quest: The Folk Music Revival and American Society, 1940–1970* (Amherst: University of Massachusetts Press, 2002), 173.

33. Doc Watson to John Cohen and Mike Seeger, June 12, 1962, John Cohen personal collection.

34. Schwarz interview (A). Tracy's biography is drawn primarily from this interview.

35. Schwarz interview (C).

36. Schwarz interview (A).

37. Schwarz interview (C).

38. Schwarz interview (A).

39. Schwarz interview (A).

40. Schwarz interview (A).

41. Mike Seeger to Tracy Schwarz, June 16, 1962, Tracy Schwarz personal collection.

42. Seeger interview (E).

CHAPTER 6. SEEGER, COHEN, AND SCHWARZ PERFORM THE FOLK

1. Jon Pankake and Paul Nelson, "The Old and the New Lost City Ramblers," *Little Sandy Review* 28 (ca. January–February 1964): 17–21.

2. Israel Young, "Frets and Frail," *Sing Out!* 12 (October–November 1962): 51.

3. Tom Paley to Mike Seeger and John Cohen, September 10, 1962, Tom Paley file, Moses and Frances Asch Collection, RRFAC.

4. Tom Paley to Mike Seeger, n.d. (ca. fall 1962), Tom Paley file, Moses and Frances Asch Collection, RRFAC.

5. Benson & Israelson Counselors at Law to Mike Seeger and John Cohen, October 25, 1962, NLCR file, Moses and Frances Asch Collection, RRFAC.

6. Benson & Israelson Counselors at Law to Manuel Greenhill, October 26, 1962, NLCR file, Moses and Frances Asch Collection, RRFAC.

7. Unsigned agreement between Tom Paley and Mike Seeger, John Cohen, and Tracy Schwarz, NLCR file, Moses and Frances Asch Collection, RRFAC. Under the agreement Tom would continue to receive royalties for all previous Folkways recordings he had made with the Ramblers.

8. Tom Paley probably to Moe Asch, n.d. (ca. early 1964), Tom Paley file, Moses and Frances Asch Collection, RRFAC.

9. Schwarz interview (C).

10. Bob Dylan, *Chronicles Volume One* (New York: Simon & Schuster, 2004), 238.

11. "Folklore Concert #3: Well Received Experiment," *Broadside*, November 16, 1962, 7.

12. Burton Michaels, "Folk Trio Shows Authenticity," *Michigan Daily*, December 16, 1962.

13. C. T. Moynihan, "New Lost City Ramblers Perform Country Music," unidentified Minneapolis newspaper clipping, January 24, 1963, Mike Seeger personal collection.

14. New Lost City Ramblers University of Chicago Folk Festival concert recording, February 1, 1963, tape FT-9719, Mike Seeger Collection, SFC.

15. "The New Lost City Ramblers," *Chicago Maroon*, January 25, 1963.

16. New Lost City Ramblers Ash Grove concert recording, Los Angeles, April 4, 1963, tape FT-5622, Mike Seeger Collection, SFC.

17. As cited in Ronald Cohen, *Rainbow Quest: The Folk Music Revival and American Society, 1940–1970* (Amherst: University of Massachusetts Press, 2002), 200.

18. David King Dunaway, *How Can I Keep from Singing? The Ballad of Pete Seeger* (New York: Villard Books, 2008), 258.

19. Cohen, *Rainbow Quest*, 189–91.

20. For background on *Broadside*, see Cohen, *Rainbow Quest*, 179–81.

21. For more on the intersection of the folk revival and the civil rights movement, see Cohen, *Rainbow Quest*, 183–87. See also Robert Shelton, "Singing for Freedom: Music in the Integration Movement," *Sing Out!* 12 (December–January 1962): 4–7.

22. For more on Pete Seeger's congressional trial and eventual acquittal, see Dunaway, *How Can I Keep from Singing*, 246–60.

23. For more on *Hootenanny* and the boycott, see Cohen, *Rainbow Quest*, 194–98.

24. Cohen, *Rainbow Quest*, 198. See also Pete Seeger, "Johnny Appleseed, Jr.," *Sing Out!* 13 (April–May 1963): 63.

25. Seeger interview (F).

26. "John Cohen I," in *Wasn't That a Time!: First Hand Accounts of the Folk Music Revival*, ed. Ronald Cohen (Lanham, MD: Scarecrow Press, 1995), 28–29.

27. John recounts Gottlieb's snub at the *Hootenanny* audition in Cohen, *Wasn't That a Time*, 29. Gottlieb had a different interpretation of the event and countered that John would never have taken the time to listen to an entire Limeliters song ("Lou Gottlieb," in Cohen, *Wasn't That a Time*, 152).

28. Seeger interview (F).

29. Irwin Silber, "News and Notes," *Sing Out!* 14 (April–May 1964): 4. Tom's comments appeared in "Will the Real NLCR Stand Up Please," *Folk Weekly*, August 15, 1964, a newsletter of the British magazine *Folk Music*. Clipping from Mike Seeger personal collection.

30. Cohen, *Rainbow Quest*, 195.

31. Bill Malone, *Country Music U.S.A.* (Austin: University of Texas Press, 1968), 35.

32. Schwarz interview (A).

33. A 1965 recording of Robertson playing "Leather Britches" can be heard on *Close to Home: Old-Time Music from Mike Seeger's Collection, 1952–1967* (Smithsonian Folkways CD 40097, 1997). He can be heard playing with the Ramblers at the 1965 Newport Folk Festival on *The New Lost City Ramblers: Old Time Music* (Vanguard Records VGDC 770112, 1994).

34. Malone, *Country Music U.S.A.*, 64–65.

35. Cohen interview (C).

36. Maybelle Carter can be heard singing "Wildwood Flower" and "The Old Gospel

Ship," backed by the Ramblers at the 1965 Newport Folk Festival, on *The New Lost City Ramblers: Old Time Music*.

37. D. K. Wilgus, *Anglo-American Folk Song Scholarship since 1898* (New Brunswick, N.J.: Rutgers University Press, 1959). In 1965 Wilgus served as editor for a special issue of the *Journal of American Folklore* devoted to hillbilly music, the first serious treatment of the material by folk song scholars. See Wilgus, "An Introduction to the Study of Hillbilly Music," *Journal of American Folklore* 78 (July–September 1965): 195–203.

38. UCLA Folk Festival brochure, May 3–5, 1963, Archie Green Papers, SFC.

39. Mike Seeger, album notes to *Dock Boggs* (Folkways Records FA 3251, 1964).

40. In addition to the above-cited Boggs LP, Mike produced *Excerpts from Interviews with Dock Boggs, Legendary Banjo Player and Singer* (Folkways Records FA 5458, 1965); *Dock Boggs, Volume 2* (Folkways Records FA 2932, 1965); and *Dock Boggs, Volume 3* (Folkways Records FA 3903, 1970).

41. Robert Cantwell, *When We Were Good: The Folk Revival* (Cambridge, MA: Harvard University Press, 1996), 208.

42. See Ralph Rinzler's analysis of Boggs's singing and banjo styles in the liner notes to *Dock Boggs* (Folkways Records FA 3251, 1964).

43. Dock Boggs FOTM concert recording by Peter Siegel, New York City, December 13, 1963, Peter Siegel personal collection.

44. "Welcome," *Newport Folk Festival, 1963 Festival Booklet*, Mike Seeger personal collection.

45. Ralph Rinzler, "The Friends of Old Time Music," *Newport Folk Festival, 1963 Festival Booklet*, Mike Seeger personal collection.

46. Jon Pankake and Paul Nelson, "The Old and the New Lost City Ramblers," *Little Sandy Review* 28 (ca. January 1964): 18–19.

47. Pankake and Nelson, "The Old and the New," 18.

48. Pankake and Nelson, "The Old and the New," 20.

49. An income of $8,000 in 1963 would be approximately equivalent to $53,642 in 2007 dollars. Likewise, $500 in royalty payments would be approximately equivalent to $3,353 in 2007 dollars. Inflation calculations from http://www.westegg.com/inflation/infl.cgi.

50. Thomas Scanlan, "Folk Concert Tonight No Hootenanny," *Minnesota Daily*, January 28, 1964.

51. Archie Green to Dan Auerbach, February 13, 1964, Archie Green Papers, SFC.

52. John Cohen, liner notes to *The New Lost City Ramblers with Cousin Emmy* (Folkways Records FT 1015, 1968).

53. Jon Pankake and Paul Nelson, "The New Lost City Ramblers: String Band Instrumentals," *Little Sandy Review* 30 (ca. 1965): 38–39.

54. Cohen interview (C).

55. John Cohen and Mike Seeger, eds., *The New Lost City Ramblers Songbook* (New York:

Oak Publications, 1964), republished as *Old-Time String Band Songbook* (New York: Oak Publications/Music Sales Limited, 1976). All page references are to the 1976 edition.

56. According to historian Ivan Tribe, Hattie Stoneman lent the Dunford photograph to Mike in the mid-1950s. *The Stonemans: An Appalachian Family and the Music That Shaped Their Lives* (Urbana: University of Illinois Press, 1993), photo caption opposite p. 74.

57. *Old-Time String Band Songbook*, 6.

58. *Old-Time String Band Songbook*, 22.

59. *Old-Time String Band Songbook*, 23.

60. *Old-Time String Band Songbook*, 31.

61. *Old-Time String Band Songbook*, 18.

62. Hally Wood to John Cohen, quoted by Irwin Silber in *Old-Time String Band Songbook*, 3.

63. To further confuse the situation, the header for "Don't Let Your Deal Go Down" lists the original key as F, when in fact both the Ramblers and Charlie Poole recordings are in the key of G (*Old-Time String Band Songbook*, 182).

64. Review of *The New Lost City Ramblers Song Book*, *Saturday Review*, May 15, 1965.

65. Robert Shelton, "Book Review: The New Lost City Ramblers," *Sing Out!* 15 (November 1965): 93.

66. Tom's initial comments on why he left the Ramblers appeared in the British magazine *Folk Music*, ca. summer 1964. Clipping from Mike Seeger personal collection. The article "Will the Real NLCR Stand Up Please" appears in the August 15, 1964, edition of *Folk Weekly*, a newsletter of *Folk Music* magazine. Clipping from Mike Seeger personal collection.

67. Roy Guest to Mike Seeger, September 15, 1964, Mike Seeger personal collection.

68. Tony Millard, "Who Are the Real New City Ramblers?" *Combo Musical Weekly*, November 27, 1964. Clipping from Mike Seeger personal collection.

69. Mike Seeger, "Regarding Tom Paley's Departure from the New Lost City Ramblers," statement sent to the British magazine *Folk Music*, dated August 25 and copied to Moe Asch, Mike Seeger file, Moses and Frances Asch Collection, RRFAC.

70. Russell Karp to Moe Asch, November 2, 1964, NLCR file, Moses and Frances Asch Collection, RRFAC.

71. Tom Paley to Mike Seeger, August 11, 1965, Mike Seeger file, Moses and Frances Asch Collection, RRFAC.

72. Agreement signed by Tom Paley, September 3, 1965, Tom Paley file, Moses and Frances Asch Collection, RRFAC.

73. Tom Paley to Mike Seeger, September 5, 1965, Tom Paley file, Moses and Frances Asch Collection, RRFAC.

74. The exploits of Kesey and the Merry Pranksters are well chronicled in Tom Wolfe's *The Electric Kool-Aid Acid Test* (New York: Bantam Books, 1968).

75. Cohen interview (D).

76. For an account of the December 2, 1964, Berkeley FSM sit-in see David Burner, *Making Peace with the 60s* (Princeton, NJ: Princeton University Press, 1996), 139–42.

77. Cohen interview (D).

78. Mike Seeger, liner notes to *The New Lost City Ramblers: Rural Delivery No. 1* (Folkways Records FA 2496, 1964).

79. John Cohen, liner notes to *The New Lost City Ramblers: Rural Delivery No. 1* (Folkways Records FA 2496, 1964).

CHAPTER 7. GONE TO THE COUNTRY

1. Cohen interview (E).

2. Schwartz interview (A).

3. Seeger interview (G).

4. For more on Moe Asch's agreement with Verve/MGM, see Peter Goldsmith, *Making People's Music: Moe Asch and Folkways Records* (Washington, DC: Smithsonian Institution Press, 1998), 326–27.

5. Folkways/Verve record statement, December 1965, Mike Seeger personal collection.

6. Flyer announcing January 30, 1965, concert at Town Hall, Mike Seeger personal collection.

7. Robert Shelton, "Lost City Ramblers Back after 4 Years," *New York Times*, February 1, 1965.

8. John Cohen to Archie Green, April 30, 1965; Archie Green to John Cohen, May 11, 1965, Archie Green Papers, SFC.

9. D. K. Wilgus, liner notes to *Mike Seeger* (Vanguard Records VSD 97150, 1964).

10. Jon Pankake, "Mike Seeger: The Style of Tradition," *Sing Out!* 14 (July 1964): 7.

11. Nat Hentoff, "Record Reviews," *Mountain Music of Kentucky, Reporter*, July 7, 1960, 59.

12. D. K. Wilgus, "From the Record Review Editor," *Journal of American Folklore* 73 (October–December 1960): 357.

13. See *Mountain Music of Kentucky* (FW 02317, 1960), *The Music of Roscoe Holcomb and Wade Ward* (FW 2363, 1962), and *Roscoe Holcomb: The High Lonesome Sound* (FW 02368, 1965).

14. See John Cohen's notes to the two Elektra albums *Old Time Banjo Project* (EKL 276, 1965) and *String Band Project* (EKL 292, 1965).

15. Edgar Waters, "Battle of the Ballad," *Australian*, May 22, 1965. Clipping from Mike Seeger personal collection.

16. Edgar Waters, "Folk Revivalists Really Are," *Australian*, June 1, 1965. Clipping from Mike Seeger personal collection.

17. Richard Zachariah, "Heady as Corn Liquor," May 26, 1965. Unidentified newspaper review of Melbourne concert, clipping from Melbourne concert. Clipping from Mike Seeger personal collection.

18. Seeger interview (J); Cohen interview (H); Schwarz, e-mail communication with Ray Allen, January 15, 2008.

19. See Irwin Silber's review of the June Carnegie Hall festival in "What's Happening," *Sing Out!* 15 (September 1965): 5, 97.

20. Ralph Rinzler, "The Newport Folk Foundation: Keeping the Roots of Music Alive," in *Newport Folk Festival, July 23–26, 1964 Festival Booklet*, 4–7, Mike Seeger personal collection.

21. Mike's comments on the need for small workshops conducive to artist-audience interchange appear in *Newport Folk Festival, July 22–25, 1965 Festival Booklet*, 3, Mike Seeger personal collection.

22. Robert Shelton, "Folklorists Give Talks at Newport," *New York Times*, July 24, 1965. Lomax allegedly introduced the Butterfield band by saying, "Today you've heard some of the greatest blues musicians in the world playing their simple music on simple instruments. Let's find out if these guys can play at all." A fistfight between Lomax and Grossman broke out backstage when the latter, who hoped to manage the Butterfield band, shouted, "What kind of fuckin' introduction was that?" See Ronald Cohen, *Rainbow Quest: The Folk Music Revival and American Society, 1940–1970* (Amherst: University of Massachusetts Press, 2002), 235.

23. Concert and workshop recordings made at the 1963 and 1965 Newport Folk Festivals with the Ramblers and Carter, Robertson, McGee, Boggs, and Cousin Emmy can be heard on *The New Lost City Ramblers: Old Time Music* (Vanguard Records, VGDC 770112, 1994).

24. Mike's remarks on the history of the banjo and his performance of "Leather Britches" at the 1965 Newport Folk Festival banjo workshop can be heard on *The New Lost City Ramblers: Old Time Music*. The liner notes mistakenly attribute the banjo workshop to the 1963 festival, but the participants indicate the recording was made at the 1965 event.

25. Accounts of Bob Dylan's appearance at the 1965 Newport Folk Festival abound. Recent sources include Joe Boyd, *White Bicycles: Making Music in the 1960s* (London: Serpent's Tail, 2006), 102–6; George Wein, *Myself among Others: A Life in Music* (New York: Da Capo Press, 2003), 332–34; Ronald Cohen, *A History of Folk Music Festivals in the United States: Feasts of Musical Celebration* (Lanham, MD: Scarecrow Press, 2008), 93–96; and Benjamin Filene, *Romancing the Folk: Public Memory and American Roots Music* (Chapel Hill: University of North Carolina Press, 2000), 184–85.

26. Filene, *Romancing the Folk*, 218–32.

27. John Cohen to Archie Green, April 30, 1965, John Cohen personal collection.

28. Wein, *Myself among Others*, 334.

29. D. K. Wilgus, "An Introduction to the Study of Hillbilly Music," *Journal of American Folklore* 78 (July–September 1965): 203.

30. D. K. Wilgus, "Current Hillbilly Recordings: A Review Article," *Journal of American Folklore* 78 (July–September 1965): 267–86.

31. For more on the history of County Records see Charles Wolfe, "Dave Freeman and

County Records," *Bluegrass Unlimited* 15 (December 1980): 50–55; and Wolfe, "County Records and Blue Ridge Music," *Appalachian Journal* 7 (Spring 1980): 234–38.

32. Charles Benson, "The New Lost City Ramblers at Laurie Hall," *Country & Western Roundup*, November–December 1965, 19. Clipping from Mike Seeger personal collection.

33. F.G., "Ramblers' Mixture," *Eastern Daily Press*, November 10, 1965. Clipping from Mike Seeger personal collection.

34. Cohen interview (H).

35. Mike Seeger, "A Contemporary Folk Esthetic," *Sing Out!* 16 (February–March 1966): 61.

36. The December 1965 episode featuring the Ramblers is available on *Pete Seeger's Rainbow Quest* (Shanachie DVD 608, 2005).

37. Seeger, "Contemporary Folk Esthetic," 59–61.

38. Alan Dundes, "Texture, Text, and Context," in *Interpreting Folklore* (Bloomington: Indiana University Press, 1980), 22–24. The essay was originally published in *Southern Folklore Quarterly* 28 (1964): 251–65.

39. "Introduction" in *Transforming Tradition: Folk Music Revivals Examined*, ed. Neil V. Rosenberg (Urbana: University of Illinois Press, 1993), 16–17.

40. For more on Stekert's experience studying folklore at Indiana University and Dorson's hostility toward the folk music revival, see Ellen Stekert, "Autobiography of a Woman Folklorist," *Journal of American Folklore* 100 (October–December 1987): 579–85.

41. Ellen Stekert, "Cents and Nonsense in the Urban Folk Song Movement: 1930–66," in Rosenberg, *Transforming Tradition*, 96–97. The essay was originally published in Bruce Jackson, ed., *Folklore and Society: Essays in Honor of Benjamin A. Botkin* (Hatboro, PA: Folklore Associates, 1966), 153–68.

42. Stekert, "Cents and Nonsense," 87. Stekert's comments appear in her introduction to the 1993 reprint of "Cents and Nonsense" in Rosenberg, *Transforming Tradition*.

43. Jan Brunvand, *Folklore: A Study and Research Guide* (New York: St. Martin's Press, 1976), 23.

44. David Culhane (London correspondent), "British Tapping Toes to Pure Folk Music," *Baltimore Sun*, March 20, 1966; R.F.D.G., "Museum Piece U.S. Country Music," *London Daily Telegraph*, March 12, 1966. Clippings from Mike Seeger personal collection.

45. For further recollections by the Ramblers on the 1966 tour and all quotations by the Ramblers, see *American Folk and Country Festival* booklet, Bear Family CD (BCD 16849 BK, 2007).

46. Cohen interview (D).

47. "Record Review," *Sing Out!* 17 (June–July 1967): 43.

48. Mike's quotes are from the liner notes to *Remembrance of Things to Come* (Verve/Folkways FT/FTS 3018, 1967).

49. Cajun and zydeco music scholar Mark DeWitt suggests that the 1964 appearance

of the Balfa Family at the Newport Folk Festival and the subsequent recording of "Parlez-Nous a Boire" by the Ramblers were key in introducing Cajun music to the folk music revival. See DeWitt, *Cajun and Zydeco Dance Music in Northern California: Modern Pleasures in a Postmodern World* (Jackson: University Press of Mississippi, 2008), 119.

50. Background on the efforts of S. Dillon Ripley and James Morris to institute early programming on the National Mall is found in Richard Kurin, *Smithsonian Folklife Festival: Culture of, by, and for the People* (Washington, DC: Center for Folklife Programs and Cultural Studies, Smithsonian Institution, 1998), 103–4; and in Richard Kurin, *Reflections of a Culture Broker: A View from the Smithsonian* (Washington, DC: Smithsonian Institution Press, 1997), 110–11.

51. Tony Wilson, "Keeping the Country Music Flag Flying," *Melody Maker*, February 25, 1967. Clipping from Mike Seeger personal collection.

52. Archie Green's introduction to the August 10, 1966, Smithsonian Ramblers program as well as the music and additional commentary can be heard on tapes FT-9789–93, Mike Seeger Collection, SFC.

53. Joseph C. Hickerson, "Folk Tunes Delight Crowd," *Washington Evening Star*, August 11, 1966.

54. Eric Winter, "Gimmie That Old-Timey Music," *Music Maker* 1 (February 1967): 35. Clipping from Mike Seeger personal collection.

55. Wilson, "Keeping the Country Music Flag Flying."

56. Peter Coulston, "New Lost City Ramblers at the Albert Hall," *Country News and Views* 5 (April 1967): 9, clipping from Mike Seeger personal collection.

57. Mike Stott, "New Lost City Ramblers in Leeds," *Country News and Views* 5 (April 1967): 8, clipping from Mike Seeger personal collection.

58. Maurice Rosenbaum, "Song-Rituals Enacted by Watersons," *Daily Telegraph*, February 13, 1967. Clipping from Mike Seeger personal collection.

59. Coulston, "New Lost City Ramblers at the Albert Hall," 9.

60. John Cohen to Moe Asch, n.d. (ca. 1967), quoted in Goldsmith, *Making People's Music*, 337–38.

61. Moe Asch to John Cohen, February 18, 1967, quoted in Goldsmith, *Making People's Music*, 338.

62. Cohen interview (H).

63. "Folk Tour Fills Cabell," *Virginia Weekly*, ca. April 1, 1967. Clipping from Mike Seeger personal collection.

64. Tracy Schwarz, e-mail to Ray Allen, February 7, 2008.

65. Cohen interview (D).

66. See Mike's comments on folk music and politics in Seeger, "Contemporary Folk Esthetic," 59.

67. Cohen interview (D).

68. "The New Lost City Ramblers: With Their Music They Bring the Country to the City, They're Three Young Men with a Mission," *Woman's Day*, June 7, 1965.

69. Cohen interview (D).

70. Tracy Schwarz, e-mail to Ray Allen, February 7, 2008.

71. These record-sales figures do not count the sales of the Folkways/Verve LPs *Rural Delivery No. 1* and *Remembrances of Things to Come*. None of the Ramblers have records of the Folkways/Verve LP sales.

72. John Cohen, "Chicago Festival," *Sing Out!* 18 (June–July 1968): 65.

73. *Third Annual Southern Folk Festival* program book, 1968, Anne Romaine Papers, SFC.

74. All quotes in reference to the 1968 Southern Folk Culture Revival Project tour are from Seeger interview (K); John Cohen, e-mail to Ray Allen, February 1, 2008; and Tracy Schwarz, e-mail to Ray Allen, February 7, 2008.

75. John's comments are from the liner notes to *Modern Times* (Folkways Records, FTS 31027, 1968).

76. Robert Shelton, "Lost City Ramblers Start on 11th Year," *New York Times*, November 25, 1968.

77. Jon Pankake, "Ten Years in the New Lost City," *Sing Out!* 18 (October–November 1968): 30–31, 73, 75.

CHAPTER 8. A SECOND DECADE

1. John cites Sara Katz in his liner notes essay, "The Tradition Lives," for *Jerry Garcia and David Grisman: Shady Grove* (Acoustic Disk ACD-21, 1996).

2. NLCR Family Dog concert recording, San Francisco, August 16, 1969, tape FT-9796 LC, Mike Seeger Collection, SFC. The live recording of "Wildwood Weed" was issued on *The New Lost City Ramblers: 40 Years of Concert Recordings* (Rounder Records 82161–0481–2, 2001).

3. Cohen interview (E).

4. Cohen interview (E).

5. Cohen interview (E).

6. Tom Miller, "A Melting Pot at Sky River Festival," *Rolling Stone*, October 4, 1969.

7. Jim Henderson, "Rambling But Not Lost," *Virginia Pilot*, May 18, 1969. Clipping from Mike Seeger personal collection.

8. Michael Scully, *The Never-Ending Revival: Rounder Records and the Folk Alliance* (Urbana: University of Illinois Press, 2008), 42.

9. Happy Traum, "What's Happening," *Sing Out!* 19 (Winter 1969–70): 34.

10. Ralph Rinzler, "Festival of American Folklife," in Smithsonian Festival of American Folklife program booklet, 1971. For history of the Smithsonian Festival of American Folklife, see Richard Kurin, *Reflections of a Cultural Broker: A View from the Smithsonian* (Washington, DC: Smithsonian Institution Press, 1997), 109–37. See also Robert Cantwell's criti-

cism in "Feasts of the Unnaming: Folklife Festivals and the Representation of Folklife," in *Public Folklore*, ed. Robert Baron and Nicholas Spitzer (Washington, DC: Smithsonian Institution Press, 1992), 263–305.

11. The NLCR stage introduction by Ralph Rinzler at the Festival of American Folklife concert on July 3, 1970, was taken from a recording stored in the RRFAC.

12. See Burt Feintuch's essay "Introduction: Folklorists and the Public Sector" for background on the establishment of the NEA Folk Arts Program, the American Folklife Center, and other government-sponsored folklore initiatives dating back to the Depression era WPA projects in *The Conservation of Culture: Folklorists and the Public Sector*, ed. Burt Feintuch (Lexington: University of Kentucky Press, 1988), 1–16. See also the essays in Baron and Spitzer, *Public Folklore*.

13. Alan Jabbour to Cathie Whitesides, published in "Issues in Old-Time Music," *Old-Time Herald* (Winter 1993–94): 25.

14. See Jabbour's comments on the problems of the authentic/imitative dichotomy with respect to festivals and other folklife programs in Philip Gura, "Some Thoughts on the Revival: Alan Jabbour and Old-Time Music," *Old-Time Herald* (Summer 1991), 28.

15. The history of the National Folk Festival is well chronicled in Michael Ann Williams, *Staging Tradition: John Lair and Sarah Gertrude Knott* (Urbana: University of Illinois Press, 2006). See pages 144–51 for the festival's transformation in the 1970s under sponsorship by the National Parks Service and Joe Wilson's direction. Mac Benford's piece "Folklorists and US—An Account of Our Curious and Changing Relationship (with More Personal Reminiscences)" appears in the *Old-Time Herald* (Spring 1989), 22–27; Joe Wilson's response, "Confession of a Folklorist," appears in the *Old-Time Herald* (Spring 1990), 25–31, 43. See Michael Scully's commentary on the Benford-Wilson exchange and its implications for the folk music authenticity debate in *Never-Ending Revival*, 126–27.

16. Cited from booklet to *Where'd You Come From? Where'd You Go?: The New Lost City Ramblers at 50* (Smithsonian Folkways CD 40180, 2009), 34.

17. Mike Seeger, liner notes to *Berkeley Farms* (Folkways Records FA 2436, 1972).

18. Background on the Highwoods Stringband is found in Alice Gerrard, "Colby Street to New York & Points South: The Highwoods Stringband," *Old-Time Herald* (Summer 1992), 26–33; and in Mike Greenstein, "New York Stringbands: The Highwoods & Cranberry Lake," *Bluegrass Unlimited* (February 1979), 36–41. See also Scully, *Never-Ending Revival*, 120–24.

19. *Highwoods Stringband: Fire on the Mountain* (Rounder Records 0023, 1973) and *Highwoods Stringband: Dance All Night* (Rounder Records 0045, 1975) are reviewed in *Bluegrass Unlimited* (June 1976), 44–45; *Highwoods Stringband No. 3 Special* (Rounder Records 0071, 1978) is reviewed in *Bluegrass Unlimited* (July 1978), 30.

20. Mac Benford, quoted in liner notes to *Berkeley Farms*.

21. Walt Koken, "Hysterical Note," in liner notes to *The Highwoods Stringband: Feed Your Babies Onions* (Rounder Records CD 11569, 1994).

22. Mac Benford quoted in Greenstein, "New York Stringbands," 38.

23. Mike Seeger quoted in Gerrard, "Colby Street," 28.

24. Liner notes to *Highwoods Stringband: Fire on the Mountain* (Rounder Records 0023, 1973).

25. Mike Seeger quoted in Gerrard, "Colby Street," 30.

26. Mike and John's tributes to Highwoods are found in the liner notes to *The Highwoods Stringband: Feed Your Babies Onions*.

27. Greenstein, "New York Stringbands," 37, 40.

28. Alan Jabbour initially shared this perspective with me in an e-mail of February 15, 2008. His position regarding the role the Ramblers played in the larger instrumental folk music revival is further discussed in "Hollow Rock and the Ramblers: A Memoir and Some Reflections," paper delivered at the October 2008 meeting of the American Folklore Society, Louisville, KY. Used with permission of the author.

29. Alan Jabbour, "The Hollow Rock String Band Remembered a Generation Later," www.originalredclayramblers.com. See also Scully, *Never-Ending Revival*, 118–19. The original 1968 Hollow Rock String Band LP has been reissued by County Records as *The Hollow Rock String Band: Traditional Dance Tunes* (CO-2715-CD, 1997).

30. Thomas Carter, "Looking for Henry Reed: Confessions of a Revivalist," in *Sounds of the South*, ed. Daniel Patterson (Durham, NC: Duke University Press, 1991). Carter's discussion of the differences between Hollow Rock and the Ramblers is found on pages 79–80; his remembrance of first hearing the Ramblers in 1964 appears on page 74; the picture of the Hippo Choral String Band is on page 76.

31. Bill Hicks, "Where'd They Come From? Where'd They Go? A Brief History of the Fuzzy Mountain String Band," *Old-Time Herald* (Spring 1995), 21.

32. Background on the Fuzzy Mountain String Band is found in Hicks, "Where'd They Come From?" 20–21. See also Scully, *Never-Ending Revival*, 118–20, and Bill Hicks, Blanton Owen, and Sharon Sandomirsky, "The Roots of the Red Clay Ramblers: The Fuzzy Mountain String Band," www.originalredclayramblers.com.

33. I am grateful to Burt Feintuch for sharing this insight with me in an e-mail dated June 17, 2009.

34. Clive Barnes, "*Diamond Studs: a Saloon Musical*, Is Sheer Delight," *New York Times*, January 15, 1975.

35. For a loosely written history of the Red Clay Ramblers, see Bill Hicks, "Blurred Time," www.originalredclayramblers.com.

36. Tommy Thompson quotes are taken from his liner notes to *The Red Clay Ramblers with Fiddlin' Al McCanless* (Folkways Records FTS 31039, 1974).

37. Cohen interview (E).

38. David Axler, "Record Reviews," *Sing Out!* 21 (March–April 1972): 34.

39. Richard Spottswood, liner notes to *Strange Creek Singers* (Arhoolie CD 9003, 1972, 1997).

40. Seeger interview (L).

41. Axler, "Record Reviews," 34.

42. Jon Pankake, "Records," *Rolling Stone*, July 20, 1972, 50.

43. Bob Norman, "Record Reviews," *Sing Out!* 22 (September–October 1973): 43.

44. Seeger interview (M).

45. Cohen interview (I).

46. John Cohen, liner note to *Putnam String County Band* (Rounder Records 3003, 1973).

47. Michael Goodwin, review of *The End of an Old Song*, *Rolling Stone*, March 18, 1971. *The End of an Old Song* and *The High Lonesome Sound* have been re-released on the DVD *The High Lonesome Sound* (Shanachie 1404, 2002).

48. Schwarz interview (A).

49. Schwarz interview (D).

50. Tracy Schwarz, liner notes to *Look Out! Here It Comes* (Folkways Records FA 2419, 1975).

51. Tracy Schwarz, liner notes to *Cajun Fiddle Old & New with Dewey Balfa* (Folkways Records FM 8362, 1977).

52. Mike Seeger to John Cohen, May 9, 1975, John Cohen personal collection.

53. Mike Seeger to John Cohen, July 30, 1975, John Cohen personal collection.

54. John Cohen to Mike Seeger, August 12, 1975, Mike Seeger personal collection.

55. Mike Seeger to John Cohen, October 10, 1975, John Cohen personal collection.

56. Mike Seeger to Manny Greenhill, October 25, 1975, Mike Seeger personal collection.

57. Philip Elwood, "Folk 'Authentics' from the Big City," *San Francisco Examiner*, September 13, 1973; Joel Selvin, "Joyous Night: New Lost City Ramblers," *San Francisco Chronicle*, September 13, 1973.

58. John Cohen, liner notes to *On the Great Divide* (Folkways Records FTS 31041, 1975).

59. Jerry Leichtling, "Ramblers Still Wear Vests," *Village Voice*, March 21, 1977; Robert Palmer, "Traditional Idioms of Folk Music Mixed by the New Lost City Ramblers," *New York Times*, March 14, 1977; Billy Altman, "Riffs: Twenty Years of Unselfconsciousness," *Village Voice*, October 9, 1978.

60. Highlights of the September 20, 1978, show are heard on the *New Lost City Ramblers 20th Anniversary Concert* (Flying Fish Records FF 70090, 1986, 1993).

61. Mark Greenberg, "Performances: The New Lost City Ramblers Are Found in New York," *Vermont Vanguard Press*, October 10, 1978.

62. Harold Leventhal Management, letter and financial statement, to John Cohen, Mike Seeger, and Tracy Schwarz, October 6, 1978. Mike's request to have the group pay expenses for Cotten and the Highwoods comes from his December 12, 1978, letter to John and Tracy. Both letters from John Cohen personal collection.

63. Tracy Schwarz to Mike Seeger and John Cohen, June 26, 1979, Tracy Schwarz personal collection.

64. General Announcement from Mike Seeger, August 1, 1979, Mike Seeger personal collection.

CHAPTER 9. THINKING LEGACY AND MOVING ON

1. Mark Greenberg, "New Lost City Ramblers: Energetic Traditionalists," *Frets* 1 (October 1979): 19–23. The editors' note regarding the Ramblers' retirement is found at the end of the Greenberg article on page 23.

2. Review of *The New Lost Ramblers: On the Great Divide*, *Bluegrass Unlimited* (July 1975), 37.

3. Doug Tuchman, "The New Lost City Ramblers," *Pickin'* 2 (March 1975): 4–6, 8–10, 12–13.

4. Rhonda Mattern, "Country Music Renaissance: Twenty Years with the New Lost City Ramblers," *Sing Out!* 27 (May–June 1978): 2.

5. D. K. Wilgus, "From the Record Review Editor: Revival and Traditional," *Journal of American Folklore* 81 (April–June 1968): 173.

6. Jens Lund and R. Serge Denisoff, "The Folk Music Revival and the Counter Culture: Contributions and Contradictions," *Journal of American Folklore* 84 (October 1971): 393, 399, 400.

7. David Evans, "Record Reviews: Folk Music Revival," *Journal of American Folklore* 92 (January–March 1979): 108–9.

8. Robert Cantwell, *Bluegrass Breakdown: The Making of the Old Southern Sound* (Urbana: University of Illinois Press, 1984), 197.

9. Neil Rosenberg, *Bluegrass: A History* (Urbana: University of Illinois Press, 1985, 2005), 173–74.

10. Ray Alden, liner notes to *The Young Fogies* (Heritage Records 056, 1985).

11. Quote from *The Young Fogies Gazette*, insert to Alden, *The Young Fogies*.

12. Mark Greenberg, review of *There Ain't No Way Out* CD, *Sing Out!* 42 (Fall 1997): 130.

13. Alan Jabbour, "Hollow Rock and the Ramblers: A Memoir and Some Reflections," paper delivered at the October 2008 meeting of the American Folklore Society, Louisville, KY. Used with permission of the author.

14. Quote from Robert Cantwell, *When We Were Good: The Folk Revival* (Cambridge, MA: Harvard University Press), 329–30. See also Burt Feintuch, "Musical Revival as Musical Transformation," in *Transforming Tradition: Folk Music Revivals Examined*, ed. Neil Rosen-

berg (Urbana: University of Illinois Press, 1993), 186; and Ronald Cohen, *Rainbow Quest* (Amherst: University of Massachusetts Press, 2002), 143–44.

15. Jon Pankake, liner notes to *The New Lost City Ramblers—The Early Years, 1958–1962* (Smithsonian Folkways CD 40036, 1991).

16. Jon Pankake, liner notes to *The New Lost City Ramblers Volume II, 1963–1973—Out Standing in Their Field* (Smithsonian Folkways CD 40040, 1993).

17. Philip Gura, "Roots and Branches: Forty Years of the New Lost City Ramblers, Part 1," *Old-Time Herald* (Winter 1999), 30.

18. Philip Gura, "Roots and Branches: Forty Years of the New Lost City Ramblers, Part 2," *Old-Time Herald*, (Spring 2000), 24.

19. Archie Green's interview can be seen in the documentary film *The New Lost Ramblers in Always Been a Rambler* (Arhoolie DVD AFV-204, 2009).

20. Cantwell, *When We Were Good*, 313–37.

21. Barbara Kirshenblatt-Gimblett, "The Future of Folklore Studies in America: The Urban Frontier," *Folklore Forum* 16, no. 2 (1983): 179–80.

22. Burt Feintuch, "Musical Revival and Musical Transformation," in Rosenberg, *Transforming Tradition*, 192.

23. Philip Bohlman, *The Study of Folk Music in the Modern World* (Bloomington: Indiana University Press, 1988), 130.

24. Benjamin Filene, *Romancing the Folk: Public Memory and American Roots Music* (Chapel Hill: University of North Carolina Press, 2000), 5.

25. Filene, *Romancing the Folk*, 5.

26. Filene, *Romancing the Folk*, 59–65.

27. Filene, *Romancing the Folk*, 65–75.

28. Michael Lowy and Robert Sayre, *Romanticism Against the Tide of Modernity* (Durham, NC: Duke University Press, 2001), 17.

29. Lowy and Sayre, *Romanticism*, 21.

30. John's inclination to make aesthetic and philosophical connections between modern art and folk revivalism is examined in Brian Jones, "Finding the Avant-garde in the Old-Time: John Cohen in the American Folk Revival," MA thesis, Brigham Young University, 2009, 62–67.

31. Mark Slobin, "Rethinking 'Revival' of American Ethnic Music," *New York Folklore* 9 (Winter 1983): 39.

32. A full listing of Mike Seeger's recordings, grants, and honors is found at www.mikeseeger.info.

33. www.rexfoundation.org/awardsmaster.html.

34. Cohen interview (J).

35. A full listing of John Cohen's recordings and films is found at www.johncohenworks.com.

36. A full Tom Paley discography is found at www.wirz.de/music/paleyfrm.htm.

37. A full listing of Tracy's recordings and recent activities is found at www.ginnyandtracy.com.

38. Quotes from Mike Seeger, "23 Years Between Recordings," booklet essay to *The New Lost City Ramblers: There Ain't No Way Out* (Smithsonian Folkways CD 40098, 1997).

39. Lyle Lofgren, review of *There Ain't No Way Out* CD, *Old-Time Herald* (Winter 1998–99), 40; review of *There Ain't No Way Out* CD, *Bluegrass Unlimited* (October 1997), 76.

40. Greenberg review, 130, 132.

41. Quotes from Seeger, "23 Years Between Recordings," and John Cohen, "The Lost Rambler Years," booklet essays to *There Ain't No Way Out*.

CHAPTER 10. PASSING FOR TRADITIONAL AND RETHINKING FOLK REVIVALISM

1. Tracy Schwarz to Ray Allen, e-mail, July 13, 2008.

2. Tracy Schwarz, letter, *Old-Time Herald* 2 (Winter 1989–90), 27.

3. Peter Schwarz to Ray Allen, e-mail, July 29, 2008.

4. See Neil Rosenberg's discussion of the etymology of the term *revival* and its linkage with the term *folk* in the introduction to *Transforming Tradition: Folk Music Revivals Examined* (Urbana: University of Illinois Press, 1993), 17–18.

5. Cohen interview (J).

6. Mike Seeger, "23 Years Between Recordings," booklet essay to *The New Lost City Ramblers: There Ain't No Way Out* (Smithsonian Folkways CD 40098, 1997).

7. Burt Feintuch, "Revivals on the Edge: Northumberland and Cape Breton—A Keynote," *Yearbook for Traditional Music* 38 (2006): 2.

8. Tamara Livingston, "Music Revivals: Towards a General Theory," *Ethnomusicology* 43, no. 1 (1999): 68.

9. See, for example, Mark Slobin, *Fiddler on the Move: Exploring the Klezmer World* (New York: Oxford University Press, 2000).

10. NEA Folk and Traditional Arts guidelines can be accessed at www.arts.endow.gov/grants.

11. Michael Scully, *The Never-Ending Revival: Rounder Records and the Folk Alliance* (Urbana: University of Illinois Press, 2006), 47.

12. Benjamin Filene, *Romancing the Folk: Public Memory and American Roots Music* (Chapel Hill: University of North Carolina Press, 2000), 4.

13. Barbara Kirshenblatt-Gimblett, "Sound and Sensibility," in *American Klezmer: Its Roots and Offshoots*, ed. Mark Slobin (Berkeley: University of California Press, 2000), 133–34.

14. Rosenberg, "Named-Systems Revivals," in *Transforming Tradition*, 177–78.

15. See my attempt to apply Anthony Wallace's concept of revitalization movements to the old-time string-band revival in Ray Allen, "Old-Time Music and the Urban Folk Revival," *New York Folklore* 7 (Summer 1981): 78–79.

16. Kirshenblatt-Gimblett observes that the historical development of klezmer music is not necessarily characterized by the dramatic temporal rupture implied by revival: "Instead, old and new are in a perpetual equivocal relationship," "Sound and Sensibility," 138.

17. See, for example, Scully, *Never-Ending Revival*, 28–37; Michael Ann Williams, *Staging Tradition: John Lair and Sarah Gertrude Knott* (Urbana: University of Illinois Press, 2006), 11–15; and Filene, *Romancing the Folk*, 9–75.

18. Scully, *Never-Ending Revival*, 18.

19. Scully, *Never-Ending Revival*, 49.

20. Mark Slobin, "Rethinking 'Revival' of American Ethnic Music," *New York Folklore* 9 (Winter 1983): 37.

INDEX

tour, 1966, 178; family background, 26–29; films in Kentucky, 163; first appearance with Mike and Tom, 39–40; founds New Lost City Ramblers, 2, 9–10, 24; Holcomb album, 162; on image choice, 83; inspired by Pete Seeger, 27; introduction to folk music, 30; introduction to hillbilly music, 27; marries Penny Seeger, 26, 138; on Marxism and bluegrass, 111; meets Eck Robertson, 131; *Mountain Music of Kentucky* (Folkways album), 61–62, 77, 163; moves to the country, 156–57, 158; at Newport, 1959, 68, 69; at Newport, 1963, 134; at Newport, 1965, 167; at 1958 recording session, 46; *Old Time Banjo Project* (Elektra Records album), 163–64; on oral folk tradition, 58; in Peru, 35, 152–53, 163; photographs, 35–36, 164, 237; playing with Tom Paley at Yale hoots, 32; post-Ramblers activities, 236, 237–39; promotes trio, 41–42; in Putnam String County Band, 209–10; on Ramblers musical experience, 114–15; records west coast musicians, 200; second album, 163; solo pursuits, 162–63, 238; on the Stanley Brothers, 100; *String Band Project* (Elektra Records album), 163–64; teaching, 186, 195, 210; tensions with Tom Paley, 95–96; 117; tensions with Mike Seeger and Tracy Schwarz, 164, 208, 213–15; on topical songs, 70–71, 72; traditional artist audio-recordings, 163, 238; at University of Chicago, 1960s, 232; views on segregation, 95–97; at Washington Square, 1958, 43; at Yale, 42

Cohen, Mike, 27, 33; concert productions, 37, 58
Cohen, Norm, 170
Cohen, Ronald, 4, 131; on folk music in 1957–1958, 36
Cohen, Rufus, 237
Cohen, Sonya, 156, 166, 237
Colby Street house, Berkeley, 226
Cold Mountain (film), 238, 249
A Collection of Mountain Fiddle Music (Country Records CD), 170
Collins, Judy, 138, 164, 165
"Colored Aristocracy" (tune), 9, 78, 262n22; LOC recording, 51, 53, 54
Composer's Collective, 11
Conference for New Politics, Chicago, 285
"A Contemporary Folk Esthetic" (essay), 173
"The Coo Coo Bird," 94
Cooder, Ry, 208
Cooney, Michael, 187
copyrighting controversy, 149
Cornett, Bill and JC, 61
Correct Tones, 225
Cotten, Elizabeth, 23; New York City debut, 89; plays Town Hall, New York, 159; relationship with Seeger family, 60, 61, 145; on *Second Annual Farewell Reunion*, 208; writes "Freight Trian" (song), 60; at University of Chicago Folk Festival, 1961, 90
"Cotton Mill Colic," 184
Coulston, Peter, 182, 183
Country Gentlemen, 119, 237
Country Joe and the Fish, 194
Country Music U.S.A. (book), 113
Country News and Views, 182
Country & Western Roundup, 172

Driftwood, Jimmy, 84, 85

Dunaway, David, 16

Dundes, Alan, 174

Dunford, Eck, 146, 148

Durham/Chapel Hill folk scene, 204

Dust Bowl Ballads (Woody Guthrie Victor Records album), 27, 258n3

Dyer-Bennett, Richard, 37, 114

Dykes Magic City Serenades, 53

Dylan, Bob, 6, 109, 248; contributes to *Broadside*, 128; controversial appearance at Newport Folk Festival, 1965, 1–3, 167–68; first album, 128; memoirs, 4; on New Lost City Ramblers, 125; at Newport, 1963, 138; on *Third Annual Farewell Reunion*, 237

Earle, Gene, 80

Earth is Earth (New Lost City Bang Boys Folkways EP), 107, 268n11

"East Virginia" (song), 52, 53

Edelman, Myron, hosting hoots in Baltimore, 19, 38

Elektra Records, 84, 163

Elliot, Cass, 168

Elliott, Jack, 114

Elwood, Philip, 21

Emmy, Cousin, 2, 28, 144; European tour, 1966, 175, 176, 178; at Newport 1965, 166

The End of an Old Song (film), 163, 210

English Folk Songs from the Southern Appalachians (song collection), 247

European tours by Ramblers, 144, 151–52

Evans, David, 223

Evans, Walker, 73, 147; *Let Us Now Praise Famous Men*, 163

"Everyday Night" (tune), 81

Faier, Billy, 68

Fat City String Band, 200, 226

"Feast Here Tonight," 110

Feintuch, Burt, 230–31, 280n33

Fiddle Country Style with Tracy Schwarz (album), 162–63

field recordings, 170; by Alan Lomax, 9, 13, 56, 247; by John Cohen, 61–62, 238; by John Lomax, 9, 247; Library of Congress, 29, 38, 54; by Mike Seeger, 21–23, 237; by Tracy Schwarz, 212

Filene, Benjamin, 4, 6, 168, 231; on Lomaxes, 232; on roots music, 246

Fire on the Mountain (Highwood's Stringband, Rounder Records album), 202

Fisk University Jubilee Singers, 223

Flatt, Lester, 84

Flatt and Scruggs: at the Ash Grove, 87; on *Hootenanny*, 131

Fleischer, Mike, 82, 90

"Fly Around My Pretty Little Miss" (tune), 101

Flying Fish record label, 205, 226

Foggy Mountain Boys, 84

"Foggy Mountain Top" (song), 84, 107, 110

Folk Alliance, 248

folk-based songs, 173

Folklife and the Representation of Culture (book), 5

Folklore: A Study and Research Guide (book), 175

Folklore Center (Greenwich Village), 30, 36; concerts, 37

folk music: aesthetics, 173; alternative terms, 246; commercial, 36; commercial viability, 25; community based, 197; interface with rock, 195;

authenticity, 56, 80–81, 83, 86, 99; background, 2; at Berkeley Folk Festival, 1960, 85; blacklisted, 108; in California, 1961, 2; Carl Fischer Hall concert, 70–71; change in personnel, 116, 121; coffeehouse appearances, 77–78; college audiences, 81, 104–5, 109–10; at Columbia, 77; in commercial show business, 88; concert patter, 110–12, 113; concert persona, 44–45, 65, 78, 87, 95; concert reviews, 58–59; criticisms of, 234; disdain for Kingston Trio, 99; distrust of recording industry, 98–99; early broadcasts, 9; early concerts, 42, 45–46, 104; economic straits, 77, 121; emphasis on performance style, 224; formation, 26, 41; at Gate of Horn, 82, 83; humor, 60, 63–64, 85, 99, 109, 112; at Indian Neck Folk Festival, 77; as individual musicians, 40, 54–55; individual personalities, 106; inspire old-time string bands, 80, 230; instrumental choices, 39–40, 50–53, 54; legacy, 221–35; managers, 102, 108; Mills College Theater concert, 62, 65; move to Chicago, 83; name choice, 45; at Newport Folk Festival, 69, 84, 120; place in folk music revival, 6, 67–68, 69; pursue music full time, 76, 103, 105; recognition, 239, 246; recording sessions, 45; relationship to commercial market, 49; relationship with Folkways, 77; and romanticism, 233–34; scholarly recognition, 223; second album, 59; sources, 80; southern concerts, 94–95, 112–14, 228; on tour, 1960, 82; trademark vests, 83; tuning habits, 59, 78, 109;

at University of Chicago Folk Festival, 89–91, 109–10; vocals, 55, 56, 75, 81, 101, 112; Washington Theater Club appearance, 97

New Lost City Ramblers (Mike Seeger, John Cohen, Tracy Schwarz): aid Newport evolution, 169; album sales, 183; appear with Bill Malone, 135; college audiences, 126, 161, 177, 184, 187; conflict with civil rights advocates, 129; disband, 220; on Dylan controversy, 168; early appearances, 125–26; on electric folk, 168–69; engagements dwindle, 195, 214–15, 218; and government support, 198; *Hootenanny* controversy, 129–30; income, 126, 143, 153, 161, 173, 186, 214; at initial Smithsonian concert, 180–81; instrumental configuration, 126–27; international tours, 164–65, 169, 175–78, 182–83; with Johnny Cash, 133; last California tour, 1973, 215; with Maybelle Carter, 133; at Newport Folk Festival, 1–3, 137–38, 167, 184, 196; 1971 Festival of American Folklife, 199; and 1960s counterculture, 153–54, 155, 185–86, 193–94; political ventures, 184–85; relationship to commercial folk music, 128; relationship with folklorists, 175; relationship with Moe Asch, 183–84; renewed interest in bluegrass, 127; Southern Folk Festival appearances, 184, 187–88; squabbles within, 161; stage presentations, 127; ten-year anniversary, 190; topical songs, 188–89; Town Hall appearance, 161; twentieth anniversary concert, 1978, 202, 218–20; at UCLA festival, 134; at

on limitations of transcription, 150; on revival-survival dichotomy, 22; at UCLA Folk Festival, 133, 134

Seeger, Christopher, 105, 157

Seeger, Constance Edson, 10

Seeger, Jeremy, 157

Seeger, Kim, 88, 157

Seeger, Marge, 77; sits in for Tom Paley, 117

Seeger, Mike, 1, 2, 9, 26, 32; on Alan Lomax, 114; album notes, 61; on the Almanac Singers, 114; *American Banjo* (album), 18, 21; appearances with Peggy, 18; approach to folk music, 16; arranges Pierce Hall concert, 60; on "art" folksingers, 114; bluegrass background, 19; on board of National Folk Festival, 199; on Bob Dylan, 173; on Buck Owens, 173; on Burl Ives, 114; on Charles Seeger, 114; childhood, 9–24; compiles library of traditional material, 17–18; conscientious objector status, 19; on D. K. Wilgus, 114; on Ewan MacColl, 173; on folk aesthetics, 173; on folk music revival, 245; on folk revival in England, 172; founds New Lost City Ramblers, 2, 39–40; Grammy nominations, 236; on the Greenbrier Boys, 107; involvement with Smithsonian festival, 197; on Jack Elliott, 14; on Jim Nesbitt, 173; on Johnny Cash, 173; on Kingston Trio, 114; learns the banjo, 257n23; marries Alexia Smith, 236; marries Alice Gerrard, 207; marries Marge Ostrow, 77; on Marxism and bluegrass, 111; meets Ralph Rinzler, 257n28; meets Tom Paley, 38; meets Tracy Schwarz, 120; moves to Baltimore, 21; moves to D.C., 58, 206; moves to Lexington, VA, 236; *Music from the True Vine* album, 207; at Newport, 68, 84, 137, 167, 177; as Newport advisor, 94; at 1958 recording session, 46; *Oldtime Country Music* album, 161–62; organizes American Old-Time Music Festival, 1975, 208; on popular topical songs, 72; Ramblers' English tour, 1965, 171; on Ramblers' European tour, 1966, 176–77; on Ramblers musical experience, 114–15; records *American Folk Songs Sung by the Seegers* (album) with Peggy Seeger and Ralph Rinzler, 22–23; records traditional musicians, 21–23, 135–36, 237; records west coast musicians, 200; reflects on early sessions, 43, 44; relationship with Pete Seeger, 16, 114; on Richard Dyer-Bennett, 114; on Roger Miller, 173; on *Second Annual Farewell Reunion*, 208; second bluegrass album, 69; serves on Newport Folk Foundation board, 166; small-town home, 157–58; solo career, 88, 143, 186, 195; on southern string band music revival, 244; teaching at Fresno, 208; tensions with John, 161, 213–15; on *Third Annual Farewell Reunion*, 236; on *Tipple, Loom and Rail: Songs of the Industrialization of the South Sung and Played by Mike Seeger* (album), 161; Travis-style guitar picking, 59; at University of Chicago, 1960s, 232; views on segregation, 95–97; at Washington Square, 1958, 43; on Weavers, 114; on William Clauson, 114; wins Galax contest, 42; working as recording engineer, 76

Seeger, Peggy, 10, 11, 16, 32, 164; Actor's

RAY ALLEN is a professor
of music and American studies at
Brooklyn College, City University
of New York.

MUSIC IN AMERICAN LIFE

Race, Rock, and Elvis   *Michael T. Bertrand*

Theremin: Ether Music and Espionage   *Albert Glinsky*

Poetry and Violence: The Ballad Tradition of Mexico's Costa Chica   *John H. McDowell*

The Bill Monroe Reader   *Edited by Tom Ewing*

Music in Lubavitcher Life   *Ellen Koskoff*

Zarzuela: Spanish Operetta, American Stage   *Janet L. Sturman*

Bluegrass Odyssey: A Documentary in Pictures and Words, 1966–86   *Carl Fleischhauer
    and Neil V. Rosenberg*

That Old-Time Rock & Roll: A Chronicle of an Era, 1954–63   *Richard Aquila*

Labor's Troubadour   *Joe Glazer*

American Opera   *Elise K. Kirk*

Don't Get above Your Raisin': Country Music and the Southern Working Class
    Bill C. Malone

John Alden Carpenter: A Chicago Composer   *Howard Pollack*

Heartbeat of the People: Music and Dance of the Northern Pow-wow   *Tara Browner*

My Lord, What a Morning: An Autobiography   *Marian Anderson*

Marian Anderson: A Singer's Journey   *Allan Keiler*

Charles Ives Remembered: An Oral History   *Vivian Perlis*

Henry Cowell, Bohemian   *Michael Hicks*

Rap Music and Street Consciousness   *Cheryl L. Keyes*

Louis Prima   *Garry Boulard*

Marian McPartland's Jazz World: All in Good Time   *Marian McPartland*

Robert Johnson: Lost and Found   *Barry Lee Pearson and Bill McCulloch*

Bound for America: Three British Composers   *Nicholas Temperley*

Lost Sounds: Blacks and the Birth of the Recording Industry, 1890–1919   *Tim Brooks*

Burn, Baby! BURN! The Autobiography of Magnificent Montague
    Magnificent Montague with Bob Baker

Way Up North in Dixie: A Black Family's Claim to the Confederate Anthem
    Howard L. Sacks and Judith Rose Sacks

The Bluegrass Reader   *Edited by Thomas Goldsmith*

Colin McPhee: Composer in Two Worlds   *Carol J. Oja*

Robert Johnson, Mythmaking, and Contemporary American Culture
    Patricia R. Schroeder

Composing a World: Lou Harrison, Musical Wayfarer   *Leta E. Miller and Fredric Lieberman*

Fritz Reiner, Maestro and Martinet   *Kenneth Morgan*

That Toddlin' Town: Chicago's White Dance Bands and Orchestras, 1900–1950
    Charles A. Sengstock Jr.

Dewey and Elvis: The Life and Times of a Rock 'n' Roll Deejay   *Louis Cantor*

Come Hither to Go Yonder: Playing Bluegrass with Bill Monroe   *Bob Black*

Chicago Blues: Portraits and Stories   *David Whiteis*

The Incredible Band of John Philip Sousa   *Paul E. Bierley*

The University of Illinois Press
is a founding member of the
Association of American University Presses.

Designed by Rich Hendel
Composed in 10/14 Quadraat
with Sluicebox display
by Jim Proefrock
at the University of Illinois Press
Manufactured by Sheridan Books, Inc.

University of Illinois Press
1325 South Oak Street
Champaign, IL 61820-6903
www.press.uillinois.edu